GEORGE MEANY

AND HIS TIMES

A BIOGRAPHY

Archie Robinson

SIMON AND SCHUSTER
New York

SIMON AND SCHUSTER and colophon are trademarks of Simon & Schuster.
Designed by Irving Perkins and Associates
Photo Editor—Vincent Virga
Manufactured in the United States of America
Printed and bound by
American Book–Stratford Press, Inc.

1 3 5 7 9 10 8 6 4 2

Library of Congress Cataloging in Publication Data

Robinson, Archie.
George Meany and his times.

"George Meany's own story, told largely in his
own words excerpted from taped interviews that
began in late 1975 and ended in July 1979"—Acknowledgements.
Bibliography: p.
Includes index.
1. Meany, George, 1894–1980.   2. American
Federation of Labor and Congress of Industrial
Organizations—History.   3. Trade-unions—United
States—Officials and employees—Biography.
I. Meany, George, 1894–1980.   II. Title.
HD6509.M4R6   331.88′33′0924   [B]   81-13616
ISBN 0-671-42163-8   AACR2

ACKNOWLEDGMENTS

This is George Meany's own story, told largely in his own words excerpted from taped interviews that began in late 1975 and ended in July 1979, when, only six months before his death, he was wracked by pain but still determined to tie up loose ends. For years AFL-CIO staff members had urged their president to cooperate on an account of his life and times, but he had felt he was too busy handling current problems to deal with the record. To their surprise, in 1975 he changed his mind. Thereafter he gave his complete cooperation. He set up a schedule of weekly interviews in a conference room adjoining his office, and every Monday morning at ten o'clock except when he had an unavoidable meeting or was testifying at a congressional hearing, he would take a seat in front of the windows overlooking the White House across Lafayette Square, light a cigar and begin to ruminate.

It was a unique opportunity to explore his relations with eight U.S. Presidents, beginning with Franklin D. Roosevelt, to learn of behind-the-scenes maneuvers involving important political and labor events, and to hear his reasons for taking the actions he did. His photographic memory, a memory that produced minute details of events decades earlier, was an invaluable tool. When he mentioned a meeting— whether of a month or of sixty years earlier—he supplied the exact date, the hour and day of the week, plus the weather at times. Meany wanted to tell his story in chronological order because that was the way events were stored in his mind, and that is the way the story is told here.

To ensure accuracy, Meany examined the transcripts of the interview as they were typed. In addition, he opened the AFL-CIO's confidential files, including the minutes of the Executive Council's closed-door sessions. Also, texts of his press conferences along with copies of every speech he delivered between 1940 and his retirement in late 1979 were provided. (Incidentally, his public remarks about events and his remarks recorded in the interviews sometimes were identical, and almost invariably were identical as to key facts.) Wherever possible, his recollections were checked against independent sources, and in those rare instances in which his memory slipped, his version was omitted from the manuscript. Any facts needed for clarification were added without attribution to him.

Close associates and family members also were generous in submitting to extended recorded interviews to verify Meany's account and to supply anecdotes showing the private side of this very public yet reticent man. Special thanks are gratefully given to Albert J. Zack, Lane Kirkland, Virginia Tehas, Andrew J. Biemiller and to George Meany's daughters and sons-in-law, Eileen and Ernest S. Lee, Regina and Robert C. Mayer and Genevieve and John S. Lutz, for their helpful recollections and encouragement of the project. Special thanks go, too, to Carole Maloney for typing the manuscript and to Sidney Brechner for technical assistance on the recordings.

Of course, my deepest appreciation is to George Meany for the lifetime this book seeks to reflect, and for countless acts of friendship in the years this authorized biography was being written and during the thirty-seven years I reported on labor's activities for the Detroit *News* and then *U.S. News & World Report.*

Archie Robinson

To Lois and Helen,
in memory of Katherine

CONTENTS

NOTE

Excerpts from the taped interviews with George Meany on which this book is based are indented in the text, as are occasional extended quotations from his speeches and press conferences. Except when otherwise indicated (in text or in "Notes"), all Meany quotations are taken from the interviews for this book.

1

THE MAN

To my God go my prayers—prayers of thanks for granting me more than one man's share of happiness and rewards, and prayers for His continued blessing on this nation and on this movement and on each of you.

When George Meany, choking with emotion, concluded his retirement speech at the AFL-CIO 1979 convention with the prayer above, he appeared to sense that his life—as well as his long career—was coming to an end. Eight weeks later, on January 10, 1980, the crippling arthritis and complications that kept him in a wheelchair for the farewell took their final toll. Death from cardiac arrest came sixty-three years to the day after his admission, as a journeyman plumber, into Local 463 of the Plumbers International Union. After six decades of demanding more—more progressive legislation, more compassion for the poor, elderly and minorities, more regard for human rights at home and abroad, and more money for workers—George Meany, political activist and leader of American labor for more than a quarter-century, left the political and labor arenas at the age of eighty-five.

He was a controversial figure from the beginning, with more than a dash of vitriol—a burly Irishman from the Bronx, who made up his mind in the early 1920s that he would make a career of labor leadership. At the time, he was the obscure "business agent" of the Bronx local he had joined at the age of twenty-two. But he knew where he wanted to go. Extremely strong-willed, he fought hard to get there.

And almost inexorably, it seemed, he succeeded, becoming the spokes-man for fourteen million American workers and millions of other peo-ple as the president of the American Federation of Labor and Congress of Industrial Organizations.

On the way he made enemies with his sharp verbal attacks on oppo-nents, but he made more friends. He made mistakes, too, which he ad-mitted afterward (pre-eminently his unqualified support of American involvement in the Vietnam War). Controversy stormed around him, primarily because the changes he proposed, both for the labor federa-tion and for society, were important. Those profiting from existing conditions fought him tooth and nail. Meany lost very few disputes in-side the labor movement but suffered many setbacks on national issues. Enactment of a national health insurance program, for instance, re-mained high on his agenda to the end.

His career was unparalleled in American labor history. Besides deal-ing with eight U.S. Presidents, he knew scores of world political and labor leaders, hundreds of members of Congress and thousands of American union officials. He chatted with Popes, royalty, sports and media figures, and, when his sympathies were engaged, exiles like Aleksandr Solzhenitsyn.

From business agent, Meany rose through leadership roles in New York City labor to the presidency of the New York State Federation of Labor. In 1940 he went to Washington as secretary-treasurer of the AFL; he moved up to the presidency in 1952. Three years later he brought about the merger of the AFL and CIO after convincing pow-erful union chiefs in both organizations that they had to end the inter-necine war that had been underway for twenty years. Then he strug-gled for more than a decade to prevent a new split threatened by the United Auto Workers' Walter P. Reuther.

An amazing aspect of Meany's career was the transformation of a plumbers' business agent into the most influential national lobbyist for progressive social legislation. He started his career in a notably restric-tive trade union, one that accepted only close relatives of members. Ev-eryone else was discriminated against—white and black—and when jobs were scarce, members voted to close the doors even to their own sons. Yet from the 1940s to the end, Meany fought against discrimina-tion in and outside the unions. He set up machinery within the AFL-CIO to root out discriminatory practices and lobbied successfully for fair employment provisions in federal law—provisions that, inciden-tally, apply to unions as well as employers.

He worked closely with black union leaders in opening up the skilled construction trades to minority workers and in instituting training programs for both blacks and whites in those unions.* Together with the national craft-union leaders and with the cooperation of national black leaders such as A. Philip Randolph, he set up an apprentice recruitment program, called Operation Outreach. Because the unions had discovered that few young blacks were willing to go through the several years of training courses operated by unions, contractors and the U.S. Labor Department, the Outreach program was organized to convince them that the training (for which they were paid) was necessary if one was to hold a skilled job.

The American craft unions—such as those of the plumbers, carpenters, printers, cigar makers—regarded themselves as descendants of the medieval guilds. Skilled workers, proud of their trade, they looked down on lower-paid factory labor and devoted themselves to improving their crafts. It was "bread-and-butter unionism." Meany, with not only a father but two uncles in the Plumbers union, grew up in that craft atmosphere, and yet he revised his thinking and actions as society, technology and industry changed. He saw the need for industrial unions to represent all employees in a particular workplace regardless of skill, as well as the need for all workers to bargain collectively to offset the growing power of the big corporation. (That, parenthetically, was what the CIO was set up to do. As a powerless delegate at the 1935 AFL convention, Meany watched the heads of big unions battle while John L. Lewis of the Mine Workers split the labor movement by creating the CIO. In recalling that period, Meany blamed the AFL's craft leaders along with Lewis for the split. He also thought that President Franklin D. Roosevelt had had a part in the creation of the CIO, for his own political reasons.) Likewise, Meany revised his thinking as society turned to new social problems; he led the labor movement into intensive lobbying for laws benefiting everyone. The old "bread-and-butter unionism" was discarded.

* Meany was harshly criticized in the 1970s because a few of those local unions and certain affiliates resisted taking in minority applicants. Much of the condemnation was prompted by his reaction—and the crafts' reaction—to the Richard M. Nixon Administration's ill-fated "Philadelphia Plan," which compelled building contractors working on federally financed projects to employ a specified percentage of minority workers. Meany opposed the plan as unfair to the very minorities it was supposed to help, on the ground that the new minority employees were not adequately trained for complicated construction jobs and consequently, when they lost their jobs on completion of the federal projects, most would be unable to get work on private projects not covered by the law. He thought this time would be better spent learning a trade paying high wages for years ahead.

This broadening process carried Meany into the field of foreign affairs as well, where his implacable hatred of Soviet communism provoked attacks from many American liberals and from socialist labor leaders abroad. They advocated "bridge building" to Soviet Russia in search of world peace; he saw Russians pouring across that "bridge" to extend communist conquest through subversion or military action.

Meany's concern about communism and U.S. foreign policy in general went to the heart of the man. It began in the decade before Adolf Hitler's rise to power in 1933. Meany's interest increased after an anti-Nazi campaign in this country was launched that year by AFL leaders in a New York City meeting. As he summarized his theory:

> In the final analysis, no matter what type of dictator takes over a country, the first thing he does is destroy worker freedom. If he's going to dictate, he has to have control over the means of production, he has to have control of the workers. That's the reason every dictator—whether military, right wing or left wing—began by wiping out the freedom of workers. They wipe out free trade unions and substitute a system of government controls.

Meany held that workers everywhere need unions to protect them, that unions cannot exist without democratic government, and that democracies need free trade unions as a protection against concentrated wealth. Military and far-right dictatorships were just as abhorrent to him as was the communist variety. His hatred of right-wing dictatorships, such as Francisco Franco's in Spain, was not as well known as was his opposition to communist dictatorships, but he and the American labor movement strongly opposed the State Department's tolerance of Spanish fascism throughout Franco's reign.

Organized labor in America had taken an interest in this area for years, and Meany was no exception. Soon after Hitler took office, Meany and other AFL leaders began a secret operation that saved many German union leaders from detention camps. Donations from American workers financed agents aiding those persecuted by Hitler to flee to Allied countries. After World War II, as secretary-treasurer of the national Federation, Meany directed efforts to rebuild the free labor movements of West Germany, France and Italy as a buffer against communism.

Meany clearly saw the crucial role of labor movements in international developments, especially where dictatorships were involved.

Certain that dictators would destroy free unions, he was equally sure
that organized labor could do much to combat such tyranny elsewhere.

What happens in foreign affairs—especially our economic relations with other countries—has a direct bearing on jobs here, on
conditions here. We have a higher standard of life. If the standards
of living all over the world kept going down, inevitably ours would
go down.

We're the most prominent trade union movement in the world. I
say that without trying to brag or anything; this is true. While in
percentage of the work force organized we're certainly not up on
top, in effectiveness over the years we can show far better results
than any other group in the world.

There are only a certain number of areas in the world where labor
is free, and we feel that if that number is reduced it represents a
threat to our own freedom. Let's take the picture here of the Western
Hemisphere. You've got Canada and the United States and a few
Latin-American countries where labor is free. Most of the countries
in Latin-America have a dictatorship of some kind, and labor is not
effective under a dictatorship.

What if, for instance, all of Latin-America beginning with Mexico
went the way of Castro? This would mean that the only two free
labor movements left in the Western Hemisphere would be those of
the United States and Canada. We would be pretty well isolated,
and we feel that would be a threat to our continued existence as a
free movement.

That's one of the reasons we're interested in foreign affairs; another is that we have a sentimental interest in labor all over the
world. Certainly we have an interest in European labor because, in
fact, the founders of our movement were Europeans who came here
during the nineteenth century and helped establish the American
labor movement. We feel that if they go down the drain, if they lose
their freedom, then we're threatened.

We have an interest in foreign affairs as Americans. We want to
maintain the American system, the only system under which labor
can make progress.

Meany was not opposed to working with socialists. He cooperated
with socialist union leaders in Israel and Europe—with reservations, at
times, about the Europeans. However, AFL founder Samuel Gompers
had had a serious problem with American socialists, and Meany never
forgot it:

Socialists were very active and had a lot of supporters in the AFL unions, especially those made up of recently arrived immigrants from Europe. They had been oppressed in their homelands. A good many socialists came to this country, and other workers became socialists here. Gompers was never done debating with the socialists, who were always criticizing what they called "Gompers' bread-and-butter unionism."

Gompers believed that the way to improve workers' conditions was to use whatever means you had under the law, by striking, organizing and so forth, to raise your standards—not at the ballot box. The socialist idea was to elect socialists and change things from the top; Gompers' idea was to go on strike and change things right there and then.

Most American workers rejected both socialism and communism, while many European workers joined unions that were influenced by one or the other. British workers had a Labour party with socialist ideas, but not so the AFL-CIO:

Our attitude has been that we are able to make greater progress for our workers, get them better wages, better working conditions, through the direct economic pressures we can put on through strikes, boycotts and things like that. Our point of view has been: Why should we set up a labor party when we're more successful without a labor party? That doesn't mean we are not active politically, but we certainly don't look to the political structure for our wages and working conditions: we get them our way.

When you compare what we have done—the only measuring rod you can use is what's happened to the conditions of the workers. So why should we waste our time asserting that we want to run the country when we're able to do better without that sort of political ambition?

Meany, in fact, had positive reasons for avoiding that kind of political involvement, and characteristically he did not shrink from voicing them:

The Canadian trade union has its own political party; practically every trade union movement in the free world is tied in some way to a political party. In a good many nations the trade union movement is split along political lines: different divisions have an alliance with a different political party.

When you tie yourself to a political party and that party assumes control of the government, you then are faced with the obligation, more or less, to cooperate with that political party and come up with a policy of moderation: "We now control the government, so you've got to behave and not get out of line, not make your demands too heavy."

We are the only trade union movement in the world that is truly independent—politically and every other way. We don't have any political party speaking for us; we don't have our own political party. We maintain an arms-length arrangement with the political parties. We have very little to do with the Republican party; we have a lot to do with the Democratic party, but we don't run the Democratic party and they don't run us.

Meany's labor philosophy was part pragmatism and part unshakable principle. Love of country, church, family and unionism underpinned his thinking. Liberals were more flexible than he was. His anticommunism was one factor that led him to support American intervention in the Vietnam War, a stand deplored by some labor leaders. Another was his long-standing belief that decisions of the President as Commander in Chief regarding military operations abroad should be supported because the President has information not available to the public. Scrupulously honest himself, Meany assumed that President Nixon would not lie to the American public. That also was the position of the labor movement as a whole. Meany predicted in 1976, however, that labor leaders would no longer automatically back such military moves. Their minds, like his, had been changed, he said, by Nixon's lies to Americans about what he was doing in the war—particularly the scope of American bombing and the extent of the invasion of Cambodia in 1970. At that time, Meany endorsed the invasion—only to concede four years later, on the basis of postwar information, that he had made a mistake.

Not only Presidents were held to a strict standard of honesty. Meany applied the same rule to labor leaders. If he caught a union official (or politician) lying to him, he never trusted that person again. As for himself, he was incapable of dissembling; those who dealt with him at any level soon found that he stated clearly and simply where he stood.

His honesty probably was one reason he scorned the idea of "improving his image" by softer language, fewer vitriolic blasts. His sense of humor was another reason. His disdain for "imagery" made him almost a unique figure in the days when an entire industry was devoted to that cosmetic science. In Meany's case, the ever-present cigar magnified the belligerent look in any argument. Smiles hardly come easily from a mouth grimly clamped on a stogy.

Meany was equally well known for his consistency. If he started out on one side in an argument, he remained on that side throughout; his word was his bond. He never forgave President Gerald R. Ford for failing to sign an important piece of legislation after promising to do so.

Stealing union members' money was, in Meany's opinion, a crime tantamount to treason. Therefore, he convinced an AFL-CIO convention to expel the Federation's largest dues-payer, the powerful Teamsters Union, after disclosures of misuse of union funds by its executives James R. (Jimmy) Hoffa and Dave Beck. Meany led the fights to oust several other affiliates and to clean up still others.

Well known as his views were, the AFL-CIO president was a problem for those who insist on putting public figures into neat categories according to their beliefs. Many conservatives considered Meany to be a flaming liberal, or perhaps a radical, while some liberals outside the labor movement rated him a conservative.

Meany never thought of himself as a liberal or conservative; he supported a cause when he decided it was good for people in general. His positions often were supported by the professional liberals, who joined forces with him on the minimum wage, human rights, jobs for blacks, the Equal Rights Amendment, Social Security. But he and the old AFL began advocating national health insurance long before professional liberals took up the banner. A particular social program won his endorsement because he felt it was needed—not because it was on a list of liberal causes.

In foreign affairs, Meany sometimes lined up with the hawks and conservatives but not always, as witness his opposition to right-wing dictators. Also, on the Panama Canal treaties, he strongly backed President Jimmy Carter while the hawks denounced the agreements as practically treason. The AFL-CIO was the first major national organization to support return of the Canal to Panama. It was easy for Meany to decide on that position: he said that America had stolen the Zone in the first place and thus ought to return it.*

* The detente policy pursued by Nixon and Secretary of State Henry A. Kissinger, on the other hand, was criticized frequently by Meany, who called it, among other things, "just ordinary appeasement" and "blackmail" that never works. He also saw it as a giveaway program aiding Russia without reciprocal benefits for the United States. America, he said, was making all the concessions. (Nevertheless, Kissinger continued to give the labor leader private briefings.) Although the AFL-CIO, through Meany, had exerted considerable in-

Meany's insistence on integrity made itself felt in domestic matters as well. He made perfectly clear at the time what he thought about Nixon and Watergate. At Meany's instigation, the Federation became the first national organization to demand the President's resignation or impeachment. It kept up a drumbeat of documented reasons why he should be impeached. This was only three years after Nixon had staged the most elaborate dinner honoring organized labor ever held at the White House.

Heavy odds against success never dissuaded Meany from taking an action he believed was right. An example: the AFL-CIO's opposition to two of Nixon's Supreme Court appointments. After blocking the first one on his anti-black, anti-labor record, Meany insisted on trying to block the second. When aides protested that the Senate was not likely to vote against two nominees in a row—especially when the second nominee's decisions had not involved labor issues—Meany argued that anyone who was anti-black was bound to be anti-labor, too. He launched the effort, and won.

His thick frame, balding head, large jaw, and horn-rimmed glasses were an inviting target for photographers and cartoonists. He enjoyed the cartoons and lined his office walls with them. Why not? The look of brusqueness coupled with his photographic memory and keen mind enhanced any "power" that he exercised and, as spokesman for millions of workers, he felt he had a responsibility and right to present the Federation's position and problems to Presidents and members of Congress.

Presidents sometimes disregarded the keen Meany mind, but not for long. From Franklin D. Roosevelt on, they learned that behind the blunt talk lay wisdom developed in many a political or legislative battle. Both Roosevelt and Harry S Truman had sharp disputes with him. Yet Dwight D. Eisenhower, despite the Federation's support of his Democratic opponent on two occasions, welcomed his sometimes uncongenial views. Indeed, the two became such close friends that Eisenhower, on his last full day in office, had Meany over to the White House for a ninety-minute chat. Presidents John F. Kennedy and Lyndon B. Johnson freely tapped Meany's mind, especially about the concerns that became the legislative proposals of the Johnson years. Presi-

fluence on U.S. foreign policy during Democratic administrations, Meany also failed to dissuade Carter from what he called "one-sided detente." Ironically, as Meany's life was ending, the Russian invasion of Afghanistan prompted Carter's disillusionment with the doctrine.

dent Nixon, unable to end the chaos of a nationwide postal strike, appealed to Meany, who worked out a compromise. President Ford asked for and got Meany's help in prying loose from committee an important foreign-aid bill, which was then steered successfully through Congress.

All eight Presidents with whom Meany dealt also learned that when the labor leader said "I can't buy that" in connection with a proposal or pending legislation, they were facing a tough fight.

A sample of Meany's lobbying was provided by Murray H. Finley, a member of the AFL-CIO Executive Council, who recalled a session of President Ford's labor-management advisory committee, on which Finley served. Present were prominent business executives as well as labor leaders. Finley said he later told his Amalgamated Clothing and Textile Workers board that if strangers from Mars had seen and heard the session they would have concluded that the President of the United States was George Meany. Seated on Ford's right, clearly the center of attention, Meany outlined, in an off-the-cuff speech of some length, what he thought should be done to create more jobs. When he politely but firmly explained to Ford that the AFL-CIO objected to the Administration's policies, "you could see Ford wiggling a little bit," Finley recalled. The Clothing Workers' president described the meeting as a great example of democracy in action, with a private citizen presenting "strongly, forcefully and eloquently his total disagreement with the President." Meany never was disrespectful, however, and in concluding his remarks on that occasion, grinned and said, "That's my speech, Mr. President."

Dick Cavett asked Meany about his meetings with Presidents soon after Ford took office. On his television show, Cavett inquired, "Have you ever had a President shout at you, in or out of office, had harsh words with you?"

"No. No. Never."

"Always pleasant?"

"Always. Didn't always agree with them and they knew that but, never, never, on a personal basis."

"You are not in awe of the President, though?"

"No, no, not after thirty-five years in and out of the White House. You couldn't be in awe of him."

It wasn't only Presidents who showed respect for Meany. The feeling was shared by many who never met him—from corporation heads to taxi drivers, who based their respect on a Meany TV appearance, his printed comments or his actions. Cynical reporters, too, after sufficient exposure, discovered to their amazement that he said exactly what he thought, as unfashionable as that was in the image era.

A high official of the Export-Import Bank indicated one reason for the trust put in Meany's statements. Introducing an aide of Meany's, the banker told an audience that the aide—Andrew J. Biemiller—followed the same practice as Meany: "We know what's on his mind; he doesn't try to fudge issues with us. We know exactly where he stands, and that's a mark of both George Meany and Andy Biemiller."

Meany was seen by many Americans as a person speaking out clearly for all the people—the retired elderly, the poor, the workers both union and non-union. The media thought that too, as indicated when, after a President had vetoed a bill passed by Congress or announced a new policy, the cameras were more likely to seek out the reaction of George Meany than those of members of Congress or spokesmen for the Chamber of Commerce.

Why was Meany accepted so widely as a spokesman for the people? One opinion was offered by the head of the Building Trades Department of the Federation, Robert A. Georgine:

"I think because he has credibility, because he is honest, because no one can ever say that George Meany—at least to my knowledge—is guilty of some sub-rosa deal, some stab in the back. He has done one thing that a lot of people can't do; he has reached tremendous power and influence and success in what he has done—but he hasn't changed. He hasn't become something other than what he started out to be: he was a plumber, he's still a plumber. I think that is why people accept him and recognize him as the voice of the workingman: he is still a workingman."

A sailor's view of Meany's leadership qualities was offered by Paul Hall, Seafarers Union president and a member of the AFL-CIO Executive Council:

"George was ideally equipped at a time when he was called on to put together varying personalities. You give me one good guy on a ship who knows what he's doing and I'll give you a united crew with a single purpose. There is a certain type of quality about varying types of leadership. Meany has that quality. If Meany comes into a room and nobody knows who he is, he has the quality to attract the attention of other men. If you go aboard a ship and meet in the mess hall over a cup of coffee, you'll soon see who the leader is. They call that built-in-leadership quality, and this Meany has.

"Not only is he a guy with the goddamn instincts and that certain touch, but it was the right time for that kind of leadership [in 1952]. Had the movement set out with its best craftsmen to build someone with leadership qualifications, George, who was long on those qualifications, would have been the one they crafted."

Hall also had some observations about the way Meany talked to Presidents and cabinet officers:

"George Meany is, I think, constitutionally incapable of having two sides, two positions. That goes with every meeting that I've sat in on with him, whether it was with Nixon, Ford, Johnson or you name them, and it goes also for cabinet-level people. I can tell you that there is no difference.

"Whatever George Meany says to the [AFL-CIO] Executive Council and puts forth as a position for agreement by the group—that's what he presents at the White House. If the President disagrees, George will come right in and say, 'Wait a minute here'—so-and-so-and-so-and-so. It doesn't mean that everybody loves George on every issue. Of course, not. I know we've had differences on issues but, by God, he's about the most predictable person I've ever sat with. This is what makes George's leadership unique.

"A lot of great leadership people have their good days and bad days relative to attitudes on issues. But I can sit here and pretty much tell you, on most issues that have been previously discussed, what George Meany will do. That doesn't make him simple; it makes him consistent. What George gives is something that is terribly important, and that is a continuity of leadership, position and attitudes."

Meany's ties with Israel were marked by the same constancy, and former Prime Minister Golda Meir and Meany were longtime friends. Her regard for him was shown in a cablegram she sent to him during Israel's 1977 diplomatic problems:

"Thank God that George Meany is there. In this world where expediency is the governing consideration, when oil and brutality dictate policy and set the pattern for values of the most powerful, you are one of the very few that Israel can depend upon. You are not prepared to wait till Israel is in 'mortal danger.' You simply speak up to prevent it being in danger. I feel more than I can say. My love to Mrs. Meany."

Meany's compassion was more real than apparent. Ernest S. Lee, director of international affairs for the AFL-CIO and one of Meany's three sons-in-law, with ample opportunity to see Meany at work and at ease, commented: "There is a great warmth about the man that I don't think the general public sees. They talk about him being rough and abrupt, but he has great wit, great humor and great warmth. It's not simply for grandchildren or relatives; it's for people he has known or for people who particularly have suffered some indignity or some privation or some mishap.

"He's one of the most sympathetic people that I know of—for honest causes. And one of the most ruthless I have ever seen for the charlatan or the crook."

During a federal investigation of reputedly improper banking practices by Bert Lance, President Carter's Director of Management and Budget, Lee said that Meany did not have "any deep animosity" toward Lance. "It wouldn't even be categorized as disgust; it would be simple: Why does a man have to resort to that sort of thing who already has quite a bit, and why should someone try to chisel? Chiseling is something that he has never understood, and so the chiseler doesn't have much of a place in his heart or his time."

Patience was another Meany attribute. He knew, for example, that labor could not expect to win every legislative battle it engaged in, so it must keep on fighting and eventually the victory probably would come. As Meany mentioned in a 1952 speech:

"You make progress by fighting for progress. You will only retain the gains you have made by constant vigilance and by a demonstrated willingness to fight again. So when we look back to our gains, let us do so not for the purpose of indulging ourselves in the luxury of a feeling of satisfaction or complacency but for the knowledge and inspiration needed to carry on in the direction of even a better day."

He demonstrated the same patience and flexibility in deliberations of the AFL-CIO Executive Council. In discussing the Council actions for this book, he said, "There are lots of cases where I find myself in the minority—not very often—but I don't get upset about it."

From comments of Council members, the governing part of that remark would appear to be "not very often," and minutes of the meetings bear it out. Few roll calls were taken in the Council's closed sessions, although any member might call for a formal vote or register his own position on the record. Meany, however, was an expert at operating by consensus.

The Council sets the official policy between the biennial conventions, where delegates have the final say. The news media tended to personalize any AFL-CIO action, saying that "Meany did" this or that, but, in fact, he was careful to clear his proposals with the other thirty-four members of the Council or with the convention. He sounded out key members in advance to get their reactions and suggested changes, if any. He revised or dropped any idea if there seemed to be heavy opposition.

Often there was extended debate in the Council over important issues, but, judging from the news reports, the public assumed that Meany alone made the decisions. It was not generally realized that most of the Council members were presidents of big unions and did not take orders from Meany or anyone else.

Meany's blunt remarks at press conferences and elsewhere reinforced the picture of a dictator, but several family members and close associates saw his blunt public demeanor as a protective shield for a shy nature. To be sure, no shyness surfaced at his press conferences or at the occasional parties that reporters held with him as guest of honor and raconteur extraordinaire on the good old days of the labor movement or on his favorite baseball players. He clearly enjoyed a party when he knew those present, but he would become reticent if surrounded by strangers.

For eight years after he went to Washington to become the AFL's secretary-treasurer, Meany took the train home to the Bronx on weekends. The reason he gave for the long delay in moving the family to Washington was that the girls should be allowed to finish high school with their friends, but there were other reasons. Mrs. Eugenie Meany loved her native New York and hated to move away from relatives and longtime friends, and it had been agreed from the outset of her marriage that their home would be sacrosanct.*

In Washington or in the Bronx, as the girls were growing up, it was the mother who disciplined them whenever necessary. Their father could direct the affairs of a big labor federation, but at home he issued few orders. (Reporters always thought he was joking when he made remarks about being "dominated" by a house full of women, but he wasn't entirely.)

The daughters remember that, soon after their father went to Wash-

---

* The reluctant move to Washington finally was made in 1948—when Genevieve, the youngest daughter, finished high school—but the daughters seem to think there would have been further delays except for one fact. The family doctor told Mrs. Meany the weekly train trips had brought on a sinus condition and were too tiring for her husband. (During the commuting years, the patient father brought home phonograph records ordered each Wednesday in a daughter's telephone call.)

ington, a magazine described his voice in union meetings as shaking the chandeliers. Mrs. Meany, one daughter reported, "said, 'There will be no chandelier shaking in my house' and there never was."

"I've never heard him raise his voice; I've never heard him swear," another said. "The only thing I ever heard him say is, maybe, hell or damn. But, you see, he lived in a house full of women, and in those days there was no women's lib. We used to say, 'If they think he yells, they should hear mother.' Because mother had all the discipline on her shoulders. She would say, 'You had better do it or when your father comes home he'll see about it.' He would come home and he never raised his voice. He was a very loving father."

She remembers, however that on the few occasions when "he told me to do something, I did it!" because she knew "he meant it."

In fact, the public knew practically nothing about Meany's private life. He was a devoted husband, father and grandfather. Away from the limelight, he was an easy mark for his fourteen grandchildren, a devout Catholic, an avid golfer, a self-taught pianist and organist, a singer of Irish ballads, an amateur painter*—and much else.

Until Mrs. Meany died in early 1979, the couple led an extremely quiet domestic life in Bethesda, Maryland, with all three of their daughters' homes nearby.

Meany's first grandchild tagged him "Pop Pop" and the other thirteen thought it a good idea. As they grew up, Pop Pop kept a closet filled with toys and games and had a billiard table installed in the basement. He enjoyed competing with the children and helping them with math problems.

Off the job, Meany was a changed man: only the cigar and Bronx accent of his public persona remained. Humor replaced blunt talk; smiles drove away scowls. When that changed man appeared in his favorite neighborhood restaurant with Mrs. Meany, a daughter and son-in-law, he surprised strangers. So much so that on one trip a man came to the Meany table to ask if he realized he looked like George Meany. Advised that "a lot of people have told me that," the man insisted, "Well, you really do!"

Despite Meany's efforts to protect his family by erecting a wall between public and private lives, the frequent bitter attacks on him in

---

* A daughter's joke gift to him of a paint-by-numbers set inspired him to take up the art seriously. He said he became so engrossed that he let his cigar go out and "even forgot the economy."

the media must have hurt the family members. His own reaction to attacks, as he once said, was: "I started in this business many years ago, and I don't look upon it as a popularity contest. I have no desire to be popular. I have a job to be done."

How he did that job, and why, he describes in the following chapters.

2

THE ORGANIZER

I can remember when I was sworn in as a new member of the local union and lined up at a meeting to take the pledge of allegiance to the local and go through the ritual. I remember five hundred people there booing their heads off. They didn't want any new members. They saw every new member as a threat to whatever jobs there were.

That was George Meany's recollection of the January 10, 1917, evening when he became a full-fledged member of Plumbers Local 463 in the Bronx, at the age of twenty-two. (Later, it became Local 2.)

The hostile welcome to union brotherhood could have aborted Meany's long career as a labor leader if he had been less determined about entering the trade of his father and uncles. But, as many labor leaders and national politicians were to discover later, Meany with his mind made up was a difficult man to stop.

By 1917, Meany already had proven his stubbornness, having defied his father's wish that he complete his high school education and take up some line of work other than plumbing. Young Meany had gone behind his father's back to seek a job as a plumber's helper and had struggled through five years of training to pass his "journeyman" test on the second attempt.

The rise to journeyman status happened to coincide with one of the rare periods when the Bronx local was accepting new members. Often it was "closed"—taking in no one. Nearly sixty years later, Meany still vividly recalled that hostile greeting by the "brothers":

The local was very definitely closed at times. For a while it would be open and then they would close it again. The situation was we had a union of about 3,600 members and in May, June, July and August of practically every year all of those people were working. Come October and November, sixty or seventy percent would be unemployed and they would be unemployed all during the winter. This, of course, was on everybody's mind. It was a constant source of irritation within the local union.

At times, they would open the books to members' sons and members' brothers. They didn't want members' sons, they didn't want anybody, but that was a concession they would make. There always was pressure from the employers to bring in new members because sometimes there would be a shortage of workers during the season when there was a lot of work, especially in the summertime. The employer wanted a full supply.

There was always the question of what you do with apprentices who had spent four or five years learning the trade. It was completely unfair to them, but this was the way it was. They would close the books. Then the pressure would come on and they would open the books. They'd be open for two or three months and they would take in quite a few members. Then someone would get up and make a wild speech and make a motion that the books be closed. The books would be closed again.

The real reason for it was fear of unemployment and the idea that those new people would reduce the share of work for the people who already were members.

That was a common practice in many of the skilled crafts then, but Meany helped open up the union doors in later years. It was one phase of his transition from the closed-union background of his youth to his insistence as head of the AFL and AFL-CIO that all affiliates accept blacks as members, that the "lily-white" local unions and the black-only locals be merged.

Over the years, too, he changed from a craft-oriented union official to an advocate of industrial unionism, and from a bread-and-butter unionist to a crusader for social-welfare programs to aid the public as well as union and non-union workers.

Meany's early urge to be of service to his fellow plumbers as a union business-agent broadened into a desire to help all workers and the poor and underprivileged. Brought up in a skilled craftsman's family, he never experienced poverty and starvation at home, but he saw them in other homes in his working-class Bronx neighborhood. During the Depression of the 1930s, he cut his own salary and often begged union contractors to give a needy unemployed member a week's work to save a family.

This background influenced Meany in his Washington years. He never forgot that Depression. In his view, about the harshest criticism he could make against a public official was that the official was never even acquainted with a workingman and thus had no sympathy for his problems. Meany thought of himself as a plumber for decades after he put down his tools.

Michael J. Meany, his plumber father, was born in 1864 in New York's lower Harlem, his family having come from Ireland eleven years earlier—soon after that country's Great Famine. In 1891, Mike Meany married Anne Cullen, a native New Yorker whose grandparents also fled Ireland in 1853. George was the second of their eight children.

George Meany drew a vast amount of inspiration and moral principle from that Irish background, as he explained in a 1976 speech in New York to the American Irish Historical Society when it awarded him its medal:

> Tonight you honor a grandson of the Meanys of West Meath. They came to these shores in the 1850's and had established a line of reasonably competent and successful plumbers—until I was drawn off into other pursuits. . . .
>
> I grew up among the Irish of St. Luke's parish in a household where Ireland and its troubles and history were subjects of daily discussion. I found out, for instance, that my grandfather (my mother's father) was the champion cross-country runner in his native county, Longford. There can be no doubt on this— he told me so himself. I recall also his fruitless efforts to teach the children of the family to speak Gaelic. . . .
>
> The dominant political party [in New York] then, as now, was the Democratic Party, headed up by a Murphy in Manhattan and another Murphy in the Bronx with a McCooey in Brooklyn and a Connally in Queens. . . . The Catholic Church, with a hierarchy that was predominantly Irish, also was a major factor in this city's civic and religious life and also, believe it or not, in the political power structure of those days.
>
> And while the early development of the American trade union movement was brought about by people of varied ethnic backgrounds, it can not be denied that there again the American Irish made a significant contribution. . . .

Now, it may be true that the Irish rose to leadership in American labor because of their inherited flair for language and love of the spoken word—but I like to think that they were equally spurred by the deep, centuries-old indignation which injustice stirred in them. They had been schooled in justice, freedom, equality and human dignity—and where they found those things absent they rose to do battle.

The yearning for freedom—the insistence on human dignity—are forever enshrined as part of the Irish character. Similarly, they are the well-spring of the American trade union movement. Oh, yes, we spend lots of time in negotiating for wages and hours and working conditions but these are simply the material manifestations of the achievement of worker dignity. The basis of our trade union movement, and the reason why it continues strong, is that men and women see in it the vehicle for enduring recognition of their human dignity. They see it—correctly—as the device through which they can band together to help themselves and help one another assert that dignity and thereby improve their lot and that of their children.

The lessons I learned in the Bronx and the lessons I learned as the son of Irish forebears have stayed with me through the years. The love of God, family and country and the dedication to a freedom based upon the dignity of the individual has been a valid guidepost all my life.

The details of that life, as Meany recalled them in interviews, characteristically skirted the private domain of his religious beliefs. Also characteristically, they began at the beginning:

I was born August 16, 1894, at 125th Street and Madison Avenue in the Harlem section of Manhattan, just across from the Bronx. What was generally considered to be Harlem in those days was from 110th Street up to 155th Street. That became Black Harlem, but the area where I was born at the time was pretty much Irish-American. When I was five years old my family moved across the river to the Bronx. That was in 1899. My mother's home had been in the Bronx. I suppose my parents moved to the Bronx to get away from the congestion that was developing in Harlem.

In those days, right after the turn of the century, the Bronx was a series of small communities connected by a trolley system that ran in all directions through the East Bronx, Central Bronx and West Bronx. All of those trolley lines terminated across the Third Avenue Bridge in Manhattan, where at about 127th Street and Second Avenue there was a great open space where the cars came in from the Bronx and made a big circle before starting out again.

In the portion of the Bronx closest to Manhattan there were some apartment houses and a few small one-family homes. In the other portions of the Bronx running all the way up to the Westchester County line, there was one small community after another, consisting mainly of small houses with gardens but including some quite pretentious houses, too—almost the mansion type.

The section of the Bronx where I grew up—the southeast corner—was known as Port Morris. It was at this point that the East River broadened into Long Island Sound.

I had a very pleasant boyhood in that area; I played a lot of baseball. In the winter there always was plenty of snow. During the summer months we spent most of our time swimming in Long Island Sound, right down from where I lived, and there was good fishing at that time—that's how clear the water was. The area where I lived is the exact spot where today the Triborough Bridge reaches the mainland, at 133rd Street and Southern Boulevard.

When I was growing up, our neighborhood was mostly Irish; the Germans were second and there were a lot of Scots, Scotch-English and some Scandinavians. They were mostly workingmen—it was what you would call "middle class." There were building-trades mechanics and bricklayers and German immigrants who came to work in the fifteen piano factories scattered through this local area.

The Ludwig piano factory was directly in back of our house. We had a little row house with a garden in the backyard. Back of our rear fence was this five-story piano factory and, especially in the spring, summer and fall when our windows were open, you could hear them tuning the pianos: Bang, bang, bang, it would go constantly.

Between 1905 and 1915 the character of our Bronx neighborhood started to change; there was less open space and more and more apartment houses. I went to public school right there, and then for a year and a half I went to high school, before I dropped out and went to work on my first job.

Back when I was still in school, I delivered what was known as the official race-entry card. It was put up mostly in saloons—a daily bulletin on heavy paper about twenty-four inches by fourteen inches. It fitted into a frame and it had the race results up until the fifth race—they wouldn't have them all. In addition, it listed the baseball scores that were in at the time. All of this was on the front; on the reverse side were the race entries for the next day.

We would start delivering them about six o'clock in the evening
on a regular route. I went to thirty-five or forty places. For that I got
a dollar fifty a week. Well, we made a little more. Four or five of us
would start from the same general area in the South Bronx, so we
worked out a plan by which one boy would go each day and get all
the cards and bring them to the elevated station, where we would
meet before we started delivering. That meant we made an extra ten
cents each day; we saved the carfare.

For a couple of years, around the same time as the race-card job, I
had another job delivering orders from a bakery, beginning about
six o'clock in the morning—running around with a big basket with a
dozen rolls for this house, a loaf of bread for that—a regular bakery
route. It paid the same amount as the other job, a dollar fifty a week,
but in addition when I went back after delivering my last load I
would get a big bag of buns to take home, so that was a little extra.

Meany also recalled a vacation job he had running errands for a
shop manufacturing briar pipes. That was when he discovered he
really had been named William George Meany. He had to obtain a
birth certificate in order to get working papers. His mother confirmed
the extra name, explaining that although he was baptized "William,"
they had never called him that. Meany said, "So, I just dropped it."

George Meany's memory helped to get him as far as he went in high
school. One of his daughters recalls that he told her he never was a
really good student but that "I never had any trouble passing tests because the minute I read anything over once I remembered it. I didn't
really get through on anything but an excellent memory."

Meany's skill at mathematics also helped him in school, he told a
crowd of newspaper business writers in 1975 after being introduced
with praise for his economic predictions: "I certainly am thankful to
God that I am not an economist. I look back when I was a high school
dropout. I think now that if I had gone on I might have wound up
being an economist. And, to me, this is kind of a sad profession. Although it is the one profession in which you can gain great eminence
without ever being right. And I point to Arthur [Burns, then Federal
Reserve Board chairman] as a prime example of that."

Math problems had another use, he told his grandchildren. When he
was a boy, he recalled, he would lie in bed and do math problems until
he fell asleep—instead of the usual counting-sheep routine. Later,
Meany frequently worked out in his head the conclusion to be drawn

from complicated statistics before staffers could provide the answer.

At age fourteen, Meany left high school to work for the George Batten Company, an advertising agency which later became Batten, Barton, Durstine & Osborn. He enjoyed working there because it was "a lively sort of a place, with a lot going on." There he met author Elbert Hubbard and Otto Harbach, the musical comedy writer, who was a copywriter at Batten's.

Young Meany didn't have to go to work to assist the family. "My first job as an errand boy," he said, "paid four dollars a week and I'm sure that didn't make any difference in the family income. I just couldn't stand the indoors. I wanted to get out."

After about seventeen months as a messenger, Meany said, "I became determined I wanted to work at my father's trade." But Mike Meany didn't want his son to become a plumber. As George Meany recalled it, his father never explained his reasons for the opposition, "but he just said, 'You know this is awfully hard work,' and it was very hard work. I imagine it was harder work in those days than it is today, although I think that today, with construction what it is, it demands much more skill than it did in those days. But the work then was hard physical labor."

It was natural for young George to aim at the trade that was his father's lifetime occupation. George grew up in a union home as well, his father having been president of the Bronx local. Also, the Meanys' home was a favorite gathering place for union plumbers. Perhaps the union atmosphere was the more important factor.

"I have never had much interest in anything else but the trade union movement," Meany recalled at the 1953 AFL convention. "Many, many years ago, before I knew what a union was—in fact, before I knew too much of anything; I had just reached what is known as the age of reason—I can remember little groups of people coming to our home on a Sunday afternoon. There were no movies in those days and not many automobiles around, and people visited each other on Sundays.

"Practically all of the visitors who came to my home were officers and members of the union, because my father at that time was president of the local union to which I still belong.

"I can remember in those days these men talking about something known as 'the Organization' . . . and they called it, 'Organ-I-zation.' But I can remember the reverence with which they used the term, and inculcated into my mind at that time was the thought that whatever the Organ-I-zation was, it was something these men put almost on a par with their religion."

One of those visitors, on a Sunday afternoon in October, 1910, was a plumbing foreman on a big building project in the Hunt's Point section of the Bronx. Meany never forgot that day:

> As this foreman, Mr. Duggan, was walking down the street, I ran up and asked him if he would give me a job as a helper. I told him, "My father isn't anxious for me to work in plumbing, but I'd like to work at it."
>
> He replied, "Well, there is no reason you shouldn't if you want to."
>
> So, the next morning, I went to work, but when I came home from work that evening, my father asked, "You went to work at plumbing?" When I said "yes" he told me, "Fine. You go over and register at the trade school."
>
> And for three nights a week for the next two years I went to trade school at 138th and Fifth Avenue. I was working in the daytime, and three nights a week I was going to this public vocational trade school—and I thought I was through school! That was kind of a shock, but it worked out all right.

Meany was sixteen when he began work, at $6.88 a week. Work on mansions of the wealthy Whitney family in the New York area provided part of that training, as he gradually advanced up the craft's ladder of skills. His employer at that time, "a high-class jobbing shop," did all the construction work on the Fifth Avenue residences of Harry Payne Whitney and his brother, Payne Whitney. The "enormous" Long Island estate of Harry Payne Whitney was another part of that training ground. Meany said the construction workers would go by railroad to Roslyn, Long Island, every Monday morning and live in a boardinghouse during the week, riding out to the estate by horse-drawn wagon.

In spare time on the construction site, Meany often played baseball with other workers. "George was a pretty nimble fellow; he could move around well for a man of his size," recalled William T. Dodd, who worked with Meany on a building project at Camp Upton, on Long Island. "George had athletic ability." (Dodd also later chose a union career, but he rose through the ranks of the Plumbers International to become general secretary-treasurer, while Meany chose a different route to national office.)

On Sundays, the plumbing apprentice was catcher on a semipro team called the Bronx Professionals. Meany received from $7.50 to $10 a game—more than the outfielder's $5 but less than the pitcher's $20, as he remembered it. He described it as "really a sort of junior semipro team," adding:

I didn't play every Sunday. On Sundays in New York there was no professional baseball in those days—no Giants and Yankees. The semipro teams were all over the city and they drew tremendous crowds. There were two great black teams: the Lincoln Giants at 136th Street and Madison Avenue and the Lincoln Stars just nine blocks away, up at 145th Street and Lenox Avenue. The big one was the Lincoln Giants, but the Lincoln Stars, hell, they would also have several thousand people in their park on Sunday.

The audience was at least fifty percent white; they came because you saw good baseball. I often went over to Black Harlem to watch those games. We played the Negro teams, both of them; we played many other teams. I played from 1913 to about 1918, when the war knocked it all out.

The black teams had great players, but they were barred from professional baseball. What the hell, the ordinary citizen had nothing to do with that. They were barred by the owners and I think it was on the theory that baseball was a white man's game. Of course, that was silly, because time has proved that baseball is a great sport for blacks, with a lot of great black stars. The good teams have black after black, so this proves that they can play baseball, and they could play it, too, when I was a kid.

When I was a young fellow the word "discrimination" didn't mean a thing, really, because I was brought up in New York City. There was discrimination—it was sort of accepted in employment, with certain jobs and certain areas barred to blacks—but there was no discussion on it; it was not an issue. You couldn't have much discrimination in your heart and be born in New York City. The neighborhood where I was brought up had ethnic groups of all types and people who suffered from discrimination.

I don't recall it, but my parents and grandparents told me about the discrimination against Irish Catholics. They were quite aware of that, but it had pretty much disappeared. There was a certain amount of discrimination against Jews, but actually it was not a serious thing and in New York you accepted everybody. I think New York was the most tolerant city in the world.

By 1915, after five years of training, Meany was ready to try his luck before the local union's journeyman examining board, which could make him eligible for full union status—if the union rolls happened to be open at the time. But the twenty-one-year-old Meany flunked the examination and had to wait six months before he could try again. His father did not intervene to help him pass, although the men who conducted the test had been appointed by the elder Meany. "When I flunked," the son said, "he was very, very peeved—not at them but at me."

George Meany was still an apprentice when his father died in 1916, after serving for more than a decade as president of Plumbers local unions in Manhattan and the Bronx. Some years earlier, Mike Meany had been promoted to foreman plumber for the city parks in the Bronx. His son recalled:

> My father died of a heart attack following pneumonia. He was a big, powerful man, only fifty-one. He contracted pneumonia. We lived in a little row house up in the Bronx and I remember seeing him in the afternoon, late in February, sitting in the front of the house and the sun was shining. He had recovered from pneumonia. But he went up to bed that night—up a flight of stairs—and he never got to the top. So, actually it was a weakened heart, as a result of pneumonia.

Early the next year, George Meany was admitted to full membership in that hostile union meeting, boosting his pay from $3.50 a day to $5.50 a day—well below today's hourly rate. Being elevated to journeyman status meant he could go to the union meetings, held every Wednesday and "quite well attended." He admitted, however, that after a few weeks of regular attendance he began to skip the sessions for months at a time because "I didn't pay much attention to it."

But his first union meeting did make a lasting impression on him, as he recounted in 1957 to a labor conference:

> At the very first union meeting I ever attended, more than 40 years ago, as I went into the meeting hall there was a little white pamphlet on every seat in the hall. . . . It was a report of every single penny expended by that local union in the previous 90 days, right down to the towels and the soap that went to the office. . . . That's the way it should be, because the most important thing in the philos-

ophy of the trade union movement is that the unions belong to the members—not to Meany . . . or anyone else. While it is the job of the leaders to lead, it is the job of the members to decide.

The new journeyman plumber barely had gotten started in his trade when his older brother, John, enlisted in the Army—one week after the United States declared war against Germany, April 6, 1917. Coming so soon after the father's death, this was a severe financial blow to the Meany household. It meant that George was the sole financial support of his mother, six younger brothers and sisters and George's maternal grandfather, who lived with the Meanys.

John, who had been a pressman at the New York *World,* came to the building project where George was working to announce his enlistment. When George asked John why he had done it so soon after war broke out, John replied, "I figured that one of the two older boys had to go and one had to stay home. I figured you should stay home because of the very simple reason that you make more money than I do."

At that time, Meany also recalled, he was making $30.25 a week as a journeyman plumber when work was available. He was only twenty-two years old.

John Meany was in the front line trenches in France by the end of October, his brother said, and was badly wounded in July 1918 when a dumdum bullet went through his stomach. After being released from the hospital, John rejoined his regiment and in 1919 returned from Germany with it. But his war injury soon sent him to a veterans' hospital, where he died in 1920.

George, meanwhile, was finding out that he had chosen a difficult trade:

> The working conditions were good, but the work was terrifically hard because it was all competitive. It was not unusual for a fellow to work for four or five days on the job and then get fired because he was not producing as much as the others. It was very hard work. You worked against time always; it was a competitive business. These contractors would have bid on the work and, as they said, they really had to sharpen their pencils and their estimates to get the contract. The union conditions were all right except that you just had to work hard all day long or you would fall behind. That was true on 90 percent of the work.
>
> On other projects, like telephone work, the emphasis was on qual-

ity rather than on the quantity of the work. On the fine-residence projects the emphasis also was on quality of work. That wasn't nearly as competitive, not as hard.

When jobs were scarce for plumbers, in 1918, he tried the carpenter's trade, but only briefly, as he related to a Carpenters Union dinner in 1971:

> I worked as a dock builder for about three weeks. They were short of dock builders over in Port Newark in the early months of 1918 . . . and they just said, "Well, any member of the building trades with a paid-up card can work. We need some people who can work as dock builders constructing this facility which the Government needs badly." But after about three weeks I discovered that plumbing was much better than dock building.

The struggle to earn enough money to support the Meany household kept the young plumber busy, but there was some time for dates with his future wife, Eugenie McMahon. The courtship began in 1915 and continued for four years, with dancing a mutual interest. "In those days everybody saved their money before they got married; no one lived on credit," a daughter said, adding, "To this day, they both think that buying anything on credit is terrible."

Meany described his courtship years in a magazine article he wrote in 1957:

> We had a great deal in common. We were both of Irish extraction. We both lived in the Bronx and we both had to go to work at an early age to supplement the family income. [The long courtship] was not due to indecision on our part or parental opposition. It was a matter of economic necessity. I had become the family breadwinner due to the passing of my father and the [approaching] death of an elder brother.

Mrs. Meany often told her daughters about the dances she and her husband-to-be attended, and the trip home. Eileen Meany Lee recalls:

"They danced a lot. Mother tells a charming story of how she lived in West Farms, the Bronx. Now it is really a slum area, but in those days it was literally a farm. My father would bring her home from a date where they had been dancing and walk her to her house, which evidently was quite far from the trolley line, and then he would walk, she said, through the snow, ice and cold back to the trolley line to go home. She always said that there must have been something that brought him way out there to the country.

"Her memories are of home things, where people came and played the piano and danced. She decries the fact that no one dances anymore, at least the way they did. But she said my father was always bright and humorous, always steps ahead of anybody else—with his mind and his humor.

"My father came from a large family, a family where the door was always open. My grandmother's house was always full of people playing cards, and the kitchen was full. She always had a cake in the oven. They didn't have much money, but they had a good time; they were a very open, outgoing Irish family."

When Eugenie and George were married on November 26, 1919, her annual earnings were larger than his because she was a skilled factory worker with year-round work while he often was unemployed in the seasonal construction industry. Their first home was in a Bronx apartment house on 167th Street near Hoe Avenue. As he recalled:

> We lived in the apartment house several years and then in 1925 I went way up near Pelham Bay Park and bought a lot and built my own house. I hired contractors, but I did quite a bit of it myself. I didn't give any contract for plumbing and my brother was an electrician so we didn't give any contract out for the electrical work. We built a nice house; it's still there.

With his marriage and added responsibilities, meanwhile, he began to take more interest in union affairs:

> I don't know why, but every single Wednesday I would go to the union meeting. A year later [1920] they had an election and one of my friends who worked with me on the job said, "I think there's a chance to break in as a member of the executive board and I think you should run." So I decided to run even though I personally had very few acquaintances in the union, which had about 3,600 members—quite a large union. I think the largest plumbers' union at that time was in Chicago and I think our local in New York was the second largest.

Meany said he was elected to the local board "strictly because my name was Meany." The voting lasted from 8 A.M. to 6 P.M. on a Saturday and, by custom, the candidates lined up at the door to hand out cards with their names on them. "A lot of the fellows," Meany recalled, "came along and looked at the card saying, 'Are you Mike Meany's son?' " Mike's boy won.

At twenty-five, Meany was the youngest member of the board "by far"—with the other members "well up there in their forties and fifties." It was a part-time job, paying $100 a year, and Meany remained a working plumber.

Two years later the young labor politician decided to make a run for a full-time position as one of the business agents of the local union. The work included checking up on the wages being paid and the working conditions to ensure that the union contract was lived up to by the employer. The agent also had to see that the workers abided by each contract, and had to settle disputes between the members and the employer. Leading the infrequent strikes and negotiating new contracts were among the duties.

The decision to seek the agent's post was a turning point in Meany's life, and it was a difficult decision to make. Should he remain in the trade he had been so anxious to enter or should he lay aside his tools and enter the trade of union administrator? Officers of the local union and board members had few duties; the agents were the full-time managers of the union.

In the race for the agent post, Meany was the "clean" candidate. He ran against a man who had held the job for more than ten years, until forced to resign several months before the election because he was being investigated in a city-wide building-trades scandal. When he was cleared, just before the election, the former agent decided to recover his post and he seemed unbeatable because, despite the scandal, he had remained popular with many members. Several others who planned to seek the job dropped out when the veteran agent entered the race. But not Meany; he had made up his mind and would not back off even if the odds seemed overwhelming. Meany won the two-man contest by a 5 to 1 margin, helped by his anti-corruption stand and his father's reputation.

Although no one realized it at the time, when Meany took the agent's job his father's wish had come true: never again did he work as a plumber. He had found a new and more exciting occupation.

> It was the attraction of getting into the union business. I liked very much the discussions on the floor of the union. I'd get up and say my piece. Then, of course, when I became business agent there

was a financial attraction there because a business agent's pay was maybe twenty percent higher than a journeyman's pay, and it was a year-round job. I think my first business agent pay was $60 a week and $15 expenses. This was when the wage of the plumber was $49.50 a week—$9 a day for 5½ days.

From all reports, business agent Meany ran a tight ship. He enforced the contract terms on the members as well as on the employers. It was excellent training for his later union posts. The plumber agent's blunt talk and tough attitude showed up later in Meany's national leadership roles, in which he was bargaining not for three cents more an hour for plumbers but for a new Social Security law or a higher minimum wage for the country's lower-wage workers—most of whom were not union members.

Meany's home life also soon changed, with the arrival of one daughter and later two others. But one thing remained the same. Mrs. Meany refused to let him bring union business home; home was for the family and not for union associates' visits.

"She never mixed in with the union business," Mrs. Lee said. "She was always something outside. My mother was the kind of a woman—well, they were both like that—people whose life-style was very practical, but very private. She didn't like him bringing people home, and he didn't—that kind of thing. So when we were a family, when he did come home to us, we were on our own. We sort of had him all to ourselves, which was a pleasure because we didn't have him very often in the early days.

"He was fun and then he would turn around and do things for us, so his complete concern and his complete interest at that point was focused into the family. In that sense, we never shared him at home. It was like closing one door and opening another."

Meany's growing interest in making a career of the labor movement was shown by his attendance at the New York State Federation's convention in 1922, the year he became business agent. At that meeting, in Poughkeepsie, he was introduced to the founder of the AFL, Samuel Gompers. For the first time, Meany heard Gompers address a gathering:

He was a very, very effective speaker. His speeches were quite lucid, very much to the point. He had a flair for the dramatic; he had a bit of the actor in him. I met him again in El Paso in Novem-

ber 1924, at the hotel just prior to the AFL convention. I had no real
contact with him, as he died shortly after that, in the first week of
December 1924.

By that time, I had already made up my mind that I was going to
stay in the labor movement because I was doing what I wanted to
do. I was doing something that to me was quite satisfying. I felt that
I was on the side of industrial disputes where I wanted to be and it
was quite rewarding to me and it always has been, right up to this
present moment. I never regretted my decision on that.

I became quite well acquainted with Gompers years later by
reading a great many of his speeches and by reading testimony he
gave before congressional committees way back. Gompers was really
an outstanding labor leader.

Reading Gompers' speeches was part of Meany's thorough study of
earlier AFL convention proceedings, contained in books kept on file at
the state Federation office. Meany absorbed the Gompers philosophy
and still could quote it from memory in the late 1970s, although in
practice he revamped it and modernized it.

It was in 1922—the year he first heard Gompers—that Meany
broadened his own area of operations by joining a campaign to clean
up the city-wide council for the building trades in New York. For years
it had been headed by Robert P. Brindell, the dock builders' business
agent, who was sentenced to five to ten years in prison for taking a
bribe in return for ending a construction strike:

> That was a case where a fellow became drunk with power and he
> had pretty much control of the building trades in New York. He just
> gave orders to shut down a building under construction and he
> wouldn't explain to anyone why he was shutting it down—he'd shut
> it down, take the men off the building.
>
> Then he would collect, and when he collected he would let the
> men go back to work. It was bare-faced extortion. He finally got
> clipped and they sent him to jail. That was a big scandal around
> New York and those things hurt the unions, there's no question
> about it.

Brindell's extortion conviction in 1921 was a small part of the
sweeping investigation ordered by the State Legislature. Meany's
union, only indirectly involved through the accusations against the former business agent, withdrew from the Brindell council along with fifteen other unions.

These local unions asked the national AFL to let them form a new council and in February 1923 the new organization was chartered by the AFL's Building Trades Department as the official building-trades council for the city. The old council lost its charter but remained in business.

The new group elected Meany as secretary, a nonpaying post with duties not conflicting with his business-agent job. Finally, in 1927, the national leaders got the two councils to merge and Meany went on the new executive board.*

The board position was part-time and also unpaid and Meany was busy in his business-agent work. It didn't take him long to get involved in jurisdictional disputes—inter-union battles over the right to perform a particular type of work. This costly warfare, which plagued unions in various industries for decades, continued to create major problems for Meany in his various union positions until he forced through a disputes-settlement procedure in the AFL-CIO in the 1960s. This is how he described his own local union's problem and the broader jurisdictional quarrels:

> The steamfitters had a local union that belonged to the same international [as the plumbers did] and there were certain areas of work that were on the borderline between the two trades. There was constant bickering and fighting between the two trades. When I became business agent that fight was at its very height and I felt that the only enemy my union had was the Steamfitters Union. But that sort of faded out after a few years and it doesn't exist now. There was quite a bit of fighting in those days, though.
>
> It started over jobs. It was the effort on the part of the plumbers on one side and the steamfitters on the other to get as many jobs as they could, especially in industrial work, like powerhouses. There was a tremendous argument over different types of piping; it meant jobs. The plumber and the steamfitter fought it out, despite the fact that there was an agreement in existence when the International Plumbers and the International Steamfitters unions merged about 1915. The so-called jurisdictional agreement set up a line of demarcation between the two trades. Actually, looking back, it was kind of a silly dispute, but, still, there it was.

* Meany's own reaction to the Brindell scandal revealed his abhorrence of corruption in unions—stemming in part perhaps from that deep reverence for the "Organ-I-zation" he had seen in the family home. Shortly after he became AFL president in 1952 he was to startle the old-timers by an unprecedented crackdown on crooked officers in national affiliates, through a drastic revision of Gompers' doctrine that the Federation could not interfere with internal affairs of its member unions.

In the building trades there were a great many jurisdictional disputes. They came about mainly because of changes in the methods of installation, changes in the types of materials. Let me give you a very simple example. The plastering of a ceiling is the work of the plasterer. When you substitute plaster board or acoustical tile, which is not put up with a trowel, then the argument starts with the carpenters. They say, "We are the fellows who use the hammer and we're the fellows who drive the nails; that's our work." And the plasterers say, "We're the fellows who finish off the ceiling." That's just one example of how disputes start.

It isn't a case where these trades were just looking for a reason to fight. Actually, when someone came along with a new method of installation or with a new material that was substituted for an old material, they were fighting for jobs.

There also were a great many arguments in those days about materials that would be put together in factories and shipped to the jobs, where building-trades mechanics would install them. I know we had it in our trade. I remember one time we wouldn't use brass tubing because we saw brass tubing as a threat to our jobs; it eliminated the cutting of threads and a lot of work.

Actually, when the unions finally got to the point of saying there is no sense fighting this thing, it brought more work because it was easier to install and was less expensive.

Years later, the building-trades unions established their own machinery to settle the jurisdictional disputes, with binding arbitration by a neutral umpire as the final step. Meany called it good machinery that works, although there are occasional cases in which one trade will go on strike because it doesn't like the decision of the arbitrator.

When Meany was a business agent, the building trades spent a lot of time and energy fighting one another over a few jobs but scorned the idea of trying to unionize workers in the industrial plants. He discussed the attitude of his Bronx members in a 1957 speech:

I can tell you what was on my mind as an officer. . . . We talked about jurisdiction. Did we try to organize the skilled people in our trade who worked in industrial plants? We did not.

My union was a closed union, closed in . . . that it didn't take in new members. It had a closed shop agreement with a closed association of employers. When we had industrial work crop up that we felt we should do, we made an effort—if we had any weight, any pressure—to get that work for our contractors. We wouldn't work for anyone but our own contractors.

We didn't want the people that were on the work; we merely wanted the work. So far as the people who were on the work were concerned, for our part they could drop dead.... We even went so far that we wouldn't even take clearance cards [allowing out-of-town union men to work]. I am not bragging about it. I am not proud of it.

Another example of the attitude of craft-union members was cited by Meany years later as further proof that the AFL's leadership in the pre-CIO days had support for the absence of serious organizing drives in the mass-production industries:

I recall an effort to organize marine pipe fitters around New York. There was considerable work in the marine shops on both the East River and the Hudson. In my own International Union some effort was made to bring them in, and the opposition in my local union was absolutely unanimous. We didn't want them.

Then some industrial work came in when the garment industry had a tremendous building boom along Seventh Avenue, where they put up big loft buildings. A lot of pipe work went into those structures after they were finished: pipe racks to hold clothes. Small shops did that work—they weren't plumbing shops or heating shops, just pipe shops that specialized in putting up pipe racks.

After construction of the building was finished, there still would be a lot of the pipe work to do, and it was the same type of work that both plumbers and steamfitters did. They installed certain equipment for pressing, which also was pipe work. When that work would start while the new construction people still had control of the building—when the building wasn't really completed—the union had some leverage there and they would stop the pipe work being done by others.

I'm talking now about my own local union. We would demand that work and in some cases we would get it. As soon as the building was completely finished we were out and we didn't get any. It went to these other people.

I remember that the suggestion was made at that time why not organize these people and bring them into the union, but the opposition was practically unanimous. These were low-wage people. Nobody wanted them in the union, because of a fear that then they would be competing with our people for the regular jobs to whatever extent they could perform the regular work.

When a member of the local union was in trouble, however, the others rallied round. In a 1969 press conference, Meany referred to his own local union days in explaining that the pressure for legislation comes from the membership. He talked of the push to force through an insurance system to cover injuries on the job:

> Workmen's Compensation came right out of the shop. It came out of the local union. It came to the top [the AFL]. When a workman was injured on the job when I was a kid, we would run a raffle. You would take a collection up at the union meeting to help this guy out until he could get back on the job. We formed little committees. And then, of course, you would have the bad cases, where a fellow would really lose his power to earn at all and he would be shoved on the scrap heap, as it were. The company charitably might find some sort of a job for him to do that would pay him maybe one-fifth of his normal wages.

But at that local union level there was little interest in political action in those years, as Meany told a convention in 1952:

> The tradition of the American worker for many, many years was to stay out of politics. I heard it from my own union, where a man would get up and start to talk about politics and the chairman would say, "Politics is out; don't want no politics." The attitude of the average American worker was that the union was to meet his bread-and-butter problems, his economic problems, but the union had nothing to do with two things and that was the members' politics or the members' religion.

Meany, however, was conscious of political action early in life, as he recalled:

> I remember when I was a boy of twelve or thirteen and on election day I would go over to the election district where my father was an election-district captain for the Democratic party. I recall pretty well that the voting strength in that election district was 360 or 370 registered voters.
>
> I would go over there about four o'clock—the polls closed at seven o'clock—and my father would hand me a slip of paper. I would run to the homes and say, "Mr. Smith, my father told me to come around and ask you if you could get over to the polls and vote." I was getting out the vote. I would run around to perhaps fifteen or twenty places between four and six o'clock, getting out the people. They had voting lists and they would see who hadn't voted.

The elder Meany's involvement in politics probably had some influence on his son's political participation later on, but in his early years as business agent the latter had to contend with those bread-and-butter issues that were of more interest to his members. William Dodd, the onetime coworker, described how Meany operated as agent:

"George was a very vocal individual. He was looked up to by the men in the union because of his quick mind and his ability to analyze a problem, his ability to furnish an answer his membership felt was a proper answer at the time for the problem. In general, I would say that he assumed leadership very early in his political life. He was the youngest full-time salaried officer we had and he was one of the very youngest, I guess, who had ever been elected up to that time as an officer.

"When a problem arose—a matter of the collective bargaining agreement or some jurisdictional dispute with another union or problems they felt were bread-and-butter problems—George eventually, if not immediately, saw it and got the floor of the union meeting. He gave his version of the difficulty and his interpretation of what could be done to alleviate the trouble. He was pretty much listened to all the time; only rarely were his opinions disputed.

"Many times they were only disputed by someone who was drunk. I remember being present one time when a drunken member interrupted the meeting and particularly interrupted George when he was talking. George walked across in front of the chairman and over to this individual. George bear-hugged him, carried him out the door and closed the door behind him.

"George was well liked by the men. He was respected by the employer. George was not a radical. He was a person who knew there were limitations in what the contractor could or could not do, and I think he stayed within those bounds all the time."

Nor did Meany's realism check the demands only of other union members. The Great Depression proved that, Dodd recalled:

"No matter how good a mechanic a fellow was, that didn't mean he was going to get a job. Jobs, during that period, were based on a lot of other things besides mechanical ability, and I'm not downgrading mechanical ability, because that is highly important. For instance, people got jobs because they belonged to the Masonic Order. People might get a job because they were Knights of Columbus, others because they went to the same synagogue, or because they were friends of an employer.

"The local union started running out of funds and was unable to pay the officers the salaries due them. They took voluntary reductions in salary."

Asked about the pay cuts, Meany recalled:

> We cut our own pay, kept cutting it and kept cutting it. We cut it ten dollars and another ten dollars and then we got down to the point where it was exactly the same as the journeyman's and the question came up: If we cut below the journeyman's rate, we would be committing the cardinal sin of working below the union rate.
>
> So what I suggested was: "We won't cut it any further and we'll get paid every other week. We keep working; we won't get paid one week and the next week we will get paid." Several years later they paid me—the president of the union gave me a check for, I think, eleven or twelve hundred dollars. When the union got on its feet, they said, "We owe this money to these fellows." So they paid us for the payless weeks.

> In the 1932 election, there was a Democratic sweep, a reaction to the Depression. The people blamed the Depression, rightly or wrongly, on the Republicans. In fact, an awful lot of people, especially working people, blamed it on [Herbert] Hoover personally.
>
> I didn't agree with that; I didn't think it was true. I think the Depression came because of the way the system worked. We had this so-called boom of the twenties and then we had the bust. We had the stock market running wild. I don't think Hoover was to blame. I think he failed to respond to the problems caused by the Depression.
>
> I think, really, in 1932 things were so bad that it didn't make any difference who the Democrats ran. I don't think it was Roosevelt; I think it was just a nationwide revulsion against the people in charge.

As the Depression deepened in late 1932, Meany took another step into a broader field of union activities. He became a board member of the "Central Body" in New York City, which coordinated activities of the city's local unions. In this he was going beyond the building trades to deal with problems affecting all the AFL workers in the country's largest metropolis.

For technical reasons, this move proved to be difficult at first, until Meany's determination to get ahead won out. He told how he maneuvered it:

> My local union had been a member of the Central Body for as long as I can remember. But a great many of the building-trades

unions were not members and the question came up as to how I could become a member of the executive board of the Central Body when I was not a delegate to the Central Body. The appointed delegates from my local were men who worked at the trade, and as business agent I couldn't push one of them out.

So I hit upon the idea of getting the Building Trades Council to affiliate with the Central Body. This took a little doing because the building trades didn't think much of the Central Body. They used to look upon it as a local debating society of some kind. I went to see John Halketi, the head of the building trades and with whom I was quite friendly. I suggested that the Building Trades Council, as a council, become a member of the Central Body, which had never happened before, because the Central Body is made up of local unions.

He was horrified at the idea, saying, "Join the buttonhole makers and the pants pressers and all that?" Anyway, I convinced him that it was the thing to do and it didn't cost a lot of money. For a union the dues amounted to maybe five or ten dollars a month. I then went to the Central Body as a representative of the Building Trades Council and was elected to the executive board. I got a number of building-trades unions that had never belonged before to join the Central Body.

This was in the depths of the Depression. I became fairly active and was appointed chairman of a three-man special committee to iron out problems involving the various work-relief programs.

During his service on the Central Body, Meany witnessed a new attempt of Communist party members to seize power in the labor movement. He talked of it in a 1953 interview:

The first idea of the Communists way back in the '20s was to tear our people away from us. They had what they called the TUUL, the Trade Union Unity League, and that was sort of a dual movement, pulling our people out. That went on for five or six years, but they weren't successful. Then, the next thing was to infiltrate. And they did infiltrate. They did bore from within.

We had a weak spot in our local central bodies. A central body is a coordinating organization and could be a very convenient sounding board in any city. The average trade union official, who was busy with the affairs of his local union, would not be a delegate to the local central body. He'd give that post to some member who had no experience, as a means of education in the trade-union movement.

So what happened was that the Communists figured this out and they got into the local central bodies. They got in because they were sent there by people who didn't know they were Communists, but they got into those central bodies and the first thing you know they were raising hell. . . . That was in the late '20s and early '30s. We licked them on that. We had quite a time with them, however.

But then, in 1935, our AFL Communist problem was solved completely and finally. The CIO were formed and, boy, the Communists lapped it up. They were welcomed with open arms into the CIO at that time. They are, incidentally, very, very good organizers.

Meanwhile, Meany had participated in a protest meeting against Adolf Hitler and his brand of totalitarianism. In a 1970 speech he talked about it and the old AFL's concern about the foreign policy of the U.S.:

> We have had a longtime interest in the foreign policy of our country going back many, many years, long before the involvement in this present difficult war in Indochina. We have done this . . . because we feel that what our nation does in the field of foreign policy affects the millions of people who are members of our unions.
>
> As a sample, I can tell you of a meeting held in New York City in 1933 at which William Green [AFL president], David Dubinsky and Matthew Woll [AFL vice-presidents] were present. I was there, too, but just as a young observer—oh, just out of curiosity, let's say; I was there as an officer of my own union. And at that meeting in April of 1933 there were two organizations formed: one known as the Anti-Nazi Non-Sectarian League and the other known as the German Labor Chest.
>
> The Anti-Nazi Non-Sectarian League was set up to boycott German-made goods that were being turned out by the regime of Adolf Hitler. The German Labor Chest was set up to collect funds for the rescue and relief of labor leaders who were either in exile from their homeland in Germany or who were in concentration camps, put there by Hitler.
>
> We did this because of our belief that we had a stake in what was happening in Germany in those days, because we knew—and we knew from sad experience—that the first victim of any dictator, whether he is a dictator of the Left or of the Right . . . must be the workingman, because nobody can dictate to any country unless he controls the means of production.
>
> So the significance of this little incident I am telling you is this: It took place in April of 1933 at a time when the vast majority of the American people were unaware that there was any threat to their

future by the actions of this madman 4000 miles away. And the date of April 1933 is significant because Hitler only came to power on January 30, 1933. Less than three months later, American labor was participating with others in the formation of organizations to fight Hitler at a time when the vast majority of our people in this country were isolationists.

Concern over Hitler's rise was just one example of how the outlook of the Bronx plumber was being extended into fields far from the wage-and-working-conditions issues handled by a business agent of a local union. In addition, Meany's growing activities on the board of the Central Body—especially his efforts to help unemployed workers gain relief jobs—brought him into contact with city and state officials. He had dealt with Franklin Delano Roosevelt during the Roosevelt terms as governor and he had begun a lifetime friendship with Herbert H. Lehman, lieutenant governor and then governor and later U.S. senator.

Meany was continuing as one of the business agents of the Bronx Local Union—it was his only paycheck—but he was able to devote more and more time to city-wide labor matters. By 1934 his New York City duties, and problems, were expanded to statewide horizons. The business agent was about to become Meany the Lobbyist.

3

THE LOBBYIST

When I got into legislative work, I would have been satisfied to stay there for the rest of my life, because I liked it. I knew the state, I knew the people of the state. I knew the legislative work; I used to enjoy it. It was very tiring and all that, but, hell, I was really a young man and I had no idea of going any other place. After one year in the job, they doubled my salary. Of course, the salaries weren't very high. I had no opposition, I was going on.

Some people say that Meany was never involved in a strike, but we did have a couple of strikes in my own local union. Strikes in my union were very uninteresting because there were no picket lines. Why? Because there was no attempt to replace the strikers.
I've been criticized on grounds that I never carried a picket sign. That is true. I never had any reason to carry a picket sign. But to say I never was involved in a strike—I was involved in a strike against a pretty powerful employer: Uncle Sam.

In the Depression of the 1930s, George Meany chose a path through the internal political maze of the AFL that seemed to offer him absolutely no chance of advancing to national leadership. In 1935 he led a city-wide strike of skilled workers in New York against the federal government, and specifically President Roosevelt's jobs program to get people off relief rolls. The controversial strike, and prolonged deadlock with FDR, alone might have ruined Meany's chances at higher union office, but the odds against a promotion multiplied when he decided to become "a Federation man."

In 1932 the president of my local union came to see me early in the spring and said, "There's going to be an opening on the executive board of the State Federation." The board consisted of the president, the secretary-treasurer, and thirteen vice presidents. Six of the vice presidents came from New York City, six from north of Westchester County, and the other from Westchester County.

You had six from the City of New York, you had the head of the Westchester County Federation of Labor, you had an electrical worker from Albany, a carpenter from Utica by the name of Bill Brown, a painter by the name of Al Sherman from Syracuse, a hotel and restaurant worker by the name of Manny Koveleski from Rochester, a streetcar man from Buffalo, Clarence Conway, and the sixth upstate man was Jerry Ryan from Binghamton, a printer.

Tradition—always potent in the AFL—held that there should not be more than one board member from any trade. However, this had been violated; there were two steamfitters on the board, and one, a business agent in New York City, was retiring. His successor as local agent also was seeking the board position.

The president of Meany's local pointed out that Meany would have tradition on his side—there was no plumber on the board. Meany, thirty-eight, was young for a union office then. It was ironic that tradition gave him a boost, because he never again relied on this factor; in fact, he broke more than his share of precedents.

Other factors helped: from attending the conventions since 1923, he knew many of the delegates, and State Fed President John Sullivan supported his candidacy. Meany went on the board at the August convention.

He was beginning the career of union leadership he desired, but he had no thought then of national office. He knew that a State Fed post was not the way to national leadership, because, in those days more than now, the lines of advancement were rigidly drawn. For example, in the Plumbers Union, a man usually moved up from a local union office to an officer's post at national headquarters of the Plumbers. Officials of the American Federation of Labor customarily were elected from high positions in the national unions. AFL President William Green formerly had been secretary-treasurer of the Mine Workers, for instance.

Meany's state post as board member was only a part-time office with occasional meetings to attend, and he could retain his union offices in New York City. Then, some sixteen months after Meany went on the state board, Sullivan resigned the presidency to accept a state government post. The vacancy was to be filled by the state board until the next convention.

The favorite to win was Emanuel Koveleski, of Rochester, who was the senior member after twenty-four years on the board. The members from upstate areas were backing him. But seniority did not stop Meany, the newest and youngest member, when the voting began December 6, 1933. Meany expected to get seven of the thirteen board votes but ended up with six: a New York City Teamster member he assumed would back a fellow New Yorker voted for the upstate man and elected him. Meany explained that the Teamster Union leadership in New York City had opposed him because Longshoremen President Joseph P. Ryan, who had endorsed Meany, was a political enemy.

That was the first and last time Meany lost a race for union office. Determined to wipe out the stigma, he declared his candidacy again the following year and conducted what the press called the most vigorous campaign in state labor history.

Delegates disregarded seniority to elect Meany, 233 to 185, over Koveleski in the customary caucus and, the next day, formally made it unanimous in the public session. He was the youngest man to hold the office in forty years, the surprised press reported. He had been elevated from his lowly position as twelfth vice president to the top. (Meany was re-elected to four more annual terms without opposition.)

For his first eleven months in office he received $5,307.48 in salary and $1,140.40 in travel expenses, according to the secretary-treasurer's report. Meany resigned as business agent of the local in the Bronx, although remaining active on the Central Body in New York City, an unpaid post.

In his acceptance speech at the convention, the new president set a pattern of brief ceremonial addresses he was to follow throughout his career. This one had only ninety-four words, including: "The problems that we are facing now are difficult and complex and I feel that, with the spirit shown at this convention, we can face them in an optimistic frame of mind."

It was amazing that, with the Depression and its problems, this forty-year-old business agent, entering an entirely new line of work, could speak confidently of the future. The next year's legislative results, however, proved he had the right idea.

At that time the New York Federation was one of the largest in the

country, with almost 800 local unions affiliated; it spoke for an estimated 850,000 workers—more than one-fifth of all union members in
the United States. Meany enlarged that membership—partly by convincing David Dubinsky, head of the Ladies Garment Workers, to send
his local unions in. At first Dubinsky argued, "That organization is run
by Tammany Hall," but Meany told him, "It isn't going to be run by
Tammany Hall anymore; I'm going to run it." The locals came in, and
Meany ran the Federation.

He also threw more energy into the state presidency than any of his
predecessors had, as he met with national and state officials, pushed for
new laws, conferred with AFL union leaders around the state. In his
first eleven months, the record shows, he made 38 formal speeches,
gave 8 radio addresses, and attended 202 conferences or meetings. He
took 38 train trips between Albany and New York City plus 22 railroad journeys to other cities. He often held a meeting in New York
City in the morning, rode the train to Albany that afternoon and attended sessions of the Legislature or other meetings that evening. For
all of those speeches, Meany never took lessons in public speaking. Social events also kept him busy, as Meany explained:

> I was about as busy as a man could be—and enjoying every min-
> ute of it. I had a lot of nights out. I was home as much as I could be,
> but a lot of these things took place at night. The so-called social side
> of it was pretty difficult to avoid, to say no to them. It might be the
> twenty-fifth anniversary of the establishment of a local union or the
> twentieth anniversary of a man holding the presidency, and they put
> a dinner on for him. They would expect the president of the State
> Fed to come there.

Some lobbying took place on train rides between New York City and
Albany.

> The routine would be to take the Empire State Express that left
> Grand Central Station at nine o'clock in the morning and got you in
> Albany around noon on Monday. Then, coming back on Wednes-
> day nights, it was like a great big party from Albany to New York—
> not much lobbying but a little drinking and a lot of talk. The train
> would be absolutely jammed with legislators and staff members,
> people who lived in New York and worked in Albany. When they
> got toward the end of the session, it would be seven days a week,
> practically [in Albany].

Often Meany would drive to and from Albany during the sessions. Between trips, he spent weekends with his family at their Bronx home, as he did later during the first eight years he was in Washington. Daughter Eileen Lee described her father's role at home in those days practically as that of a cherished visitor.

"It was my mother, basically, who raised us. It was Mother who was the disciplinarian. He was always someone who, when he appeared, was a family signal for rejoicing and a good time. We went everywhere. When he came home, he took us as a family every weekend to ice shows at the Garden or the circus or just Sunday dinner out on Long Island.

"This was my concept of my father as a disciplinarian: he was somebody who came on the weekend and it signaled a good time as a family. Mother did all the hard work, so far as raising us was concerned—and, yet, he was always close."

Cigar smoke in the house was a welcome signal to Meany's oldest daughter, Regina Mayer, because her father's appearance on weekends was such a happy occasion: "That's one of the reasons I like the smell of cigar smoke. I opened the door and I could smell cigar smoke and I knew my father was home: I can't remember him without one." (Meany once said he never smoked cigarettes but took up cigars because he thought his father "looked elegant with a cigar.")

Mrs. Mayer agreed that Mrs. Meany was the disciplinarian: "He's too much of a softy; he would like to stay out of it. He always backed up my mother."

Father disappeared when repairs were being made to the house, Mrs. Lee recalled: "We always joked in the family that whenever anything had to be done around the house—if the painters came—my father would leave town. Then he would call up and say, 'How are the painters doing?' We'd say fine, and then he would reappear as they left. He was never there when there was any trouble or turmoil; he always managed to avoid the thing. His timing was exquisite."

Asked if her father's memory enabled him to keep track if they failed to carry out an order of his, Mrs. Lee laughed: "But he never ordered!" The daughters ranged in age from four to eleven when Meany began his five-year stint in Albany.

The years in Albany were among the happiest of his life, Mrs. Lee believes. "Those were his best years. They [her parents] loved being in New York; they were young, they've always had good health, both of them, on the whole. My father had a very good, rich life. In summer we went to Lake Luzerne and spent a month or so. When the Legislature was in session at the time—if there was a crisis of sorts—he would go back and forth to it.

"My father would drive us from the Bronx to the cottage; it was fifty miles north of Albany and in those days the trip took all day. He was the only driver; my mother did not drive. He had three little girls in the car who needed to go to the bathroom or were hungry or who sang. I was told, and I don't remember, that I said my prayers aloud, which I think drove my mother almost bananas. We would stop for lunch and my father would say he had to rest his eyes; we would all get out of the car and he would have about half an hour's nap. I often have wondered at his patience. In a month or six weeks, we would do the whole thing in reverse—a car full of giggling girls."

Union chores such as politics cut into the happy family times, although political action then was nothing compared with the modern labor effort:

> Those were the days when labor's political activity amounted to very, very little. We followed the general policy of the American Federation of Labor at the time: we didn't spout politics, but we passed resolutions of endorsement of a particular candidate. When a man was running for re-election, we would pass a resolution and send him a letter in which we told him we passed the resolution, that we liked the things he was doing.
>
> The only thing he could do with that letter, the only political effect he could get with it, was put it in a pamphlet and distribute it. We didn't make speeches, we didn't campaign, we didn't do any of the things we do today.

Meany's philosophy on lobbying in Albany, on the other hand, has been carried over into modern-day legislative efforts in Washington:

> My general policies on lobbying then and now are the same, exactly the same. I told Biemiller in 1956 when we designated him [AFL-CIO] legislative director: "Andy, in lobbying there are just a couple of things that I want you to remember. You never beg and you never threaten. And always keep in the back of your mind that the other guy may be right. That's it."
>
> I don't think we're always right on the things that we want. Some of them, when put to the test, don't work out. I don't think we're perfect. I think generally what we try to do is good—not just for our members but good for the country as a whole. For instance, protecting the consumers of America is good for America.

But I never believed in threatening. I never believed in saying to a
fellow, "If you don't vote for this bill we'll get you next November."

In Albany, four and a half months a year were devoted to lobbying. The month before the Legislature session opened was devoted to
getting bills prepared. Six months out of the year were spent on legislative work and the other six on traveling around the state, keeping
in contact with local unions, getting local unions to join the State
Fed, and attending social affairs.

On national issues of policy, the state federations are required to follow the lead of the national Federation, but in the matter of state laws
a state fed runs its own affairs, as Meany explained:

You have to look at the structure of the AFL-CIO and of the old
AFL because the structure is the same for state feds. The AFL was,
and the AFL-CIO is, a federation of national and international
unions with, presently, 106 of these unions. The AFL-CIO is a coordinating organization; it does for these unions collectively what they
feel can best be done that way—such as seeking national legislation.

The state federations of labor are practically duplications of the
AFL-CIO in the various states. They combine the local unions of the
various national unions; they form coordinating organizations and
are chartered by the AFL-CIO. They do not have the autonomy
that the national unions have; they must follow national policy of
the AFL-CIO. Outside of that, however, the state feds manage their
own affairs within their own state. Any position they take on state
legislation or in relation to state agencies they are perfectly free to
take, unless it would be a position that in some way contravenes national AFL-CIO policy.

Thus, Meany had great leeway on state issues and legislative proposals. In the 1935 legislative session he testified before committees on
some 112 bills. As the bills reached the voting stage, he used his secret
weapon: an address book containing home and office telephone numbers of every important AFL union official in the state. After making a
head count, if he found that some friend of labor was about to oppose
the bill favored by the Federation, he would alert unionists in the legis-
lator's home town and suggest a call be made on the straying friend.

It was very effective. I can recall talking to the chairman of a
committee in Albany early in the evening and being told, "I can't go
with you on this particular bill" and then meeting him two or three

hours later, when he would ask, "What the hell are you doing to me?" He'd been hearing from back home.

I've always felt, while we had good lobbying effort here in Washington, that if we really want to put pressure on an individual congressman the place to put pressure on is right back where he gets elected. I did that in Albany years ago and I did it very simply with that little book in my pocket, and all those telephone numbers of everybody.

Prospects for labor victories in the 1935 session, he said, were excellent:

> We had a very friendly governor, [Democrat] Herbert Lehman, who not only would endorse a bill but would fight for it just the same as we did. He didn't just give it pro forma endorsement. He would follow it up and find out what happened [in committee]. It really became his program. For the first time in twenty-two years, the Assembly and Senate were controlled by the Democratic party. So we did have a rather unique situation that enabled us to pass this legislation.

Meany himself felt that those five years in Albany were the highlight of his career, as he told a 1969 press conference when asked if, looking back, he might have preferred some other line of work: "I don't know of anything that could ever possibly have given me the excitement—if you want to put it that way—the interest or the satisfaction."

During the Albany years, he said, "we put more legislation on the statute books of that state in favor of labor than had ever been put on in any period before or since by any other state." He continued:

> I worked hard, but I was damn lucky. . . . I came in there at the depth of the Depression. It is an amazing thing how the attitude of a state legislature toward labor can be influenced by a Depression. During the so-called boom days in the twenties, during the [Calvin] Coolidge and Hoover days, it was a rare thing to get two labor bills through the State Legislature, but when labor was flat on its back— it was a very odd thing. I suppose it was due to the fact that these people had to run for office and they knew that these workers needed this sort of help. . . .
>
> I had a governor who was without parallel, in my book, in the field of public service: Herbert Lehman. . . . We presented him with a program in the fall of 1934 . . . and he took all but one [proposed

bill]. He put them in his campaign [and later] proceeded to go to the Legislature with legislation that we helped to draw up on every one of those items.

Meany also praised Lehman highly in interviews for this book:

> When Lehman became governor—he had been a lifetime Democrat and his whole family were Democrats—he said he would appoint only Democrats to public office, provided they were qualified. Oh, the old Tammany crowd didn't like that at all because their idea was that you rewarded the clubhouse guys by giving them the appointments.
>
> Lehman told them, "I will fill every appointive job that's at my disposal with organization Democrats and I will take the recommendations from all the leaders in various segments of the Democratic party, but I will not appoint anybody to any job who is not qualified."
>
> People realized very quickly that he was not a political hack and wasn't going to go along with political hacks. I can remember, though, meeting some of these Tammany guys who would say, "Goddamn Jew banker, why the hell did we ever pick him?"
>
> He was a very good governor and he kept to his promises.

Herbert Lehman, who was fifty-four years old when first elected governor, did not look, or act, like a politician. Short, almost bald, with a fringe of gray hair and a round face above a stiff collar, he was solemn and reserved. His rather dull, but fact-packed, speeches were delivered without expression. He was the opposite of the flamboyant politician who avoids facts but depends on dramatic delivery and personality.

His father had helped found Lehman Brothers, a New York investment banking firm, and he grew up in a German-Jewish society vastly different from Meany's Irish one. He was an honor-society student at Williams College, while Meany was self-educated. Yet Meany teamed up with this man of such a contrasting background to push through a flood of laws.

There were close calls, however, because the margin in the Assembly was dangerously slim: 76 Democrats and 74 Republicans. The danger was dramatized by the voting on labor's top-priority measure, the Unemployment Insurance Act. This pioneering state law was credited with materially helping to get Congress to enact a national statute in this field.

The New York Senate approved the bill, but there was a long delay in the Assembly with the measure tied up in committee. Finally, Lehman made a phone call to the Speaker of the Assembly, and the bill went to the floor. Meany recalled the close margin:

> A young assemblyman from the Bronx was one of the seventy-six Democratic votes. We needed seventy-six to pass a bill, but we had figured on seventy-seven because we had a Republican assemblyman from Yonkers who had publicly supported this bill. But the Bronx man had a severe heart attack and never got back to the session.
>
> That meant we had seventy-six votes on this particular bill, and there was a tremendous battle. The State Manufacturers Association put up a very bitter fight. The floor opposition was led by Irving Ives, the Minority Leader.
>
> The Governor originally was opposed to the Unemployment Insurance Bill. This was not surprising, as he was a banker. But we talked to him at length and worked with his assistant, Charles Poletti. Once he changed his mind, he was just as strong an advocate of unemployment insurance as I was.
>
> What Lehman did was very interesting, because Lehman didn't think politically—so he was the best kind of politician. When the bill came up in the Assembly, he sent his assistant secretary, with a tally sheet, to sit alongside the clerk as he called the roll. It was really intimidation, in a way, but I'm sure Lehman didn't even think of that. He just wanted to make sure that he got a count and got it quickly.

The Republican from Yonkers joined with the 75 Democrats to adopt the bill. Under a procedure to allow switching after passage of a bill, the final count was 102 favorable votes.

Ironically, the State Federation was able to lobby for the insurance legislation that year only because the national AFL had reversed its position in July 1932 on a similar national measure. Until then, national AFL leaders had opposed such insurance plans.

> They took the old-fashioned approach that we don't want insurance; if the employer has got any money to set aside to insure against unemployment, let him put it in the pay envelope. They changed their position, and what brought that about was quite obvious: the events had caught up with them. They were not dealing with a social theory now; they were dealing with the fact of fourteen percent unemployment or whatever—the millions of people unemployed in 1932.

Another progressive measure put on the books was the Security Awards Law, designed to make sure that money awarded to workers seriously injured on the job—or to families of workers killed—would be paid under the existing Workmen's Compensation Act. Meany had been shocked to discover that some six thousand compensation awards were unpaid because the insurance firms had gone bankrupt.

Insurance companies fought to block the measure, taking thousands of their employees and supporters to Albany by special trains to pack a committee hearing room. Meany and two other Federation officials and their witnesses were the only proponents of the bill present. Despite the numerical odds, the measure became law.

During the session, labor and Governor Lehman pushed through legislation that had been sought for decades in some instances. All in all, in three and a half months, the State Fed lobbied for 108 bills and saw 62 of them enacted. Sixteen were major pieces of legislation.

In a 1963 speech Lehman described Meany's lobbying role this way: "Of course, George Meany's main concern was to advance the cause of the men and women of labor he was serving, and to raise their standard of living. But, over and above that, he always took into consideration the interest—the paramount interest, of course—not only of labor but of the American people. . . . He never asked me for a thing, either as Governor or as a member of the United States Senate, that I had the right to question so far as his sincerity, as far as his patriotic interest was concerned."

Only three months after the end of the productive 1935 legislative session, Meany entered his crucial confrontation with President Roosevelt over wage rates for skilled workers on public-works projects that were creating jobs for the unemployed. Meany's leadership of the resulting strike was a bit of labor history unknown to union workers in later decades, when the Auto Workers' Walter Reuther and the Teamsters' Frank E. Fitzsimmons were voicing claims that the AFL-CIO president had never led a strike.*

Early in his state federation career, Meany had been appointed chairman of a committee set up by the Central Body in New York City to coordinate relations between the various trades and government officials running the work-relief programs. Now, in 1935, a major prob-

---

* Reuther raised this "issue" in his bitter attacks on Meany during the 1960s, hoping to convince the rank-and-filers that the Federation head was not a labor warrior like Reuther but was merely an office man, a "pie-carder." Fitzsimmons made the same noises in his general grumbling about the man who had led the AFL-CIO in expelling his union from the AFL-CIO.

lem had developed, one affecting not only New York craftsmen but those in other big cities, as Meany explained:

> The federal government decided that they were going to change the whole method of paying this relief money. Everyone was going to be equal. Earlier they had been paying them on a varied hourly rate, paying the legal prevailing wage.
>
> The prevailing wage laws had been on the New York statute books for some twenty years at that time. The principle, we felt, was quite sound, and I still think it is quite sound. When government goes into the field to do work or to purchase materials or equipment made by private employers, they are in a sense injecting themselves into the general economy.
>
> If the government says, "We, because we are the government, are going to buy as cheaply as we can buy and we're not going to pay any attention to legal standards or conditions," it's pretty bad. The government should be a fair competitor and should at least pay the prevailing rates—the wage which is paid to the most people in a particular industry in a particular area. It should not depress wages in the labor market.

In June, worried federal officials sent General Hugh Johnson to administer the new policy in New York. Meany understood that Washington was fearful of resistance to its policy, "which meant a breakdown of the prevailing rate all over the country." If they could put it in effect in New York, it would be easier to enforce it elsewhere.

On July 1, Meany met with Johnson and several others, with most of the persuading being handled by Edward F. McGrady, a troubleshooter for Roosevelt and a former AFL organizer.

> McGrady did most of the talking. He was explaining this new government policy and how everybody was going to be treated equal. After a long-winded explanation, he said, "Now, you'll go along with that, won't you, George?"
>
> "I will like hell go along with that," I replied. "I'll not go along with any proposal that asks my union men to work for less than the union rate of wages."
>
> Up to that time, Hugh Johnson had been sitting on the side, absolutely quiet; he hadn't opened his mouth except to say hello when we shook hands. When I made that response to McGrady, Hugh Johnson's hands hit the table and he said, "Goddamn it! I knew there was some catch here. I knew that this wasn't as nice as they were telling me it was going to be. I knew there was some catch."

I told him, "You're asking me will I go along with a plan by which my people will be merged with everybody else, completely equal. It doesn't make any difference whether you have any skill to contribute or not. What you're saying is, you want union people to forget the prevailing rate of wages because they are in trouble and have to work for the government to prevent starvation. You're asking me to cooperate. The answer is absolutely no! I will not cooperate!"

After the meeting broke up I made arrangements to meet with Johnson again—this was about a month in advance of the time the plan was to go into effect about August first. I had quite a bit of contact with Johnson and I discovered that he was completely in agreement with my approach on this thing but he was an Army man and he was sent there by the Commander in Chief to do a job under these conditions. He was quite unhappy and he tried to change the Administration's position. I developed a very good personal relationship with him.

Johnson and Meany later went to Washington to see Harry Hopkins, in charge of the national program, but Hopkins declined to talk to Meany. Back in New York, Meany met with officials from all the skilled-trade unions to make strike plans. Some 2,300 building-trades mechanics were among the 60,000 or so workers on the public works projects in the city.

On these projects of the Works Progress Administration, Meany explained, where skills were required, officials assigned a craftsman to each gang of ten or more unskilled workers. The union craftsman showed them how to perform the jobs.

When the WPA ordered the new rate system put into effect in August, the union craftsmen voted to strike on August 9. Meany and Johnson shared time on a radio broadcast the following night, with Meany explaining:

> What we are trying to do is to uphold the wage standards that have taken years of intensive effort to build. . . . We now say to our Government, if you can afford to allot our people $60, $70, $40, or $50 per month, we have absolutely no complaint, but we must firmly say to you that, whatever you want to allot, do so at the standard legal rate in order that we may be able to maintain that which is dear to every union man, a standard rate of wages.

As the strike dragged on, the unskilled workers on the projects continued on the job but were not able to work without the guidance of the craftsmen. Meany and Johnson made several radio speeches, and, to avoid unfair comments, exchanged copies in advance, during pre-broadcast dinners together. One New York newspaper termed the strike "Mutiny on the Bounty," and the press generally attacked the walkout. But the decision on ending the strike, Meany felt, had to be made in Washington; there were no negotiations in New York. Finally, Johnson telephoned Meany from Washington to say, "I got this thing worked out, on one condition."

The condition was that Meany and the other union officials would not cry victory. Meany said he had no interest in claiming a victory. When they met in New York subsequently, Johnson asked how it was to be worked out and was given a list showing the number of hours each trade would work per month to collect that trade's prevailing wage and keep the man's total within the government's wage of $93.50 a month. For example, a worker normally getting $2 an hour would work about forty-seven hours a month under the plan.

Johnson announced the schedule the next morning and the strike ended on September 15. A few days later a group of reporters checked out the union hourly rates with Meany and discovered that the settlement had retained the prevailing-wage principle. One editorial declared that Johnson had been "outmaneuvered," but there was no great publicity about it.

In the discussion for this book—from which the above is summarized—Meany was asked why he agreed with Johnson not to claim a victory. He replied:

> I have no desire to brag about winning. If you win one here, you lose plenty of them, too. To me, if you're fighting for a principle and you win— that's the satisfaction. I'm certainly not much of a political animal. But there is no question that the people in the White House at the time said, "All right, go back and get it settled somehow, but we don't want any victory cry." Well, there wasn't any victory cry, no great announcement.

Despite the adverse economic situation, the New York unions had preserved the principle of the prevailing wage and the national AFL wanted to extend the rule elsewhere. On January 16, 1936, Bricklayers President Harry C. Bates told fellow members of the AFL Executive Council that the "bitter fight against the security wage" had been won in New York but "in many sections of the country the wages on WPA

projects are so low that they are breaking down wage standards established by the organized labor movement."

William Green, the president of the national AFL, assured Bates
that Harry Hopkins had indicated that the prevailing-wage rule would
be extended to the other areas. Green was recorded in the official minutes of the closed meeting as reporting on a confidential talk he had
had with Hopkins, who was quoted as telling President Roosevelt that
the security wage had failed, that they "just couldn't put it over." The
minutes went on to say: "The President in a large way agreed with this.
Mr. Hopkins pointed out to the President that the people who are dis-
satisfied and protesting against this are the masses of the people and
the papers supporting it are against the President anyhow."

Meany had won his only big strike, but he didn't get much time to
think about that. Almost immediately, he would witness one of the
most important and dramatic moments of American labor history.

4

THE BIG SPLIT

Roosevelt was thinking politically. . . . He wanted to split the AFL because the old Executive Council of the AFL was, by and large, very conservative, very conservative. They were not supportive of the Democratic party. . . . I'm quite sure that those forming the CIO received great encouragement from the White House at the time.

Franklin D. Roosevelt was high on George Meany's list of those who caused the Big Split in the 1930s, a split that completely restructured the U.S. labor movement and vastly expanded its membership and power. In an odd quirk of history, Meany was a powerless delegate at the 1935 convention, where John L. Lewis, the Mine Workers' president, made his final moves for a massive organization drive that would create the CIO. At first his organization was called the Committee for Industrial Organization; later, as a permanent entity, it became the Congress of Industrial Organizations.

Meany had only one vote in 1935—a "one-lunger" in AFL parlance—because he represented a state federation. National unions such as the Mine Workers cast one vote for every one hundred members. Thus, Lewis, with four thousand votes, had clout, and probably didn't know that Meany existed. Yet they would clash later in crucial labor showdowns, with Meany emerging the winner. As an observer of the action and from his subsequent intensive research, Meany drew the following conclusions:

I think Lewis set up the CIO strictly as a basis for a political machine. I don't think there's any question about it. He was following an old Lenin doctrine that the way to be politically active was to organize workers as a mass. That was the reason Lenin opposed the American trade-union structure, because it was not effective politically. It was set up in craft unions and not one employer, one union. When Lewis and Sidney Hillman [president of the Clothing Workers] created the CIO, I think that's what they had in mind—political power.

I have no hard evidence, but it was pretty well known around that forming the CIO had a political side: that Roosevelt wanted to be assured of labor support and felt that he could never get it out of the conservative AFL.

The CIO was created, of course, by Lewis and Hillman, and the basis for the CIO was laid here in Washington at the AFL's 1933 convention. I had one conversation with Hillman in 1935 or 1936 and he made a prediction to me that the AFL would disintegrate within six months. So we got the notion that was one of the things they had in mind, but the AFL didn't disintegrate.

Hillman was very close to Roosevelt, and Roosevelt, like every other President, was just elected [in 1932] when he was starting to think about the next election. It looked as if Roosevelt was going to seek more active political support and he didn't figure that he would get it through the old AFL Executive Council, which was fairly conservative.

I always took the position—and said so many times—that there was no good trade-union reason for this split. There might have been a political reason; there might have been a personal reason. There might have been Lewis' drive for power and, of course, anybody who knew Lewis and was associated with him over those years will concede, they would have to concede, that this was the driving motivation: personal power. He wanted to run the American labor movement in the same one-man fashion he ran the United Mine Workers for many, many years—it was a one-man affair.

A lot of the people who were with Lewis on issues and on problems did not want Lewis to be in full charge, because, I think, they had a certain fear of him.

Political motives were mentioned by Meany in a 1953 interview, but he didn't mention Roosevelt by name:

CIO was not really formed to carry the ball for industrial unionism. The CIO was set up because there were several men in this country who felt that they needed a political arm among the workers of the nation. The industrial-union idea was a bugaboo designed to cover up the political motives of the sponsors of the CIO.

John L. Lewis was the best dramatic actor ever to mount the platform of a labor convention. A massive head and a mane of coal-black hair plus the trademark bushy eyebrows and jutting jaw made him an impressive, often terrifying figure. He was nearly six feet tall, with a prominent paunch. Cold, gray eyes glared down opponents. He never smiled on stage, on camera, unless the script demanded a faint smirk to show that some slighting reference to himself was meant to be—and obviously must be—merely a joke.

Lewis never underestimated his own importance (which sometimes led to oversized errors of strategy). From the arrogant tilt of his black fedora to the way he walked, he showed he was in charge. His voice could be played like an organ, from booming denunciation to confidential whisper. With all that equipment, Lewis was a master of not only dramatics but public relations. He delighted newsmen with biting descriptions of his enemies and sonorous quotations from the Bible and William Shakespeare.

If television had been available then, Lewis might have had a run for the U.S. Presidency—a goal he obviously had in mind but missed owing to miscalculations and inflation of the ego, not to mention lack of qualifications and public support.

As a delegate at AFL conventions, Lewis at the time was respected, if feared, by his peers. His Mine Workers Union was the largest in the Federation and also the leading industrial type of organization—taking in everyone working at the mine from skilled machinist to day laborer, as well as miners. That meant his union crossed craft lines, the "jurisdictions" carved out by the Carpenters, Plumbers, Cigar Makers and other unions which had formed the AFL's predecessor organization in 1881. However, by the 1930s, millions of factory hands worked in the mass-production industries without representation by unions. As Meany explained:

> There was no sentiment among the old AFL craft unions for industrial-type unions, as far as I can see, and the craft unions were the ones that controlled the AFL; they had the majority voting strength. They were the building trades, Machinists, Electrical Workers and unions like that. Our biggest industrial union in the AFL at the time was the Miners. We had a small steelworkers union, the old Amalga-

mated Iron, Steel and Tin Workers, but it had never gotten off the ground.

So when Lewis was fighting for the AFL to really get off its butt and get out to try to organize these mass-production industries, he didn't have much chance of success. The craft union situation in the AFL was still very strong and I think that the Ladies Garment Workers and many of the other unions felt that this was holding the AFL back—that they would never organize mass industries if they had to organize them into ten or fifteen separate unions on the basis of craft jurisdiction.

I think they were right in that. I've always felt that Lewis could have avoided the split by just going along the way he was going. Lewis, in my opinion, could have had his way inside the AFL. I don't think there was any question about that. I think it might have taken another year or so. He had been rebuked quite soundly [in 1921] when he ran against Samuel Gompers for the AFL presidency and lost by a two to one vote. But there was a growing agreement with Lewis' philosophy, Lewis' desire to move the AFL, to modernize it and get it into the big industrial field. There was a lot of such sentiment among the unions: Printers, Garment Workers, Hatters, almost everybody outside the building trades and some metal trades.

But there was always this reservation that they didn't want Lewis to head up the AFL. They'd go along with him, but they would not—it was a funny thing: they were afraid of him. They were willing to follow him, but they didn't want him to head the AFL. I'm sure he knew that in a couple of years he would have his way [with industrial unionism], but he couldn't get Green out [of the president's job].

What precluded any drive in the mass-production industries was the attitude of the AFL at that time, and this included the building trades and a good many other unions that are now big industrial unions. It certainly included the Machinists. Their attitude was: You can organize any mass-production industry you feel like as long as you give us the people that should be members of our union.

They looked down on factory workers. They looked down on them, first, because they were not union men and, second, because their wages were so low compared to the high wages in the building trades. It was the attitude of a skilled man toward an unskilled man. It wasn't as if they wanted to kill them or anything like that. It was just that "he's unskilled, and he's not in the class with us skilled men."

Back in the 1920s, the craft attitude was: If you went into a factory to organize and there were some painters, they wanted those painters in the Painters Union. If there were a few machinists, they wanted those in the Machinists Union; the electricians they wanted in the Electrical Union. They didn't want any industrial union that put them all in one union.

The craft unions are successors of the old European guilds and the one dominating feature of the guilds was skill. A man would be an apprentice first, but he could never be admitted to the guild until he attained the skill that was necessary. This idea of the people in the craft unions getting paid a wage comparable to their skills is not new. It goes way, way back.

In these industries that Lewis wanted to organize the wages were miserable. They were miles away from the printers or the building trades, and there was always a fear that, by opening the doors and bringing these people in, it would add to the job problem.

It was not just the opposition of the leadership. The opposition of the leadership reflected the feeling of the members. It was not a very progressive approach, but they were trying to cling to something. The fear was that by bringing in low-wage people they would be, in some way, a threat to maintenance of high wages, which the union members already had in the shops that were organized.

In building-trades conventions that I went to in those days—my first building-trades department convention was in 1924—all of the time at the meetings was spent in arguing jurisdiction between their own unions. That's pretty much behind us now. But that was a way of life for them; they just argued jurisdiction. When they had the separate conventions of their own unions, this would be a big topic of discussion: what some other union was doing trying to take their members away and all that sort of thing.

Fights went on for years. Actually, they involved very, very few members, but that didn't make any difference. They used to say, "It isn't the number of members, it's the principle: Do we maintain jurisdiction? If we lost our jurisdiction our union would be destroyed."

These fellows didn't sit up all night trying to find something to argue about, but when a job appeared that they felt belonged to them, they argued. For example, the Carpenters had a knock-down, drag-out fight with the Machinists that went on for twenty-nine years until it finally was settled, about the early 1950s. This was an argument over conveyors and conveyor belts [which, once carried on wooden rollers, were then carried on metal].

It was that sort of thing that would bring on the jurisdictional dispute. The introduction of different methods, different materials, would immediately bring on a jurisdictional dispute, and from the

viewpoint of the trades that were losing the work, they were losing
jobs. That was what their interests were: to try to maintain jobs. It
was the workers who lost jobs that prompted the disputes.

Craft unions had fared better financially than the Mine Workers did
during the recession of the 1920s, which nearly destroyed Lewis' union.
Its dues-paying members, according to one authority, declined from
more than 400,000 in 1920 to fewer than 150,000 or possibly as low as
60,000 by 1930 because many unionized mines had to close. Lewis ordered "no backward step!" and miners struck to preserve their contract
wage scale.

> Roosevelt put Lewis on his feet after Lewis' organization in the
> twenties was starving. I remember being on a "Save the Miners
> Committee" in 1928 in New York. We were collecting money, blan-
> kets and clothing and sending them out to Pennsylvania. Other
> unions tried to save the miners. One particular winter there were
> thousands of miners living in tents because they had been put out of
> their homes, which were owned by the companies. It was all part of
> the miners' way of life in those days, and it was pretty desperate.
> I don't think the Miners Union got into a position of relative fi-
> nancial security until the early days of the Roosevelt Administra-
> tion. Roosevelt was pressuring mine owners to unionize and using
> the powers of the President—whatever power he had—on the Con-
> gress to be helpful to the Miners [through the National Industrial
> Recovery Act and, later, the Guffey-Snyder Act].
> Part of the agreement the operators had with Roosevelt was that
> if legislation was enacted they would stop their resistance to union-
> ization, particularly in the West Virginia mines. These mines had
> been non-union for forty years or more. The basic idea of the Guffey
> coal bill was to allow the mine companies to fix prices without get-
> ting clipped by the antitrust laws. It was an escape from the anti-
> trust provisions, the theory being that this was a distressed industry
> and needed government help. The mine operators wanted the right
> to hold up prices, and I'm sure they held up prices by some kind of
> agreement. The Guffey Coal Law gave them that right.
> The result was that the Miners Union started to become finan-
> cially secure, because every time Lewis signed up a non-union mine
> there was a checkoff of union dues, which went to the Washington
> headquarters of the Miners Union.

At the 1933 AFL convention, Meany, who was a spectator, recalled,
Lewis "displayed a good deal of muscle." One of his victories involved

the admission of Sidney Hillman's Amalgamated Clothing Workers into the AFL. The clothing union had been formed in 1914 by rebellious local unions that left the AFL's United Garment Workers, which now had the power under AFL rules to block the entrance of the Amalgamated.

An arrangement was maneuvered by Lewis in the convention to bring the Amalgamated into the AFL. It was agreed that the Amalgamated would buy union labels from the Garment Workers in return for the charter. An alliance was formed by Hillman and Lewis. It was political; I'm sure that was the big idea back of it. It really was the foundation of what happened in 1934.

I believe that when Lewis got into this fight in 1933 and 1934 he deliberately planned to break away from the AFL, that he did not really plan to work inside the AFL, although he did set up a committee to work inside. He set up the Committee for Industrial Organization knowing full well that would be considered a violation of the AFL constitution and disloyal. That was the first step. [The second step was the formation of a permanent, rival organization to AFL.] The real start was made in the AFL convention of 1933 in Washington.

Hillman was very close to Roosevelt, and Roosevelt was thinking politically. He wanted the break; he wanted to split the AFL because the old Executive Council of the AFL was, by and large, very conservative, very conservative. They were not supportive of the Democratic party, while, of course, Roosevelt had a lot of support there. The so-called hierarchy of the AFL at the time was Matt [Matthew] Woll, very conservative and prone to go Republican, and Gus [G. M.] Bugniazet of the Electrical Workers, an out-and-out conservative Republican.

I don't have any evidence, but what I really believe is that when Lewis brought Hillman into the AFL and made this deal—sort of forced this thing over—it was the forerunner of a political setup. I'm quite sure that those forming the CIO received great encouragement from the White House at the time. I think Roosevelt wanted it to happen, although it wasn't very long [before] Lewis fell out with Roosevelt. When they brought Hillman in and made the fight in San Francisco in 1934 and then followed up in 1935 in Atlantic City, the whole purpose was political as much as anything else.

Lewis had been a staunch Republican and supporter of the Penrose machine in Pennsylvania; he supported Republican candidates in Pennsylvania for quite a few years.

Meany's contention that as early as 1933 Lewis was plotting to break away from the AFL appears to be confirmed by Saul Alinsky in his generally friendly biography of Lewis. Alinsky reports that the Miners president told him he began planning for the creation of the CIO in the spring of 1933. Lewis, by that account, tried to convince AFL President Green that the Federation should launch a vast organizing drive in the big industries because of expected New Deal legislation that would aid unionization. Lewis is quoted as stating that when Green rejected the idea Lewis "knew it was up to me" and "the next day I began to plan the CIO."

Having won some tactical victories in 1933, Lewis moved on to the 1934 AFL gathering, as Meany explained:

> Lewis in 1934 was feeling quite secure as far as miners were concerned and he started this campaign to really take over control of the AFL; no question about it, that was his purpose. At the convention in San Francisco, Lewis started his revolt and he picked up a lot of allies.
>
> He came up with one-third of the vote and it was quite obvious that it would not take very long for John to win out, because the Miners were in good shape then. On some of the key issues he was able to force the Executive Council to make concessions to him. They did agree to do something about organizing the large mass-production industries.
>
> Now, they didn't follow through and keep that promise, but they did make the commitment.

Lewis was able to use the split among the building-trades unions to get some craft votes for industrial unionism—quite a tribute to his skill. Three of the most powerful unions, the Carpenters, Bricklayers and Electrical Workers, had pulled out of the construction department a few years earlier. That was the usual ploy: If a big union was defeated in some inter-union battle, it quit the department, or the AFL itself.

These three dissenters, however, now had reason for returning to the department; membership there gave added clout in administration of the so-called "Blue Eagle" regulatory codes of the National Recovery Administration (NRA), which fixed prices, wages and hours of work in each industry. The department got Green's assistance in bringing them back. It was optional whether an affiliate of the AFL joined the department. But after the trio sent in their credentials for the 1934 de-

partmental convention, it became known that they had made a deal
with some of the unions in the department that gave them a majority
of the votes.

To prevent the takeover by the Carpenters, Bricklayers and Electrical Workers, Meany explained, the ruling group there—headed by the
Plumbers—rejected the credentials of the Big Three. Green denounced
the move, because a department has to accept any union that is eligible if it cares to come in. The issue went to the AFL's own convention,
which overwhelmingly ordered admission of the three unions. (It
wasn't until 1936 that the Carpenters, Bricklayers and Electrical
Workers were taken back—and promptly defeated the "old crowd" in
election of officers.)

Meany recounted how Lewis operated at the 1934 AFL convention:

> Lewis took advantage of this building-trades split, playing one
> group off against the other. He also made noises about supporting
> the Brewery Workers in their fight with the Teamsters, which the
> Brewery Workers lost. As a result of his maneuvering, he was able to
> force the Executive Council to make concessions to him. One was
> the enlargement of the Council [making room for Lewis and six
> others].
>
> The other concession was the adoption of a resolution pledging
> the AFL to organize the mass-production industries—to really do a
> job in organizing them. When they left the San Francisco conven-
> tion, Lewis had the support of these additional leaders and he had a
> commitment on organizing.

The convention directed the Council to issue charters for national
unions "in the automotive, cement, aluminum and such other mass
production and miscellaneous industries as in the judgment of the Executive Council may be necessary to meet the situation." A recruiting
drive in the iron and steel industry also was ordered. The Council, for a
provisional period, was to direct the policies of these new unions and
appoint their officers.

The craft leaders were marching into the modern industrial age, but
they were dragging their feet all the way, reassured by this portion of
the resolution: "We consider it our duty to formulate policies which
will fully protect the jurisdictional rights of all trade unions organized
upon craft lines and afford every opportunity for development and ac-
cession of those workers engaged upon work over which these organizations exercise jurisdiction."

Lewis, a member of the resolutions committee, joined in the unanimous approval by the committee of this drastic policy revision—the first rewriting since the 1901 convention adopted a "Declaration of Jurisdiction," which founder Gompers helped draft. Lewis appeared to be happy with the new policy, and he also had won a seat on the powerful Council. Meany in 1969 commented that in the 1934 convention Lewis "put up quite a fight and made a very good showing, if you were looking at it politically—one fellow fighting the Executive Council, as it were."

But the "victory" had repercussions almost immediately. The Council heatedly debated over how large the jurisdiction of the proposed auto union would be. Finally, it was awarded the assembly and parts plants—without various skilled craftsmen working there. At the first United Auto Workers convention in August 1935, Green delivered the charter and appointed the officers, with AFL organizer Francis Dillon as president. Rubber workers in the tire factories refused to accept the limited charter and appointment of officers and continued to recruit among skilled workers eligible for the craft unions.

Representatives of the few local automobile and tire unions attended the 1935 AFL convention seeking to get wider authority and independence. As president of the New York State Federation of Labor, Meany had a single vote in the meetings, since the votes of the local unions in that state were cast by their national union at the AFL's annual conventions. Therefore, they did not get a second vote through their state federations. (The same practice is followed in the AFL-CIO today.)

At AFL conventions the power brokers were the heads of the national unions, such as Lewis, with his four thousand votes at that meeting, and William L. (Big Bill) Hutcheson of the Carpenters, with two thousand. Voting strength was based on the per capita "tax" paid to the AFL—one vote for every one hundred members, at that time. The most influential of these titans were on the Executive Council, which ran the Federation between the annual conventions.

Meany had a surprisingly objective view of the impending split—coming, as he did, from one of the strong craft unions—and he offered this assessment:

> Between October 1934 and October 1935, the date of the next convention, the Executive Council did nothing to implement the action of the thirty-four convention—which gave Lewis his big argu-

ment. He said, in effect, "You promised me and you didn't keep your promise"—and, of course, that was true.

When we got to Atlantic City in 1935, the fight was renewed and this time Lewis was playing with the other faction in the building trades, against the Carpenters, Bricklayers and Electrical Workers. They played along with him and he was looking for their votes on the industrial-union issue, but he didn't get them. It was a case of double-crossing a double-crosser, somebody said at the time. There was a lot of politics involved and Lewis lost in that 1935 convention. He got quite a good vote, but he lost on a number of issues.

Lewis said that the Council [in its 1934 resolution] had seduced him with fair words. He said they hadn't kept their word and they hadn't. Lewis had gotten promises that they would really put on a drive to organize mass-production industry. Of course, that never happened, because inside the AFL at the time the crafts jealously protected their desire to maintain everybody in the craft unions.

As the crucial debate began at the convention on October 7, John P. Frey, secretary of the resolutions committee, spoke for the proposed resolution rejecting creation of plantwide unions. Frey argued that the Federation had made a contract with the craft unions guaranteeing "jurisdiction over all workmen doing the work of a specified craft or occupation covered by the organization," as well as complete autonomy over internal affairs.

A minority report by six of the fifteen men on the committee stated that after fifty-five years the AFL had only 3.5 million members out of the 39 million "organizable" workers in the U.S. Organizing of mass-production industries was blocked by workers' fears that they would be divided among the craft unions. Lewis' minority wanted to compel the Council to remove restrictions and begin an aggressive recruiting campaign.

Committee Chairman Matthew Woll protested against the proposal to take from the Council the right to use its own discretion in issuing charters. Woll reported he had heard of threats that unless the industrial charters were granted "there might be secession and the organization of another federation of labor." He said he thought the threat was a bluff.

When the prolonged debate ended at nearly midnight, the Lewis minority's report lost by 10,933 to 18,024, and by voice vote the convention adopted the majority report reaffirming the 1934 policy. Thus, the Council kept its discretionary authority to issue the charters.

Days later, after disposing of other matters, the convention took up a request from the new Rubber Workers Union for full jurisdiction over all rubber workers. The resolutions committee recommended rejection of the plea, to protect craft claims.

Big Bill Hutcheson of the Carpenters interrupted the speech of a Rubber Workers' delegate with a point of order: "The industrial-union proposition has been previously settled by this convention."

A glowering Lewis shouted that "this thing of raising points of order all the time on minor delegates is rather small potatoes." To which Hutcheson retorted, "I was raised on small potatoes. That is why I am so small," as he drew himself up to his six-foot-two height. He accused Lewis of wasting time "attempting, in a dramatic way, to impress the delegates with his sincerity."

President Green sustained Hutcheson's point of order and the ruling was approved. Then, as Lewis returned to his delegation's table— across the aisle from the Carpenters—a blow was struck that went down in labor history.

The official word-for-word transcript of proceedings fails to mention the incident, but witnesses reported that Lewis landed a punch on Big Bill's nose as they met paunch-to-paunch in the aisle. The Carpenters' chief overturned his table as he fell back, while Lewis calmly relit the cigar that had been in his mouth throughout.

Some observers said Hutcheson had called Lewis "a bastard" before that single blow was struck. Others thought Lewis had staged the "fight" to get publicity for his upcoming organizing drive and to offset his defeat in the convention voting.* In any case, brief as it was, the incident drew newspaper headlines across the country and dramatized the Lewis crusade for industrial unionism. Thus, Lewis lost in the voting but won in the headlines.

Hutcheson, Meany recalled, had been angry with Lewis at that convention but not over the industrial-union issue. He was sore because Lewis, after being on his side in 1934 in the building-trades fight, now was backing the opposition faction—only to have it double-cross him by opposing plantwide unions. Actually, Hutcheson and Dan [Daniel J.] Tobin of the Teamsters did not take a leading role against Lewis in the industrial-union dispute. "Their approach to the Lewis thing was

* The Alinsky biography of Lewis quotes him as saying, "An act of some kind, an act dramatic to the degree that it would inspire and enthuse the workers of this country, was necessary. . . . It was essential. With this in mind, I laid my plans and Bill Hutcheson, unknowingly, was to be one of the main actors of the cast. . . ."

really that they didn't want Lewis to run the show. It wasn't a question of craft unionism, because the Carpenters' was pretty strong back in those days."

The Machinist Union, under Arthur O. Wharton, however, was engaged in fighting the emerging industrial types of unions.

> Wharton's union originally was pure craft. He wanted his machinist; he didn't want anybody but his machinist. He didn't care how many production workers there were; he wanted his machinist—this was the craft approach.
>
> Of course, when the CIO got going, Wharton dropped that completely; he became just as industrial-union-minded as anybody else. He took in anybody and everybody. But before he began expanding, Wharton did not take in the machine operator, the production worker. The machinist was the man who built the machine and repaired it—all sorts of machines.

The records show that Meany not only didn't speak in the debate but didn't always cast his lone vote on convention issues. He wasn't part of any machine. His powerlessness in those early years helped enormously in his later peacemaking role.

> I was just a little stranger from New York and my acquaintanceship was mainly with my own international union and with other building trades that I had gotten to know over the years. For instance, I had never met Arthur Wharton or Dan Tobin then and I knew Hutcheson only through a chance meeting at a New York social affair. I had met a few others of the building trades.

As for relations with the Miners' chief, Meany said Lewis ignored his existence for years. In 1969, Meany gave this analysis of Lewis' 1935 situation:

> His strength had grown tremendously. He had over 35 percent of the vote and that was a tremendous showing. I can recall some of the old-timers saying, "Give him another year or so and he is going to be all right."
>
> But he didn't want a year or so. He didn't want to control; he wanted to split. He didn't want the things he was fighting for; that was just the test of strength. So he split and formed a committee. He

said he was not forming a rival organization, just forming a committee. But it was only [three years] later that he transformed that
committee into a permanent organization.*

In any event, the Lewis group set up the Committee for Industrial
Organization on November 9, 1935. Its members were eight union
chiefs: Lewis, as chairman; Charles P. Howard, Typographical Union,
as secretary; Sidney Hillman, Clothing Workers; David Dubinsky,
Ladies Garment Workers; Thomas F. McMahon, Textile Workers;
Harvey C. Fremming, Oil Workers; Thomas H. Brown, Mine, Mill
Workers; and Max Zaritsky, Cap department of the Hatters.

In a letter to the CIO, President Green expressed "feelings of appre-
hension over the grave consequences" that might follow formation of
an organization within the AFL, and the CIO's secretary replied. The
debate-by-mail continued until the AFL Council in January ordered
the CIO to dissolve immediately. This was followed by filing of formal
charges of "dual unionism" by two craft-union leaders. Finally, the
CIO unions were ordered to "come home" by September 5, 1936, or
face suspension. Nobody came, and ten former AFL affiliates in the
CIO were suspended. (Nine charters were revoked by the AFL in
1938.)

While all this maneuvering was going on, the young CIO began the
recruiting drive which in two years or so was to change whole industries from "open shop" to unionized shops. Never before had there
been such a huge organizing crusade as the CIO launched in 1936, in
fields like steel, autos, rubber, farm equipment, electrical products and
textiles.

CIO organizers told millions of workers that "President Roosevelt
wants you to join the union" and pointed to the new Wagner Act (National Labor Relations Act). That statute put the government on
record as encouraging workers to join unions to bargain collectively
with their employers. The National Labor Relations Board stood
ready to punish any company that fired workers for union activity.
Meany explained the law's help to organized labor:

> The Wagner Act came along in 1935 to establish collective bar-
> gaining as a right under law. A lot of the old-timers weren't so en-
> thusiastic about the Wagner Act. Their philosophy was, "Why do
> you have to have the law tell us that we have the right to collective

* Contrary to claims by top AFL officials, Meany said that he thought the creation of a
committee within the AFL to promote industrial unionization was "legal" under the Federation's constitution.

bargaining? We've got that!" I can remember one old-timer saying, "God gave us that right. We don't need the Congress."

But the point is that there were a lot of people who were denied this right, and the Wagner Act opened it up for them.

Way back in the 1920s and 1930s the blacklist was a common thing. A man would try to start a union in a shop and he would not only lose his job; he couldn't find a job in that industry.

Before the Wagner Act, there were strike-breaking agencies whose sole purpose was to deny the right of collective bargaining. They would not only break strikes, but they would infiltrate the union. A man would be very active at a union meeting and the next day he would be fired for something he said at the meeting. Without the Wagner Act I don't think we could have organized the mass-production industries.

Lewis seized the initiative, but with mixed results.

Lewis picked up the best organizers there were. I say "organizers"; I'm not talking about people to run unions. I'm talking about people to get workers in. He picked up Commies—every Commie he could—and the Commies were all good organizers.

What they offered these workers was a union that was going to do a great deal for them. The old AFL theory was you join a union to see what you can do to help make the union go. These CIO workers were told, "You don't have to do anything. You just join and we'll take care of everything." So in the early days the CIO was very successful in organizing, but they were not successful in holding members and building stability in the union.

The CIO was organizing on a different basis than AFL unions did. In the old AFL, you joined the union, you became a member almost the same as you became a member of a church. Lewis brought in all the hot-shots, the radicals and the Communists that were in other unions. They all flocked to Lewis and he took them all in. They were outstanding organizers; they could get people to join. They were not very good in conducting the affairs of a union.

Observers have argued as to whether Lewis, in hiring the Communists as organizers, was using them or whether they were using him. Meany thought "it ended up with them using him."

He was so egotistical. When Dubinsky was arguing about using Communists as organizers, he said to Dubinsky, "Well, who gets the bird—the hunter or the dog?" In other words, the Commie organizer was the dog and Lewis was the hunter.

One of the techniques the CIO adopted was that when you joined you paid nothing; you paid no dues and no initiation fee. The theory was that you didn't start paying dues until the union did something for you.

In the old AFL, you joined a union and you paid your dues whether you were working or not, because you were trying to preserve the union as an instrumentality to build up work standards. Therefore, the loyalty of workers to the union was much stronger in the old AFL than it was in the CIO. In fact, that loyalty really didn't exist in the CIO.

Looking back on the early CIO, Meany said he thought the split between the AFL and CIO "could have been avoided by John L. Lewis accepting something less than full control of the AFL." He felt that Lewis did have legitimate grievances on the industrial-union issue— "no question about it." And he thought the AFL's craft-union leaders should have compromised with Lewis on that issue. Moreover, he conceded that the CIO was a help to the labor movement. But he added that he didn't believe Lewis had "set it up for that"—but for political reasons:

The fact that the CIO was set up had a tremendous effect on the industrial workers. When this split came, the old AFL conservatives were under attack, and they got off their butts and went to work. Unions that had been in the doldrums for years, just maintaining a certain level of membership and satisfied with that membership, went out and started organizing.

When it came to organizing, while the CIO did a very good job in the sense that they organized a lot of people, the AFL unions did a better job because the people they organized they kept. The CIO would organize them and, with their tremendous turnover, would lose them.

It had to happen sometime. I think when Lewis set up the CIO one of his best trade-union arguments was the failure of the AFL to organize the mass-production industries. I think that would have happened without the CIO; eventually the very big industries would have been organized. But the CIO certainly brought some of the largest corporations into unions.

Thus, Meany could be critical of both craft- and industrial-union leaders in assessing the blame for the split, and was so at the final convention of the old AFL in 1955, on the eve of merger with the CIO:

I have no desire to rehash ancient history, to review the type of argument that brought about the division. . . . I am convinced beyond any doubt by my study and by my own knowledge of that period that these differences of opinion that caused the split could have been worked out within the framework of the American Federation of Labor as it was at that time. There was no need for a split.

In the heavy-industry states, meanwhile, there was plenty of action from the CIO organizers. The United Rubber Workers and United Auto Workers formally joined the CIO in 1936. The tire workers experimented with the sit-down strike, in which the employees took over the factories and occupied them until management surrendered on a contract. By early 1937 some 45,000 workers were seizing various General Motors plants for six weeks, until Lewis negotiated an agreement that eventually led to unionization of the auto companies.

Turning steel into a union industry took longer, but CIO unions spread through much of American industry. As a wave of CIO strikes hit the country, the AFL decided to fight back.

By 1937 the dispute with CIO really got hot; [on May 23] there was a closed convention of the AFL in Cincinnati, with no press and no outsiders. It was sort of a council of war. It was at this point that the AFL really started to move; all the AFL unions started to organize.

They were organizing without regard to jurisdiction or anything else. They were organizing any industry they could. Frankly, they did a pretty good job because by World War II there was no question that the AFL had the most members. The CIO membership went up drastically during the early days of the war, but then it went down just as drastically right after the war.

The war helped, since the government was much interested in production and expanded factory employment. Also, we had the War Labor Board and there were a number of things that certainly were to the advantage of union organizing. In the beginning, the CIO picked up hundreds of thousands of members—whom they promptly lost as soon as the war ended.

By 1945 they were concealing their membership; they wouldn't tell anybody how many members there were; they wouldn't even make a report to their convention on those figures.

The AFL unions were really much stronger—there was a certain amount of tradition there.

One difference between the rival federations was that while CIO headquarters took charge of organizing drives and financing them, the AFL turned the job over to its affiliates.

> As soon as the CIO really got to be a going concern, all of these craft unions without exception stepped right out and organized. I'll give you an example: the Structural Iron Workers had about 40,000 members. They had had that 40,000 members for quite a few years and they paid very little attention to any part of their business except the structural end. That's where the big money was.
>
> When the CIO threat came in 1937, they turned around and started organizing. Boy! They organized; they tripled their membership in about three years—after being stagnant as far as organization is concerned for maybe twenty years before that. So when Lewis got organizing anybody who would let you put his name on the list, that served as an impetus to the old AFL people. From that point of view, it didn't do any harm. The AFL membership went up and up.

Dues-paying AFL membership rose from about 2.9 million in the early fall of 1937 to more than 3.6 million a year later, and to nearly 7.6 million by 1947. In late 1937 the AFL thought it had an agreement on ending the split after two subcommittees representing the AFL and the CIO met off and on for two months. Meany, not involved, mentioned these talks at the 1952 AFL convention:

> After a number of sessions, they brought in a report and were prepared to release it to the press. It was completely agreed as to the method of bringing these organizations back into the AFL.
>
> Phil Murray [one of the CIO negotiators] presented that to John L. Lewis in his office, and John Lewis walked over the window, looked out the window for about ten minutes and then solemnly strode back to his desk, tore the proposal up and put it in the wastebasket without reading it.

Asked for this book if he thought the unity negotiations in 1937 were conducted in good faith, Meany said he had no way of knowing as he wasn't in Washington then, but he added: "From the grapevine, I have the impression that they never got close together. Why, I don't know. I don't think you talk about good faith, knowing Lewis. I don't think there was any good faith on his side. At that point he was determined, for his own purposes, to have a separate labor movement. Of course, after 1940, he also, for his own purpose, took another line."

Lewis in 1937 was in full charge of the CIO side in the negotiations, Meany felt. "The shots were being called by Lewis, without consultation with anyone. He wasn't in the habit of consulting people he considered subordinate to him—and people that he considered subordinate to him included all people. That was the monumental ego he had."

The document Lewis rejected—read or unread—included agreement of the negotiators that there was no jurisdictional obstacle to the return to the AFL of the twelve unions that had been suspended or had left the AFL, according to an AFL report to its 1938 convention. However, it stated that "since the CIO had established twenty additional unions in the same fields occupied by AFL unions, it would be necessary to consider each of these twenty new CIO unions separately in an effort to remove the conflict with the AFL unions."

Thus, the report added, the twelve former AFL unions would not be readmitted to the AFL until "all matters" affecting the twenty other unions were adjusted. (When Meany in 1955 achieved the merger of the AFL and the CIO, he agreed to immediate affiliation of all the CIO unions, without questions of "jurisdiction"—the exact opposite of the 1937 terms.)

As Meany had expected from the beginning, on November 14, 1938, the Committee for Industrial Organization took the formal step of converting itself into the Congress of Industrial Organizations and conceding that it was a separate federation. Leaders claimed a total membership of 4,037,877 among the thirty-two national unions and nine organizing committees. Formation of a permanent federation prompted the Ladies Garment Workers and United Textile Workers to leave the CIO.

CIO's membership figures were often exaggerated, insiders admit, and were not supported by information on actual dues-payers. The more than 4 million claimed compared with a dues-paying membership of 3,623,087 for August 1938 reported by the AFL. The report estimated that an additional 1.4 million members were unemployed, bringing the AFL total to more than 5 million—the largest in its history up to then. The AFL's organizing drive had more than replaced the million lost when the CIO founders were expelled.

Meany, however, was not involved in this recruiting campaign. He was busy in New York State showing that he was as good a politician as he was a lobbyist.

5

THE POLITICIAN

*I felt many years ago and still feel that under the U.S. system, which
Gompers used to refer to as "bread-and-butter trade unionism," we made
more progress for our workers than did the workers in democratic countries
who had a definite tie to a labor party.*

The infant CIO was moving into politics as well as organizing workers and, in 1936, its political efforts in New York State happened to
coincide with Meany's own desire to re-elect Roosevelt. Meany proved
to be an extremely pragmatic politician—in fact, somewhat of a tight-
rope walker.

He set up his own state AFL committee to support Roosevelt, but he
also was asked to cooperate with the newly formed American Labor
party, which had the same objective. It was a branch of Labor's Non-
Partisan League, which had been launched in April 1936 by the CIO's
John Lewis and Sidney Hillman and by George L. Berry, president of
the AFL Printing Pressmen.

Although working with a labor party was directly contrary to
Meany's philosophy (and that of Gompers), Meany decided there were
practical reasons for an exception in this instance. Even so, his cooperation definitely was arm's-length:

> In the 1932 election, Roosevelt got no official support from any of
> the Socialists. They had their candidates, and there was a tremen-
> dous membership—a good deal of it either first- or second-genera-

tion American—in New York. They just wanted no part of the Republican party—as the reactionary party—or the Democratic party, because they identified the Democratic party with Tammany Hall, corruption, and so on.

So Roosevelt—I imagine it was Roosevelt—James A. Farley and maybe Hillman came up with the idea of setting up in New York State what they called the American Labor party. The idea was to get those Socialist votes for Roosevelt in the 1936 election. The AFL had no policy on that at all; this was something happening only in New York State.

Farley called me up and asked me to come over to see him. He told me frankly what they were doing and its purpose. One thing about Jim Farley: he would never lie to you; he was just as straight as a die. My immediate response was "I don't want anything to do with any labor party."

"I know that," Farley said, "but this is for the thirty-six campaign and we don't want any friction. You people are for Roosevelt; these people who are forming the American Labor party are for Roosevelt, too."

So, as a result, we not only didn't get in a battle with them—they did their business and we did ours—but I agreed to let them copy the mailing list of the New York Federation of Labor for the purpose of sending out mailings. They had trouble organizing the Labor party upstate. They had no trouble in New York City, but there were few Socialists among the labor people upstate. They were pretty much Democrats and a strong representation of Republicans, especially in the rural areas. I cooperated with Farley during that campaign.

The State Fed mailing list also was helpful in gathering the required number of voter signatures to put the party on the ballot. It helped volunteers, headed by Morris S. Novik, to contact upstate AFL adherents. Novik stresses that, under Meany's orders, he burned this entire roster after the election so that it could not be used by the Labor party in later campaigns. Meany was intent on aiding this party only for the sake of Roosevelt.

For the first, and only, time in his life, Meany was on a ballot in that contest. The same list of New York electors had to be used by both the Labor and Democratic parties, and he agreed to go on it with other union leaders. The Labor party polled 274,924 votes for Roosevelt.

Meany's campaigning for Roosevelt and for Governor Lehman was done through the State Fed's Non-Partisan Committee, as authorized

unanimously by the Federation convention. It was possible for a state
federation to endorse a Presidential candidate because the national
AFL had taken no position. Meany told the next New York Fed convention that the 1936 effort gave "practical effect to the traditional
AFL policy of rewarding our friends in public office." In later years, he
was to go much further in giving "practical effect" to the old Gompers
policy in national politics. But after the 1936 election, Meany had
nothing more to do with the Labor party.

It was a one-shot deal, something for that election. Then the Communists came in and grabbed control of it. They split and the non-
Commie element created the Liberal party, which still exists in New
York. The Commie end just sort of disappeared, although there are
local splinter parties here and there.

As for a permanent labor party, Meany always opposed the idea:

The greatest thing about Gompers was that he decided he wanted
a labor movement that was purely American. He was an immigrant
and a good many of the people who were active in the American
labor movement at that time were also immigrants. Gompers was in
a constant fight with what he called Socialists in those days—people
who had these ideas: One, the Socialists wanted a labor party; two,
the Socialists believed in municipal ownership of transportation and
so on. I wasn't against municipal ownership. I can't recall that, as far
as philosophy is concerned, I was very far away from the Socialists at
all. But I was in complete agreement with Gompers, and am still in
agreement, that a labor party for American workers is not the answer to our problem.

We look around the world—this is not just today, this is going
back seventy-five years—and we see the major labor movements in
the free world have a definite, solid tie to a political party. For instance, in Britain the British Labour party is a creation of the British
labor movement; it is in a sense the property of the British labor
movement, which finances it and plays a tremendous role in deter-
mining the policy. There always is a little conflict between the people in the Labour party who are not directly from the labor movement and the people who go to the annual conferences of the party
representing unions.

If you're going to measure the efficiency of a labor movement on
the basis of what it does for the standard of life and work for its
members—and I don't know any other measuring rod—the American trade-union movement has accomplished more for the Ameri-

can worker than has the trade-union movement of any other country on earth.

I take a very practical view and Gompers took a very practical view that he did not want to run the country. When you set up a labor party—I don't care where it is—and you tie yourself to a labor party, you are saying, in effect, we not only want better conditions for the people we represent, we not only want to raise the standard of life, we want to run the country. Gompers took the position that it was not our job to run the country. Our job was to be nonpartisan; our job was to try to make progress for the people we represented by economic strikes—by withholding our labor—by boycotts, by using our purchasing power through the use of union labels, and by legislative action.

Legislative action means that you must be political, you must be engaged in political activities, because you wouldn't get anywhere in legislative activity unless you were able to influence to some degree the composition of the State Legislature and the national Congress.

This was Gompers' theory: That we could best advance the standard of life of American workers by withholding our labor, by going on strike if necessary, and by using our power at the ballot box—not through a political party but through endorsing candidates we felt were favorable to the things that were important for the great mass of American workers.

The Gompers philosophy was not to be nonpolitical, it was to be nonpartisan. The Gompers philosophy basically was that labor should not tie itself to a political party in any way at all. That is still our policy and I don't think there was any better demonstration of it than in 1972 when we said we wouldn't go with the Presidential candidates of either party. We had a perfect right to say, no, we didn't like either candidate.

I've heard it said in Britain that when they elect their own government they're always told, "Don't rock the boat; we're running the country now and we've got to be careful." I've heard that from British labor leaders, but I'm not passing judgment. I merely say we have done better through our methods of putting pressure on public officials for the things we want than they have done.

Gompers established a labor movement in this country and shaped it so it fitted into the American scene. That is why it was more or less accepted over the years by the American people. That doesn't mean that the vast majority of the American people agree with us on some of the things we advocate. But I think that they do agree that it is not a bad thing for this nation to have a pretty strong labor movement. I think this was the real legacy of Samuel Gompers for the American worker.

In line with Gompers' belief in legislative activity, Meany sought to continue in the 1936 session of the Legislature the highly successful lobbying of the previous year. However, the Republicans in the 1935 election had recaptured control of the Assembly, ending the brief period of Democratic dominance over both houses. Labor was fortunate to have Governor Lehman on hand to veto bills aimed at destroying progressive measures.

Meany conceded that far fewer pro-labor laws were passed during the balance of his stay in Albany but pointed out that, having achieved nearly all its major goals in 1935, the Federation didn't have many measures to push for in the following sessions.

Twenty-two bills proposed or endorsed by the Federation were enacted in the 1937 Legislature. Lehman's Social Security program was among them, as were laws creating a State Labor Relations Board—as part of a "little Wagner Act"—and a State Mediation Board for labor-management disputes.

A new law to fix minimum wages for women and children was enacted also, after the U.S. Supreme Court had reversed its decision invalidating a 1933 New York statute. Meany put the State Federation on record as heartily favoring protection for women and children and also headed a large group urging ratification of the Child Labor Amendment to the U.S. Constitution. Meany later recalled the crucial Assembly hearing:

> A powerful element in the Catholic Church was opposed to the Child Labor Amendment. We were campaigning for its approval, and at the hearing we were doing very well. All of the left-wing organizations were supporting the amendment, too. The Assembly chamber was packed to the doors.
>
> The Catholic bishop of Albany came in his ecclesiastical robes and he was bitterly opposed to the amendment. We lost it right at that hearing because the galleries were full of the Commies and the radical groups and they just booed and booed and booed—which was exactly what the opponents of the amendment wanted.
>
> It was a rather disgraceful episode, and we lost enough votes even though we had some very prominent Catholic members of the Assembly openly fighting on our side.

In connection with that session of the Legislature, Meany long afterward revealed how he helped convert Republican Irving Ives from "conservative" to "very liberal and very fair." Ives had led the fight against unemployment insurance in 1935 as the Minority Leader of the Assembly and had moved up to the Speaker's post in 1936 with his party's capture of majority control.

> In the summer of 1936, I made a speech that was very critical of Ives and his record. This was at a Printers Union convention in Binghamton, only eleven or twelve mile away from Ives' home town, Norwich, and the speech was rather widely quoted in the papers in that area.
>
> In January 1937 there was an internal fight in the Republican party—a real knock-down, drag-out fight, sort of a revolution— which the papers said was staged by the "Young Turks" in the Assembly. They put on a tremendous campaign against Ives and defeated him for the position of Speaker, although he was supposed to be automatically made Speaker. One of the things they used— strangely enough—inside the Republican party was that Ives had no standing with labor, and they distributed copies of the speech I had made the previous August.

As a compromise, Meany recalled, the Republican caucus elected a new Speaker but put Ives in as Majority Leader. Ives soon asked for a meeting with Meany and admitted, "I don't know anything about labor problems." The response was an acid "You do a lot of voting." But Meany said it was a pleasant meeting "and I really struck up a friendship with him as a result."

> Ives took a very definite turn toward a liberal. I wouldn't say he became pro-labor, but he became very liberal and very fair in his approach to legislation. He was fairly helpful in the Legislature from that time on. He also got an idea for a labor school and I think it was from that experience that the labor school [at Cornell] really developed. He was the father of that school; he pushed the legislation through.
>
> Ives came to Washington afterward [as a U.S. senator]. I got to admire him very much; he was a very sincere sort of fellow.

Soon after the Legislature adjourned, Meany went to work in the successful 1937 campaign to re-elect Mayor Fiorello H. LaGuardia. While he had never been an official or staff worker of the Democratic party, Meany said he voted for that party's candidates most of the time he was in New York. He campaigned for Roosevelt and Lehman in 1932, obtained State Fed endorsement and spoke at political rallies held by the AFL unions. In 1933, Meany voted for the Democratic opponent of LaGuardia, an independent candidate whom Meany later supported enthuasiastically.

"We looked upon LaGuardia in those days [1933] with some suspicion; we looked upon him as a Socialist who was a gadfly," Meany said. "We didn't take him seriously. But when he was elected mayor he promptly started to support union labor in the subways, in heavy construction, in school construction, in printing."

A quarrel over wiretapping of union officials by special prosecutor Thomas E. Dewey, however, interrupted the Meany-LaGuardia friendship for six months starting in late 1936. This affair revealed two traits of the future AFL-CIO president that often were demonstrated publicly during his career: (1) a basic belief that everyone—citizen, police and U.S. President—should obey the laws, and (2) an intense hatred of corruption in labor unions.

Because Meany had caused a complaint to be filed with Mayor LaGuardia about the reported wiretapping, the mayor called a closed meeting of the City Board of Estimate to hear both sides:

Dewey, of course, stalled around. He was very entertaining, talked about organized crime. He took the board all over the country, told us about the Purple Gang, the Capone Gang, the Jersey Mob and the Kansas City racketeers.

He stopped to get his breath and I said, "Now, Mr. Dewey, you say you're not tapping the wires of union officials in this town?"

He stalled around but finally said, "Do you know what it takes to tap a wire? It takes nine policemen—three shifts."

The wires had to be tapped by policemen. Under the New York City charter, the mayor controls the Police Department—absolutely. It's his.

Dewey finally admitted, yes, he had tapped a few wires. I paid no more attention to him and turned to LaGuardia. I gave LaGuardia quite a dressing-down; "You're the great liberal, the great liberal crusader. You're the fellow who demonstrated your liberalness ten years ago by making beer on the Capitol steps in Washington."

I really lit into him. He was the only non-Democrat on the Board of Estimate. He was squirming and he got arguing with me: "What are you trying to do; protect racketeers?" I said, "No. I don't believe in wiretapping without a court order. I know positively they are tapping." I knew without question because the police officials who were following the Mayor's instructions in tapping the wires told us.

LaGuardia never admitted that he had permitted the wires to be tapped. I just said, "Any wires that were tapped, you're responsible for. You own the Police Department and no wire can be tapped without your signing for it." On Monday morning, he took all the taps off.

Afterwards, Dewey continued his investigation and he did turn up a lot of corruption, especially in the hotel and restaurant industry. He sent some employers to jail and he sent some union people to jail in that industry. I'm sure he did some [more] wiretapping, but I'm sure he did it under court order. I was delighted to get rid of the racketeers.

Despite the fact that Meany subsequently had reason to believe his own wire was tapped, Meany and LaGuardia restored their friendship shortly thereafter.

In May of 1937, LaGuardia sent one of his commissioners to ask me to come in and talk. I told him I was willing to support him. At that point, I resumed my close association with LaGuardia.

I could get LaGuardia any hour of the day or night—in his office, car or home. He lived on the top floor of an apartment house at 109th Street and Fifth Avenue. He had a telephone in his car—remember, this was almost forty years ago—and he could be reached by calling the Fire Department; his phone was tied in with the Department's communications system.

I'd call him and say I wanted to talk to him and he would say, "Meet me in the morning." I'd meet him about a quarter after eight at his home. I had a little Ford and he would sit in the little Ford with me while I drove him to City Hall. His chauffeured limousine would go ahead, empty. When I let him out, all my business would be done. I would do that maybe once every couple of months, and I would maintain very good communications with him. I think he was really a good fellow—a real showman in lots of ways.

The 1937 LaGuardia campaign was the first real political campaign I was involved in. I organized a committee of three hundred; we had nearly every business agent of every union. We raised money, put banners up all over the front of City Hall, in Brooklyn, and in Union Square. We put a banner in Times Square, had placards all over, and held big meetings. In that race there was no question of the support of the labor people—although they were practically all Democrats and LaGuardia was an independent.

There was, however, one exception:

Joe Ryan was very close to the Democratic machinery, but he came on the committee to re-elect LaGuardia. Of course, all of us were Democrats; I don't think we could find ten Republicans. We put Ryan on our steering committee. After the first meeting, the head of the Teamsters' joint council, Mike Cashal, told me, "George, he's going to double-cross you." I said, "He's shown no indication," but Cashal said, "I know him and I know his connection. He's going to wait until you get to the campaign and then he's going to start a desertion movement—labor starts to desert."

Sure enough, when I left to go to Denver for the AFL convention, around the end of September 1937, Ryan announced that he was going to support Jerry Mahoney, a lawyer and former judge, who was the Democratic candidate. It was the old political game—Ryan joined us in order to desert us. He was very prominent—he was the president of the Central Body and of the International Longshoremen. So I called a meeting in Denver of all the New Yorkers who were there. I had about fifteen there.

"Ryan has walked away from us," I told them. "He's now supporting Mahoney. Right after the election there is an election in the Central Body and I think we should just take care of Mr. Ryan." And we did. We booted him the hell out. He didn't run for re-election. We had the votes and we elected Tom Lyons from the Teamsters as president.

I went to Ryan when we came back from Denver and told him what we were going to do: "Joe, we've got the votes and we're going to beat you, so you can run if you want to." He said, "Well, I'm not going to get beaten," and he knew we had the votes.

Two other political parties added to Meany's work load that year: the Communists and the organization he had aided in the Roosevelt campaign—the American Labor party. Directly involved was Michael J. Quill's Transport Workers Union, which switched allegiance from the AFL to the CIO.

At that time, the Transport Workers Union was under the control of the Communist party. They were still in the AFL but preparing to leave. Quill had joined the Communist party and the Commu-

nists had put a lot of money into his union. They were organizing all
around. They started as a little local union of about three hundred
mechanics in the city subway system and overnight they became active.

A Hungarian Communist by the name of John Santos came with
the money. The Communist party gave a first payment to Quill of
$150,000 and they threw it all into organizing. Santos was really the
boss of the union at the time. Quill afterwards broke with the Communists and they just walked away.

Santos was assistant to the president; he was not an elected officer.
He was given some title, but every place that Quill went, he was
right alongside of him; he never, never left. He was running the show
and he had control of the purse strings.

The Communist Soviet philosophy back in those days was to try
to bore into the American industrial scheme and they looked upon
communication and transport as being very important, very vital.
They would have liked to get control of the radio system—anything
to do with communication. They would have liked to get control of
trucking if they could; city transportation was very important to
them.

They did get control of radio operators on ships; that union became strictly under control of the Communists. They had control of
certain shipping; they had control of the National Maritime Union
at the time. Joseph Curran was the NMU president. [He split with
the Communists later.] So, the Transport Workers Union in the nation's largest city was to them an important target and I can understand why they threw a lot of money in there.

In early 1937, Lewis came to New York, and the Transport Workers voted to go CIO, and within two or three months they were tying
the city up in a knot. They had a powerhouse sitdown strike in
Brooklyn. They bought a headquarters building, although they
came from a union that had absolutely no treasury. They became
quite affluent overnight, put thirty organizers on the payroll—they
were really organized. They were following these subway workers to
their homes, forcing them, really, to join. They were using every tactic they could.

The New York local, which at that time was the whole damn international union, had a fellow by the name of Joe English as legislative agent. He came up to Albany in March 1937 and went to the
chairman of the committee handling the Transport Unification Bill,
which would bring all of the New York subway workers under Civil
Service. They were unifying the whole system, and the private corporations were being paid off; the city was taking over the property.

English was trying to make changes in the legislation without consulting Meany, as was required under Federation procedures. When the Legislature's leaders learned of English's tactics, "they just killed the bill," Meany recalled. When the State Fed reintroduced the bill in 1938, the American Labor party wanted to revise it. That year the party had five members in the Assembly headed by Nat Minkoff.

> John L. Lewis thought it was very important that the bill not pass because it was sponsored by the New York Federation of Labor. He didn't know what was in the bill and he didn't care. It was a good bill to protect the workers, but these people started to raise minor objections.
>
> I told English, "We handle the legislation and it will not move unless we approve. It's our legislation; we drafted the bill for all the transit workers—for thousands of workers who are not your members."
>
> Then I went to see this fellow Nat Minkoff. He had three or four objections and I said, "All right, these things are completely minor; I'll change them all and I'll get the committee to amend the bill just as you want. Now will you support the bill?"
>
> He said, "I'll have to call Alex Rose in New York [leader of the American Labor party]." Of course, I sort of chewed him out. But we passed the bill in 1939; it was still our bill and it was a real good bill. They were still going through the motions of opposing it with these trivial objections. They did not want the AFL to pass the bill and get credit for it.

Because of this and other Labor party machinations, at the 1938 AFL convention in Houston Meany delivered a slashing attack on Lewis' political operations. Meany recalled that Green had asked him to make the speech—his first address to an AFL conclave—because Green was trying "to stop our people from being dragooned by Lewis into his political machine." Meany had studied the historical record of AFL conventions and he spoke from bitter personal experience:

> The New York State Branch of Labor's Non-Partisan League is known as the American Labor party. . . . The American Federation of Labor, according to the record, on forty-five occasions during the last fifty-seven conventions has reiterated the nonpartisan policy, the policy that labor should be neutral insofar as party politics are concerned. On twelve of these forty-five occasions the reaffirmation has taken the form of a direct refusal to sponsor or inaugurate or ap-

prove of the formation of a labor party . . . but I want to assure you that if there was any necessity of proving that the nonpartisan policy of the American Federation of Labor was a sound policy, we have that proof in New York State, where we are not dealing with an abstract theory or with an academic problem of labor participation in politics.

We have labor participating in politics through a Labor party controlled by John L. Lewis' and Sidney Hillman's Non-Partisan League, and we know what it is to contend with labor in politics. Nothing that has happened in the previous conventions of the AFL presents such substantial proof that there should not be a labor party. . . .

We had experience in New York State, where the American Labor party deliberately and officially set out to thwart the thoughts of the rank and file of one of our AFL unions [the subway bargaining-rights bill]. . . .

Mr. Lee Pressman [CIO general counsel] came into New York City and called a meeting of the CIO representatives and announced that they were opposed to this particular bill. . . . The very next day . . . this so-called American Labor party decided they were also opposed to that particular bill. . . . The CIO union that was involved was contributing to the American Labor party and the leaders of the American Labor party who used their influence to defeat this bill told me very frankly that the employees of the independent subway system of the City of New York could not have the benefits of collective bargaining by law because they were not contributing to the Labor party.

Is there any more contemptible or sordid reason that ever was used to turn down a labor proposition before the people of that or any other state? . . .

On another occasion a bill which every union member should have been interested in was defeated in the State Legislature last year by the efforts of the American Labor party. This bill was to stop the police from interfering with legitimate, decent and honest picketing, to stop the police from framing up pickets on phony charges of disorderly conduct. [The bill was defeated] because the members of the American Labor party who were there decided it was too important a bill to have put through under the sponsorship of another political party. . . .

A labor party such as we see it in New York State is a class party, and there is no place in America for a party founded on class or caste lines. . . .

The delegates also were told that the New York Fed convention a month earlier had unanimously condemned the activities of the Labor party and reaffirmed support of the AFL's nonpartisan policy. Meany accused the Labor party of being controlled by the Communist party, declaring: "We are not going to surrender to John L. Lewis in the industrial field and we are certainly not going to allow him to pull the wool over our eyes in the political field."

The national convention went on record approving existing AFL policy barring participation of AFL unions in Labor's Non-Partisan League. Policy of the AFL could change, however, at times, and one time was when President Roosevelt proposed a federal minimum-wage and maximum-hours law. Meany recalled the craft attitude:

> Gompers set the philosophy of the American trade union movement. . . . Back in those early days they really wanted very little interference from government. It wasn't until the Great Depression that that changed.
>
> The AFL was very suspicious of the whole idea of a minimum wage law. We didn't get that law until 1938 as the result of that old-fashioned theory. It reflected the independence of these old-time trade-union leaders; they didn't want any interference from government. They said, "You look to government for something, government can give you something. If government gives you something, government can take it away." Gompers was quoted one time as saying that the government was like the law; what the law giveth, the law taketh away.
>
> One reason for this reluctance to buy the idea of the minimum wage was the fact that the unions which really counted were highly paid. Comparatively, the printing trades and the building trades were well paid and they felt: "Wait a minute! If we accept the idea of a minimum wage aren't we also accepting the idea of a maximum wage? Is government going to tell us we can't get anything more? If they tell us we can't get any less, can they tell us we can't have any more?"
>
> That whole attitude changed, and I think this is a feature of the American trade-union movement that few people recognize: the movement tries to live with the times. It tries to live as of today; it doesn't stick to some line, or thought, or activity, or philosophy that's become outmoded. It does adjust.
>
> We realize now that, although the minimum wage does not directly affect our membership as a whole—we have few members getting less than the minimum rate—it does affect us. It affects the

whole economy by bringing these people up to the point where they can, at least, play some part as consumers. If a person gets a dollar fifty an hour, about all the family can do is eat. They can't buy the things we make, can't buy a car, can't buy a television set and things like that. The further you get his wages up, the more you get him into the general market as a consumer. We figure it's mass purchasing power at the bottom of the economic structure which is the key to whatever prosperity we are going to enjoy—or fail to enjoy.

In August 1939, Meany was able to tell delegates at the State Fed convention in New York City that, despite a national wave of anti-labor legislation in state legislatures, New York labor had been spared any repressive laws that year. Governor Lehman had used his veto power on several bills passed by the Republican majorities in both houses.

Nevertheless, when six local unions submitted resolutions asking for convention endorsement of Roosevelt for a third term, Meany blocked action with a speech pointing out that the election was more than a year away:

> I took a stand against the third term. This was a full year before the nominations. People were talking about a third term and I just said I was against a third term for anyone. When 1940 came around, I had a choice between Wendell Willkie and Roosevelt. There was no question that it was Roosevelt.

A massive labor parade in which, Meany said, some 100,000 workers marched was a feature of the 1939 State Fed meeting—and probably gave him a boost for a promotion, but it wasn't planned for that.

> The World's Fair was on in New York that year and several of the upstate fellows said to me, "Why shouldn't we have a convention in New York, instead of having the New Yorkers come upstate?" I forced that year's convention into New York solely because of the World's Fair.
>
> Then some of the fellows around the city Central Labor body said, "We haven't had a Labor Day parade in many years. Let's have a parade." So the idea came out of the Central Body; it wasn't my idea, but I certainly wasn't opposed to it. We got great cooperation from LaGuardia. It was on a Saturday and he closed off Fifth Avenue for us. It was really a great parade; it started about nine A.M. and wound up at nine P.M. They just marched all day long—and

that's when I really realized that people like parades: our people and everybody else.

LaGuardia and I went down that morning and met Roosevelt on the cruiser *Tuscaloosa*. We had problems in regard to the WPA and other things.

LaGuardia and I came back to the parade. He had marched in the first contingent, with the Air Line Pilots Union. He was a member of it, and he had a uniform on. Whether he ever flew as a commercial pilot I don't know. There wasn't any connection at all in my mind between the parade and the AFL convention.

Several members of the AFL Executive Council did watch the big parade, and Meany heard that at least one of them—Teamster President Daniel Tobin—"was very much impressed by the parade." Tobin played a key role in what happened six weeks later at the AFL's national convention to drastically change Meany's life—and the American labor movement.

6

MEANY AND F.D.R.

I saw Roosevelt many times. . . . You would be with him forty minutes and he hadn't gotten to your problems at all. He would be spouting off, with that cigarette at a snappy angle. He was a great conversationalist—very, very entertaining.

Taking an overall view of the Presidents that I knew in my lifetime, I would have to say that the fellow who made the greatest contribution to the solution of America's problems was Franklin Roosevelt.

I was perfectly happy where I was as president of the State Fed. I was doing quite well. . . . I was not looking for a change, but I got to thinking it over—

Meany faced a crucial career decision at the annual AFL convention late in 1939. The decision, whether to leave his probably lifetime post in New York to gamble on survival in national office, was thrust on him with hardly more than a moment's notice, albeit some labor leaders, himself not included, may have seen it foreshadowed in September of that year. As Meany recalled:

Sometime in September of 1939 there was a move by a small New York local of the Marble Polishers condemning Bill Green and nominating me for president of the AFL in his place. They gave it to the press and it appeared in the New York papers just prior to the AFL convention in Cincinnati.

I recall very vividly going to that convention—I had one vote. When I got to Cincinnati my international union president, John Coefield, sort of growled at me: "What's this about you running for president?" I said, "Forget it, John; that's a lot of damn nonsense. I'm not running." He said, "That's what I told these people around here."

The New York story embarrassed me so much—the reporters were bothering me—that I went to the opening session and didn't attend another session all that week. I deliberately stayed away because I didn't want the reporters bothering me and I didn't want to be seen around there—to kill this idea that I was going to be a candidate against Green. The idea was so completely ridiculous—me with my one vote.

Meany was not staying at the convention hotel, the Netherlands Plaza. But on the fourth day of the convention, as he passed the hotel after dinner, he was told by a friend that Bricklayers President Harry Bates was looking for him. Meany found that Bates had gone to bed; it was about 10 P.M. As he prepared to leave, Teamsters President Tobin hailed him and took him aside, saying that AFL Secretary-Treasurer Frank Morrison "is in his dotage and we have to retire him. We got the votes and we can put you in the job, and it pays ten thousand a year."

"Wait a minute," Meany replied. "As far as ten thousand dollars is concerned, I'm already getting ten thousand."

Still, Meany promised to think about it and to talk to the Bricklayers president.

The following morning, I talked to Bates. I knew Bates much better than I knew Tobin; I was quite close to him. He told me that Morrison was eighty years old and his eyesight was failing and so on.

"Harry," I said, "I don't know. You've got to give me some time to think about this. I don't know whether I want to go to Washington." I still didn't go near the convention. I called New York to tell my wife that this was a possibility. She just said very simply, "I don't like the idea of moving to Washington under any circumstances, but if that's what you want it's all right."

The way I looked at it was: I was perfectly happy where I was as president of the State Fed. I was doing quite well; I knew the people and I knew the legislation. I knew the political situation; Lehman was governor and he was my friend. I was not looking for a change, but I got to thinking it over: After all, this is what I am doing. I am in the labor movement. This is my life, more or less, and this is definitely a big promotion.

Close friends from New York urged Meany to remain there, pointing out that, at forty-five, he would be regarded as too young by the elderly chieftains, whose large blocks of votes might later be turned on him, and that he would be going over the heads of veteran national vice-presidents. Meany made his decision before accompanying Bates to the last game of that year's World Series between the New York Yankees and the Cincinnati Reds.

> There was a throw from the outfield and one run came in, I think, from third base. Joe DiMaggio was on second and he got to third. Ernie Lombardi, the Reds' catcher, missed the ball and it rolled about fifteen feet away. He fell down on his stomach, and while he was lying on his stomach, trying to get up to get the ball, Joe Di-Maggio came in with the winning run. It was a very interesting Series.
>
> After the game, in Bates' room at the Netherlands Plaza, I told him, "Harry, I've made a decision. I will take this job under certain conditions. Number 1, I will not run against Morrison. I'd be crazy to run against Morrison even though I had the votes. Do you think I want to get this job by defeating a man eighty years of age who's been holding the job for forty-three years? In addition, he's a friend of mine.
>
> "Secondly, I have to get this job under the sponsorship of my international union. I'm a State Fed guy with one vote and no constituency. That means John Coefield has got to agree to support me for this job. He would be the one I would want to nominate me, provided Morrison is going to retire."

At breakfast the next morning, Coefield told Meany that he "knew damn well you wouldn't run against Morrison" and agreed to explain the situation to Morrison. It was arranged that if Morrison retired there would be a special pension (at that time the AFL did not have a regular pension plan). While the maneuvering was going on, the president of the AFL was not consulted about the selection of the Number Two man:

> Green played no part in this at all—absolutely no part. He wasn't consulted. He didn't talk to me about it until after I was elected. I

got along with him, but that was Green's way. They re-elected him and that was what he was interested in.

The result was that on the second Thursday of the convention I was nominated and elected, and that's it. There was no opposition at all.

Green and the delegates learned on that second Thursday of the convention that Secretary-Treasurer Morrison wished to step down from the office he had held since 1897. Unanimously, Morrison was voted a pension of six thousand dollars a year and praised for his services. (He lived nine more years—"my friend, a very, very wonderful old gentleman.")

Meany's nomination to fill the secretary-treasurer post came later that day, with Plumbers' chief Coefield describing his candidate as "a young man who has become quite prominent in the labor world, a young man who I think has made more progress in the last few years in the position that he holds than any other labor representative I know of. . . . He is at present holding a responsible position, president of an organization composed of about one-fourth of the membership of the entire American Federation of Labor. He has properly represented that organization and it is generally conceded that he is at least one of the best, if not the best, president we ever had in the position he holds."

Coefield also referred to the fact that they were going outside the ranks of national union leaders. He assured delegates that his man "is as well known as any man . . . who has not been an international president or secretary . . . a man of very fine habits, a clean-living young man who is not addicted to the bad habits that some people are. . . ." Coefield ended by acclaiming Meany "an honest plumber."

Tobin, one of the seconding speakers, said that in the past the New York Federation's officers had devoted their time "principally to providing political jobs for themselves." He reported that Meany "changed all this and he has done many things, but he cleaned up a bad situation and he worked for the labor movement in New York and not for a job for George Meany."

Describing his candidate as "second to none on the platform and in debates in legislative halls," Tobin declared that Meany could assist in the Washington lobbying when Green was unable to testify at hearings. He alluded to criticism of Green's legislative work by reporting that senators and congressmen had complained about the "weakness of our legislative department in presenting the case of labor before congressional committees."

Nominating speeches filled nearly six columns of the printed proceedings while Meany used only a half-column—187 words—to express thanks and pledge he would "do all in my power to make this organization even a better Federation, to make it a better instrumentality for the welfare and advancement of the workers of our great nation."

Meany arrived in Washington on New Year's Day 1940, by train from New York, and appeared at his office ready to work the next morning. In addition to the regular duties of the secretary-treasurer, he was looking forward to doing some lobbying on Capitol Hill, the best part of the job as outlined to him by his sponsors.

But Meany was disappointed. His long career in Washington got off to a slow start—such a bad beginning, in fact, that he seriously considered dropping out and going back to New York. The problem was that the duties of the secretary-treasurer were severely limited by the AFL's constitution and customs; the office was something like the U.S. Vice Presidency, without the glory.

Added to this was the attitude of the AFL president, who declined to assign any other work to the new man in the office. Green was following tradition in not allowing Meany to do what he was most noted for in New York. Green must have been startled, and worried, at the sudden arrival of this young, strong and tireless leader, because Green was not a powerful leader, as shown by the fact that he was not consulted on the promotion. And there was substance to his fear.

According to William Dodd, then the president of Meany's home local union, the promotion "was no great surprise to the union people of New York. There was all sorts of talk amongst the union people that he was qualified . . . that they would like to see George Meany go immediately into Green's position. It was anticipated that something would happen, somehow or some way."

Green, who was sixty-six years old, obviously was thinking about that possibility, too. A forty-five-year-old head of a subordinate state federation suddenly had been elevated to national office by a group of union presidents who really ran the AFL. True, there was no tradition of promoting the AFL secretary-treasurer to the top post (Green had been secretary of the United Mine Workers when elected at Gompers' death). But Meany was the type of strong leader who seemed to defy tradition, as witness his unorthodox rise.

Green certainly noticed the threat inherent in Tobin's suggestion that the new officer lend a hand at the lobbying chore, contrary to tradition. For Green let his Number Two man testify before congressional committees only once during the thirteen years Meany was secretary-treasurer. Meany recalled the situation with obvious regret:

> Actually, and I say this without any malice at all, Green did not do a good job on the legislative end. He would read a long statement; it seemed that he liked long statements. He would read for fifty minutes without stopping and then, when the questions were asked, he didn't have the answers. He would say, "We'll check on that and send you a letter on that." Around the Capitol, they used to say that when Green got on the stand most of the committee members would find something else to do. But he would go on and on, reading statements that were given him by various members of the staff.
>
> I know that both Tobin and Hutcheson had no regard for Green's ability on the legislative end. Tobin told me that the Executive Council members felt I would be helpful to Green because of my five years' experience in legislative work. When I got here, Green wouldn't let me handle the legislative end of it and, of course, we didn't have any argument about it. He wanted to handle it himself and that was his right as president.
>
> In 1942, members of Congress were introducing some rather rigid legislation—the Smith-Connally bill and others—which denied labor's right to strike. Hutcheson came to me and asked me if I would testify.
>
> "Yes, of course I will testify," I said, "providing Green agrees that I testify. It would be ridiculous for me to testify without having his agreement. After all, he is the president."
>
> On this particular occasion, Hutcheson went to Green and got Green to agree that I would help him out on the legislative work. Green gave me an assignment to testify on the anti-strike bill. But on the day I was to testify he said that he had made a decision: "I don't think either of us should testify, George. I don't think it would be helpful."
>
> The only time I did testify was on a similar bill when Green was away and asked me to go before the Rules Committee of the House. I got a little more attention, I guess, than they liked. Fulton Lewis commented and there was an item in the paper.
>
> When I came here I had the impression that I was going to do the legislative work and I think the people who asked me to come here had that impression.

But for the war, Meany might have given up in despair. He was still debating returning to New York (where his family still lived) when the Japanese attacked Pearl Harbor. As he recalled in 1957:

About four days after the Pearl Harbor attack on December 7, 1941, Bill Green and I had a conference with President Roosevelt—a conference that had been scheduled even before Pearl Harbor. We thought we would get a telephone call that he couldn't see us, because of the events of the time, but we didn't get that call.

We went over and met a very, very calm Chief Executive. I have never seen a man more calm in the face of the furor which seemed to pervade official Washington at that time when those officials in high places and a good many citizens who were in contact with those officials knew of the terrific blow that we had suffered, knew what had happened to our Navy, and knew that we were in a tremendously difficult position. I can't forget what President Roosevelt said at that time.

He said, "We can out-produce the Axis powers. We have the know-how; we have the material resources; we have the skilled labor and we have a united population in this country today. But all these things are meaningless unless we put them to work. We are not going to win the war by telling Hitler or even convincing Hitler that we can out-produce the Axis nations and that we can put an army into the field that certainly will not be second to the Nazi army.

"Telling him that and convincing him of that means very little; we have got to do it. In other words, we have got to make use of this power, of this know-how, of this resourcefulness and ingenuity of the American businessman and the skill of the American worker. We have got to get into production."

Elaborating years later, Meany said:

Roosevelt indicated that we were in trouble. Our navy had been badly hurt by Pearl Harbor, but he also indicated his complete confidence in the ability of the American people to produce and to come back.

I was sure that he had no doubts about the reaction of the American people. Now that we were in the war we would certainly produce for ourselves and for the people allied with us. Events proved he was absolutely right.

At an emergency meeting of the AFL Council, Green and Meany reported on the fast-developing moves in Washington. Meany recalled that there had been a War Labor Board of labor, public and industry members during World War I and urged creation of a similar board.

Roosevelt wrote Green, inviting him to nominate six AFL delegates to an industry-labor conference to open December 17. Green designated Meany and himself along with four AFL vice-presidents. The Council issued a statement urging compliance with the AFL's previously adopted policy of avoiding walkouts in defense plants and suggesting creation of a War Labor Board. (A special conference attended by the officers of all AFL unions on December 16 affirmed this statement.) The CIO had suggested a meeting of labor and management officials.

The Industry-Labor Conference opened the following day under the "monitorship" of lawyer-mediator William H. Davis and Senator Elbert D. Thomas, chairman of the Senate Committee on Education and Labor. CIO President Philip Murray headed the CIO group, which included Lewis, who played an unusually quiet role, Green later told his Council.

The AFL delegates suggested creation of a board to mediate disputes affecting war plants—with authority to recommend settlement terms—a pledge of no strikes or lockouts, and recognition of the right of workers to join unions. The suggestion formed the basis of a joint AFL-CIO proposal drafted by a labor subcommittee of Meany, Matthew Woll, Murray and Lewis. Years later, Meany recalled:

> At that conference, we had the Chamber of Commerce, the National Association of Manufacturers, the AFL and the CIO. There was no question in anybody's mind but that we had to come up with production: everybody was in favor.
>
> The big question, however, and really the only question, was union security. Employers wanted to freeze union security. They said that if you have a union and it's a closed-shop union you should retain it. If it's open shop or both union and non-union, or if it's non-union, it should stay non-union. This meant that as long as the war lasted there would be no progress in organizing the unions. We went around this ring-around-the-rosy for two and a half days. Davis had done most of the talking as moderator. Senator Thomas had said practically nothing.

Meany was sitting next to Thomas when they returned from lunch on December 22.

I asked Thomas, "Why don't we cut this thing short? We can't go on. If there is going to be no meeting of the minds on this, why don't we report to the President what we've agreed on: one, that there should be no strikes or lockouts during the war in war production; two, that there should be some kind of board to settle disputes; and three, the President should appoint that board. Then we say that there is a fourth point on which we do not agree."

So Thomas made this proposal that I had written down on a little piece of paper and he made a plea for it. Then we framed a letter to Roosevelt and we got a letter back saying, "Gentlemen, I see that you have agreed one, two, three." He ignored the fourth completely—the union security issue—as if it wasn't there, and he said, "Thank you very much, appreciate your efforts and I wish you all a Merry Christmas!"

That meant the whole question of union security was left completely open and, of course, this was really a victory for the labor side. We didn't want an affirmative action on the part of the government on this; we just wanted the government to say they wouldn't interfere, and this is what this meant.

This was a big disappointment for the employers. I remember Roger Lapham [later a War Labor Board industry member] was bitterly disappointed, because he was one of the leading industry fellows on this question, arguing that labor shouldn't make any organizing progress during the war.

We said, "The hell with that! We don't see why we should stop organizing just because there is a war going on. We are going to cooperate to try to win the war."

The National War Labor Board was established by Executive Order on January 12, 1942. Meany, as one of the labor members, helped rule on the problems presented by various Mine Workers' strikes—walkouts that occurred even though John L. Lewis had attended the Industry-Labor Conference. Meany insisted that "Lewis committed himself" to the conference's report. The no-strike pledge was by unanimous agreement, Meany added, "and that included Lewis."

Summing it all up later, Meany recollected:

The War Labor Board handled specific disputes that came before it—disputes that could possibly impede war production. There were disputes on wages, on organization and union security and so on. They took every dispute and held hearings on it.

After the hearings, the board would have a discussion, and the public members would propose a solution. Their solution practically always was the answer because either the labor members or the industry members would agree with them. The public members did a great job; they were very competent fellows: Bill Davis, George [W.] Taylor, Wayne Morse, Frank [P.] Graham. One of their alternates was Lloyd Garrison.

The board did a great job in keeping production going. The only big trouble was in coal, the only outstanding case of union defiance. The whole labor movement got a bad reputation only because of Lewis. He defied government and everybody else. We certainly turned to and did our part of the job of getting this tremendous war production. Aside from coal, when we had strikes, hell, we would settle them in twenty-four hours, settle them over the telephone in a good many cases. We would get them back to work and throw the case to the WLB.

We had cases where the strikes were almost incited by the employers. They would handle the dispute as if they were trying to get the boys to go on strike, which they figured would get the workers in very bad. We countered that; we saw that they didn't go on strike. I'd tell these people, "We gave a pledge and you've got to respect that pledge. Whatever your trouble is, it will be settled by the board; you're not going to get a bad deal." Lots of times we would call the presidents of the international unions and they would get after the locals. Patty Morrin, the head of the Iron Workers, for example, didn't even ask his strikers questions. He lifted their charter.

Meany amplified his war efforts in numerous speeches exhorting workers to improve production, but his cooperation on the War Labor Board, effective as it was, rested firmly on a commitment to economic justice.

In serving on the board, Meany, who was the highest ranking labor member, exhibited a characteristic noted throughout his life. On an issue of principle, he was ready to do battle relentlessly with foe or friend—even a President of the United States he had helped elect.

While working to settle labor disputes, he fought back when Roosevelt stripped some of the power from the board. Meany felt that the President's action was a violation of the no-strike agreement signed by government and unions, and to him that was a breach of faith. So he did what came naturally: In blunt language Presidents seldom hear in the Oval Office, he demanded that the NWLB be allowed to increase the wage formula to match the rise in living costs.

As he recalled in 1946:

The National War Labor Board, which came into being as a result of labor-management cooperation for victory, represented, in a sense, a willingness on the part of both labor and management for the first time in our history to accept regulation of wages and conditions of work by an agency set up under government sponsorship.

Labor agreed to accept this sort of regulation as a substitute for the free collective-bargaining method, which it had always adhered to, in order that workers could produce to the full, without interruption, the weapons of modern war so badly needed by our fighting men.

Organized labor understood and accepted wartime regulations by the War Labor Board for two basic and fundamental reasons: First, workers along with all others had a solemn duty to contribute their very best to the war effort; secondly, workers, who have always been the major victims of inflation, wished to avoid a return to this evil, so disastrous to the nation following World War I.

So when the NWLB was created in January of 1942, labor cooperated wholeheartedly in making it work. When the so-called Little Steel [wage] formula was devised in July of 1942 as a policy of the NWLB, the labor members of that tribunal, who had voted against the adoption of the formula, accepted the majority decision and cooperated fully—in an attempt to solve the many and vexing wage problems which arose—by applying the rules of the formula.

The dispute with Roosevelt arose in this way. Duties of the War Labor Board had been greatly expanded after enactment of the wage stabilization law of October 2, 1942. From a dispute-settlement agency, the WLB suddenly became the authority checking all wage increases in the country—including employers' voluntary moves to boost pay, as well as raises unions won in bargaining. Price controls were imposed, too, under another agency (the Office of Price Administration).

Then, in April 1943, the White House tightened the screws on wage boosts with a new Executive Order that brought loud protests from the NWLB's labor members. After an internal fight, with Meany a leading debater on the labor side, public and industry members joined the union men in petitioning the President for changes in the order. The board members agreed that it could not function under the new strict regulations.

Some modifications were granted on May 12, restoring much of the authority the board previously had had to correct inequities in wage scales. But the board did not regain the right to readjust the Little

Steel Formula. Meany promised that labor members intended to keep
fighting for a bigger increase in the formula to cover rising living costs.

Meany complained to the AFL Council that the White House had
switched "the board's tripartite judicial function" to make it "partially
a law-enforcement agency." He said if the board was to become merely
an enforcement agent for Presidential orders "there is no place for
labor members on that board."

A position statement submitted by Meany for himself and NWLB
member Woll was adopted by the Council. It contended in part that
the new NWLB status was "in direct conflict" with the agreement
reached at the 1941 Industry-Labor Conference. AFL representatives
at the NWLB were told to continue efforts to recover the board's original power to draft policy and not merely enforce White House rules.

Veto power over War Labor Board policies and decisions had been
given to James F. Byrnes, director of the Office of Economic Stabilization:

> Roosevelt gave Director Byrnes a veto power over the War Labor
> Board, which the WLB resented very much. At one time with Roo-
> sevelt, I brought up the question of the veto power and Roosevelt
> said there was no veto power. I argued a little and he said, "George, I
> wrote it and I know what's in there. I know what it means."
>
> I reported that back to the board and the board promptly sent a
> committee over consisting of Chairman Will Davis, myself and I
> think the employer member was Roger Lapham. We had an inter-
> view with Jimmy Byrnes, who was a soft-spoken southerner, quite an
> attractive guy. He said, "Gentlemen, I read English very well and I
> read this order. While it doesn't use the word 'veto,' it is quite obvi-
> ous that the Economic Stabilization Office has a veto power over
> any action of the War Labor Board in the wage field."
>
> So, a few days later, I went back to Roosevelt, along with Phil
> Murray, Tobin and Green and I told Roosevelt that Byrnes said he
> did have a veto power under the Presidential order. Despite what
> Roosevelt told me two weeks before, he promptly said, "Yes, of
> course he has, but it doesn't mean anything. You fellows can come in
> here and see me at any time you want to—so stop worrying about
> it."
>
> Later on, R. J. Thomas of the CIO and I presented a petition to
> the WLB claiming that the Bureau of Labor Statistics was not ade-
> quately doing its job of measuring the cost of living, that they were
> using what they called the "old market-basket formula." They did

not take into consideration that the whole work-pattern of the country had changed because of the war; it was an entirely different situation.

I publicly accused Ford Hinrichs, who was in charge of the BLS, of failing to do the job. I took the position that the Administration was not keeping down the cost of living, so they were therefore playing games with the cost-of-living index. Thomas and I made public a very comprehensive report that we made to the War Labor Board, in which we went into newspaper files and compared advertisements in 1939 and 1940 with those three years later. On the basis of that survey, we said that the cost of living index was way out of line.

There was an amusing incident when I talked to Roosevelt about that. I was there arguing this line that the cost of living was not being adequately measured. The War Labor Board had unanimously taken that position.

In our report we measured all commodities, including what were known as the sugar family of foods—syrup and sugar and candy, among other things. In a household with children, we argued that candy was an item. Roosevelt sort of pooh-poohed this whole candy idea, saying, "George this is ridiculous! We're fighting a war and you're talking about candy!"

While he was telling me that, I was staring at a box of candy on his desk—a Valentine, heart-shaped box of candy. He saw me staring at it and said, "Now, this is the first candy that has been in here for months and months. Grace Tully [his secretary] brought it in here this morning."

The labor members' survey of living costs reported that "there has been a rise in the actual cost of living of at least 43.5 percent" since January 1941, while the government's index showed an increase of about 24 percent. The Little Steel Formula had held general pay boosts to 15 percent over the period from the start of 1941.

This report and two petitions filed with the WLB by its AFL members failed to shake the "hold-the-line" policy of the Administration. In late November 1944, Meany was awaiting the President's decision on the second appeal (it was rejected later) when he told the AFL convention:

I know we have to sacrifice and no matter how this decision goes against us, no matter what the President's decision is in regard to changing the formula, we will go along, we will not rock the boat.

The demands to win the war are greater than any demands we have
for wages, but we have the right to demand that the American
worker gets justice and that the bargain made with the government
be kept.

Meany's determination to get justice for workers prompted this out-
burst against BLS Commissioner Hinrichs on June 8, 1944. Referring
to the bureau's reply to the labor complaints about the cost-of-living
index, Meany said:

> In its answer, the bureau agreed that its index does not measure
> the full increase in living costs. It attempted, however, to play down
> the importance of this inadequacy, and centered its efforts in an at-
> tempt to discredit the labor members' report. It presented no plan
> for securing the facts needed. . . .
>
> We are led to the inescapable conclusion that the bureau has be-
> come identified with an effort to freeze wages, to the extent that it is
> no longer a free agency of statistical research. We feel that for the
> present and as regards its efforts to give labor an accurate measuring
> rod for the workers' living costs, the bureau has laid aside its func-
> tion as an impartial research agency interested only in securing and
> presenting the facts and has identified itself with the objectives of a
> specific political administration. . . .
>
> [Hinrichs] has by his actions assumed the appearance of a bureau-
> cratic monkey on a stick who moves up and down in conformity
> with the dictates of administrative wage policy. As an agency of a
> department which was established by Congress to "foster, promote
> and develop wage earners' welfare," the Bureau of Labor Statistics is
> today indeed a sorry spectacle.

Meany's concern about getting all-out production of war goods
while anticipating postwar problems is found in this representative
wartime speech:

> We will not achieve peak production [in America] until the very
> early months of 1944. . . . This is no time for complacency . . . for
> overconfidence. . . . Labor's Number One job is production. . . . We
> should keep that one supreme objective in our minds: producing,
> producing and producing for eventual victory.
>
> But while we keep our eye on that objective and while we bend
> our efforts in the direction of more and more production, we have a
> right as soldiers of the home front . . . to turn our eyes also in the di-
> rection of our ultimate objectives when peace comes. . . .

> We refuse to accept the theory that there must be a major depression following this war. We refuse to accept the theory that will bring us the dole and the breadline. We look upon this problem as another challenge to our democratic system.

Just as the democratic system showed it could wage war, Meany continued, "I say to you that democracy can meet the next challenge." The AFL's program, which he outlined, included full benefits for returning veterans, jobs for everyone, a public-works program, and an expanded Social Security program.

Meany had seen that democratic system working to win the war even before America became directly involved. He had served on the National Defense Mediation Board established by the President in March 1941—with a tripartite membership like the War Labor Board—as it averted most of the threatened strikes in arms-manufacturing plants. The board handled 114 such disputes involving 1.2 million workers to keep armaments rolling for U.S. allies and for its own defense buildup. The only enforcement machinery of the board consisted of referring unresolved cases to the White House for seizure of the manufacturing facility and only three seizures were required.

After Pearl Harbor the national defense program became the war production effort, the Defense Mediation Board became the War Labor Board, and Secretary-Treasurer Meany further expanded his own duties in Washington.

A few days after the War Labor Board was set up, John L. Lewis announced a proposal that embarrassed Meany, Green and CIO President Murray. The AFL Council's minutes for January 17, the final day of the winter session, disclosed that Green reported receipt of a letter from Lewis and that Murray also had been sent one. It said: "It is obvious that if accouplement [merger] could be achieved, with unified and competent leadership, the results would be advantageous and in the public interest. . . . America needs unity in every phase of its national economy."

Lewis, referring to his membership on the CIO's standing committee, proposed a meeting with the AFL negotiators. Meany said the story was "leaked" to *The New York Times:*

> It said that Lewis' plan was to have Green retire, have me become president of the AFL with the CIO people back in there and have Murray take my place as secretary.
> At that time, I didn't even know Lewis, I hadn't even met him,

and I was puzzled by this business. Lewis made his announcement without ever consulting Murray. Murray was down South; he wasn't well at that time. He came back to Washington and in an interview said that nobody was going to make him a secretary-treasurer without his permission—something like that. But, as I said, I didn't even know Lewis and why they shot my name into it I don't know.

The thing came out of the clear sky as far as I was concerned. Lewis sent a hand-delivered letter to the Council, which was meeting here in Washington. The letter contained a check for sixty thousand dollars, and this was to be his payment for re-entry into the AFL. [Carpenters President] Hutcheson brought the letter to the meeting.

The thing to me was a matter of amusement because as far as I was concerned there was certainly something fishy about a scheme that was going to make me the head of a combined organization and the fellow who was promoting it was a guy I didn't know and had never talked to—and nobody had ever talked to me about it.

We sort of laid the letter on the table and I just put the check in my desk. It lay there for months. Some years later, Lewis indicated that he blamed me for ditching his plan, and to some extent he was right, but there was no enthusiasm among our people. The only one who was trying to promote accouplement was Hutch; everybody else looked upon it with suspicion. This thing came out of the blue. Nobody bought it; nobody even paid any attention to it.

What I think Lewis blamed me for was he said I took the check and didn't even answer, didn't even acknowledge it. Which was true; there was no action taken on it. I stuck the check in the drawer. Later we sent it back to him. [The Council] just didn't trust him.

On January 22 the President created what he called the Combined Labor War Board, also known as the Combined Labor Victory Committee, consisting of three members each from the AFL and CIO: Green, Meany, and Daniel Tobin representing the AFL and Murray, R. J. Thomas of the Auto Workers and Julius Emspak of the Electrical Workers representing the CIO. The committee meetings were "very free and open," Meany recalled, estimating that the committee met with Roosevelt every two weeks. Roosevelt created the panel, Meany thought, "to preserve the CIO."

Establishment of the Combined Committee helped to isolate Lewis, pointedly left out of it. Lewis' letter also aggravated the feuding in the CIO between Lewis' adherents and Murray's faction. An angry Murray and the CIO Executive Board repudiated the Lewis invitation to renew negotiations (broken off in 1939). The Miners chief, after all, hadn't bothered to check out the idea with the current CIO leadership.

The AFL Executive Council's reaction to the accouplement letter was to have Green reply immediately with an offer to resume the talks that Lewis had broken off three years earlier.

"Peace talks" between the AFL and CIO never amounted to much from that time on until Meany became AFL president. Officials of both organizations became engrossed in the win-the-war efforts, in which they cooperated with each other and with the Administration.

John Lewis, however, renewed his attempt to reaffiliate his Miners Union with the AFL despite failure of his accouplement stunt. He formally severed relations with Murray and the CIO on October 7, 1942, by having his convention vote to quit the movement he had set up seven years earlier. Then, on May 17, 1943, Lewis wrote to the AFL Council applying for readmission.

With a check for sixty thousand dollars for dues payment, Lewis wrote that the UMW "accepts the AFL as it now exists and expects the AFL to accept the UMW as it now exists." He added that his union "has no interest in questions of hypothetical jurisdiction"—which, of course, the Executive Council of AFL definitely had an interest in. After talks with Lewis, a committee reported back to the Council meeting in August.

During Council discussion, Green said he felt that the UMW never would agree to give up the members of its District 50—a miscellaneous unit with members in a variety of fields, especially in the chemical industry.

Meany argued that "we cannot take them back in on the basis of the proposal" and he listed several possible moves but stressed that any counter-proposal must make it clear that the UMW had to give up to other unions any non-coal workers taken into UMW since it left the AFL in 1935. The Council objected to Lewis' expansion into other industries where the AFL already had unions.

The coal union's application was referred to the AFL convention in October, which endorsed a committee report rejecting return of the UMW on the basis of Lewis' take-all-or-nothing condition. Delegates approved further talks with UMW officials in an attempt to settle the jursidictional problems. Various AFL unions filed complaints about the UMW's invasion of their domains.

Meany was one of the five Council members who met with Lewis on December 10. Meany reported to the Council's January 1944 session that after three hours of discussion with Lewis the conferees "were just exactly where we were at the start," with Lewis insisting on return of the union as is.

Council minutes also quote Meany as saying that Lewis had rejected his suggestion that the AFL establish a new union for chemical workers who belonged either to District 50 of UMW or to AFL local unions. Lewis, he reported, said the Miners would never give up any of its chemical members.

When further negotiations failed, Lewis withdrew the application on May 8 and got back his sixty-thousand-dollar check. To protect the territory of its unions, the Council had passed up a gain of about a half million UMW members.*

Late in 1944, Meany correctly predicted that the war would end before the fall of the following year—which, it turned out, Roosevelt would not live to see. During the war, in the periodic meetings with the President and labor leaders, Meany thought that Roosevelt was in complete command of the war effort and fully acquainted with developments. But in January 1945, on the eve of the President's trip to Yalta, Meany thought "he was really a wreck then; he was not the old Roosevelt at all. He was nowhere near as sharp as before." This did not worry Meany at the time:

> After all, I am not a physician. I don't look at a fellow from that point of view. When he finally died in April of 1945, of course, it was a shock, but as I looked back at it I said to myself, well, it was not unexpected. I had seen him going downhill quite rapidly.

Meany was able to see the vast difference between Roosevelt's appearance in 1939, when they conferred in New York harbor, and at that final visit before Yalta. He described the typical Roosevelt conference with the labor leaders between those years:

> I saw Roosevelt many times during that period. When Bill Green and I would go in to see him, we generally had a problem to discuss. You would be with him forty minutes and he hadn't gotten to your problem at all. He would be spouting off, with that cigarette at a snappy angle. He was a great conversationalist—very, very entertaining.

* But Meany had reported that at the end of 1942 the AFL had become "the largest trade union organization in the world" with 5,954,434 dues-paying members. That was a rise of 3,093,501 since the original CIO unions had pulled out five years earlier.

He had a fellow, General [Edwin M.] Watson, who was sort of his handyman at the White House, and he would open the door, which was a signal that somebody else was waiting. But Roosevelt used to just wave him out.

The meetings were about labor matters, but he also would discuss the progress of the war. Actually, these meetings did not reach any decisions or anything like that. There would be an hour's social conversation and a few little problems would be brought up. But no great policy decisions were made. Everybody chimed in; it was a very free discussion.

A surprising political decision of Meany's was prompted by one of those Oval Office sessions. It wasn't known at the time, but Meany cast his vote for Republican Thomas E. Dewey rather than for Roosevelt in the 1944 Presidential election.

It was very simple. I liked FDR, but all during that period prior to forty-four—beginning back in forty-one—I had been in and out of the White House many times. I was convinced that we were going to have real problems with the Russians after the war was over. I had seen FDR during that forty-four period and I came to the conclusion that, physically and mentally, he had gone downhill very, very fast; that he was not the FDR we knew a few years before; that he didn't have the pep. Actually he looked almost the picture of death in forty-four. I just came to the conclusion that I couldn't vote for him.

It wasn't anything that he did to me; it wasn't any bitterness, or anything else. I just felt that in dealing with the Russians after the war, we would be better off with Dewey. So I voted for Dewey, but I didn't campaign for him; I wasn't on any committee. It was just a personal decision.

Roosevelt, however, got Meany's vote as the greatest U.S. President he'd known:

It's a hard thing to make a definitive judgment on just who is the best. Taking an overall view of the Presidents that I knew in my lifetime, I would have to say that the fellow who made the greatest contribution to the solutions of America's problems was Franklin Roosevelt.

Take when he became President on the fourth of March, 1933: we were in an absolutely catastrophic situation. You remember that the banks were failing all over the place. What he did was to close the banks in order to get some stability there. The Federal Deposit In-

surance Act was one of the greatest things that ever happened.
Those runs on the banks used to come for any number of reasons. If
something went wrong at the bank and hit the paper, boy, everybody would line up—now that's all eliminated.

Other tremendous achievements were the wage and hour act, the
setting up of the Securities and Exchange Commission, unemployment insurance, and the Wagner Labor Relations Act. Then we had
the National Recovery Administration, one of the things set up to
combat the bad economic situation.

When Hitler threatened the entire Western world, Roosevelt was
quite alive to the problem. He inaugurated Lend-Lease to help the
British even before we got into the war. When we got in the war, we
were in terrible shape—after Pearl Harbor, we had no navy—and
Roosevelt rallied the people of the country.

In the next three or four years, we accomplished what was a production miracle: we not only produced to arm ourselves but we produced to supply our allies in the war with Hitler. We were tremendously fortunate to have a fellow like Roosevelt in there.

The contribution he made in combatting the Depression, turning
things around, and the contribution he made in leading the country
during the war were without precedent. This makes him the greatest
President, at least in this century, as far as I am concerned.

After Roosevelt's death, President Truman had the task of ending
the war and tackling the problem of how to deal with the Soviet Union
ally: continue to cooperate or move to contain the expansion of communism.

Meany and the AFL chose the cold-war solution at war's end. It took
Truman and the State Department longer.

7

THE COLD WAR

For human freedom, in my book, you have to be anti-Communist, you have to be anti-dictatorship. You have to be anti-Allende, you have to be anti-Franco, anti-Hitler, anti-Stalin, anti-South Africa.

The people who consider themselves liberal become very selective. They can be very anti-South Africa—strongly against this apartheid policy—and shrug their shoulders about Czechoslovakia and Poland and the Soviet Union. We hold them all even.

George Meany's own cold war began earlier and lasted much longer than the one waged by the U.S. Government or most labor movements abroad. His cold war extended to any dictator, of the Right or Left. He was more consistent than the State Department. Its tolerance for right-wing dictators angered the man from the Bronx. As he saw it, all dictators destroy personal freedom, with trade unions wiped out or made into puppets of the state.

Meany's attacks on Communists started in the 1920s in his own local union, where a Communist or two surfaced. The fight broadened into world dimensions long before President Truman turned on Russia after World War II.

Did any single incident or influence turn him into a militant anti-Communist? "Nothing except my feeling that I don't like to get kicked around; I don't like seeing anyone else kicked around," Meany replied. "When I saw workers being kicked around by Communists, I immediately became an anti-Communist."

This firmly established foreign policy—also followed by the old AFL and the AFL-CIO—became highly controversial at times, attacked by politicians and others, in and out of the labor movement. Meany was influential on American official policy at times, and his actions in international affairs won him friends and enemies among world political leaders as well as unions officials:

> It's not just a question of Communism; we're going to do what we can to fight any system anywhere in the world that denies workers their freedom to associate freely in order to improve the conditions under which they work and under which they live.
>
> Communism, of course, is a dictatorial system; it denies workers the rights of freedom. Workers are controlled by government through one means or another. For instance, in the Soviet Union they have what they call the All-Soviet Council of Trade Unions, and all workers are members of what they call "trade unions." The purpose of these unions is a governmental purpose: they are really set up to control workers. They have a tremendous influence on the lives of workers, and that influence is used for the purpose of the state rather than the purpose of the workers.
>
> The head of the Soviet "unions" is appointed by the politburo. [In 1974] they appointed Shelepin, who had been head of the Russian secret police. He wasn't elected by anybody. He said that his experience as head of the secret police was the type needed to run the unions!

In the United States, Meany had witnessed the attempts of Communists to invade AFL unions in the 1920s and 1930s:

> They worked very hard. Their objective was always to gain control: they used different methods. At times they would be boring from within, trying to take over unions, and they did take over some unions. At other times they would be promoting the so-called "united front."
>
> The Communist-controlled unions would join with democratic unions on the claim that even if they were Communists they were workers and we all had a common interest and should work together. Of course, the real purpose of that is to break down the democratic structure of unions—not to build up worker standards.
>
> We had a couple of Commies in our local union. Actually, they made a lot of noise and we had some excitement, but they never were a threat to our union; it was just a couple who would come to

the meeting week after week and talk against capitalism and all that stuff. They didn't have many real listeners.

We had one fellow who would come every week and make all this noise and, lo and behold, we saw his picture on the front page of one of the tabloids leading a picket line for a Communist strike of the silk workers over around Paterson, New Jersey. We asked him, "What were you doing carrying a banner in a Communist parade?" He lost whatever standing he had on that one.

While the AFL-CIO does not grant affiliation to a national or international union that is dominated or controlled by Communists or fascists, there were local unions where Communists were in control, Meany conceded:

> They are pretty low-key; they don't get out in front too much. There's always a question [about] denying membership to a fellow because he's a Communist and thus denying him the means of making a living.
>
> Actually, whatever threat Communists were to the American trade union structure is forty years behind us. They made a lot of noise in the twenties and they did get control of some unions and they caused a lot of trouble—but that's all past and gone.

In world affairs, the AFL-CIO took a stronger anti-Communist position than American businessmen, Meany felt:

> Businessmen are always looking for profits. They don't see anything wrong in making profits anywhere they can make them. If they can deal with Communists and Communist nations and feel they can make a profit, they'll go ahead. I don't say they are any less patriotic [than labor]; they're less aware of the real threat. The threat is very definite because private business goes out the window any time Communists get control.
>
> They are ready to do business with the Communist nations right today. I don't think American corporations should be allowed, under our law, to do business with Communist nations. If there was a counterpart in these nations to the American businessman—but there are no Communist businessmen.
>
> We're all here on the same globe and we can live with the Communists if we deal with them on a government-to-government basis.

This vivid description of the Russian dictatorship once was offered by Meany:

We in the trade union movement are familiar with the hocus-pocus of the Communists' terminology. They speak in terms of a "people's democracy"; they act in terms of ruthless dictatorship. Their system chains the farmer to the soil and freezes the worker to his assigned job. It robs the people of the fruits of their production and their basic liberties.

It stifles freedom of conscience and the intellect. It concentrates total economic and political power in the hands of a narrow dictatorship to which the people at large are enslaved. It takes no stock of either human rights or human life on the theory that the end justifies the means. Today it is desperately concentrating on producing the means to end freedom on earth.

Criticism of the labor movement's attacks on communism and of its general interest in foreign policy prompted Meany to state soon after he became AFL president:

The American Federation of Labor has long been active in this field. We've been criticized for this. ... You should keep this in mind: We have no hope of getting any members in Europe or Asia. We can't be accused of being mercenary. We're not trying to collect dues in any of these far-away places.

But we have a tremendous interest in seeing to it that there are free trade unions in every country in the world where it is possible to have them. Because in every country in the world where there are free trade unions there must be some semblance of democracy. Because, when democracy goes out, there just can't be a free trade union. The record of the dictator countries proves [that] beyond a question of doubt. ... If [Germany and Japan] do have strong free trade unions, it will insure some kind of a democracy and keep those countries out of the hands of the Soviet dictators and out of the Soviet orbit of influence. ...

We feel that the best safeguard for world peace is free democratic nations, and free democratic nations can come into being through the actions of a trade union.

An early appraisal of detente—then being marketed under the label of "co-existence"—appears in a 1954 speech:

Propaganda for co-existence ... is sweeping Europe and ... evidently is being taken quite seriously here in this country. It is spewed out by the *Daily Worker* and by every apologist for Moscow that there can be co-existence between the Communist countries and the democratic world. . . .

Might I ask who threatens whom? Who is it that maintains an international subversion conspiracy for the fifth-columnists all over the world? Who is it that has wiped out the freedom of more than a dozen nations and millions upon millions of people? Who is it that has grabbed millions of square miles of territory and placed the people in those areas in enslavement?

[AFL members] have always been realists, and they are realists today. We don't accept the price of co-existence with gangsters unless there is evidence of good faith by the return of freedom to those who have lost their freedom under this diabolical conspiracy which is known as international Communism.

Although he was fighting communism both abroad and at home, Meany was horrified at the excesses of Wisconsin Senator Joseph R. McCarthy's witch hunts in the congressional committee he chaired in the 1950s. McCarthy's often baseless accusations of Communist sympathies were the subject of this attack in 1955:

We are not going to gain anything in the fight on Communism if, in these Congressional investigations such as are carried on by the McCarthy committee, we throw to the winds all semblance of American fair play, by which we lower the morale of public employees from one end of the country to the other, and by which we depart from the American concept of justice by accusing people without giving them the slightest opportunity to defend themselves; by asking for the removal of federal employees from their jobs without even giving them the opportunity to know what they are accused of.

No, I think it would be well for Congress, in its fight to preserve the internal security of this country, to not lose sight of the fact that we have some essential basic freedoms to preserve, and let them come up with some sort of a code—a code of fair procedure—[so that those summoned] can face the committee like real Americans and [know] they are going to get a fair deal.

Meany became involved in attacking world communism and other forms of totalitarianism well before that McCarthy period. As early as 1933, American trade unionists launched a massive underground rescue operation to save German labor leaders from Hitler's prison camps and death squads.

Active in that effort was Jay Lovestone, who had been chairman of the U.S. Communist party from 1926 to 1929, when he was ousted by Stalin for opposing the Moscow line for the American party. Later a rabid anti-Communist, Lovestone worked with Garment Workers President David Dubinsky and, through him, became acquainted with Meany soon after Meany was elected to the Number Two AFL post.

Lovestone's background seriously worried Meany at first:

> I didn't want any part of him at all. But Dubinsky convinced me that Jay was no longer a Communist and could be trusted to work with us. When I got to know him and work with him, I had no misgivings about him at all.
>
> There was no question that he, as a young man, was a dedicated, active Communist, and after a few years he got to see communism for what it really was. Then he became anti-Russian communism. The Russians were doing everything they could to make it difficult for him.
>
> He was a very effective anti-Communist for many, many years. He had more documents and more material on Communists and their activities in various parts of the world than any other American. I don't think the U.S. Government intelligence agencies and our State Department had anything like the information that Jay Lovestone had about Communists all over the world.

Lovestone's role with the AFL for several years was informal: he made suggestions to Meany and the AFL's international affairs committee while remaining on the garment union's payroll. His advice was valuable, but he did not turn Meany into an anti-Communist. Meany had been anti-Commuist when Lovestone still was a Communist party official.

As director of the Free Trade Union Committee of the AFL, Lovestone worked closely with Meany and, in 1956, joined the staff of the Federation as an adviser on foreign affairs. He was director of the AFL-CIO's international affairs department from 1964 until his retirement in 1974.

Meany's concern with foreign affairs went through "an interesting evolution," especially in relation to Lovestone and his background, Lovestone said. He thought that Meany showed a "special amount of courage, a certain basic courage," in deciding to work with a former chairman of the Communist party.

While Meany was influenced in a large measure by internationalists Dubinsky and Matthew Woll of the AFL Council, according to Lovestone, "they did not give George the interest in international affairs; he had it himself."

The rise of Hitler aroused Meany, but he went beyond a passive opposition to fascism, Lovestone said:

"He has this capacity: when he gets interested in something, he wants to do something about it. It's no platonic affair. Personally, I was most attracted to that because a good bit of theorizing is thumb-sucking. As I worked with him, I found him to have a very clear mind, a quick mind—he's quite perceptive. He can see a point, and when he can't see, he will ask a question. When he disagrees, he'll put it very bluntly. He was positively interested in international affairs.

"Frankly, I think that without George the international work [of the Federation] would never have advanced to the stage it has. George Meany, Dubinsky and Woll were the prime forces, but George was in the [headquarters] apparatus. He was the secretary, and Green was an easygoing fellow, but it wasn't easy to get along with him. It's not easy to get along with easygoing people. . . . George felt absolutely hampered, wanted to be active. The international field was wide open and George welcomed the opportunity in that sense."

Meany's international work definitely helped advance his position at home and abroad, Lovestone felt.

David Dubinsky, in his 1977 autobiography, shared Lovestone's enthusiasm.

"Taken in its totality . . . the role of the AFL in foreign affairs, especially in the immediate period after World War II, is one that does great credit to American labor. It was a special credit to George Meany, who came out of the most parochial section of the labor movement, that he did more than any of us to broaden the horizons of labor's interest in helping workers everywhere create free unions and defeat the threat of totalitarianism, whether with a swastika or with a hammer and sickle as its emblem."

Part of Meany's foreign activity involved the International Labor Organization, an agency of the old League of Nations and, later, of the United Nations.

Meany's interest in the ILO contrasted with Green's disdain. Green was appointed a worker delegate from the United States, but for several years after the U.S. joined, he sent alternates.

The first opportunity Meany had to participate in the ILO sessions came in 1936, two years after America entered:

> Gompers was the major factor in the establishment of the ILO. He was at the Versailles peace conference [after World War I] with President Woodrow Wilson, and Gompers had inserted into the Treaty of Versailles the clause calling for establishment of the ILO. Membership in ILO was limited to countries which held membership in the League of Nations. The United States did not go into the League, which meant that we established the ILO and then couldn't take up membership in it.
>
> But the ILO changed its constitution and, under President Franklin Roosevelt, our country joined the ILO. Green called me out of a clear sky early in November 1936 and when he started to tell me he wanted me to go to Geneva, I really didn't know what he was talking about. Every once in a while the State Federation president would get an assignment from Green to go somewhere in the state where there were some problems. I was thinking of Geneva, New York, wondering what's going on up there.
>
> He said that [Labor Secretary] "Frances Perkins will arrange for you to get your passport" and it dawned on me that he wanted me to go to Geneva, Switzerland. I got myself together—that was just a week before I left.

In the early days, he felt, the ILO did a good job, but when the Soviet Union, which dropped out in 1939, was readmitted in 1954, "They just turned the thing into a political propaganda sounding-board and practically destroyed the effectiveness of the ILO. The ILO became a political debating society and its real work, more or less, was cast aside. But in the early days I think it did a great deal."

The AFL opposed admission of the so-called union delegation from Soviet Russia because the unions were part of government, but the AFL was outvoted. As conceived by Gompers, the ILO is tripartite, with government, labor and industry representatives. Employer delegates refused to accept Soviet "employer" delegates as voting members of their group.

As a world conscience, the ILO is supposed to adopt what amounts to treaties regarding workers and working conditions, but these do not become binding on a nation until it approves the document. U.S. legislators have been slow to adopt even the relatively lenient ILO standards.

To get more practical results, American labor had to form its own committees to help workers abroad. Soon after becoming AFL's secretary-treasurer, Meany was appointed honorary secretary of the Labor League for Human Rights, set up by the Federation in 1938. He also became a member of the AFL's committee on international relations when it was formed in 1943.

The committee, of Council members, had general authority over the work abroad. AFL's relief effort spread through Europe and Asia as the war expanded, with many refugee unionists sustained throughout the conflict. In all, some $25 million was contributed through the Labor League in relief to war victims.

Lovestone was operating head of the Labor League and its successor agencies. In 1944 the AFL convention created an umbrella panel—the Free Trade Union Committee, or FTUC—with Meany an active officer from the start.

Although raising money in World War II to aid British workers, AFL leaders quarreled with their British friends over how to cooperate with Soviet Russia's "unions" after Russia became an ally. In May 1942, Sir Walter Citrine, leader of the British Trades Union Congress, or TUC, brought a delegation to America, Meany recalled in 1954:

> We were asked then to enter into a Soviet-Anglo-American alliance for the purpose of labor cooperation in the war effort. We took the position at that time that we would not go into an alliance with an organization which in fact did not exist. . . . There were no Russian trade unions, and, of course, we have not deviated from that position.

The Anglo-American Trade Union Committee, nevertheless, was established at the suggestion of the AFL in July 1942, with the understanding that the existing Anglo-Soviet Trade Union Committee and the new panel would exchange views. In this way, the British became the conduit for keeping Russian and American labor informed on anything of mutual interest during the war.

"During the war," Meany explained, "Citrine tried to get us to go into an alliance with the Soviets and we wouldn't do it. They finally got the CIO to go in, and in 1945 they formed the World Federation of Trade Unions [WFTU]."

Meany's habit of blunt speech, stating exactly what was on his mind notwithstanding an audience's hostile reaction, never was better illustrated than at a riotous labor gathering in England that year.

Before the formal establishment of the WFTU, Meany made his first appearance as "fraternal delegate" to the British TUC, at Blackpool in September 1945. The visit was long remembered by the British unionists. On the platform also was the Russian "fraternal delegate"—adding to the drama.

As the American opened a furious attack on the Russian "unions," the audience booed loudly, jeered, shouted, "Shame!" and "Tommyrot!" in an effort to halt the speech. The unhappy chairman rang his bell desperately and begged for obedience to the British tradition for free speech. Among other things, Meany said above the racket:

> By unanimous action of our convention and of our Executive Council we have refused to participate in the formation of this so-called world organization [WFTU] and I say to you very simply and directly that if, as and when this organization is formed, we still will not seek, nor will we accept, membership in it. . . .
>
> The two most vital reasons . . . for our decision not to affiliate . . . are (1) the inclusion in the conference of representatives of the CIO, and (2) the inclusion . . . of representatives of the pseudo trade unions of Russia. . . . The measure of recognition your great movement has so far given to the dual group in America has already served to delay the possibility of labor unity there. . . .
>
> [Regarding] our refusal to sit with the so-called representatives of Russian labor, let there be no quibbling or misunderstanding: we do not recognize or concede that the Russian worker groups are trade unions. The Soviet worker groups are formally and actually instruments of the State. They are official branches of the government and of its ruling dictatorial political party. These so-called unions are designed to protect the interests of the Soviet state, even if this means that the interests of the workers themselves must be subordinated or ignored. . . .
>
> What common ground for discussion could we find in cooperating with those who pretend to speak for workers but in reality represent the government itself? What could we talk about? The latest innovations being used by the secret police to ensnare those who think in opposition to the group in power? Or perhaps bigger and better concentration camps for political prisoners?

Ignoring the riot, Meany proceeded to point to the AFL's support of America's actions to rearm Britain, at a time when the Communist faction in the CIO was opposing all U.S. defense measures.

Newspapers reported that Meany finally was cheered by delegates when he declared in closing: "I hope I have not offended anyone, but it would be silly to come 3400 miles and then go home without saying what was on my mind."

When asked about that incident years later Meany said his speech "was routine; I told them what I thought of their WFTU and how they went into it, and what went on." He also discussed the background of WFTU's creation:

> The British were really responsible for WFTU. After 1940, Ernest Bevin had gone into the coalition cabinet with Churchill, and, as minister of labor, was in charge of war production. He was the fellow who had to get British labor to produce under the very, very difficult conditions; they had to shift people around.
>
> Citrine was the general secretary of the TUC; he had no influence in the political structure at all. The Number One labor fellow, recognized by labor and everyone, was Bevin. I always had the feeling that Citrine wanted to do something to build up his standing as a rival of Bevin's. There was a certain amount of jealousy there.
>
> Citrine, I imagine, assumed that as the prime mover [in creating the WFTU] he was going to be Number One, but suddenly he discovered that the Russians hadn't any such idea. Even before they went through the founding convention, Citrine realized that he had been had by the Soviets, working in conjunction with the CIO. He tried desperately to get control of it.
>
> When they finally set up the WFTU, he only had a ceremonial position; the actual head was the general secretary, a French Communist by the name of Louis Saillant. They got all the Europeans in, the CIO and the British TUC. Within two years [the non-Communist unions] were disillusioned, and one by one they dropped out, the Scandinavians dropped out, the British dropped out, and so on.

After the war a labor battle for Germany began, with Russian Communists and AFL leaders agreeing on one thing: Germany was the key to expansion of communism into Western Europe. The AFL's thinking was explained by Meany:

> We recognized that Germany was the key to Europe and, in fact, today Germany is still the key to Europe. Russia was ready to move any place they could. But they couldn't very well move into the British, French and American occupation Zones, which covered what today we call West Germany. The Russians were in East Germany.
>
> We didn't have any doubt about what their intentions were. We

felt that the best safeguard against infiltration and starting of a so-
called people's rebellion would be a free trade-union movement;
that is why we concentrated on the trade unions. Also we had a sentimental interest in preservation of German labor, because a great
deal of the development of American labor came about through the
influence of German immigrants a century or so ago.

We were aware of what was going on in France and Italy—the
determined effort of the Commies to take everything.

We felt that as soon as the [Alllied] military loosened its grip in
West Germany they would move in there. We felt that the best way
to stop them was to have the workers organized into one national
trade-union center, and we had a great deal to do with that.

Before the war, Germany's trade union movement was divided
along religious lines as in a good many European countries—Socialist, Catholic and Protestant. We were afraid that if they reorganized
on that basis this would present a divided union setup and the Communists certainly would move in to take advantage of it. So we
worked hard during forty-seven and forty-eight to get them to come
together. Father [later Monsignor] George G. Higgins went to Germany from Washington and used what influence he had to see that
the Germans did not go back to their traditional way of organizing.

There was a movement in the United States to punish the German people by making Germany into an agricultural country and
shipping the industrial production out of Germany. The Russians
were quite busy doing just that. We made representations to John J.
McCloy and other American [occupation] authorities and brought
that to a halt, even though there were very prominent people here in
this country who were all for the plan. They were going to render
Germany impotent as an industrial nation. It was known as the
Morgenthau Plan. [CIO leader] Sidney Hillman also was pushing it,
but the plan didn't last very long.

If the AFL had not helped rebuild the labor movement, Meany felt,
Germany probably would have been made into a Russian satellite like
so many other countries. As it is, he added, "that movement is the
strongest trade-union movement in the world outside of the American
or possibly the British."

American Communists and their fellow travelers employed by the
U.S. military's manpower division in Germany had considerable success, at first, in preventing the former union leaders from regaining
their old posts. Irving Brown, then an AFL staffer in Europe, and later

the AFL-CIO representative, said that the American military's ignorance of labor matters played into the hands of the Communists.

The most prominent member of the pro-Communist group was George Shaw Wheeler, who had "enormous influence" inside the military headquarters, according to Jay Lovestone. When AFL representatives Brown and Joseph D. Keenan offered evidence of Wheeler's activities, it was rejected by officials, who believed the charges only when Wheeler fled to Czechoslovakia.

"Before he defected," Meany recalled, "Wheeler was doing everything he could to upset what we were trying to do in Germany. He was a Communist agent; no question about that."

As a result of AFL pressure in Washington and Germany, the U.S. Military Governor General Lucius B. Clay, wrote Green on June 3, 1946, listing numerous steps he had taken at the Federation's urging to assist revival of the German labor movement. Among them were restoration of prewar union property and office equipment, permission to publish a union newspaper, and labor access to radio broadcasts. Clay thanked the AFL for its help and asked for further cooperation and advice.*

Meany also directed the Federation's day-to-day operations aimed at helping to establish free unions in France and Italy. In discussing that period decades later, he played down his own part, and credited Dubinsky and other garment union officials for helping the Christian Democrats block a Communist attempt to win control of the Italian Government in a 1948 election. Meany explained in 1964:

> [Our unions] played a strong part in both Italy and France . . . in keeping the Communists from taking over. We financed a split in the Communist-controlled union in France. We sent American trade union money; we set up their offices; we gave them supplies and everything else so that we could weaken the Communist front. In Italy . . . we had our people there; we assisted the non-Communist unions and the so-called Christian Democratic unions and we brought them together and they are still together. . . .
>
> We want to preserve the type of society under which it is possible to have a free trade-union. . . . When [the Soviets] say I am an agent of Wall Street—if they mean . . . that I am an agent of the American

---

* Earlier, Clay had reported that the German unions were growing in membership, adding: "Since unions are a basic pillar in the construction of future democratic Germany, every effort must be made to expedite that improvement."

system—as far as I'm concerned, I accept that. I am an agent of the American system and quite proud of it. This does not mean that we are satisfied. . . . We always want to do a little better.

The labor federation's involvement was equally instrumental in assuring the success of the Marshall Plan.

After Secretary of State George C. Marshall proposed the massive recovery-aid program for Europe's war-torn economy, Truman appointed a committee chaired by Commerce Secretary Averell Harriman to find out if the U.S. economy would be able to finance the effort. Meany, who was on that committee, recalled that its answer was: "Yes, we can do it. The American economy can stand it and the American people are all for it." America forged ahead with the great humanitarian program.

Meany's insistence that European workers be given a voice in the relief program and receive some of the assistance undoubtedly played a part in preventing Communist union leaders on the French docks from blocking the delivery of supplies from America. In the committee sessions and at congressional hearings he urged that the democratic unions in the stricken countries be brought into the Plan operations. He was able to get a provision in the legislation that set aside a percentage of the Plan relief money to strengthen the labor movements and build housing projects for workers.

Also at his suggestion, European free union leaders were invited to create a labor advisory committee for the Plan. Representatives of the AFL and CIO were appointed to important posts in the Plan's Paris headquarters.

This participation of labor in the whole effort encouraged the members of the free trade-unions to keep supplies moving through the French ports for the relief program and for the North Atlantic Treaty Organization (NATO), despite massive efforts of the Communists to disrupt them.

When General Eisenhower headed NATO's military headquarters in Paris, Irving Brown recalled, Meany arranged for special briefings from Ike for friendly European union chiefs, thus further bringing labor into the program.

John L. Lewis discovered the extent of Meany's enthusiasm for the Marshall Plan at the 1947 AFL convention. Jay Lovestone had prepared the draft of a resolution endorsing the Marshall Plan, but, at a committee meeting, Lewis crossed out that section and rejected all of

Lovestone's arguments for its restoration. When Meany was told of this—he had been unable to attend the meeting—he convened another meeting and got the endorsement back in. Lewis was at this meeting as well, Lovestone recalled, "but never said a word" in opposition.

Soon afterward, in a radio speech, Meany referred to actions of the European Communists:

> Mr. Stalin, the Russian Hitler, and all his agents and henchmen are trying to move heaven and earth to block the Marshall Plan. There is no mystery about their motives. They know that if France and Italy and the other non-Communist countries fail to receive assistance they will fall into the Russian basket. Nothing helps the Communist cause more effectively than hunger and economic chaos.

Meany explained the AFL's independent course in foreign affairs in a 1951 speech:

> In its fight against Communism, in its positive fight for democracy, the AFL conducts its activities as an independent force. We are totally independent of any government control or influence. At times we may agree and cooperate. At times we may disagree. But at no time can we serve or act as an agency or dependent of our government.
>
> It is this entirely independent role of the AFL which has lent great potency, prestige and effectiveness to our domestic and foreign activities against the Communist scourge. We are labor, we fight as labor, we fight for labor. We fight against the termites in the house of labor.

Cooperation of the AFL and U.S. Government in opposing Communist expansion in Europe—plus the increasingly desperate Soviet attempts to stop the rehabilitation program—soon weakened the party-line World Federation of Trade Unions. By late 1947 and 1948, non-Communist labor organizations began to regret their ties to the WFTU. An open attack by WFTU on the Marshall Plan was too much for some and withdrawal was authorized by the CIO and the British TUC conventions. Nearly all other non-Communist groups also left, except for Israel's Histadrut, which had to worry about possible Soviet reprisals against the country. (Histadrut later quit, in May 1950.)

In the meantime the British prepared a new world labor organization.

In March of 1949 a British delegation came to Washington. They were through with the WFTU. They said it was an instrumentality of the Soviet Union, propagandizing all over the world for the Soviet cause. They felt they had to set something up to combat it. They were prepared to do that if they got the cooperation of the Americans. They insisted they not only wanted the AFL but they wanted the CIO, too.

We had a meeting of our committee: Dubinsky, Woll, George Harrison, [William J.] McSorley, Green and myself. Now, up to that time the AFL had always objected to giving the CIO any recognition in any international field. However, we felt that here was an opportunity to set up a world organization of free unions, and we agreed that, all right, we'll withdraw our objections to the CIO coming in. The only fellow who wouldn't go along with that was Green, and we sat and talked to him and finally outvoted him on it. Green was very upset, but he went along, although he was pretty bitter about it.

The experience the CIO and the Europeans had had with Communists in the WFTU promised a successful new direction for the new organization, Meany felt. Groundwork was laid at a Geneva meeting in June 1949 and the founding congress was held in London late that year, creating the International Confederation of Free Trade Unions, or ICFTU:

We had quite a few disputes with the British right from the start. For instance, they had told us they wanted to set up a world federation that would embrace all non-Communist unions throughout the world. To us, that included the Christians [Christian Democrats] but they barred the Christian unions. They immediately double-crossed us. Walter Reuther and I fought for their admission together, shoulder-to-shoulder. The British would not keep their word on that.

This weakened the organization because there were very strong Christian unions in certain countries. The old prejudices [of the Socialists] still prevailed. The Christian unions in most of these countries were rivals—like the CIO was to the AFL for twenty years here. The Christian unions never got in ICFTU. We felt that the British had broken their commitment to us. We [had] put aside our factional differences at the request of the British and agreed the CIO and the AFL both would go in, despite the fact that we were rivals here.

From the beginning, the British also blocked the Israelis from joining, but we finally did get them in. They invited the Israelis to come to the first meeting as observers but then barred them as members because the British and Israeli [governments] were doing battle at the time. This was right after Israeli independence.

At that opening meeting of ICFTU, Meany outlined a series of basic principles being suggested by the AFL. Among these principles was a ban on big-power politics in the organization, protection for the rights of both large and small union movements, and extension of the organization to all parts of the world. Meany warned, however, against allowing "any specific political ideology" to dominate the organization. "There should be no intention of attempting to force our way of life upon trade unionists in other parts of the world, nor will we permit others to force their political or ideological beliefs on us."

This was Meany's notice to the British and other Socialist-oriented federations that the AFL did not want them using the ICFTU to spread their political doctrines into the newer labor movements. In rejecting big-power politics, he was telling the British not to try to dominate the ICFTU and promising that the AFL would also refrain.

Labor movements from about fifty countries attended the founding congress of ICFTU. They represented some fifty million workers.

By this time, the CIO had ousted the Communist-dominated unions from its own ranks and thus could join the new confederation without internal dissent. The fact that the ouster had taken place also made it easier for the AFL to cooperate with the rival American federation.*

When the ICFTU established a Western Hemisphere branch, called ORIT, or Organización Regional Inter-Americano de Trabajadores, Meany headed the AFL delegation to the first meeting in Mexico City in January 1951. Unions from twenty-one countries were represented there. He insisted that the government-controlled unions of Argentina be rejected; they were, with only Mexican labor dissenting. Meany was made a member of the nine-man executive committee.

---

* Meany's willingness to work with Walter Reuther and others on the CIO delegation to ICFTU undoubtedly was a help in negotiating the eventual merger of the CIO and AFL, where Reuther again was a key factor. The men, who were rivals inside the U.S., learned to cooperate in the politics of international labor. As Jay Lovestone said: "It is true that the CIO was one of the later ones to leave the WFTU, but I must say in fairness that was not the fault of Walter Reuther. He never was enthusiastic about the WFTU. I think George saw that in Walter and welcomed it." The two men didn't always agree on issues, but the CIO officials found that Meany was an AFL man they could respect for integrity and ability.

8

THE TAFT-HARTLEY STRUGGLE

Before Taft-Hartley was put on the statute books over Truman's veto, I didn't push for what you might call a political machine. . . . It wasn't until Taft-Hartley in 1947 that the AFL really went into the business of working at elections.

The Cold War battles were only a sideline for George Meany during the Truman years. On the home front, organized labor was waging a word war against big business' attempts to clamp new restrictions on unions through tougher federal laws.

Union leaders found they were not as welcome at the Truman White House as they had been at the Roosevelt one. The wartime strikes of the coal miners plus a postwar wave of industry-wide walkouts, largely by CIO unions, helped conservatives push the Taft-Hartley Act through Congress, despite Truman's veto. Labor called it the "Slave Labor Act."

The President had convened a labor-management conference in November 1945—three months after the fighting in World War II ended—to propose ways to improve labor relations in industry. Meany was on the AFL delegation, although Green was its spokesman. Also present were representatives of the CIO, the National Association of

Manufacturers, the Chamber of Commerce of the United States and the independent unions such as the United Mine Workers.

After the sessions ended without recommendations on such issues as legislation to curb the wave of postwar strikes, Truman proposed to Congress that the fact-finding procedures of the Railway Labor Act be extended to industry generally. Recommendations of these fact-finding boards are not binding on either side.

Congress rejected the suggestion, but the President used his own executive powers to set up such boards for major disputes at General Motors and in the basic steel industry. The following year the White House employed this weapon extensively as a record number of big walkouts slowed the economy, Meany recalled:

> I was never opposed to the fact-finding boards and I didn't look upon that as an enormous intrusion on the part of the government. I had the same feeling about fact-finding boards as Bob [Ohio Senator Robert A.] Taft did; he was very much opposed to fact-finding boards—for the same reason that I was for them.
>
> My experience has shown that in ninety percent of the cases where fact-finding boards were involved—and were actually fact finders and not playing games—the union came out on top. I remember in one discussion, about 1947, this question of fact-finding boards came up and Taft blurted out that "these boards always find on the side of labor." So, I liked the idea. All I wanted to know was that we had fact finders who were straight and honest, who would give us the facts as they found them.

Meany and the AFL opposed Truman's request for legislation authorizing appointment of these boards.

> We would not object to fact-finding on an ad hoc basis, but to write a law would be entirely different, because that would have an influence on collective bargaining right from the start. Everybody involved would be looking at the law down the road. No, we couldn't buy that. We objected to the idea of a law because a law on fact-finding, in my book, would be just the first step toward complete government control.
>
> With fact-finding on an ad hoc basis it always left the union free to say, "We won't take it." Mostly, they did take it. But [boards set up by law] would be just like a labor court. Instead of having fact finders that were chosen by agreement—with third parties suggest-

ing names and the union and employer agreeing—you would have
fact finders that were political and, to some extent, permanent. No,
we wouldn't buy a law on compulsory fact-finding any more than
we would buy a law providing compulsion against strikes.

 You couldn't write such a law without also saying employees have
to keep working while the fact-finding process is going on. Of course,
I certainly would favor keeping them working, but to write a law is
an entirely different thing.

To President Truman's shock and surprise, even the fact-finding
procedures of the Railway Labor Act could not prevent a shutdown of
the nation's railroads in May 1946 because of a strike of the Locomo-
tive Engineers and the Trainmen, supported by other crafts.

 In turn, Truman shocked the labor unions by asking Congress to empower him to draft the strikers into the military service. He already
had seized the railroads under war powers that were still on the statute
books and he had ordered the employees to remain at work, but they
walked out.

 While Truman was making his dramatic appeal to a special joint
session of the Congress he was handed a note saying that the unions
had called off the strike. He read the note to the legislators but still
asked for the law. The House gave immediate approval, while senators,
led by conservative Taft, balked at the extreme measure; it was allowed to die.

 The striking rail unions were not affiliates of the AFL or CIO, but
Meany remembered the shock of Truman's actions:

  We were not directly involved in that at all. The unions did not
  belong to the AFL, but we had a good relationship with all of the
  rail brotherhoods. We were very much concerned about anti-strike
  legislation, any move to prevent strikes or to terminate strikes by
  government fiat.

  We worked like hell with the railroad unions to try to straighten it
  out, but Truman got himself in real bad with the railroad unions.
  The odd part of it was that the railroad unions up to then had been
  his friends. There was a very close relationship between Truman and
  the rail brotherhoods. He made no bones about the fact that he [was
  re-elected] as a senator in 1940 through the action of the railroad
  unions—that he didn't have a chance [without them].

 Still, the draft-strikers proposal did not seriously impair the AFL's
relations with Truman.

It was one of those things. We looked on Truman as a good friend; we certainly didn't look upon him as a reactionary. But we felt that he was dead wrong in this one, that he had overreacted to the situation.

Reports at that time held that Truman knew before starting his speech to Congress on the draft bill that the strike had been called off. Meany thought so then and in restrospect:

> Everything I know indicates that was true—that just before he took the action he knew that he didn't have to do it. He was determined to give them a little spanking or something; he went ahead.
>
> Truman got in bad with everybody on that, especially the [union] leadership. The word went around that when he made that speech it was unnecessary because the railroad unions had already indicated, "All right, we'll capitulate." But he beat them over the head.
>
> Of course, two years later the same people, along with the AFL, very strongly supported Truman's re-election. It was not any permanent break, because while labor was certainly unhappy about that action of Truman's, there were a lot of pluses in Truman's record.*

John L. Lewis gave Truman another problem a few months later by threatening a coal miners' walkout on November 20. The mines still were operating under federal control after having been seized in a spring walkout. Truman got a temporary restraining order barring the new stoppage, but miners walked out of the pits on schedule. A court agreed with the government that Lewis was in contempt of court and fined the Mine Workers $3.5 million and Lewis, personally, $10,000. (Later the Supreme Court reduced the union's penalty to $700,000.)

Aroused by the coal strike and other postwar walkouts throughout the country, Congress decided it had to reform the labor law, as had been demanded by industrialists. The result was Taft-Hartley, which, among other restrictions, barred the closed shop.

Meany recalled how organized labor lost a friend—Fred A. Hartley, Jr.—in a key spot in Congress—and big business won an ally:

> In the congressional election of 1946, you would think that labor would get some credit for its tremendous contribution to the war effort, but, instead, all the reactionary forces turned against us. A tre-

---

* The pluses, in Meany's view, included "recognizing the Soviet threat" in Western Europe after World War II, "reacting to the threats in Turkey and Greece with the Truman Doctrine, reaction to the threat in Korea. He was a very ordinary sort of a fellow, but he really was a first-class American. He was tough. He was a great President."

mendous anti-labor sentiment was developed by the big business interests. In that election, the Democrats got defeated; they lost both
Houses of Congress.

Industry as a whole resented the fact that labor made progress.
This was a throwback to industry's position [at the 1941 Industry-
Labor Conference]. They wanted to freeze the non-union shop, keep
it non-union, and freeze the closed shop—no change during the war.
We wouldn't buy that and Roosevelt didn't buy it, either.

So, for about four years we continued to organize; we made a lot
of progress. The CIO picked up hundreds of thousands of members
during the war.

The anti-union forces in industry, which were pretty strong in
those days, resented this very much, and the minute the war was
over they declared war on us. That's why we had the bad deal in
1946, when we got a very bad Congress, an anti-labor Congress. I
can show you how well this was organized.

The second-ranking Republican on the House Labor Committee
was Fred Hartley. The ranking Republican was a fellow named
[Richard J.] Welsh, of California—from the San Francisco Mission
district, a very liberal Republican who was actually very friendly to
labor.

Hartley had been quite friendly to labor up to that time; he had
strong labor support when he was first elected in Essex County, New
Jersey. We looked upon Hartley as a friend, and Bill Hushing, our
legislative representative, had a very close personal relationship with
Hartley.

Believe it or not, the building trades were largely Republican up
in that area—conservative Republicans. They actually financed
Hartley in his first campaign. Billy Lyons, a strong trade-union
leader from the Bricklayers, raised a lot of money and loaned money
to Hartley.

After the 1946 election, the Republicans put the pressure on
Welsh, who as the ranking member was due to become committee
chairman. They pressured him to step aside; he was too liberal for
them. They made a deal with Hartley. Hartley sat down with his old
friend Bill Hushing and said bluntly, "Bill, we are parting company."

When Bill asked what he meant, he said, "I have been with you
fellows all along, but now, forget it. I am only going to be here one
more term and I'm going to make friends that will be helpful to me
so that I can make a living when I get out of here. I am going to take
care of myself. I expect to do quite well financially. I am no longer

Michael and Anne Meany and their son George, age 11, in the school yard of P.S. 29 in the Bronx, New York.

George Meany, second from left, with baseball teammates at St. Luke's Field Club in 1912, and [BELOW] with state federation colleagues in Atlantic City, N.J., shortly after his marriage to Eugenie McMahon, shown in 1919, the year of their wedding.

[ABOVE] Addressing building-trades union members in New York City in 1935 when he was president of the state labor federation, and [BELOW] as AFL national secretary-treasurer, with President Roosevelt and Federation President William Green, in May 1941.

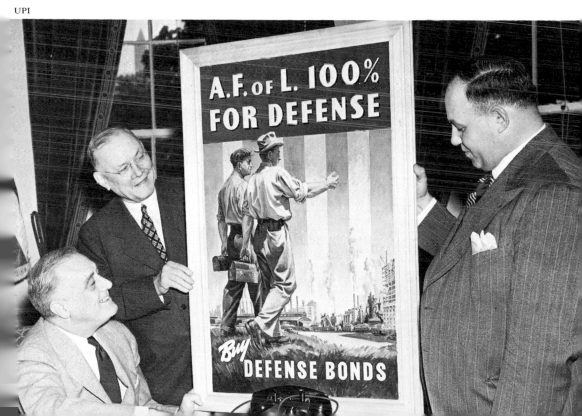

Family man with wife and daughters—from left, Genevieve, Regina and Eileen—and Regina's husband, Robert Mayer; and [BELOW] national leader, second from right, with Anna Rosenberg of the War Manpower Commission, William Green, both center foreground, CIO President Philip Murray, far left, and other labor leaders.

FRANK ALEXANDER

[ABOVE] With Matthew Woll of Photoengravers and Teamsters President Dan Tobin at Meany's installation as federation president in 1952; and [BELOW] with President Truman at Gompers centennial dinner in 1950.

FRANK ALEXANDER

FRANK ALEXANDER

[ABOVE] Symbolically clasping hands with CIO president Walter Reuther at AFL-CIO merger convention on December 5, 1955; [OPPOSITE, TOP] testifying on Landrum-Griffin bill in May 1958; and [BOTTOM] with President Eisenhower that same year.

FRANK ALEXANDER

UPI

FRANK ALEXANDER

Meany with friends: President Kennedy, at civil rights ceremony, November 15, 1962; [OPPOSITE, TOP] Senator Hubert Humphrey, at AFL-CIO Executive Council meeting at Bal Harbour, Fla., February 1964; and [BOTTOM] with four affiliate presidents at Bal Harbour, in November 1971.

FRANK ALEXANDER

UPI

AFL-CIO

FRANK ALEXANDER

UPI

[OPPOSITE] With Presidents Johnson, Nixon, and Ford and [ABOVE AND BELOW] with Carter in two views at minimum wage bill signing in 1977.

AFL-CIO

[ABOVE] Elder statesman: with Aleksandr Solzhenitsyn at AFL-CIO official welcome in 1975; [BELOW] with reporters in September 1973 just before AFL-CIO called for Nixon's impeachment; and [OPPOSITE] relinquishing the president's gavel to Lane Kirkland on November 16, 1979, when Meany was 85.

UPI

AFL-CIQ

UPI

FRANK ALEXANDER

Retirement and death: last photo, November 19, 1979; a construction worker pays his last respects at AFL-CIO headquarters in Washington, January 14, 1980; and President Carter and others attend the funeral at St. Matthew's Cathedral in Washington.

AFL-CIO

on your side; I'm going to be sponsoring legislation that you won't like."

And he set out to do just that: to give labor the works. He became chairman of the House Education and Labor Committee. This was all arranged by the big industrial people, and Hartley immediately found his services as a lecturer were very much in demand. He stepped out of Congress and got some kind of a job.

This was a fellow who had been our friend for 12 to 14 years prior to that. This was really an organized effort by the reactionary forces in business to trim labor's sails.

The other half of the Taft-Hartley's sponsorship—Senator Taft—got mixed marks from Meany:

Bob Taft was basically conservative, generally conservative. I never looked upon Taft as an enemy of labor, by any means. For instance, on the question of housing he was with us one hundred percent. He was just as strong on public housing, government subsidies and the whole bit, back in those days. He was looked upon by Republicans, as far as housing was concerned, as being some kind of a radical.

But Taft had a mental block on one phase of labor relations and this was the secondary boycott. He couldn't understand why products made by union labor in the factories would be boycotted by building-trades workers when those products went on to a construction site. He couldn't understand the boycotting of a union-made product even though it was the CIO [in the factory] and the AFL [at the site].

It really wasn't a question of CIO versus AFL with the building trades. The building trades were all het up and had been for years on the question of loss of work. When a product would come manufactured from a factory—even one under AFL contract—and they felt it could have been made on the job, they would boycott it. This was accentuated by the CIO's organization of certain plants. Take the Sheet Metal Workers: they were always engaged in production as well as installation. On the big jobs, the Sheet Metal Workers would set up a shop on the job, and the mechanic on the job would make the sheet-metal ducts and install them, making them from the bare sheets. On smaller jobs, they would order the stuff from shops organized by the Sheet Metal International Union.

When the CIO organized some previously non-union shops the Sheet Metal Workers' members wouldn't use the product from a

CIO shop. Taft had a very strong feeling about this and it was one of the reasons he got into the Taft-Hartley Act so strongly.

We felt pretty bitter that, despite all the contributions labor had made during the war, one year later we had become sort of a whipping boy and got Taft-Hartley as a result. We fought Taft-Hartley in Congress in every way we could, but we just didn't have the votes.

Somewhere in that period, Bill Hutcheson arranged for me and two or three others to meet with Bob Taft, and we had several discussions with him. We went over a number of things that were in the bill and he was not nearly as strong for an anti-labor bill as Hartley was. Somewhere along the line he made a commitment that before he reported the bill [out of committee to the floor] he would talk to us again.

He didn't keep that commitment and, I guess, a year later—after the bill was passed—we again went over to see him. I had told Hutcheson that I thought we should see Taft just to keep the record straight. We went over to his office and I said, "You made a commitment to talk to us before you finally reported the bill."

"Yes," he said, "I know that and I didn't keep it because I thought it was a waste of time." He was in a real bad mood.

Years later, in an interview for this book, Meany conceded that the Taft-Hartley Act was not as dangerous to unions as labor claimed at the time.

We sort of overreacted. The proof is that the law has been on the books twenty-nine years this summer and we have made progress. It didn't put us out of business, but we felt highly emotional about it—just as our people feel highly emotional about 14(b) [a Taft-Hartley section allowing states to ban union-security contracts]. It is a section of the law that says in effect "here is the federal standard, but if the states want to tighten up and make it more difficult for labor to organize, they can do so. But they can't go the other way." There are very few laws on the statute books where the federal government farms out a portion of its authority to the states and then puts a limit on it. They don't say to the states, "You can legalize the closed shop." Under the federal law you can get the union shop and where the state wants to take the union shop away from you under 14(b), it can. So we feel strongly that this is discriminatory legislation. Nineteen [now twenty] states have used 14(b) and in those states people are at the lower level when it comes to workers' wages.

As Congress was writing the new law in 1947, Meany told a radio audience:

> The Hartley-NAM bill now before the House of Representatives is designed to bring about the destruction of free trade unions in our country. It proposes to achieve this nefarious purpose by enacting into law the program adopted by the National Association of Manufacturers last December. . . . Throughout the 68 pages of the Hartley bill we find the ideas and the very language of the NAM's anti-labor program lifted bodily and incorporated into the bill. . . . The [House] committee minority has stated very definitely, and I quote: "During the period of the hearings the representatives of the NAM working behind the scenes were writing the legislation."

The combined Senate and House bills that finally emerged as Taft-Hartley retained basic features of the Wagner Act of New Deal days but for the first time made unions liable for specified unfair labor practices and provided for penalties. The Wagner Act itemized a whole set of practices that were banned for employers; now the new law cited six prohibited for organized labor.

It placed new restrictions on the right to strike, with court injunctions sanctioned for illegal walkouts. In addition, unions could be sued for violations of labor-management contracts. The closed shop, which forced employers to hire only members of the union, was outlawed. Certain types of boycotts by unions were made illegal.

After twelve years of invoking the powers of the National Labor Relations Board against employers' unfair labor practices, the unions suddenly found that they, too, could be hauled before the Board or into court for "unfair practices." New provisions also made it possible for employers to delay granting union recognition after unions won elections—and to harass union organizing drives.*

When Congress overrode President Truman's veto of the Taft-Hartley Act on June 23, 1947, the officers of labor unions had an immediate

---

* One section of the new law soon became an embarrassment to its sponsors. They had assumed that only union leaders favored union-shop agreements with employers—requiring all workers to join the union. Therefore, they inserted a provision in the law requiring majority approval of such clauses in a government-run election among the employees—a majority of all the workers, not just those voting. During the first four years, however, the 5.5 million workers balloting favored the union shop by a margin of 11 to 1; in 97 percent of the elections, the security clause was approved. Something had to be done to stop this union victory; the law was supposed to hurt labor, not provide it with a propaganda weapon. Congress took the section out in 1951.

problem. One provision of the new law barred a union from using the National Labor Relations Board unless the union's officers had signed affidavits swearing they were not Communist party members. That meant a union could not hold bargaining elections or file NLRB charges against employers' unfair practices until all its officers had signed the oaths.

Many union leaders as a matter of principle objected to signing such an affidavit—especially since the employers using the Board were not forced to do so. Leaders of some CIO unions actually were Communists and had their own reasons for urging a general boycott of the affidavits.

The affidavit issue involved the AFL because it had many local unions directly chartered by the Federation and not in a national organization. Under interpretations, these local unions—called "federal unions"—would be unable to use the NLRB for protection unless all AFL officers signed the oaths. That included not only Green and Meany but other members of the Executive Council who had the title of vice president.

Most of the AFL officers were willing and able to sign. But John L. Lewis and his Mine Workers Union had been taken back into the Federation in 1946 and he was on the Council.

As usual, Lewis had his own idea of what should be done. He had a special dislike for Taft-Hartley because his coal strikes had been one of the reasons Congress passed the law. Lewis' idea was to "boycott" the new law by not signing the non-Communist affidavits. It was a dramatic move, but it could destroy weaker local unions, which needed the help of the Labor Board to win bargaining rights. Meany explained what happened inside the AFL:

> We had a meeting of the Executive Council five or six weeks before the convention in San Francisco. What Lewis did in Chicago was a rehearsal for what he did in San Francisco; he followed the same line.
> We had fought Taft-Hartley, but it became law when Congress overrode Truman's veto. As soon as it became law, practically all of the AFL's national union officers—including Tobin and Hutcheson—went in and signed the non-Communist affidavits so that their unions could operate under Taft-Hartley. If you didn't sign, you had no rights, really, under the Wagner Act anymore.
> Lewis came to Chicago and accused those Council members who had signed the affidavits of taking unilateral action. He came up

with the idea that they were really selling him out, boxing him in and committing the labor movement without the matter having been discussed in the Council.

He was dead wrong, because every union then, and every union today, is autonomous and has a right to take such actions. However, what brought the subject up was what do we do about the federal labor unions? We had 220,000 members in federal labor unions and they bore the same relation to the AFL—to Green and myself as officers—as local unions did to the Carpenters or the Miners or any other union. At that time we had thirteen vice presidents. The lawyers said that they, too, were officers and they, too, would have to sign.

We didn't want to put them into the embarrassing position of having them refuse to sign and thereby leave our several hundred federal labor unions and our 220,000 federal union members without protection. We proposed that we amend the AFL constitution so that these Council members would cease to be vice presidents—just change the title and not make them officers.

That brought a couple hours of abuse from Lewis, and it was personal abuse—not of me, because he paid no attention to me; I was just the secretary, I wasn't the head of a union. He abused Hutcheson, he abused Tobin—by name. He walked around the table as he did it. He said they had no right to sign, they were committing him.

Finally, I interrupted Lewis and sort of challenged him, went after him. He was walking up and down, bawling Green out and saying the Miners this and the Miners that, when I said, "John, are you trying to tell us the only people in the American labor movement who have any red blood in their veins are the Miners?"

He just stopped in shock. He looked at me in complete amazement, because I was the secretary, I did not represent a union—that was almost like an employee in a sense. I'll never forget: he stopped short and said, "I am not addressing myself to you, young man. I'm not concerned with you." In other words, you were just a secretary; what the hell! You don't run a union, you have no troops.

But when we got to San Francisco, I addressed myself to him.

Meany's "address" ended for all practical purposes Lewis' stature as a national union leader.

Lewis' speech [to the convention] completely disregarded the facts. He made a speech about the record of the Mine Workers on Communism; how they kicked out the Communists and how they wouldn't stand for any Communists. He didn't talk about the CIO.

When he became head of the CIO he brought them all in. He was wide open because everybody in the room knew that Phil Murray didn't bring in the Communists. Lewis did.

Phil Murray had all sorts of trouble with them because he had a Communist publicity man, Len DeCaux, a member of the Communist party, and he had a Communist who was playing a very, very active part in running the CIO—Lee Pressman. Pressman was not only general counsel of the CIO and at Murray's side every day when they got to conventions; lo and behold, the lawyer was [secretary] of the resolutions committee—not a trade unionist, not a representative, not a delegate, but the general counsel.

This was the condition that Phil Murray allowed to develop, but Phil Murray didn't bring Pressman or Len DeCaux in there; John Lewis did. I reminded him of that in my speech.

But first came Lewis' oration, which began—typically—with a Biblical reference combined with some un-Christian remarks about his fellow Council members:

" 'Thou shalt not muzzle the ox that treadeth out the corn.' So runs the Scripture. But the Congress of the United States designated 15,-000,000 workers in this country, organized into one form or another of unions, as being cattle that treadeth out the economic corn of our country, and the Congress placed an economic muzzle on each of you. What are you going to do about it? Oh, I see. You are going to change our constitution. God help us!"

Lewis went on to charge that the new law "is the first ugly, savage thrust of Fascism in America," written by legislators "who still believe in the institution of human slavery." He then declared, "It is hardly necessary for me to say that I am not a Communist" and mentioned that his Mine Workers had been in the vanguard in opposition to communism. As for the stand being taken by the AFL leaders on the affidavit issue, Lewis said it reminded him of the Biblical parable, "Lions led by asses." Later he declaimed: "On this particular issue, I don't think that the Federation has a head. I think its neck has just grown up and haired over."

Teamster President Tobin got the floor to reply to Lewis ahead of Meany, but when his turn came the secretary-treasurer pointed out the practical necessity of changing the titles of Council vice-presidents to assure the AFL's directly chartered local unions access to the NLRB. He stressed also the fact that Taft-Hartley was approved through the democratic processes of the United States and that the "only way it is

going to be changed is by our representatives under that system."
Here, from the official record, are some of Meany's further remarks:

> So far as that affidavit is concerned, I don't see why we should
> pull the Communist chestnuts out of the fire. The one major objec-
> tive ... of the Communist Party in America ... has been the de-
> struction of the American Federation of Labor.... We remember
> 1935 when they cast aside all other activities because they found a
> national home. They went into the CIO. They are there today.
>
> The president of the United Mine Workers stated not so very long
> ago that Phil Murray was the prisoner of the Communists. I agree.
> Who walked out and left him prisoner? I have no quarrel with the
> record of the United Mine Workers on Communism. ... The presi-
> dent of the United Mine Workers ... has upheld the position of the
> United Mine Workers in regard to Communism. With his right
> hand from 1935 to 1940 he has upheld the position of the UMW in
> uncompromising resistance to Communism; but with his left hand
> he made a fellowship with Harry Bridges, Julius Emspak, Michael
> Quill, Lee Merrill, and all the other stinking America-haters who
> love Moscow.
>
> So I am prepared to sign a non-Communist affidavit. I am pre-
> pared to go further and sign an affidavit that I never was a comrade
> to the comrades.*

Joseph Keenan, a long-time delegate to AFL conventions and later a
veteran member of the AFL-CIO Council, described the impact of
Meany's speech this way:

"That Meany speech at the 1947 convention was the first time that
anybody had taken on Lewis in the way he did. Everybody was afraid.
Lewis bulldozed everybody. He bulldozed poor Mr. Green terribly. I
think that was one of the highlights of Meany's career because nobody
thought that a secretary—who was dependent upon these guys—
would take him on and win."

Asked if confronting Lewis had not been an emotional ordeal,
Meany recalled:

> I didn't feel emotional about it. He was dead wrong and he was
> very unreasonable. This was a play for power, you see. If he could go
> into a convention and give the Executive Council a licking, this was

---

* The constitution was revised as Meany advocated. The vice-presidential titles were restored the next year, however, after the NLRB ruled that the law did not require affidavits
from Federation officers.

the power play. This is what he wanted, and I think this was more important than the issue itself—because his attitude on the issue was quite stupid. To begin with, how could we tell our international unions not to protect their members?

After all, all of the protections that were in the Wagner Act were still in effect, with the modifications that Taft-Hartley imposed on the union shop and some other things. To refuse to cooperate meant that you couldn't get any protection, but you were still liable for any of the penalties under the Act.

There was nothing emotional bothering me. I was concerned about these 220,000 members of federal labor unions who were our special responsibility.

Lewis got a resounding defeat at that convention. He wanted no compromise, he wanted to fight. So we replaced him on the Executive Council. He didn't even run, because he knew he was going to get beaten. Lewis walked out of the convention; the last day of the convention there were no Miners' delegates in their seats; they didn't show up. He didn't pull out of the AFL at that time, but the story was that he was going to leave, and I was quite sure he was going to leave.

Toward the end of November 1947, Jay Lovestone came to me. He had always been friendly with Kathryn Lewis, John's daughter, whom I never met. She was supposed to have a very strong influence on her father. Jay had met her on a train and he had quite a chat with her. Jay told me that there was a way to keep Lewis in the AFL.

I asked what it was and he quoted Kathryn Lewis as telling him that despite the father's bitterness about what had happened in San Francisco he would stay in if it would be demonstrated to the public that the AFL wanted him to stay in. I told Lovestone, "Oh, he would like to have the chairmanship of the Political League" and Lovestone said that was right.

I said, "You just tell him to go to hell!" If he had gotten the chairmanship of the League—the way he would have handled it—the League would have been more important than the AFL itself.

On December 12, 1947, Lewis wrote a note on a piece of scratch paper and sent it over to the AFL headquarters. It said merely, "Green: We disaffiliate. Lewis." Once again, the Mine Workers Union was an independent; it was still outside the main stream of organized labor when Meany died. Lewis retired as UMW president in 1960; he died in 1969. Meany never relented.

Lewis was a wonderful orator; he could be a very entertaining person. He was destroyed by his ego; he had absolute contempt for humanity—all humanity, and that included his own membership.

It included the employers. When he shut down the coal mines during World War II, he would shut them down with a snap of his fingers. He was working against the interests of his own industry because at the time people were converting to oil for heating and industrial production, and each strike that made coal unavailable had more and more people going to oil.

The membership of the United Mine Workers fifty years ago consisted of 600,000 coal miners. By the time Lewis retired, the membership was down to about 100,000 miners and 200,000 other members in District Fifty [working in other industries]. I say that he hurt his own people.

Now, he had great ideas in lots of ways and he could have made a great contribution. The idea of the union's hospitals was a great idea, but he financed the hospitals by a royalty on coal and he defied all actuarial advice completely. When he decided to raise the royalty, he did, and forced it down the coal operators' throats. The net result was that those hospitals went down the drain; he lost them. He couldn't operate them; they were set up in a non-economic way. Yet he had these millions of dollars from royalties.

What he did with the members' money when he bought the bank in Washington [with union money] was unconscionable, in my view. How the authorities let him get away with it I don't know. They finally brought the matter to court a few years ago, after Lewis was dead and gone. He kept millions of dollars [of pension funds] in the bank the union owned and it wasn't drawing a penny of interest. This was terrible. The beneficiary was the union rather than the members. The idea that a union could benefit and the members not benefit doesn't make sense.

Perhaps Meany summed up the Lewis story best when he said in a 1967 speech that Lewis had the ability "to play a very, very important part" in the labor movement but "was temperamentally unsuited for it because John couldn't play on a team. . . . John just was John and that's all there was to that."

But, at the same time, Meany acknowledged Lewis' major contribution to labor in organizing mass-production industries through creation of the CIO. After the CIO's great gains, he acknowledged, the leaders of AFL unions woke up and organized hundreds of thousands of factory hands they had previously scorned.

Taft-Hartley, meanwhile, had exerted another powerful influence, and, once again, one that greatly affected Meany's career.

> Before Taft-Hartley was put on the statute books over Truman's veto, I didn't push for what you might call a political machine. Like everybody else, I was content to have the national AFL stay more or less neutral and let AFL Democrats do what they wanted to do locally, and Republicans, the same. [Nationally] we confined our activities more or less to dispatching letters to members of Congress with good labor records—a very nice letter signed by Green and myself. They could use the letter and put it in a pamphlet or do anything else. We didn't really [engage in] political activity; it was all sort of cosmetic.
>
> Even during the Roosevelt days, when John Lewis and George Berry formed Labor's Non-Partisan League they took no action at all at the precinct level or at the local level. [Later] the CIO had a much more active political unit [the Political Action Committee, or PAC].
>
> It wasn't until Taft-Hartley in 1947 that the AFL really went into the business of working at elections. We set up Labor's League for Political Education [or LLPE].

In the late 1940s, the strongest advocate of strenuous political activities on the AFL's Council was Meany. In Council sessions and in speeches at union conventions he kept urging that the Federation defend itself against employer-promoted laws by creating a full-time political machine. Because of his experience in practical politics, New York style, and perhaps his father's work as a precinct captain, Meany fought Council members, among them the presidents of the big Carpenters and Teamsters unions, who believed that endorsement letters were enough.

> There was a lot of pressure to set up a real political machine, but there was a lot of resistance. The most prominent politicians in the AFL then were Bill Hutcheson, a Republican, and Dan Tobin, a Democrat. Neither wanted any part of any League or any direct political action. For many years, during Presidential campaigns, Tobin headed the Democratic Labor Committee and Hutcheson headed the Republican Labor Committee. They did no work, sent out a few circular letters, but they both enjoyed the honor of being committee chairmen.
>
> After Taft-Hartley, I became very strong on establishing a politi-

cal machine and in January 1948 we set up the LLPE. George Harrison of the Railway Clerks and Joe Keenan of the Electrical Workers and a few others also were very strong for that. Hutcheson and Tobin were dragging their feet on it; they didn't want any sort of action, so the Carpenters and Teamsters boycotted the League. In 1948, LLPE worked hard and helped bring about the election of Truman.

Resolutions submitted by various unions demanded that the 1947 AFL convention get active politically, to punish those in Congress who voted for the "slave-labor law" and to elect friends who would repeal it. Delegates approved the creation of Labor's Educational and Political League—later renamed Labor's League for Political Education.

Federation leaders moved quickly to set up a full-time staff for the League:

> There was a little grumbling from Tobin and Hutcheson, who liked the old way of the committees they headed, but this was [only a few months] after the override of Truman's veto of Taft-Hartley—that was the compelling thing. Everybody recognized that we had to change our method of operation, and actually have a political machine.
>
> The real argument came at our Council meeting late in January 1948 and it was about who would be the director. Burt [Burton K.] Wheeler, the former U.S. Senator—a good friend of Bill Green's and a strong liberal—showed up and was talking to different people. He didn't talk to me, but it was very obvious that Green was setting this up to bring him in.
>
> Green felt that a politician was needed to run the machine, it wasn't that Green was trying to control it, but his idea was if you're going to have a political machine, get an experienced politician. Burt Wheeler certainly was an experienced politician, a high-type guy as far as I was concerned, a very brilliant lawyer.
>
> I fought the Wheeler idea very bitterly, saying I wanted something run by labor. I proposed to the Council that I take a leave of absence as secretary-treasurer for a year and run the League. Tobin bitterly opposed that. He didn't want me to run the League and I'm quite sure that he had a suspicion I might run it successfully, which would end his prominence as the AFL's Number One Democrat.
>
> A meeting of a small group of Council members and others interested in politics recommended that we put Joe Keenan at the head of the League. Except for Green, the Council members had no

great sentiment for Wheeler. He was identified with partisan politics, and we wanted somebody who would be independent politically, strictly labor. We put Joe Keenan in as director, staffed the
League, set up a headquarters and got people out in the field. I think
we did a very creditable job in the forty-eight campaign.

Keenan, the first director of the League, had been active in Demo-
cratic politics in Chicago as secretary of the Chicago Central Labor
Body. Green was made chairman and Meany secretary-treasurer.
Asked if Green, a prominent Democrat, had taken a leading role,
Keenan said:

"Oh, no. He went along. That's the way it was with Green: he went
along. He didn't take the lead in it. The fellow that put the whole
thing together, got it going, rented the hall, put us in business was
Meany. I think Meany and George Harrison worked with David Dubinsky; they were the three who got support from various others who
helped."

Keenan also said that Tobin refused to take a post in the campaign
because "he didn't think we had a chance." Most of the labor leaders,
he said, didn't think Truman could win—a sentiment shared by nearly
every newspaper in the country. Meany was one of the few who
"stayed with us and kept us going," Keenan recalled.

"Repeal Taft-Hartley!" was organized labor's slogan for the 1948
congressional races, and labor aimed to defeat members of Congress
who had voted for the legislation. Recalling the campaign, Meany said
years later that in 1948 he did not think there was then any real chance
even of amending Taft-Hartley, although he did think there was in
1950.

Concerning the Presidential race, in August the Executive Council
discussed whether to endorse a candidate or continue the past practice
of remaining neutral. Green, according to the minutes, argued that any
attempt to endorse would mean a divided AFL and possibly serious
injury to the Federation. Meany was quoted as pointing out that the
convention action in setting up the League was aimed at working for
repeal of the Taft-Hartley Act and for defeat of those who had voted
for it and for election of those with good records.

The decision not to endorse went contrary to the wishes of those
most active in the AFL's new political arm, LLPE, according to
Keenan's recollection in 1976. He said he worked closely with the
CIO's political-action officials to get votes for Truman; the CIO offi-

cially endorsed the President. Keenan—and Meany—recalled that various other AFL officials, including Meany, worked hard for Truman through a separate labor committee.

Truman's upset victory over Thomas E. Dewey was wonderful news for labor. Also, nine senators and fifty-seven representatives who voted for the Taft-Hartley Act were defeated, while not one of those who voted to sustain the Truman veto failed of re-election. (Hartley did not seek re-election. Taft was re-elected in 1950 in spite of labor's opposition.) Nevertheless, supporters of the Act still held majorities in both houses of Congress in 1949.

A warning to members of Congress, and some advice, was given by Meany in a speech to that year's AFL convention.

> I think I can voice the sentiment of this convention when I say that we are not prepared to compromise with those who put the Taft-Hartley Bill on the statute books, that we are prepared to talk to people who are friendly to the organized labor movement on any measures that might be proposed for the improvement of collective bargaining. . . .
>
> We expect those who were successful in this election to do the job that they promised in their platform and in the public speeches that they made—simply repeal the Taft-Hartley Act and put us back where we were in June 1947.

Thereafter, Meany and others sought to get compromise amendments through Congress to soften features of the hated law.

> Sometime along in 1949 several of us got talking to Taft and he took an entirely different look at the whole thing. He was perfectly willing to try to amend certain sections which I imagine he was not really the sponsor of. These were sections that we felt were real bad. He introduced legislation with some changes.
>
> I think there was a calculated decision made by the Democrats in Congress that they would not pass the Taft amendments. They felt that was too good an issue to lose. In fact, I, myself, heard Senator Claude Pepper say this at a cocktail party. He said, "We would be better off with the issue than disposing of it." In other words, this was a purely political decision.

The Senate passed Taft's 1949 bill, as revised, by 49 to 44, but it died in a House committee. News reports in 1950 said Democratic leaders in Congress made it clear that they had no hope of getting a new labor

law that year but would await election results in November. Meanwhile, it was said, they hoped to prevent Senator Taft from getting a
vote on his proposed changes, which Democrats said were not extensive
enough.

In the meantime also, the Korean War had begun, and, after voicing
strong support for the Truman Administration's intervention while
warning against a new surge of inflation, Meany called for controls on
prices and rents, saying that with such controls "it will be possible to
stabilize wages also." Decisions on such matters, he argued, "should be
made by those who know the score: by the representatives of business,
labor and agriculture. . . . Up to the present time the government has
denied labor a role in making policy and in making decisions in the
defense program."

When that situation remained unchanged, the AFL and the CIO
put aside their own feuds and, in December 1950, formed the United
Labor Policy Committee to seek a bigger role for labor. And when the
Committee then failed to breach the businessmen's wall at the defense
agencies, it called for the resignation of all union staffers in the agencies. Meany and others charged that in the tripartite Wage Stabilization Board the public members were taking orders from the industry
men heading defense agencies, and then imposing the orders on labor
with the help of the Board's employer members.

Circumstances of the walkout from the Board and other defense
posts were described by Meany in a June 1951 speech:

> When the national defense program began to take shape in Wash-
> ington, we suddenly found ourselves included out. Quietly but effec-
> tively, big business had moved into all the key positions in the de-
> fense program and taken complete control. We began to feel the
> effects of that takeover with price-control orders which forced
> the cost of living higher, and with a wage-control order which froze
> the income of the nation's workers so tightly that no room was left
> for the correction of gross inequities and manifest injustices, and this
> was being allowed to happen at the time when the first essential was
> to mobilize full and united support behind the defense effort by as-
> suring equality of sacrifice. . . .
>
> We protested, we appealed, and we conferred, and we nego-
> tiated—and we got nowhere. So we, at last, decided that the time
> had come to fight with no holds barred, to fight as we have learned
> to fight against injustices in the early days of trade unionism, when
> the odds against us could never intimidate or discourage our march

to progress. . . . It was anticipated that the press might try to put us in the position of striking against the government in time of war and in the midst of a national emergency, but we were not striking against the government. We were fighting as free citizens must for good government, for the protection of the great majority of the American people. We were fighting to break the stranglehold of big business over the defense program and to regain our democratic right to a voice in determination of the defense policies necessary to meet this emergency.

Well, what was the public reaction? Did they react with boos? No, they did not. We found support in many unexpected quarters . . . and within a few weeks we won the first phase of that fight. We were granted the right to participate in defense policy-making at the very highest level and we are now exercising that right.

We were accorded representation in key defense agencies. Official resistance to special interest pressure on price ceilings stiffened. The Wage Stabilization Board was reorganized and reestablished on a more realistic and equitable basis.

The "strike" was ended when the United Labor Policy Committee unanimously voted on April 30, 1951, to send the union officials back to the various agencies.*

But Meany, in addition to seeking a stronger labor voice in national affairs, was still anticipating eventual AFL-CIO merger. In August, therefore, he led a move inside the AFL Council to pull out of the United Labor Policy Committee. Subsequently, Green told the other members of the committee at its final session that it had been set up on a temporary basis and now had accomplished its objective.

The reason behind the move, according to Thomas E. Harris, who, as a CIO attorney, attended some of the committee meetings, was: "I think that Meany decided that too much cooperation between the two [CIO and AFL] would tend to freeze the situation and make it easier for the CIO to keep going, and that a breakup of that type of cooperation would put more pressure on the CIO to return to the fold."

By 1952, moreover, Meany was taking on more and more of President Green's duties as Green's health rapidly failed. In that year, Meany had to take over from Green to testify before the Republican

---

* One factor in labor's victory was Meany's blunt reply, at a White House meeting, when the President outlined his solution: a labor advisory committee to make suggestions. "Now will you do this for your President?" Truman asked. While the other labor leaders nodded agreement, Meany shot back: "No, I won't agree to it." Truman was shocked. Meany explained that labor wanted more than an advisory role.

platform committee in Chicago—something Green had handled for both the Republican and Democratic conventions in the past.

> He had been failing for a couple of years, but he got real sick in Chicago. In April he had not been at all well and he was failing when we held our summer [Council] meeting in Atlantic City.
>
> He really was in awful shape at the 1952 AFL convention [in September]. He was quite ill but going through the motions. I had to handle the committees and keep the thing going, make sure everything was taken care of. He was in very poor shape; his eyesight had gone bad and he was fumbling around up there in the chair.

From that 1952 meeting, Green went to his Ohio home. Meany said that Green wrote from there asking him "to sort of watch out for everything." Green did not return to Washington headquarters before his death, even briefly.

For the first time in AFL history, the Presidential nominees of both major parties addressed the 1952 AFL convention. Previously, the conventions in Presidential election years had been held after the November balloting, but the rules had been changed and Meany thought it a good idea to invite the candidates to explain their views in September.

After hearing the nominees—and listening to Meany's praise for the Democratic platform promise of Taft-Hartley repeal—the delegates endorsed Adlai E. Stevenson rather than the Republicans' Dwight D. Eisenhower. (It was the first time that an AFL convention had endorsed a Presidential candidate, although the AFL Council had done so earlier.) This was another step in Meany's campaign to increase the Federation's political power.

Knowing that Green's health was failing rapidly, Meany then gave the AFL, and the public, a preview of policies he would stress if he became head of the Federation. The "platform" began to show up in two speeches in late 1952:

> It might be shocking and sobering to hear this statement, but let me make it: I never knew in the history of the American Federation of Labor [a time when] we had less influence on Capitol Hill than we have today.... If we're going to build on the achievements which this movement has made over the years, we have got to turn our attention to the battlefronts, to political action.
>
> I know a time when I would have been disturbed and I'm sure a good many delegates would have been disturbed over the fact that

we heard a lot of political speeches at our convention. Well, I'm not disturbed, and the more political speeches we have the better I like it because there is where the future of our movement lies. . . . I do not think we should tie ourselves to any party. . . . We can use our strength at the ballot box.

The American Federation of Labor has long been dedicated to the principle of the founding fathers of our nation that all men are created equal. The founder of our organization—the membership of which at the outset was predominantly Christian—was Samuel Gompers, a Jew. The very name of our organization was suggested by a Negro delegate present at the founding convention. Our first declaration of principles dedicated our organization to the idea of equal opportunity for all without regard for race or religion. . . .

It would be very pleasant for me to say to you here tonight that all of our affiliated organizations had strictly adhered to this principle and had put into practice what the parent organization preached. However, I cannot make such a statement to you because it would not be a true statement. . . .

For many years, some of our own member organizations had either a color bar in their constitutions or an arrangement for segregated local unions. By constant campaigns of education and persuasion by the top leadership . . . this condition has been almost entirely eliminated within our organization. I can assure you here tonight that there will be no letup in this campaign until it is completely eliminated, not only in industry but also in any trade union where racial and religious bigotry is still allowed to prevail.

Within two weeks after that Meany speech, William Green died, on November 21, 1952, at his home in Coshocton, Ohio, at the age of seventy-nine, after serving in the top AFL post for twenty-eight years.

9

AFL-CIO

My election was settled the morning of Green's funeral, before we went to the church for the services. . . . Dan Tobin wanted to put himself in as president. . . . He made a plea that he would like to be president for a year or two. . . . He got six votes and I got seven.

I told the press that the only instructions I had from the AFL Executive Council were to try to end the rift in the American labor movement. I said I was going to do that; it was my first priority.

With Green's death, American labor entered a new era that was to bring a vast expansion of its power and prestige, affecting workers' income, national politics, legislation, civil rights, the economy, foreign policy and a lot more. Some widening of the AFL's horizons had been underway, but the election of George Meany as its president on November 25, 1952, brought his skills as a Federation man into the process and accelerated it.

In accepting the post, Meany declared:

I have no other interest in life outside my family and this Federation. I have no investments. I have nothing outside of what the Federation gives me. I have no grudges. . . .

I relish this job for one thing alone. I was born in this movement. My father was a trade unionist. He was a vice president of the Plumbers Union in 1902 and he was local business agent in my union back in those days. He had a great interest in it. I learned a great deal about the trade union movement and to me this is the greatest honor that could possibly come to me in my lifetime. . . .

I say to you that I am in this job not as a building trades mechanic, not as a plumber, but as an American trade unionist. There is a job to be done. I hope to be able to do that job.*

William F. Schnitzler, president of the Bakers Union and Meany's choice for the post, was elected secretary-treasurer.

Meany's first priority, as he had promised it would be, was a merger of the AFL and CIO, and he addressed it immediately.

I told the press that the only instructions I had from the AFL Executive Council were to try to end the rift in the American labor movement. I told the Council I was going to do that . . . but I wasn't going to waste a lot of time on it. If, after a few months, I felt that there was no possible chance for a merger, I would report back and turn my attention to other things.

Green's line was "Come back to the House of Labor" and, of course, my approach after 1952 was entirely different. I took the position in fifty-two that I wasn't going to ask them to come back to the House of Labor like a group of wayward boys, that the CIO had been in existence for seventeen years at that time. It was a going concern—whether they were doing well was another thing. I dropped the come-back-home approach, which I never believed in, anyway.

I knew of the dissension in the CIO. They were going through a terrific, knock-down, drag-out fight, a tremendous internal struggle between the Reuther people and the Dave McDonald people.

At that press conference a reporter told Meany that the CIO was disintegrating; he could let it split and pick up the pieces one union at a time.† Meany's response was that it would not "be a good way to solve the problems of the American labor movement," that the CIO "represented a viable, live organization."

* In the official election, Meany had been chosen unanimously, although in an informal poll taken on the previous day by the Council members gathered for the Green funeral, Meany only had a one-vote lead over Tobin—the last time anyone ran against Meany for union office. Years later, Meany explained: "I had been pretty much in charge of running the AFL from 1947 on. Green was perfectly content to let me handle it. So, when he died I felt that I was entitled to the job."
† At the time, David J. McDonald, the president of the Steelworkers Union, was talking about pulling his union out of the CIO. The steel union was then the chief financial support of the CIO; thus its defection would have dealt the organization a serious blow.

By then Philip Murray too had died. While Murray was CIO president, Meany had had some friendly talks with him. "I was quite friendly on a personal basis with Murray," Meany recalled. "I liked him. I think Murray had a lot of respect for me, but we never really discussed any details of merger." Merger would not have been possible as long as Murray was alive, Meany thought.

> He had been part of the bitter struggle in thirty-five when we finally split. He had been one of John L. Lewis' stalwarts in that fight. I think the fact that they were all dead or retired made the merger possible, because I had no personal involvement in the split and neither did Reuther. Hell, Reuther wasn't even around. I think he was off, around that time, working in Russia.

Six days after his election, Meany indicated his feeling of urgency about merger in an interview on a national radio program. He declared that the two labor organizations had to meet and "get at this problem as trade unionists" and expressed hope "that we'll have sense enough to unify the American labor movement in the near future."

While conceding that the organizing competition resulting from creation of the CIO had been "a good thing," he found labor's split harmful with respect to national government policy. He felt it would be better to have a single organization with one policy, rather than having two federations "striving for competitive advantage."

"I don't think that it's good for the country. I don't think it's good for labor," he declared. "There's too much effort wasted in competition between unions."

Meany outlined his goals for organized labor in several speeches. In one, he said that the labor movement "must assume broader responsibilities" than its "traditional and continuing goal of obtaining a higher standard of life for the nation's workers and the American people generally."

He praised the AFL union Actors Equity for forcing desegregation of audiences in the National Theater in Washington, D.C., through its refusal to appear on the stage there. He also promised that the AFL in cooperation with civil rights organizations would carry on the fight "so that every American citizen, regardless of race, color or creed, can enjoy the full blessings of the American heritage of freedom." In a speech to the National Press Club in Washington, he promised support of the war in Korea, more gains for workers, an attempt to get the

Taft-Hartley Act revised, and assurance that the AFL would cooperate "as Americans and really not as trade unionists" to end inflation.

Reuniting the AFL and CIO, Meany said, would not be easy, although he reported there was a feeling of good faith and an absence of the bitterness of past years.

Walter Reuther also endorsed new efforts for unity in a speech to the CIO convention on December 4, at which he was elected president over the Steelworkers' candidate, Allan S. Haywood.*

Soon after the convention, Meany telephoned Reuther and proposed reopening unity talks recessed in 1950. The two new presidents agreed to meet early the next year to arrange the agenda.

When Meany and Reuther conferred in January 1953 in Reuther's Washington hotel room, Meany brought along a practical plan that he hoped would end the division. The key to success, he argued, was to halt the costly raiding of rival union ranks. Some CIO unions were trying to capture bargaining rights and members at factories where an AFL union held the contract, and some AFL unions were playing the same game at CIO plants. Meany recalled the conference with Reuther:

> The two of us met, just by ourselves. Reuther was CIO president for only about four weeks and I was AFL president for about six weeks; we were brand-new presidents. I told him that I was not going to waste a lot of time unless there was some chance of success.
>
> I put forward the proposition that we should try to end the raiding—that you could never get a merger unless you created the atmosphere for a merger. And the way to do that was to stop the raiding, to whatever extent we could stop it. Reuther agreed.
>
> I proposed exploring what the actual situation was in regard to the warfare. The warfare between the AFL and CIO was confined to a few unions; certain unions in the CIO didn't bother us, we didn't bother them. A great many of the AFL unions had no interest in raiding; they didn't have to defend themselves. But there was extensive activity within a few unions.

Meany sold his survey idea next on April 7 to the joint unity committee of the two organizations, which agreed unanimously that eliminating raiding was a necessary first step to achieving merger. A subcommittee went to work on the survey.

---

* The bitterness of that contest appeared to substantiate rumors that David McDonald was planning to take the steel union out of the CIO. McDonald reinforced the reports by a later flirtation with John L. Lewis and Teamster President Dave Beck, in what briefly looked like a move to start a new labor federation.

We set up a small technical group under George Brown, who had been my assistant at the War Labor Board, to get all the statistics on raiding from the National Labor Relations Board. [NLRB elections among employees determined which union won the bargaining rights at a plant.]

We got some very astonishing figures showing that the raiders got raided, and the net results of the raiding was zilch. Some of our large unions spent millions of dollars raiding and defending themselves against raids, with a net turnover of practically nothing. Some unions would pick up in a year five thousand members and then they would lose fifty-five hundred—things like that.

One union was involved in elections in one year involving one hundred thousand people, and we assumed that they spent a million dollars on raids and defending against raids. It gained a net of forty-two members.

We spread the survey information around among our unions. It presented rather a ridiculous picture from the point of view of real trade unionism because nobody was gaining anything in the raiding. It was a way of life: you raided and you defended yourself.

The survey put all the unions involved on the defensive as far as the merger was concerned. They couldn't very well justify maintaining the situation that had prevailed for years. They couldn't go back to their members and say they were being raided and they were raiding this and that, when their members would get the information on just how much money they were spending and what the results were.

The survey showed that during 1951 and 1952 a total of 366,470 workers were involved in 1,245 bargaining elections in which AFL and CIO unions were raiding the rival federation. The raids gained about 35,000 new members for AFL unions and about 27,000 for CIO unions. The net change of allegiance was only 8,000 members, or about 2 percent of the total workers involved. The total cost of all these raids was estimated at $11.4 million.

After the report was studied by the full unity committee, on June 2, it voted to draft a no-raiding agreement to end this costly warfare.

Because the proposed pact would not prevent raids between unions in the AFL, Meany ran into some opposition from a few leaders, including Richard J. Gray, then head of the Building Trades Department. Meany said the complaints came from only part of that department, especially from the Sheet Metal Workers and Carpenters.

Big Bill Hutcheson, then president emeritus of the Carpenters and a member of the AFL Council, and his son, Maurice A., president of the union, opposed the pact. The senior Hutcheson decided to challenge Meany's newly won authority.

> Bill Hutcheson in August 1953 made a motion in the Council to stop all merger negotiations with the CIO until all jurisdictional problems within the AFL were ironed out—and, of course, that would have been forever. When that went to a vote, he had only his own vote.

That afternoon, Maurice Hutcheson sent notice of the Carpenters Union's withdrawal from the Federation. As soon as it was read to the Council, Meany asked for a motion to accept the union's withdrawal and fill William Hutcheson's Council seat. The motion passed, and Teamster President Dave Beck was appointed to the Council.

Council members were surprised at Meany's abrupt action because threats of pulling out often had been used successfully in the past when the Council acted contrary to the big unions' wishes. The AFL had no firm hold on affiliates; they could leave or return at will and did not have to pay their per capita tax to the Federation for the period they were out.

The pull-out threat had worked on Green, but Big Bill guessed wrong on Meany, even though Meany had been president less than a year.

> Hutch had been throwing his weight around. He was sort of telling me it was going to be run his way and I just said that wasn't going to happen. It was sort of a test, and it worked out all right.
>
> I was calling his bluff. One of the Council members, Matt Woll, told me, "George, you know Bill Hutch as well as I do, and you know it is a bluff on his part. You know that you and I can go upstairs to his room and have him down here sitting at the table within another fifteen or twenty minutes."
>
> "Yes, by making some concessions to him," I said, "and I don't have any concessions to make to him on this problem. As far as I am concerned, he has withdrawn, he has resigned from the Council; there is a vacancy. We fill the vacancy and let it go at that. We will accept his withdrawal."
>
> Officials of the Carpenters Union went back to Indianapolis [the union headquarters] and practically retired Hutch right then and there. He found out that the Carpenters were not ready to leave the AFL.

In a three-day period, we got wires from Carpenters Union members all over the country saying they were not leaving the AFL and wanted special AFL charters. The Kentucky State Carpenters, which happened to be in a meeting, voted unanimously to apply for an AFL charter; they would leave the Carpenters Union.

Two days after the Council acted I received a call from Harry Bates [Bricklayers president] asking if I would talk to Maurice Hutcheson. I said I'd be glad to, and the following week I conferred with Maurice in Washington. He said the Carpenters' board didn't agree with what Bill had done, so it was arranged then and there for them to come back right away. At our convention about three weeks later, Maurice came back.

We added two seats to the Council—the other one was for the Machinists, who had been out but had come back to the AFL. We elected Maurice Hutcheson and Al [A. J.] Hayes [Machinist president].

There was no more opposition from the Carpenters on the merger idea and really no opposition anywhere in the AFL with the exception of Eddie [Edward F.] Carlough, the Sheet Metal Workers' president. Eddie was just against it; he still wanted war.

With the capitulation of the Carpenters, AFL's new chief was firmly established as the Federation's leader. He had called the bluff of Big Bill Hutcheson, who had won that nickname because of his voting power—and bluffs—as well as his size. Meany had also recently bested Teamster President Dan Tobin, in the Council voting on AFL president, and, earlier, John L. Lewis, at the 1947 Convention. Thus, it was established that Meany could act on divisive issues.

In November 1953, Meany said in a magazine interview that there was a "definite possibility" of working out a merger but not a "probability." Asked why Lewis and his Miners Union were not included in the unity talks, he replied:

> Good Lord, he's the fellow who split the AFL. He's the fellow who tried to split the CIO after he got tired of that. He's the fellow who came back to the AFL in 1947 and tried to split it again. Of course, he says every once in a while that there can be no unity without the Miners. . . .We feel that the big question is getting the CIO and AFL together.

Within the AFL family, Meany still had trouble with some affiliates that refused to sign the no-raid agreement, but enough signatures were eventually obtained, and the pact was approved by the 1953 conventions of both federations. It became effective on June 9, 1954, after sixty-five AFL unions and twenty-nine CIO unions joined. At the time, thirty-eight other AFL unions failed to sign, but some of them did later. All but three CIO affiliates signed. Meany recalled that some of his AFL holdouts had no interest in the plan:

> They were very small unions that had never had any problems with other unions. A lot of them said, "Why should we sign a no-raid pact? We never did any raiding; we are not interested." Maybe a dozen important AFL unions were holding out and some of them never did sign.
>
> Actually, they didn't cause any great disturbance inside the AFL because there was no question where the Council was going; there was no question where the voting strength of the AFL was going. It was going for merger. We had committed ourselves to merger and we were going to go forward and try to consummate the merger.

Unions were not compelled to sign the no-raid agreement. Those that did sign promised to refrain from raiding a union from the other federation if that union had joined in the agreement. Those not signing were not protected against raids and were free to conduct raids. Signers agreed to abide by decisions of an umpire, David L. Cole, as to which union got the workers.

The non-signers included such big AFL unions as the Carpenters and Teamsters, while in the CIO the Steelworkers Union was a temporary holdout.

But serious negotiations on uniting the federations could proceed.

> Once we had the no-raid pact we were on our way; we had created the atmosphere under which it was possible to merge. There was no way to merge unless you eliminated the warfare. Although the warfare didn't encompass the whole movement, it was the thing that was in the way.
>
> Somewhere around the beginning of fifty-four, however, Reuther began to sort of drag his feet. I got an indication that he would have liked to drop the whole idea of merger. I didn't see too much of him and he would delay the meetings—he couldn't meet and all that sort of thing. He was making speeches attacking the AFL as having a lot of corrupt unions, saying we had to make sure the racketeers were eliminated.
>
> He was trying to indicate that he didn't want anything to do with

corrupt unionism. Yet, some years later, when he [and the United Auto workers] left the AFL-CIO, Reuther went right across the street to meet with the head of the most corrupt union in the country—the Teamsters.

Back in the [pre-merger] days, though, he was preaching union purity. The story I got from the inside of the CIO was that he was dragging his feet, that he wanted to upset the merger. He really never wanted to merge, but the sentiment in the CIO was very strong for it. I got the impression that certain elements in the CIO were forcing Reuther's hand.

Among those greatly favoring merger were, said Meany, union presidents Emil Rieve, Textile Workers; Joseph A. Beirne, Communications Workers; and Jacob S. Potofsky, Clothing Workers. Very much opposed to merger, he added, were James B. Carey, the CIO secretary-treasurer, and Walter Reuther's brother Victor. Meany said he didn't know why they were against it "except that they had these positions and felt that was where their future was." Victor was on the CIO staff.

Meany said he never thought at the time about delaying merger negotiations and picking up CIO unions as they dropped out of that organization.

I think that was always a possibility; it wouldn't have taken much at that time if you got the Steelworkers under McDonald [to come in]. I may be all wrong on that; maybe McDonald's personal attitude towards Reuther didn't represent the thinking of the Steelworkers.

There was real dissension in the CIO and I think some of it was due to the way CIO was handled.

CIO had an office here in Washington, which Reuther visited occasionally. He was running the Auto Workers; that always was his principal job. From his point of view, being head of the CIO was important but not nearly as important as being head of the Auto Workers. There was no cohesion [at the CIO headquarters]. The idea of administering the affairs of an affiliate and at the same time running the Federation just won't work.

Considerable evidence was unearthed at the time by labor reporters, including this one, that McDonald badly wanted to take his union out of the CIO because he couldn't bear being subordinate to Reuther, whom he wholeheartedly despised. The trouble was that he discovered his rank and file much preferred the CIO to Dave.

McDonald was on the CIO's unity committee, headed by Reuther, when it met the AFL group on October 15, 1954, in a Washington hotel to discuss a merger agreement. After Reuther talked at length about "principles" the CIO wanted in a merger document, Meany characteristically ignored high-flown theories and told how he saw the practical problem. It took him only forty-six words:

> We can go after unity the long way or the short way. The short way is to merge into one trade union [center] which will protect the integrity of all affiliates. The long way is to solve all of our problems before merging. Which shall it be?

Both sides immediately and unanimously chose the short way. But Reuther's conduct in subsequent unity meetings puzzled the AFL president:

> In October 1954 we had the no-raid pact all wrapped up. It certainly set the stage for merger. We had some meetings where it was quite obvious that Reuther was not really presenting the position of the CIO—from the attitude of the others.
>
> We had a big merger committee of ten from each side. At that [October] meeting we laid down what we felt were three vital principles, all running to the integrity of the individual unions: that they couldn't be destroyed, they couldn't be taken over or absorbed by a larger and more powerful union.
>
> That is what really brought about the merger: the agreement that under no circumstances would we create a merger where the larger unions could destroy the weaker ones. We guaranteed the integrity of all of our unions. The best test is that there has been no case where a large union destroyed or ate up a smaller union. There have been mergers, but they all have been voluntary.

At the October meeting a subcommittee was given the task of drafting an agreement. On it were Reuther, Carey, McDonald, Bates, Schnitzler and Meany.

Pressure for a quick marriage of AFL and CIO was starting to build up. McDonald told his own union's convention in late September that he wanted to stay in the CIO but would insist on an early merger with AFL. Delegates unanimously approved a resolution declaring that "organic unity can be achieved now."

Meany advised the AFL convention the same month that he expected "to go ahead and see if we cannot find the solution to this question of trade union unity." Declaring that the issue should not "be talked or conferenced to death," he promised that negotiations would begin as soon as CIO officials were ready.

McDonald assured the CIO convention in December that Meany "earnestly and sincerely desires honorable organic unity" and "will lend of his great strength and of his great courage" to achieve it.

Reuther told delegates that he had sent fraternal greetings to the AFL convention and pointed out that these were the first exchanged in almost seventeen years. In a major speech on the current negotiations, however, he appeared to cast doubt on their chances of success. For example, he cautioned that "there are many problems." He said they were not insurmountable providing that the negotiators on both sides "approach that task in a spirit of good faith and good will and act in the knowledge that the labor movement is not a loose federation of private empires. . . ."

Turning mysterious, Reuther advised the delegates that he had discussed with the CIO executive committee the "essential elements for honorable, sound and principled organic unity." But, he said, much as he would "love to tell that story to the whole world," there were practical reasons for not giving them to the convention with reporters present.

His hesitation to talk frankly probably was due to the fact that earlier public references to these matters had brought AFL protests that the CIO was creating roadblocks to unity. Reuther said that was not the case. He promised that he and the other CIO negotiators would do their best to get honorable unity, saying they did not "want a big umbrella that hides things that are wrong."

For a speech supporting a pro-unity resolution, it seemed a bit cold, but delegates unanimously approved the call for further negotiations toward merger.

Years later, Meany recalled that he had sent Reuther a telegram at that CIO convention, but Carey cut out the last sentence when reading the greetings to delegates. Meany accused Carey of this subsequently and was told that they didn't like the last sentence. There was a slip-up, however: the printed proceedings did include it: "It is my earnest wish that we can have a meeting of the full unity committee as soon as possible following your convention." Carey's act was a further indication of second thoughts on merger.

Still, the combined unity committee arranged to meet in February in connection with the AFL Council sessions in Miami Beach. Just before going south, Meany had a delicate chore.

> I knew we were getting close to an agreement, so I told Bill Schnitzler, "Bill, we don't want any misunderstanding. There is a good possibility that you will lose your job. The CIO will undoubtedly want the second post—the secretary-treasurer job—and they have got to get it. We can't prevent it. But I will suggest that we have an executive vice president and you will be it as well as director of organization and a member of the Executive Council."
>
> He said he understood. After all, I couldn't go into an agreement and leave Schnitzler high and dry, but if they demanded his job they would have to get it.
>
> We hadn't put anything on paper at all as to a merger plan and I assumed one of the principal things we would be talking about would be officers. I assumed that the AFL, as the larger organization, would get the presidency and that the CIO would demand the secretary-treasurer's job. I was prepared to accept that because we didn't have the right to say we wanted the two top offices.
>
> When we got to Miami, the CIO subcommittee had a six- or seven-page typewritten document on principles of the merger and I read it. They said for the initial period of the merger the officers of the new organization would be the secretary and the president and that they would come from the AFL. It had not even been discussed. I was shocked! Farther down, the paper said that there would be a director of organization, who, for the initial period, would come from the CIO.
>
> I was told by Joe Beirne later that if he had been at the meeting where they drew up this paper he would have objected strenuously. He felt that he could have gotten them [to demand] one of the two top posts. Naturally, they would have gotten the secretary spot as the smaller of the two organizations.
>
> Beirne's feeling was that Reuther did not want to take the secretary spot and, therefore, he didn't want anybody else to have it and thus outrank him. Reuther would have to give up the Auto Workers [presidency] to take the second spot. Actually, looking back on it, I think he could have made a great contribution to the labor movement if he had given up the auto union and come in here. I think I would have been able to work with him and he would have done his job all right.

The negotiations reached a climax on February 8, 1955, in Miami Beach. Present were the subcommittee members from the AFL and

CIO along with the attorneys, Arthur J. Goldberg for the CIO and
J. Albert Woll for AFL.

> We spent the morning going over the CIO document. There were
> certain things in it that we would not accept under any circum-
> stances—running to the autonomy of the affiliated unions. There
> was a very strong centralized-control: a special executive committee
> of the Executive Council with certain powers to lay out the agenda.
> This was a structure practically superimposed on the Council.
> We wouldn't buy that and we wouldn't buy anything that de-
> parted from the old voluntary idea of the AFL—the autonomy of
> the various unions. We bought the idea that you couldn't go and
> gobble up another union; we defended the integrity of every union.
> We bought the integrity of the directly affiliated local unions; we
> gave them the same rights in the merger agreement that we gave
> national unions, which was a right the locals didn't have under the
> old AFL. There they were sort of wards of the Executive Council.
> We made it quite clear at the very outset that, if they [CIO nego-
> tiators] were going to stick to their position in these things, there
> could not be a merger, because we could not sell the idea to the old
> AFL that the unions were going to lose their autonomy to a national
> trade-union center.
> The CIO had an entirely different situation. [They had thirty-two
> unions] and I would say that twenty of those unions were dependent
> financially on the CIO to keep going. We had about one hundred
> unions and none of ours depended on the AFL to keep going. That
> didn't mean there weren't times when they had strike situations and
> the AFL would help. But there was no financial arrangement with
> any of our unions to pay their expenses, their organizers or their offi-
> cers. So the national CIO at the time could commit their unions;
> they would say, well, after all, they were orphans, dependents.
> We tried to convince the CIO people that [centralized control]
> wouldn't work, that definitely we would not buy it and wouldn't
> even attempt to sell it to the AFL. Finally, McDonald, without any
> consultation with me, said he didn't think they should stick to those
> points: he agreed with the AFL. He left Reuther and Carey holding
> the bag, as it were, on this thing, and then they agreed to the
> changes we proposed.

After the all-day session, the two lawyers spent the evening putting
into legal language what the subcommittee had agreed on. The next
morning the document was completed by the subcommittee, and approved in less than an hour that afternoon by the full unity committee.

Most were surprised at the speedy completion of the agreement after all the bickering and futile negotiations of the past two decades.

Meany sat down at the grand piano in the conference room and played some happy tunes as the former enemies rejoiced at their accomplishment. They had been waiting for the agreement text to be duplicated for the press, but spirits were so high that they called the press in to share the good news. The terms were read to the astonished reporters, who had fully expected still another postponement.

The agreement, built on the original Meany alternative of the "short way," put all participating unions into the new federation. All disputes about overlapping jurisdictions were left for later. There were to be no compulsory mergers where the AFL and CIO each had a union in the same industry. It had been agreed that such unions would be encouraged to unite but would not be compelled to do so.

The heated arguments of 1935 over industrial-versus-craft unions were settled in one brief statement: "The merged federation shall be based upon a constitutional recognition that both craft and industrial unions are appropriate, equal and necessary as methods of trade union organization."

Another section pledged that the "integrity" of each affiliate would be "maintained and preserved." This was the protection for small unions.

The task of working out details of combining staffs of the CIO and AFL and other arrangements was turned over to a four-man subcommittee of the top officers of both organizations.

After the merger agreement was reached, Meany recalled, he had more contact with CIO officials because "we were going to merge and there wasn't the reluctance to have a contact with me." From CIO people, however, he confirmed what he had suspected before: Walter Reuther "for some reason or other was not too happy about the idea of merger."

The merger subcommittee had many problems on integrating the staffs of the two organizations—and the CIO's James Carey provoked a long argument at one meeting.

> Reuther, Carey, Schnitzler and I met until one A.M. We had gotten to the point where we were talking about standing committees—who was going to be head of the community-services committee and so on. I got into a real hassle with Carey. He wanted to be chairman of the civil-rights committee and he wanted George

Weaver of the CIO to be the executive director of civil rights. He wanted both positions for the CIO on the argument that the AFL never had any interest in civil rights, which, of course, was not true.

I am quite sure that CIO was more active in civil rights than we were, but we did have a civil-rights setup. We argued over that for a couple of hours. I said, "You can have the chairmanship or you can have the director, but you can't have both." When the showdown came, he took the chairmanship and let Weaver go down. We put [the AFL's] Boris Shiskin in as executive director.

By agreement, most of the staff divisions and Council committees were set up on that sharing basis: the chairman from one organization and the staff director from the other.

At that meeting in 1955, we also argued over the name, and we never agreed. I decided the name on my own. The CIO came in with "American Congress of Labor" and other things, but everything they came in with had part of the CIO title in it. Then, the AFL guys were arguing that the American Federation of Labor went back seventy years. I finally said, "I don't think there is any use arguing about this name; it is quite obvious there is not going to be an agreement, so we take the two names and put them together: "The American Federation of Labor and Congress of Industrial Organizations." It was approved without any real argument.*

Some AFL unions remained doubtful about the advantages of amalgamation with the CIO, and Meany had to do a selling job at a special conference the Federation held on August 12 in Chicago. Officials of all AFL unions were there to discuss the proposed constitution for the new organization.

In opening the discussion, Meany explained the AFL-CIO unity committee's decision of October 15, 1954: "There are no two ways to do it: we either had to do it on the basis of perfection, which would mean that you would iron out and settle all possible conflicts between organizations operating in the same field of the CIO and the AFL . . . before you merged, or you would attempt to merge under the plan which we decided upon."

The AFL chief said it was decided that "it was important to move ahead in these difficult days and try to end this schism . . . and get

* After Meany disclosed the agreement on the new name, a reporter said that newspaper editors would complain that it was too long. Meany's immediate response was: "I suppose the editors of the *Washington Post and Times Herald* will object."

going as a united organization." This was a reference to organized labor's failure to win support in Congress for relief from Taft-Hartley Act restrictions and to its fears of the "business-oriented" Eisenhower Administration. He warned that eighteen states had already passed laws barring the union shop, as permitted by Taft-Hartley.

Rumors spread by opponents of merger also were taken up by Meany, who conceded that some AFL unions still had "misgivings." To reports that the proposed constitution was designed "to gobble up the little unions," Meany declared that the new organization would be "pledged to protect the integrity and the existence of every union, no matter how small or how large it is."

Delegates were advised to "just scratch" the rumor that the proposed department of industrial organizations to be set up within the AFL-CIO would be a "competing organization." He said it would operate like existing AFL departments, such as that of the building trades, to carry out functions assigned by the AFL-CIO.

Meany had a few recollections of the Chicago session:

> The Sheet Metal Workers took a very strong position at the meeting, in opposition to merger, but they were pretty lonesome; there wasn't any backing up on it. I am sure there were a few of the old AFL unions that were not very happy about it. Dick Gray, head of the Building Trades Department, was very much opposed to merger. He had followed his line that we shouldn't even talk to the CIO until we straightened out all the internal jurisdictional problems of the AFL. That didn't make any sense and he had no buyers; nobody was going along with him.

Concern that the craft unions might be "submerged" in the new organization was voiced by George Q. Lynch, president of the Pattern Makers. Years later, Meany commented: "That was the old craft philosophy that Lynch maintained, and you could understand this because his people were very important in industry, but numerically—compared to the production workers—they were very small. They were highly skilled and didn't want to lose their identity in a big industrial union."

After the Chicago conference, the top boards of the CIO and AFL tentatively accepted the merger plan and prepared for delegate meetings in December to take formal amalgamation action.

Meany was so sure of success that he secretly told the contractor who was building a new AFL headquarters in Washington to go ahead and prepare marble blocks spelling out "AFL-CIO" for the structure's facade. Then, even before the merger convention was concluded, he ordered the new name substituted for the original "American Federation of Labor."

The day for which millions of union members had been waiting two decades—the opening of the convention legally establishing the AFL-CIO—arrived December 5, 1955, in New York City. Those sessions were preceded by brief closing conventions of the AFL and CIO.

At the AFL meeting, Meany declared that "the things that divided us in 1935 could have been settled within the house" and that "there did not have to be any split." But mostly he looked ahead: "I am sure that there is enough wisdom, enough common sense, enough dedication and loyalty to the principles of our movement in both the CIO and AFL to make this merger work."

When the proposed constitution for the AFL-CIO was brought up for AFL approval, the president of the International Typographical Union (ITU), Woodruff Randolph, offered the only discordant note in the whole meeting. He spoke at length of his union's fears that the new Federation would have too much authority, would destroy the autonomy the ITU had been protecting for many years.

Meany's reply to Randolph was a classic example of how the Bronx plumber could sell his ideas to hundreds of convention delegates and to Executive Council members in the AFL and the new AFL-CIO. He exhibited a sense of humor by jollying the delegates; he had done a thorough research job on AFL history; and he knew exactly what the proposed constitution would mean. Thus he could explain the situation in simple, if blunt, terms: The new Federation would have less, not more authority than the old. When he finished, no one else challenged him on merger.

In closing the seventy-fourth and final convention of the AFL, Meany said in part:

> A good many of the delegates to this convention, including members of the Executive Council, heads of various large unions and small unions, have had what I might call some misgivings. They feel that something new is about to happen and they are not sure just what it is.
>
> To use the vernacular of New York City, I may be a chump, but I don't have any misgivings about it. I am convinced that this agreement was entered into in good faith. I am convinced beyond question that it is an honorable settlement of the differences between the

two organizations. I haven't the slightest doubt that there will be trying moments, that there will be some of the old rivalries that will spring up inside the new organization.

But I am quite sure that if the work of the new organization is carried forward in the spirit of these months and months of negotiations, give and take, stating positions and trying to find some means of accommodation to different viewpoints . . . we can overcome any and all difficulties we may face.

At the CIO's final session, Michael J. Quill, the Transport Workers president, opposed the merger on various grounds, but he was in a small minority when the votes were cast.

That convention was marked by nostalgia about the CIO's Great Crusade of the 1930s that unionized mass-production industries for the first time. Obviously, some delegates were afraid that those rousing days of organizing were over—although the recruiting campaigns had slowed to a crawl in the 1950s.

On December 5 the two groups met in the Seventy-first Regiment Armory in New York City for the AFL-CIO's first convention. Much later, Meany commented: "Actually, the AFL-CIO convention was an historic event and all that, but everything had been agreed to. We went through four days of formalities that brought into being the AFL-CIO."

Basic differences in speaking style—and general philosophy—between Meany and Reuther showed up in their opening speeches. As temporary chairman, Reuther painted an impressive panorama of broad programs the new organization would undertake in the future, while Meany made a briefer comment. After being unanimously elected president, Meany said in part:

> I will give myself to it [the office] as best I can. I am not given to predictions. I tell you now I will never surrender principle for expediency. I tell you now that, insofar as it is my place to influence decisions, those decisions will be made without regard to where the union formerly was and without regard to how big or how little a union is.

In adopting the new constitution that had been approved by the final AFL and CIO conclaves, delegates guaranteed the integrity of the little and big unions against forced amalgamation or absorption.

The constitution also includes the principle that Meany had asserted and used to expel the International Longshoremen's Association from the old AFL soon after he became AFL head. To do it, Meany had to stretch the AFL's constitution—if not ignore it—because of the complete autonomy then granted to each affiliate. In effect, the AFL-CIO document picked up that Meany contention: "It is a basic principle of this Federation that it must be and remain free from any and all corrupt influences and from the undermining efforts of communist, fascist or other totalitarian agencies who are opposed to the basic principles of our democracy and of free and democratic trade unionism."

Under the constitution, power to investigate affiliates on such issues is granted to the Executive Council and the President, and the Council is authorized to suspend a union for infractions by a two-thirds vote. Ouster is left up to the convention.

Civil rights provisions in the new constitution were not as strong as wanted by black union leaders, such as A. Philip Randolph, president of the Sleeping Car Porters. But there was a section listing as one of the AFL-CIO's "objects and principles" encouragement of "all workers without regard to race, creed, color, national origin or ancestry to share equally in the full benefits of union organization."

During the sessions, moreover, Meany attacked the foes of desegregation of schools and praised civil rights measures. The convention adopted a strong resolution demanding, among other things, protection of equal employment opportunities for blacks.

In one session, Reuther pushed for more organizing work. Meany recalled:

> He was always urging a big organizing drive. For a number of years, about two or three times a year, his Industrial Union Department would come up with a big "organizing drive" and it was always a big, big plan to raise finances for it. Walter would make these rip-snorting speeches and there was never much of a follow-through on it.
>
> In the IUD, I think the first drive was half a million, and nothing happened, so the next time Walter made a speech he raised a million, and finally he came up with four million. They did open an office in Atlanta, I think, and another in Dallas, but they closed them within a year or so .
>
> Walter would make quite a speech. I remember that first one in the 1955 convention. A lot of AFL fellows came to me and said, "Boy! What a speech! What a speaker!" He got a lot of admirers right there and then.

I think the speech was a purpose and an end in itself in lots of cases. The idea was to make a speech, get some newspaper coverage and that was it, that was the accomplishment. On those IUD organizing stunts, he made the speeches and passed the resolutions and that was the end of it as far as he was concerned. Somebody else had to carry the ball from there.

Our concept always was that organizing should be done by the national unions and that anything we did would supplement what they did. We could help financially, with staff help and, perhaps, coordinate a drive if more than one union was involved. But the responsibility for organizing has always been with the national union: that is basic to the very structure. The AFL-CIO is a federation of national unions that have certain jurisdictions, and the job of organizing those jurisdictions is the national unions'.

Under the CIO philosophy—because of the way CIO came into being—the steel industry was organized by the CIO with the Mine Workers financing it. The CIO organized and paid for organizing a good many of its unions and then the CIO had to keep paying to keep them going.

If you are going to have a national trade-union center take over your organizing, then the center is going to have quite a bit to say as to how you are going to run your union. There is the basic problem of autonomy.

As the four-day convention neared its end, Meany outlined a broad program of action going beyond the usual scope of trade unions in assisting their own members. He promised that the AFL-CIO was prepared to make a full contribution to the welfare of the communities in which members lived and to the nation as a whole.

The convention, he said, had made "it crystal clear that we of the American trade-union movement are determined to remain free" and therefore would take a hand in relations with other countries "in order that freedom may be preserved for all mankind." He continued:

Despite these simple objectives which will stand the test of decency and morality, we find little men with loud voices and sometimes big titles who are critical of what we are doing, who seem to see something that is inimical to the welfare of the country. I would like to say to those little men that their criticism will not turn us aside from our chosen paths and that when we say we want to cooperate with all segments of the community, including management, including the employer, including the industrialist, they are not to get the wrong impression by that.

This is not going to be any milk toast movement. We are going to seek these things in the militant manner in which our organization was founded. We are going to use every legal means at the command of American citizens to organize the unorganized, to bring the benefits of the trade union movement to the millions who lack those benefits today. No little men with loud voices in either political or industrial life are going to turn us aside.

I am sure from the spirit that I have seen manifested at this convention . . . that we can do this job.

By agreement, seventeen vice presidents were elected from the old AFL unions and ten from the old CIO to make the division on the Executive Council roughly proportional to the claimed membership of the two Federations. Meany and Schnitzler also sat on the Council.

The new AFL-CIO president had one more chore: to serve as chairman and peacemaker referee of the convention establishing the IUD. As merger time approached, some presidents of AFL unions had objected to this IUD plan, fearing that Reuther would make it function as a separate federation inside the AFL-CIO. Meany recalled:

I had felt that there was no need for an IUD, but Reuther had made that one of the prime considerations for merger. Evidently what he had in mind was to preserve the CIO as an entity within the new structure by calling it the IUD. Of course, he couldn't do that and bar other unions from joining. Quite a few AFL unions said, "All right, if we are going to have an Industrial Union Department we are interested in being part of it."

I didn't think there was any comparison between the [existing AFL departments] and a department set up for unions in the industrial field, because there were very few unions that were not in the industrial field. Even the old craft unions by that time had become quite industrial.

But Reuther wanted it and I think there was no way we could have brought about merger if we had tried to knock down the idea. The Industrial Union Department has performed a service, but I want to be very frank to say that at the time the idea was broached as part of the merger agreement I didn't see any real need for an IUD. I don't know if Walter did or not, but I am quite sure he looked upon it as a political base. However, it didn't work out that way.

Dave Beck, the Teamster president, was one of the AFL leaders who were preparing to take over control of the IUD to block Reuther's plans. Beck announced that his union was going into IUD and would pay dues on behalf of its 1.2 million members. If the Teamsters and a few other large AFL unions voted their entire memberships, they would have control.

The AFL-CIO's Executive Council argued about his maneuver. Meany said he believed personally that the Teamsters and other AFL unions wishing to join IUD should vote on the basis of their membership in the industrial field, rather than counting also those in craft units—where the union did not bargain for the whole plant.

Finally, Meany was authorized by the Council to call the IUD convention, serve as its credentials committee, and preside over sessions. Any former AFL union could join the IUD but could vote only its "industrial" membership. Thus the roll-call strength of former CIO affiliates totaled about 4.5 million members for this purpose, while the old AFL affiliates were credited with 1.2 million. Beck was allowed to vote for only 400,000 rather than his 1.2 million total. The Machinists Union—one of the toughest foes of the CIO in the 1930s—was credited with 450,000; the Carpenters, 350,000; and the Brotherhood of Electrical Workers, 275,000. Reuther's Auto Workers voted for a membership of 1,350,000 and McDonald's steel union for 1.1 million.

With the craft revolt subdued, the IUD convention breezed through quickly without any roll calls or disputes. Elected without opposition to head the department, Reuther assured his friends and foes among the delegates that the department was "another subordinate body" of the AFL-CIO and "it will not be a political power bloc."

The former CIO unions got six seats on the executive board with the former AFL units having four, in line with Meany's recommendation. Meany, the mediator, had brought about a compromise, averting a disastrous quarrel that could have wrecked the AFL-CIO before it was a week old.

The AFL-CIO's founding convention embraced 135 national or international unions claiming a total of some 14 million members.* Merger was achieved because of Meany's approach to the problem. In the opinion of Lane Kirkland: "The old water-shed issue was whether

---

* Meany, however, recalled years later that, as far as the CIO's total was concerned, "we never got a solid figure. The CIO never had an honest figure on membership. The CIO counted members on the basis of what each organization claimed it had." (The AFL and the AFL-CIO counted membership according to the per-capita dues actually paid to the Federation by the affiliates.) Former CIO staffer Albert Zack estimated years later that the CIO's actual dues-paying membership was about 3 million in 1955. The AFL had more than 9.6 million dues payers at that time.

you work out the problems first and then have merger or whether you have merger first and work out the problems later. The clear-cut thing that Meany did was opt for the latter, which was a departure from the position Bill Green had always taken. Once you go that route it becomes possible, whereas Bill's line was not [simply] come back to the House of Labor but come back to the House of Labor after you capitulate on all the jurisdictional and other issues."

Meany, after accomplishing the amalgamation, knew he had still another big problem: "I was determined that, once we merged, I was going to make it work. I was not going to do anything that would upset it; there was going to be no factionalism. It was going to be a new ball game; there were going to be no grudges or anything else."

THE FIGHT AGAINST CORRUPTION

There is no reason why we have to accept corruption. Officers in the trade-union movement are paid to serve the interests of the members and of the union. In most cases they are paid quite well and if they want to get rich they should get out of the movement.

This was a very important period in the history of the American trade-union movement. As in the case of the Longshoremen, we were not going to let them use autonomy as a cloak for things that were wrong, basically corrupt.

The American labor movement was united again after twenty years, but the aftermath of merger afforded Meany little respite. Aside from the exacting job of keeping the former adversaries together, he had to address a serious and increasing threat to labor.

The issue was union corruption—and the perceived danger that in the inhospitable atmosphere in Washington in the Eisenhower era, and as a result of an impending congressional investigation, all unions were about to be penalized for the sins of a few, punished by enactment of restrictive legislation going far beyond any remedy for dishonesty.

Meany had attacked the danger several years earlier and, in fact, had gone far beyond his mandate as AFL secretary-treasurer in doing so.

The issue arose in 1952 when Garment Workers' President David Dubinsky filed a complaint with the Federation that reputed racketeers were being issued local union charters by a few AFL international unions in New York. Meany urged the Council to expel those locals. He explained in 1976:

> Some local charters were issued—not a great many—but we managed to get rid of them. After that, the same lawyers who had been operating formed their own unions and issued charters from a "paper" national union. That's still going on. I don't know how widespread it is, but I know there has been a lot of effort to stamp it out.
>
> They made sweetheart contracts with small employers, and the workers suddenly were told, "You belong to a union and it's going to cost you a dollar a week," or something like that. It still prevails: these unions are run by lawyers who keep them technically within the law, some way. They are not in the AFL-CIO. They are not really independent unions; they are racket unions.

In July of 1952, acting on his own, Meany launched an investigation of another affiliate, the United Textile Workers of America, and its officers, President Anthony Valente and Secretary-Treasurer Lloyd Klenert. The inquiry ran up against the autonomy doctrine, but Meany did what he could.

Valente and Klenert had approached Meany, he recalled, seeking a loan of $100,000 from the AFL on the ground that they needed it after taking in a breakaway group from the CIO Textile Workers. Meany said he had heard rumors about the conduct of Valente and Klenert and asked for a written financial statement and the reason for the loan. During the Executive Council's meeting in Atlantic City in August 1952, the officers handed Meany their statement showing why their treasury was depleted. Meany told them he'd examine it and see them in the morning:

> So I looked at it, and I didn't know too much about it, but it didn't take me long to realize that this absolutely was a phony statement. There were great sums of money going for incidental expenses to organizers. One organizer had two hundred dollars' incidental expenses one month and the next month ten thousand. I could see that there was something wrong about it.
>
> Next morning these two fellows were waiting to go into the Council room to make their plea for a loan. I very undiplomatically said

to them, "Your statement is phony. You can't sell me on it. But you've got a perfect right to go in and make your pitch."

"The loan," Klenert said, "is no longer important. You've made an attack on my integrity and I am going to prove that that statement is completely right."

This was about the first week in August and they agreed that they would bring up the documentary proof of the statement. When I heard nothing for three or four weeks, I called President Valente and he said they were working on the statement. In the meantime, the accountant came in to see me and repudiated his own report: "I am not responsible for that."

Finally I got another statement out of Valente which proved beyond question that the first statement was a phony. I was not satisfied with that because I felt that something was wrong in this union; they were doing something wrong with the money. I was hearing more and more stories about using union money to purchase a couple of homes.

When we got to the Council meeting prior to our 1952 convention in New York I [had] brought the matter up, saying I felt the Council had to look into the affairs of this union. I was met with the argument that these unions have autonomy and it is none of our business, and so on.

My argument was that it was our business because they had come to me and submitted these statements. In a sense I was involved because if, at some later date, they got clipped in some way—if the law caught up with them—they would say, "Mr. Meany knew all about this; we sent him statements."

I demanded that the Council set up a committee. I was very emphatic about it, and I got the committee. It consisted of myself, Dan [W.] Tracy and Bill [William C.] Doherty. The committee demanded that the board of Textile Workers meet with us. We met in the Commodore Hotel during the convention for two or three hours with the president, secretary, all the members of their executive board and their board of trustees—about twenty-four people. I went over the statements and told these people: "You got two officers here that are crooks, who are playing around with the money," and so on. Everyone was silent and these fellows said, "No, no. That's not true."

They appointed a committee of five of their board members to investigate and in January we got a report from the committee saying that all of the transactions that I complained of, while they were unorthodox, were done in the interests of the union, to preserve the union in its fight with the CIO Textile Workers.

After that hearing in New York, I had mailed copies of the transcript by registered mail to the president, secretary and each board
member. So everybody had these verbatim minutes. That ended it
as far as the AFL was concerned. We had our record, we had developed the matter beyond just our complaint. Their board had given
it a whitewash. We had tried to the extent it was possible under the
AFL constitution to get into these affairs.

The old AFL doctrine of "autonomy" blocked any further investigation at that time. The Council would not interfere with internal affairs
of an affiliate.

Meany by then had just become AFL president and, as such, he
began another controversial campaign. Late in 1952, widespread evidence of racketeering on the New York City waterfront was being uncovered by the State Crime Commission—with great publicity, much
of it blaming the AFL International Longshoremen's Association
(ILA), headed by Joseph P. Ryan.

Asked by reporters what the Federation intended to do about the
scandal, Meany said, "I'm rooting for the District Attorney and the
New York Police Department and hope they will do something about
it so that we can do something about it ourselves."

The difficulty again was the traditional autonomy rule. But, whereas
in the earlier Textile Workers' case Meany had had the excuse that the
union's officers had involved the AFL by filing a phony financial statement with him, this time he had to challenge the autonomy rule
directly.

Less than two months after taking office, the new president took the
ILA matter to the Executive Council. It was a bold move, made by a
man who so abhorred union corruption that he was willing to risk his
career. For at that time he had not been elected by a convention; he
had been chosen only by a split Council. And some of those Council
members strongly believed in the autonomous rights of affiliates. A
break with this tradition thus might mean defeat for Meany at the
next AFL convention election.

Nevertheless, he told the Council that it "must do something" about
the ILA. Minutes of that meeting quote him as declaring, "It is not our
business to prevent crime or to bring officials to justice but it is our
business to see that the union protects its members."

Meany had found another way to sidestep autonomy. He suggested
that the ILA be told it had to clean house by a stated deadline or be

suspended. (Only the convention could expel a union.) The Council went along. Saying it had no intention of changing the traditional position of autonomy, the Council did just that by declaring that "no one should make the mistake of concluding that the AFL will sit by and allow abuse of autonomy on the part of any of its affiliates to bring injury to the entire movement."

Thereafter, Meany recalled:

I got a resolution passed to the effect that we were not going to allow autonomy to be used as a cloak for corrupt activities. On that basis we proceeded against the Longshoremen. They were in very, very bad shape; the underworld had moved in along the docks in New York and had taken control. The union was doing nothing to protect the members; they were being exploited at every pier.

I remember that union way back in the twenties and thirties when it was a good union, a strong union, and Joe Ryan was a good, strong president, but he lost control of the waterfront. It was in the hands of racketeers and they were extorting money from the dock workers. There was one gangster for each pier; these guys had no official positions in the union. The employer was very deeply into this and working with the gangsters. A fellow known as "Mr. Big" controlled Ryan and everything.

It got so that, when the union agreement expired, there was no rank-and-file participation [in the contract process] at all. They'd announce a settlement and there would be quickie strikes against the settlement.

I got a resolution through the Council demanding that they make reforms—giving them until August. But there was no basic change in the situation. I did not expect them to clean up. They were stalling, trying to buy time. I don't think Joe Ryan had the power to clean it up. I got the Council to recommend expulsion.

At the convention in September, we expelled the union. That was the first time that the AFL had ever injected itself in any way into the internal affairs of a union. It was the first time that AFL had exerted the right of discipline. The penalty was expulsion. We had no right to put any other penalty on them. We said, "You're not behaving the way you should as a trade union so you can't maintain membership in the national trade-union center."

The position of the AFL prior to that was that the unions had autonomy. If there was any violation of law, any extortion or anything that was reprehensible, from the standpoint of the unions, if it was illegal it was up to the authorities, not up to the AFL. It was accepting this autonomy idea completely, and I think that reflected the thinking of the national unions at the time. They were saying, in effect, "Yeah. We will belong to this coordinating organization known as the American Federation of Labor and we'll cooperate with it, but it will have to keep its hands out of our business; we'll run our own business."

William Green had been there for all those years and the autonomy idea was accepted. Green was older than I was and he wasn't looking for that sort of controversy. He just deplored these things and said, "It's up to the authorities."

Beginning with the Longshoremen's case, there was a definite change in the attitude of the leadership of the American trade-union movement. During all that period when we were waiting for the Longshoremen to make good on their promise to clean up and then at the convention of fifty-three in St. Louis, the question of autonomy—as far as I was concerned—was never raised by anyone, never. I can't recall any opposition on the Council. The ILA thing had gotten to the point where everyone around the old AFL was ashamed of the picture. They were not happy about what was coming out of the ILA.

After kicking the ILA out, we took the position that the membership was not responsible for this, that this was the officers. We said the membership should have a right to be represented by a decent union. So we chartered a new union, the International Brotherhood of Longshoremen. This whole action was without precedent in the history of the AFL.

We spent more than a million dollars to give these people a new union, and it didn't work. It was pretty difficult because, despite all of the corruption, there was a certain loyalty to the old union on the part of the workers, especially the old fellows. Back in the twenties and thirties that was quite a good union and it deteriorated in the late thirties and early forties.

The intimidation against the dock workers was so serious that in the first election held by the National Labor Relations Board the Board ordered another vote. The Brotherhood, despite AFL support, lost that by a narrow margin; the ILA retained bargaining rights.*

There is no question where the chief credit for the cleanup campaign of the AFL and AFL-CIO belongs. It was George Meany who forced it on reluctant fellow officials of the old Federation and who expanded it

* Later, governmental agencies eliminated much of the racketeering, and then the ILA under new leadership took its own cleanup actions. In 1959 it was allowed to return to the Federation, with Meany supervising completion of the reforms.

after he asked for, and got, more authority in the merged organization. Others assisted the drive with enthusiasm, but there were doubters who had to be convinced by Meany's determination.

John Hutchinson, the author of an exhaustive survey of trade-union corruption, called Meany "the prime mover" in the expulsion of the International Longshoremen's Association from the AFL in 1953. Until then, he pointed out, "no strong AFL affiliate had ever been disciplined for corruption." Likewise, it was Meany who pressed for the corruption clause in the AFL-CIO constitution. Hutchinson's study also says that the AFL-CIO's crackdown on union crooks was largely due to "the personal influence of Meany" and that "the record strongly suggests that he dominated the process of reform." The conclusion was that it is "questionable—in the absence of such manifest personal influence as his—the Federation could have survived such draconian self-discipline."

The AFL-CIO phase of that cleanup began in earnest with establishment of the Ethical Practices Committee, appointed by Meany as authorized by the merger convention. Machinists President A. J. Hayes headed the committee of Council members which began drafting codes of ethics to guide all affiliates.

The panel also started investigations into charges filed by Meany against the Laundry Workers, the Allied Industrial Workers and the Distillery Workers. All of this happened before the Senate set up its investigating committee headed by John L. McClellan.

As Congress began its investigation into reported corruption in unions, Meany told President Eisenhower exactly what he thought of it. Meany advised the Executive Council in June 1956 that the President remarked to him, in a private chat: "I want to know what I can do to help you people to solve this question of labor racketeering. What can the federal government do to help?"

Meany's reply, he reported, was: "Well, we are not worried about any constructive investigation of racketeering of any kind. We think it is a crime and all the authorities should be after it. But we are wary of investigations that have as their purpose the hurting of the trade union movement rather than doing anything to help."

The McClellan Committee was using its subpoena power to uncover situations that AFL-CIO could not uncover without that power, Meany pointed out to a labor meeting. He saw nothing wrong with that, adding: "We have got to have a clean labor movement in these United States, not only because we think it is proper but also because

of the paramount obligation to serve the workers. You can't serve them
with dirty unions."

He recalled to another audience that, well before the Senate committee began its work, leaders of the merger had voiced concern about
corruption in a few affiliates and had set up machinery to combat it.
But even the leaders had been appalled by what they found out.

> [We] thought we knew a few things about trade union corruption
> but we didn't know the half of it, one-tenth of it, or the one-hun-
> dredth part of it.
> We didn't know . . . that we had unions where a criminal record
> was almost a prerequisite to holding office in the national union . . .
> that we had top grade union leaders who made it a practice to se-
> cretly borrow the funds of their union . . . that there were top grade
> union leaders who used the funds for phony real estate deals in
> which the victims of the fraud were their own members.
> And we didn't know that there were trade union leaders who
> charged to the union treasury such items as speed boats, perfume,
> silk stockings, brassieres, color TVs, refrigerators and everything else
> under the sun.

AFL-CIO's own attempts to clean up such situations, Meany said,
had been hampered by claims of some affiliates that the Federation
had no right to investigate. Pointing out that the AFL-CIO's new constitution authorized inquiries into corruption, Meany exclaimed: "If
they want a president who will accept obligations under a constitution
and disregard them for the convenience of some people who deserve
absolutely no consideration, well, then, they'd better get another president."

He pointed out elsewhere that the AFL and CIO while separate organizations had sought federal legislation to combat corruption in the
field of welfare plans and that in 1956 the AFL-CIO had asked both
major political parties to include such a plan in their platforms. Neither party did.

In other statements and speeches, Meany kept up his personal war
on union corruption, climaxed by his request to the AFL-CIO's Council early in 1957 for a formal declaration of policy on the issue. The
declaration he proposed said in part:

"The AFL-CIO is determined that any remaining vestige of racketeering or corruption in unions shall be completely eradicated. . . . It is
the firm policy of the AFL-CIO to cooperate fully with all proper legis-

lative committees, law enforcement agencies and other public bodies seeking fairly and objectively to keep the labor movement or any other segment of our society free from any and all corrupt influences.

"This means that all officials of the AFL-CIO and its affiliates should freely and without reservation answer all relevant questions asked by proper law enforcement agencies, legislative committees and other public bodies seeking fairly and objectively to keep the labor movement free from corruption."

The emphasis on cooperation with "proper" committees and agencies that are fair and objective resulted from Meany's often-expressed fears that Congress would write legislation that went beyond a cleanup of corruption and would destroy legitimate rights of labor. Meany also contended that a union official taking the Fifth Amendment on a union matter should be expelled from office.

In the Council's discussion, Dave Beck, president of the Teamsters Union and already under congressional investigation, protested immediately. Beck declared that his union would not allow any infringement of its "autonomous rights" and reserved the right to set its own policy. In reply, Meany declared:

> We have an allegiance to the fellow who works for a living. If the AFL-CIO follows the proposal of your organization and equivocates on this question, we will get legislation that will hurt every one of our members and hurt every one of our unions. . . . We will be under Government control. That is how far they will go. You can't have 15 million people in an organization and say to them, "We are above the law."

Walter Reuther also argued with Beck, predicting that failure to eliminate corruption would lead to a law that "will make Taft-Hartley look like a liberal, pro-labor law by comparison."

Meany said that Beck had voted twice to support the AFL-CIO's ethical-practices program, at a Council meeting and in a convention. It all ended with approval of the Meany policy statement 22 to 1—Beck being the dissenter.

The subsequent big battle with Beck was prompted by his violation of that policy statement by invoking the Fifth Amendment in declining to answer questions before the McClellan Committee. Meany said at the time that he made up his mind to call a special Council session on this issue "about ten seconds after I was told that he had taken the Fifth Amendment." Looking back on that period, Meany elaborated:

McClellan started to bring in a number of representatives of the Teamsters [on February 26, 1957]. When he brought in Beck, he immediately took the Fifth Amendment—in fact he spent a whole morning taking the Fifth on every question posed to him about union affairs and other affairs. Beck started about ten o'clock [on March 26] and the report came over the [wire-service] ticker that he was taking the Fifth. While he was still on the stand, about eleven-thirty A.M. I sent telegrams out calling for a meeting of the AFL-CIO Executive Council three days later. I didn't even wait for him to get off the stand.

We kicked Beck off the Council at that meeting on the ground that he was in violation of the ethical-practices code. We elected John [F.] English [Teamster secretary-treasurer] in his place. The Teamsters were one of our biggest organizations and they had a seat on the Council for years and years. This was to show that we didn't have animosity against the Teamsters; it was against their president, Beck. There was no question about that.

English was quite pleased to go on the Council and to get rid of Beck. Later, when we wanted to proceed against [James R.] Hoffa, English defended Hoffa all the way, but Beck he condemned. It wasn't that he was against corruption as such, but he didn't like Beck. English remained on the Council until we kicked the Teamsters out at the 1957 convention.

Interesting details of Meany's attack on Beck—and some internal problems—were revealed in the secret, verbatim minutes of that Council session. Beck, although invited, failed to appear, but that didn't stop Meany from pointing out that the AFL-CIO constitution stated that one of the organization's objectives was "to protect the labor movement from any and all corrupt influences."

Beck publicly, Meany went on, took a position "of complete disregard for the welfare of not only the members of his own union but complete disregard for the welfare of the trade union movement as a whole, and a complete and contemptuous disregard of the actions of the Executive Council." He added: "He has stated publicly that he is not bound by any codes that we set or anything that we do—that he is bound only by the constitution of the Teamsters International Union. He is not very familiar with it because he is unable to say what portions of the constitution would cover his particular case."

After quoting from Chairman McClellan's opening statement at the hearings regarding indications of "the misuse of union funds by Mr. Beck," Meany reported that Beck had taken the Fifth Amendment and other Constitutional Amendments more than ninety times at the hearing. Meany termed the hearing record "a pretty shocking story."

Calling on the Council to act, Meany said the AFL-CIO constitution "applies to all unions. It does not make any difference how large the union is or how small it is." He sought immediate action, charging Beck with "conduct detrimental to the best interests of the trade-union movement . . . in defiance of the constitution" and in defiance of Federation decisions.* The Teamsters Union "is at the present moment substantially controlled and dominated in the conduct of its affairs by corrupt influences," he said.

Harry Bates, head of the Bricklayers Union, said that he was not condoning any of Beck's actions but asked if Meany wasn't proposing that the Council "assume the obligation to try any member of any organization" who takes the Fifth before a congressional committee. Bates also raised the possibility that some building-trades unions might follow the Teamsters out of the AFL-CIO if the Meany idea was adopted.

Correcting Bates, Meany said he was not asserting any right of the Council to remove an officer of a union but he was contending that it could bring charges against a Council member and suspend him as a Council member pending a hearing.

The Meany motion to suspend Beck was passed unanimously.

On May 20, Beck appeared at another Council hearing, during which Meany made his charges in seeking to oust Beck from the AFL-CIO office:

> This is not a case of a local secretary-treasurer dipping into the funds because of trouble. This is a case of a very, very wealthy individual spending every waking moment, if you can credit the testimony, to find some way to use his union as an instrumentality for his own personal profit, even to the extent of getting a profit on money collected from the international union to create a trust fund for the widow and child of one of our people who died.

Beck contended the Council had no right to act and said he could not discuss the matters further because of a pending court hearing. The Council, however, unanimously voted to remove him as an AFL-CIO

* "The union even paid eight dollars for the repair of Beck's false teeth when he dropped them in New York," Meany quoted from the record. "It is quite obvious that the money was used as the personal property of Dave Beck. . . . He used it to buy property and then sold the property back to the union. . . . It was the most astounding record I have ever seen in all my experience."

vice president and Council member, adding, on the basis of facts presented in the congressional hearings, that there was no question "he is completely guilty of violating the basic trade union law that union funds are a sacred trust."

Next, the Federation's Ethical Practices Committee ordered the Teamsters to appear at a hearing to answer Council charges that the union was "dominated, controlled or substantially influenced in the conduct of its affairs by corrupt influences." Union officials refused to testify, regardless of the AFL-CIO constitutional requirement.

Among other things, the committee later found that Beck and Jimmy Hoffa used union funds for personal purposes and their official positions for personal profit and advantage, frequently to the detriment of the members. Hoffa also was accused of improper activities in connection with a huge union pension fund.

The Council approved the committee report, and union officials were told to answer the charges on October 24. Meanwhile, Teamster leaders had asked for time to present the committee's report to their own union convention on September 30. At the convention, however, the report was expunged from the record immediately after being read to the delegates. Hoffa had been elected Teamster president, with Beck stepping aside. Meany thought, in recalling these events years later, that Hoffa forced Beck out:

> That was the old Hoffa muscle working. Beck had no guts at all, and there were a lot of recalcitrant Teamster local unions that didn't care for the international union. When Beck became president, he needed some heavy muscle to keep people in line and the little guy he depended on was Hoffa, beause Hoffa was a tough little guy. It was Hoffa who really bulldozed Dan Tobin into quitting [as Teamster president] so Beck would get the job. Hoffa made no bones about the fact that Beck was only there temporarily.
>
> The arrangement that everybody seemed to understand was that if Hoffa was needed to help Beck in any area, Hoffa would help Beck in that area with the understanding that the area from that point on was Hoffa's—Beck had nothing to do with it. Like when Hoffa went into Philadelphia when they had trouble there—that became Hoffa territory. It was only a question of time before Hoffa pushed Beck out.
>
> Hoffa had a gangster mentality; he was not a trade unionist in my book. It was a way of life with him; he loved power; he loved to push people around. When he got to be president of the Teamsters he

concentrated all of the power in the national office, which was contrary to the whole tradition and philosophy of the Teamsters.

The old tradition was that they had sixteen or eighteen districts throughout the country, each with a vice president, and the vice president had complete authority to run that district. The International didn't interfere with them at all. Hoffa turned that around in his few years in office. He got himself the right to interfere, to take over collective bargaining and to dictate terms of a settlement. He had a power complex.

Soon after the Teamsters' convention at which Hoffa seized control of the big union, he and other officers appeared before the AFL-CIO Council's hearing on suspension of the Teamsters. Hoffa admitted, under questioning by Meany, that the Council's resolution and directive had not been submitted to his convention. Meany contended that no attempt had been made at the convention to discuss the charges.

After the Teamster officials left the hearing, Meany reminded the Council that Hoffa's promotion had come after Council charges were leveled against him. Meany declared: "I think we have come to the point where this labor movement has got to say whether or not we meant it when we wrote that constitution and when we said that we wanted to keep this movement free from corrupt influences." Meany proposed suspension of the Teamsters, to be ended only when the union ousted Hoffa and certain other officers.

Pleas for delay came from Doherty of the Letter Carriers and Bates of the Bricklayers. Bates said the building-trades unions would face a "terrible situation" if the trucking union was suspended.

"What is this idea of giving them more time after they spit in your face for five months?" Meany demanded. He warned that "the whole country" was watching, but he expressed the belief that harmful legislation could be headed off by complying with the AFL-CIO constitution.

Suspension was ordered by a vote of 25 to 4. The opposing votes came from Doherty, English, Hutcheson and Herman Winter of the Bakery Workers.

When Hoffa left the Council meeting after the vote, he was "in shock; he was talking to himself," Meany remembered. But before the full convention voted to oust him, Hoffa got in touch once again, through Meat Cutters Secretary-Treasurer Patrick E. Gorman.

Hoffa sent Pat Gorman to see me, and Pat said Hoffa wanted to talk to me. It was to be a private meeting, so private that I could walk away from the meeting and say it never happened and Hoffa could walk away and say the same thing. I said to myself, "Yeah, I will walk away and he would walk away with a photograph of me with him, or something."

I told Pat, "You tell Hoffa to go to hell. I will meet him at the office of the AFL-CIO in New York or at the office of the AFL-CIO in Washington, D.C., and whenever I meet him there will be other people there; it won't be private." So that was the end of that. He had no desire to meet me.

The fact that the trucking union was paying about 10 percent of the per-capita tax received by the Federation did not stop Meany from plunging ahead with the expulsion. (The Teamsters' payment to the AFL-CIO during the last fiscal year had amounted to $854,129.)

Building-trades officials and others opposed the ouster because they needed the Teamsters' assistance in strike situations. Although a building tradesman himself, Meany remained adamant. The principle of clean unionism was paramount.

Without wasting time, Meany brought the showdown to the convention floor on the second day, December 6. Contrary to the usual pattern, he allowed an opponent of the measure to speak first—Einar Mohn, a Teamster vice president. Mohn, and later John English, stressed the vast power of their union in assisting other unions on strike. There was no mention of regret over any transgressions, no promise of reform.

Meany's summation pointed out that officials of the Teamsters had "made no move to investigate, to refer, to live up to their own constitution in regard to these crimes against the trade union movement." He called for release of Teamster members "from this corrupt control . . . this dictatorship."

The vote for expulsion was 10,458,598 to 2,266,497. Principle won over muscle.*

Fear of violence against truck drivers was one reason for not setting up a new AFL-CIO truck union, as was done by the AFL in the ouster

---

* Despite the ouster of the Teamsters and the frequent public condemnation of Hoffa, little criticism was heard from the union's rank and file. Their loyalty apparently also survived his going to federal prison for pension fraud and jury tampering. He served nearly five years of the thirteen-year sentences before President Nixon released him with a commutation in December 1971 that barred him from union leadership until 1980. In July 1975, Hoffa disappeared under mysterious circumstances and was assumed murdered.

of the Longshoremen's Union earlier. After some delegates urged creation of a union at the 1959 AFL-CIO convention, Meany cited a case where dissidents sought an AFL-CIO charter but dropped the idea because they feared their interstate drivers would be unable to make deliveries in Teamster cities.*

Meany mentioned another reason years later.

> It would have been impossible for us to take on the Teamsters and try to destroy their union. We had the experience with the Longshoremen in 1953. We lost an election there after a long campaign in which we spent a million dollars. The biggest obstacle we had to overcome was loyalty to the union. We would get the younger members, but we couldn't get the older members. They would say, "It's our union; it may not be all we want, but it's our union. You're not going to destroy it." We never gave any thought to trying to take the Teamsters on.

The Teamsters, of course, were not the only targets of the McClellan Committee. An investigation into the United Textile Workers took up where Meany's own inquiry had ended in 1952. By a strange coincidence, an investigator of the Senate committee, while serving a subpoena at the textile-union office for documents, noticed a copy of the transcript of Meany's hearing lying on a cabinet. When he saw what it was—although he hadn't heard of its existence—the investigator carted it off with the other papers, and it gave valuable background to the committee.

Reviewing the McClellan phase for this book, Meany recalled:

> The committee cross-examined both Valente and Klenert. They still were president and secretary-treasurer of the Textile Workers when the AFL and CIO merged in 1955. When Klenert was before the McClellan committee he testified that all these expenses were legitimate. He had expenses for a hotel in Miami, where he stayed for

---

* Meany exhibited his skill as a counter-puncher at the 1961 AFL-CIO convention when Michael Quill of the Transport Workers and a few others sought to reinstate the Teamsters Union. To head off such resolutions, Meany jotted down a few notes and asked Lane Kirkland, then his assistant, to draw up a resolution from them. Approved by the resolutions committee, this document recalled how several unions had been expelled in 1957 for refusing to obey the Federation's constitution. The Council was instructed to accept an application from any expelled union if the Council determined that it would obey the constitution. Quill, caught by surprise, admitted publicly, "I have to support this resolution. There isn't another damned thing I can do . . . I am badly boxed in." Meany's simple statement of the obvious—that the constitution must be upheld—was adopted by overwhelming vote in place of the resolutions filed by Teamster sympathizers.

four or five months and brought his maid down, too. He made all
sorts of purchases in stores and put them on the hotel bill.

There was a $7,500 item up in Canada which was given to a Ca-
nadian officer by the name of "Francois" for organizing purposes,
but Klenert said he couldn't remember his second name. Gave him
$7,500!

There was a grand piano purchased by Klenert from one of the
music shops in Washington for $3,100 cash. He drew $3,000 out of
the treasury that morning "for organizing purposes" and he said
there was no relation between the two. When they asked him where
he got the money, he said, "I had $1,000 in my pocket and I bor-
rowed $1,000 from the wife and I borrowed $1,000 from Tony."
Tony was the president and just happened to have $1,000 in his
pocket and Klenert's wife just happened to have $1,000 in the house!
Anyway, it was a real mess and we finally got rid of them.

Valente and Klenert were "got rid of " through further hearings before the AFL-CIO's Ethical Practices Committee. That panel ruled
that the two Textile officers "attempted to perpetrate a fraud on the
AFL" with their false financial report in 1952 and that they "used
union funds to purchase their homes and that but for Mr. Meany's intervention" the union would have sustained a loss from the transac-
tion. Under orders of the AFL-CIO Council, the union removed the
two men from office and elected new officers at a special convention
monitored by a representative of Meany.

In announcing completion of that cleanup, Meany told the convention that Klenert had "embezzled well over a quarter of a million dollars" of union funds. As a final blow, the committee revealed, in forcing Klenert to resign, that the union had arranged to give him $100 a
week for twenty years as a pension. Meany got that rescinded.

Meany testified on the Textile Union case before the McClellan
Committee on July 22, 1957. What he recalled in an ad-lib interview
for this book in 1976 was basically the account he gave to the committee only five years after the incidents. He added, however, that the new
information discovered by the investigators would enable the AFL-
CIO to reopen its own Textile case and act—which was done with the
ouster of the two officers.

The AFL-CIO chief pointed out to the senators that his organization
lacked subpoena powers and other authority of the committee and
thus had not been able to discover, as the committee reported, that
Valente and Klenert had used $57,000 of union funds as down pay-

ment on new homes. Meany reported that the two men denied doing that earlier when questioned by him. He added: "I don't think that we should be a law enforcement agency but I think that we have a right and a duty and an obligation to our people to try to run unions just as clean as they can be run. And run them to the benefit of members and not for the benefit of George Meany or anybody else."

A rare insight into Meany's approach to the corruption problem was recalled by one of his aides during another inquiry. This investigation, of the Bakery and Confectionery Workers—involving such items as a Cadillac and diamond rings disguised as organizing expenses—also got underway prior to Senate hearings on the case. Meany had sent the aide, Nelson H. Cruikshank, to monitor the 1956 convention of the Bakers Union, to insure that union dissidents got a proper hearing. Cruikshank spent his spare time digging into the background of the case, including a visit with the district attorney, who had damaging information.

Cruikshank's report to Meany prompted Meany to ask for "everything you found out." After he received it all, Meany "looked kind of wistful," the aide recalled years later. The revealing talk went along these lines, he said:

Meany asked, "What should I do?"

"It's very easy for me to say throw them out," Cruikshank replied, "but I don't have to balance the books for this Federation and I don't have to meet the problems. You will have to meet the problems, Mr. Meany, if you throw them out."

"Oh, that never worried me a minute," Meany replied. "The only thing I am worried about is what's the right thing to do."

Cruikshank said he almost felt embarrassed that he had raised the other question. "That is the kind of massive integrity of the guy that the public doesn't always see," he added.

Six months after that Bakers' convention, Curtis R. Sims, secretary-treasurer of the union, showed Meany "documentary evidence that looked very conclusive," according to Meany. Advised by Meany that such evidence should be presented to the union and not to the Federation, Sims filed formal charges in March 1957 in his union.

James G. Cross, the Bakers president, moved quickly with his executive board, as Meany reported to the AFL-CIO 1957 convention. Cross was cleared of charges, and Sims was put on trial, with suspension from office coming a half-hour later.

Evidence collected by Sims, Meany further reported, showed that thousands of dollars of the members' money had been spent on gifts for Cross and were listed on the books as "organizing expenses."

Arguing his own case before the convention, Cross denied any wrongdoing and contended that the Federation lacked authority to force the union to fire him as its price for continued AFL-CIO affiliation.

Meany, after summing up the charges, stated:

> I can tell you quite frankly that this union is in a bad way if [Cross] continues to run its affairs, whether he runs them from one of his two homes in Palm Beach or whether he runs them from his other mansion, or whether he runs them in conjunction with the Employers' Association or with George Stuart [an officer of the Bakers] or others of that ilk.
>
> We have a job to do and it is a disagreeable job. I don't like it but we wrote a constitution. I thought it was a good constitution and I still think it is, but I did not write it alone. I had only a part in it. We are determined to keep this organization what it is intended to be, an instrumentality to serve workers, not an instrumentality to build up the personal affluence of an individual to make him a big shot in the community or make him an expert on finance, as one of our former members of the Executive Council [Beck] turned out to be.
>
> This is a workers' organization and I don't know anything else but this business. Let's keep it this way.

Meany urged delegates to empower the Council to expel the Bakers Union if it should fail in one more attempt to obtain compliance with cleanup orders. He promised he would arrange for the ouster "in about ninety minutes" if that attempt failed.

Approval of the plan came on a vote of some 11 million to 1.6 million.

Two days later, Meany told the convention that the Council had expelled the Bakers that morning.* On his recommendation, the Council subsequently chartered the American Bakery and Confectionery Workers International Union.

---

* Meany privately attacked his own Ethical Practices Committee in the Bakers Union case because the committee had softened the report recommended by its counsel, Arthur J. Goldberg, who later went on to the Supreme Court. In recounting the incident, Goldberg said, "I had to protect the committee against him once! On the Bakers case, he knew that I recommended a more severe report than the committee adopted; the committee softened it. I remember a meeting in New York where he went after [David] Dubinsky, his closest friend. I had to intervene: 'Now look, George. They can change it; they are a committee. There are many elements that enter into the committee deliberations and the committee has done pretty well. Hell, you appointed this committee and they haven't done a bad job in booting out all these unions.' George calmed down."

LANDRUM-GRIFFIN

We got along well with Ike all the time he was in the White House. We had our problems in the early days when he had a lot of rock-ribbed conservatives around him. We had our problems with [Commerce Secretary] Sinclair Weeks, who actually was trying to be President. When Weeks and Sherman Adams [Presidential assistant] were really strong, we didn't get much attention.

This was never Eisenhower. He was basically a very fair guy; he didn't know a great deal about our problems. In fact, he didn't know a great deal about his own job when he got in office.

While dealing with dock corruption in 1953, Meany had begun another attempt to get Congress to remove some of the anti-union clauses in Taft-Hartley. Even for Albany-lobbyist Meany, his testimony before a House committee must have set an endurance record, because his sparring with congressmen on one occasion that year lasted six and a half hours.

Meany stood up for the unorganized workers as well as the smaller and weaker unions in the Senate hearing on the law. John L. Lewis had suggested there that both Taft-Hartley and the basic Wagner Act be repealed. Meany's answer: "I'm opposed to that. The strong unions wouldn't need the law. But the weaker unions certainly would. And the great mass of unorganized workers would be helpless without a law spelling out their rights to organize."

The AFL's relations with the Eisenhower White House had begun badly, partly owing quite by accident to the selection of Martin P. Durkin as Secretary of Labor. Eisenhower had given Meany assurances during the election campaign that a Republican administration would seek repeal of the harsher provisions of Taft-Hartley, and Durkin, the Plumbers Union president and a respected labor official, regarded those assurances as binding.

Meany had met with Eisenhower on numerous occasions before Ike's election in 1952, and shortly after the balloting the President-elect had invited Meany to confer with him, in the absence of the ill William Green. (It was while Meany was on a train returning to Washington from that meeting that he heard of Green's death.) What happened at that private chat in New York Meany reported at the same AFL Council meeting that elected him after Green's death. Secret minutes contain this account:

Meany was "very much impressed by the fact that there is no show-manship about the General," who was "as comfortable a man as one would ever want to talk to."* Meany told Ike that he had no regrets about the AFL's endorsement of Stevenson but that the Federation in the past had cooperated with the President if he wished cooperation. Ike felt that the AFL "is doing a very good job" in foreign affairs.

Meany "emphatically urged" that a "man who understands the problems of the workers be selected" as Labor Secretary. When Eisenhower responded that he wished to name "someone who is not in labor's hate book," Meany said that labor had no hate book and predicted that the General would choose a businessman as Commerce Secretary and would "look a little beyond the point of trying to find somebody who is not in business' hate book." Because the Labor Department was created to promote the welfare of workers, the man heading it ought to come from the ranks of the workers, Meany argued. The labor movement had men capable of filling the job and "if the

---

* Their friendly personal relationship, however, did nothing to help the labor chieftain combat many of the programs drafted by Ike's millionaire cabinet. Nevertheless, Meany was invited to Ike's stag dinners, where most of the guests were corporation officers. As Meany later recalled, "Ike liked the company of men. He was not the type that would go flitting around socializing with the ladies—at least not as far as the White House was concerned. His stag dinners were really informal. Ike didn't even make a speech but would sort of mix around and chat with this one, chat with that one.

"I also spent considerable time with Ike [in the Oval Office], just talking. I had no trouble getting to see him at any time—just a telephone call and I'd get an appointment. Toward the end of his term I got to see him quite a bit—quite friendly with him. He was very honest. I had a great personal admiration for him. He liked being President. He liked other people to do a lot of his work."

General wants to appoint a CIO man we will approve it, but we want a labor man."

Eisenhower promised to give the selection careful consideration. Meany then suggested that if the Secretaryship was closed to a labor man, the President "should give us an employer, because the fellow who knows our problems best, next to ourselves, is the fellow we work for." The job should not go to a politician or college professor, he said.

The minutes also show that Meany relayed Eisenhower's explanation that he did not favor repeal of the Taft-Hartley Act but would see that Congress amended sections that were detrimental to unions.

Other details of the visit were recalled by Meany a quarter of a century later. He said he "certainly did not press" for appointment of a labor person as Secretary of Labor:

> Number one, I didn't think there was any chance of his appointing anybody from labor, and, number two, I have never been enamored with the idea that a man out of the labor movement could succeed as Secretary of Labor. I don't say that as a hard-and-fast rule, but I never felt that there was any great advantage to labor having a labor person in as Secretary, because he would be under suspicion from the minute he started.
>
> Anyway, we discussed a few possibilities and I said, "I wish you would look at a businessman." He was surprised at that. I didn't have any suggestions. Of course, what I was really trying to get him away from was the idea of somebody from the academic world.
>
> He asked why I would say a businessman. "I'm assuming," I said, "that you are going to get a businessman who has had fairly decent relations with labor; you couldn't take a businessman who spent his life fighting labor and put him in charge of the Labor Department. I just don't think that would happen. My thought is that a businessman knows more about the problems of his workers than anyone outside of a labor official."

Ike and Meany discussed Richard J. Gray, the head of the AFL's Building Trades Department, as a possibility for Labor Secretary.

> Gray had supported Eisenhower. Ike mentioned he was "too old" and I said, "He's not much older than you" or something like that. I was not recommending Gray; I didn't bring up his name—Ike did. He said he liked Gray very much but Gray was too old. [Gray was sixty-five and Eisenhower, sixty-two.]

Gray did not have the temperament for that sort of job. If Gray ever took a job like that he wouldn't last a month. He was always in a turmoil, but he did support Eisenhower in the election. Why, I don't know.

A few days after that meeting, Meany recalled, Martin P. Durkin telephoned to tell him that he was to be appointed Secretary of Labor. It was the first word Meany had received; there had been no mention that Durkin was being considered:

It was decided Friday evening, the day after Thanksgiving. They must have picked him up on the basis of his reputation for fairness and integrity. He was a straightforward, fine, decent gentleman—but he didn't last more than six or eight months [in the Cabinet].

I never knew how [the decision] came about and neither did Marty. The fellow who sold Ike that idea was said to be Herbert Brownell, who was prominent in the campaign. Marty told me he had gotten a call from Brownell, who introduced himself and said Ike wanted Marty to be Secretary of Labor. Marty told me he asked Brownell, "Listen, do you know who I am?" Brownell said he did. "Do you know I am an Illinois Democrat, lifelong Democrat?" And Brownell said, "Oh, yes, I know that, too."

Marty didn't get along with Ike. He got into a very confused sort of a situation with Ike. Durkin was convinced that he wasn't getting cooperation, and maybe he wasn't; I don't know. I'm sure that Ike didn't handle these things personally; he had others around him. Who knows? Maybe Sinclair Weeks was throwing a monkey wrench into the thing.

This was really the surface reason for Durkin's resignation: the attempts to straighten out the Taft-Hartley [amendments]. Durkin and [Under Secretary Lloyd A.] Mashburn, a labor fellow from California, a Republican, spent a lot of time on this stuff. They consulted me, but the thing got to be a real mixed-up affair—there was no head or tail to it. Finally, Durkin quit, and this was the reason he gave for quitting: that he had some promises and commitments and they weren't keeping them.

I talked to Durkin and I really couldn't understand what the problem was. I didn't realize then that Marty had a brain tumor. A few months later he collapsed and they operated. He lived a couple of years. I always felt that the thing was working on him in that period; he was not acting or talking very sensibly. It was out of character because he was a common-sense, down-to-earth sort of fellow.

Meany thought that Eisenhower was genuinely trying to correct sections of the Taft-Hartley Act he considered too harsh. Meany recalled that he spent a long evening discussing the problem with Durkin and Mashburn, "coming away in rather a confused state of mind, myself." After Eisenhower as candidate had assured the AFL's 1952 convention that he favored revising the labor law to make it fair to both labor and management, union leaders had expected that at least some of the amendments they were seeking would be enacted.

The public and the press shared Meany's confusion over the reasons behind the Secretary's resignation, which was accepted by the President on September 10 "with regret."

Then, on September 22, Durkin delivered an emotional speech to the AFL convention explaining his version of the mystery: A decision had been reached at the White House to send a Presidential message to Congress on July 31 containing nineteen amendments to the Taft-Hartley Act. When Senator Taft died on that very day, Durkin was advised that the message would be delayed out of deference to Taft, but still would go to Congress. But Eisenhower told Durkin on September 10 that he no longer could support the nineteen changes. Durkin then insisted that Ike accept the resignation he had submitted earlier. In his account, Durkin also told the convention delegates that the amendments were based on Republican proposals introduced in Congress—twelve of them by Taft—from 1949 on.

Following Durkin's explanation, Meany accused five Cabinet members, led by Commerce Secretary Weeks, of killing the amendments because of their own business ties.

Eisenhower, who had been invited to speak at the convention, sent Vice President Richard Nixon instead. Nixon denied that the President had broken his word to Durkin, explaining that "there apparently was a misunderstanding." Ike sent a message saying he still favored some changes in the Act.

The Federation's relations with the Administration improved with the appointment of James P. Mitchell, an officer of Macy's Department Store in New York, as Durkin's successor in the Labor Department, but the Administration's record still got bad marks in the Federation's Council report to the 1954 convention. Basic national policies, it said, had been reversed and the Administration had failed to halt the downward slide of the economy. Big business, it claimed, "has taken over the driver's seat in Washington" while Administration promises to labor and farmers "have been brazenly broken." Eisenhower appointees to the National Labor Relations Board were said to have "made the anti-labor provisions" of the Taft-Hartley Act more oppressive.*

No changes in Taft-Hartley were enacted in either the 1954 or 1955 sessions of Congress and the issue went over into the election year 1956.

Nevertheless, to the surprise of his new CIO associates on the Executive Council, Meany recommended against another endorsement of the Democratic candidate, Adlai E. Stevenson, or one for the Republican, Eisenhower. At that time, the Democrat was given little chance of defeating the popular President, but Meany did not base his stand on that assessment; it was a matter of principle to him:

> Whether or not a fellow can be elected has nothing to do with it. That wouldn't bother me a bit. If I felt a fellow should be endorsed, I would work for him and vote for him if he had only my vote.
>
> Basically, for years I had my reservations about the success of labor recommendations in campaigns. I admired Stevenson; I liked him as a person. I think he was a very fine man, but there were certain reservations he had that I didn't agree with.
>
> I didn't like the position he took in 1956 on school desegregation. The big problem then was in the South. I was very much for the complete withholding of any federal funds from any district that didn't comply with the Supreme Court's decision. I had a real disagreement with Stevenson on that. He kind of fudged on the issue, but I hadn't any great dislike for him.

That Meany comment in 1976 recalls his press conference remarks in February 1956, before the Council acted on a Stevenson endorsement. Meany quoted Stevenson as saying if he were President he would not withhold federal money from southern schools that continued to segregate pupils by race. Meany accused Stevenson of saying, in effect, that he would defy the U.S. Constitution, adding that he was "in complete disagreement with Stevenson on running away from that issue." The AFL-CIO leader also did not approve of Eisenhower's failure to speak out on the question of funds for segregated schools.

Minutes of the August 1956 Council meeting reveal a heated debate

---

* But Meany recalled years later: "Labor certainly made tremendous progress in health, education, medical care and things like that. It was because Nelson Rockefeller was running the Health, Education and Welfare Department, not Mrs. [Oveta Culp] Hobby. She was the Secretary; he was Under Secretary, but she wasn't with it at all. She wasn't interested; she had a lot of other interests down in Texas and she just sat back and let Nelson run the show. So the Eisenhower Administration, in my book, was by no means a bad time for labor."

over Stevenson. Meany said it was up to the Council to decide, but he thought no endorsement should be given that year. David Dubinsky pointed out that the AFL and CIO separately had backed Stevenson in 1952, while Jacob Potofsky expressed fear that if the Federation remained neutral it might help Vice President Nixon gain the White House following Ike's second term.

The AFL-CIO president conceded that in 1952 he was "one of the leading figures in getting the endorsement of Adlai Stevenson" in the AFL convention that year. But he added that in 1956 he considered both Democratic and Republican parties and their platforms to be "a mess of hypocrisy." He also remarked, "My opinion is the Republican party stinks and the Democratic party is almost as bad," with a reference to "Dixiecrats" in the latter.

In an informal poll of the Council on whether to endorse anyone, the vote was 14 to 8 for endorsing a candidate; all those opposed were former AFL men, with eight former CIO men and six from the AFL in favor. The endorsement of Stevenson was approved, with five negative votes coming from former AFL men.

The Council's decision went as a recommendation to a meeting of the General Board, representing all affiliates, and the vote there was overwhelmingly for endorsement. Meany supported Stevenson in the 1956 campaign, in line with the decision.

When Eisenhower's second term began with no Administration move to change the Taft-Hartley Act, Meany sent the President a letter reminding him of the promises made by Candidate Eisenhower at the AFL's convention prior to the 1952 election.* Meany bluntly stated that the "wholly indefensible provisions" were still on the books and being used.

The letter failed to produce results, and the AFL-CIO drive to ease the labor law soon turned into a defensive operation against new proposals for anti-labor legislation prompted by disclosures of the corruption in the Teamsters Union.

The issue was joined in the McClellan committee hearings and in a concurrent lobbying war between business and labor to influence the resulting legislation.

The year 1959 saw the crisis that Meany and other AFL-CIO officials had been expecting since Congress began its investigation of corruption in unions: the vote on the so-called Landrum-Griffin Act—of-

---

* Ike had told the convention: "I know how the law might be used to break unions. That must be changed. America wants no law licensing union-busting, and neither do I."

ficially the Labor-Management Reporting and Disclosure Act. One part of the legislation was welcomed by the Federation—the mandatory disclosure of union finances. The AFL-CIO, which regularly revealed its own finances, had been urging Congress to compel all unions to do likewise. Other sections of the measure that were opposed by unions included those setting stricter limits on organizational picketing and boycotts, with criminal penalties provided for leaders who failed to forbid the walkouts.

Among the preliminary moves in Congress was a pension and welfare bill, which, after adoption by the Senate 80 to 0, was allowed to die in the House because employers successfully opposed a section requiring financial reports to be filed by employer-managed funds where no union was involved (as well as by funds run jointly by unions and employers, and by unions alone).

Various other bills were introduced, including an anti-labor one supported by Senator John F. Kennedy. As Meany recalled,

> My impression of Kennedy at that time was that he was feeling his way [with labor]; he wanted to be friendly. I am sure he had his mind made up in fifty-eight to run for President. He began to pay a lot more attention to his Senate work. When he got into this labor stuff I really don't think at the beginning he knew too much about it. There is no question that his heart was in the right place.
>
> At an early stage of the legislation in 1958 he introduced a bill that I thought was very bad. I went over to see him about it and we got them to change it. But it indicated to me that at that time he didn't know the subject too well—which, with his background, is easy to understand.

But Kennedy learned quickly, according to a taped discussion Meany had with Arthur J. Goldberg for the Kennedy Library files in 1965. Goldberg recalled that Kennedy had found "he could talk to labor people and get dispassionate views about problems in which they were interested." Meany agreed, adding:

> My relationship with him [was such] that any time he had any of these bills he would call me on the phone or I would go over there to see him and we got so that we could just discuss any of the things on a very straightforward basis and it was quite helpful, I think, to us and I think it helped him in his career. [It gave Kennedy] a knowledge . . . of the thinking of . . . trade unionists that he did not have prior to these contacts.
>
> [In 1959] when we got what I think was unfair legislation in the

Landrum-Griffin Bill [as] it came over from the House, I'm convinced that if it were not for Senator Kennedy's knowledge of these
matters and also his sympathetic approach toward the unions and
their problems . . . the bill would have been much worse. . . . these
[McClellan Committee] exposures had put the trade-union movement
in a very bad light in public opinion and almost anything of a
punitive nature could have passed except for the fact that we had
some friends in Congress who just felt that these situations could be
met without ruining the trade-union movement. And I would say
that Senator Kennedy was one who really stood up with us at that
time of real need, because if things had been just let go with the reactions of congressmen and senators to public opinion and what the
newspapers were printing, we could have been pretty badly hurt.

With the onset of the Landrum-Griffin fight, Meany was back at the
old grind, testifying for hours at a time on new legislative proposals involving unions. He urged the Senate Labor Committee to draft legislation with a variety of anti-corruption provisions, requiring unions to
report on their finances and also employers to report on their labor-relations expenditures (which industry successfully opposed). He also
suggested a few amendments to Taft-Hartley to remove patently unfair sections.

The Labor Committee rejected an Eisenhower Administration bill
as too restrictive of unions and sent its own proposal to the Senate
floor. But there business groups succeeded in adding anti-union sections. One, sponsored by Senator McClellan, was a so-called "bill of
rights" for union members. It would place new restrictions on union
officials by giving members a greater right to speak out in union meetings, with the officers facing the possibility of a damage suit or even a
trip to prison if they were found to have violated a member's "rights."
The law also would make it more difficult to expel, suspend or fine a
member for alleged anti-union activity.*

Senator Hubert H. Humphrey, usually a staunch ally of labor, dis-
mayed Meany and other labor leaders by being out of town when the

---

* The so-called "bill of rights" section of the draft legislation raised many problems for
union leaders. The Executive Council summed up the AFL-CIO's complaint in these
words: "Could a union discipline wildcat strikers [unauthorized strikes]? Could a union officer throw a drunk out of a union hall? Must a union admit racketeers and Communists if
they 'tender the lawful requirements of membership'? These and other questions made it
clear that, even if it were proper for Congress to regulate internal union affairs, this was no
way to do it. Perhaps the most onerous provisions imposed heavy criminal penalties on
union officials for performing their sworn duties."

McClellan amendment was put to a roll-call vote, which ended in a tie, thereby enabling Vice President Nixon to cast the deciding vote for adoption. According to former AFL-CIO lobbyist Andrew Biemiller, on the day before the key vote, Majority Leader Lyndon Johnson telephoned Meany to say, "You had better get up here in a hurry; I have to talk to you. Two of your best friends are going to be away from here tomorrow and there are going to be crucial votes. I tried to dissuade them, I tried to keep them here—I can't do it."

Meany rushed to the Hill with Biemiller, and learned that Humphrey was planning to address the Oregon Legislature, while Illinois Senator Paul H. Douglas intended to be in Canada for a meeting on the water level of the Great Lakes—a key issue in his area. It was agreed that Douglas probably had the better excuse to be absent.

As Meany and Biemiller left Johnson's office disappointed they bumped into Humphrey and, as Biemiller recalled: "George grabs him and says, 'What's this about you going to be out of town?' Humphrey replied, 'Well, George, I had this date with the Oregon Legislature. I've had the date for many, many weeks and I just don't think I can break it.' I remember exactly what George told him, 'Well, all right, Hubert, I guess we'll just have to depend on Jack Kennedy from now on.' "

Humphrey told them he had a "pair"—an absent yes vote on the amendment to match his own absent no—to which Meany reportedly responded, "Your pair ain't worth a damn." Senator Homer E. Capehart of Indiana was the "pair," and he broke the agreement and voted for the amendment, Biemiller said.

Nevertheless, master-strategist Johnson managed to salvage something from the defeat. As Biemiller recalled, "Lyndon found a way to use some obscure rule of the Senate . . . to get an amendment after the McClellan amendment had passed." That served to tone down the McClellan bill of rights considerably. In preparation for the second showdown, Johnson called in Humphrey and, in front of Biemiller, "bawled the hell out of Hubert" for missing the first vote. Humphrey was present to help put over the softening amendment.

On April 25, 1959, the Senate bill was passed by a vote of 90 to 1, over the AFL-CIO's opposition, and the fight moved to the House. Up on the Hill again the AFL-CIO president testified three times in House hearings, urging passage of a measure that would halt labor racketeering but not damage workers' right to organize. When a Labor Committee bill got to the floor it was rejected as too soft on unions to satisfy labor's opponents, whereupon Representatives Phil M. Landrum, Democrat of Georgia, and Robert P. Griffin, Republican of Michigan, offered their version, which labor called "viciously anti-labor." In a TV and radio speech, Eisenhower endorsed the version, and a massive propaganda campaign was launched by industry to force it through. After an anti-corruption bill backed by labor was defeated on the floor, Landrum-Griffin was adopted, 229 to 201.

Labor sought to get the worst features killed in the conference committee, which had to reconcile the considerable differences between Senate and House measures. But the committee was loaded against labor, with five of the seven House members committed to Landrum-Griffin. Even so, Senators Kennedy, Pat McNamara, Wayne Morse and Jennings Randolph—a majority of the Senate group—managed to eliminate some of the worst anti-union sections in the bill, which then went back for the final showdown. Both houses accepted it and it was signed by Eisenhower on September 14.

In the aftermath of the battle, a bitter Meany publicly offered this analysis:

> Congress did not approve this bill on its merits. It was stampeded into doing so. First, the press tried to whip up public hysteria for punitive action against unions. Then the NAM and the Chamber of Commerce engineered a high-pressure lobbying campaign, based on deception.
>
> Even these did not work. The clincher came at the last moment in the House of Representatives when, according to widely publicized press reports, a group of Congressmen from both parties got together and made a deal. In exchange for Southern Democratic votes to put over the restrictive Landrum-Griffin bill, the Republicans reportedly promised to help block action on any civil rights legislation this year.
>
> Thus was written one of the most dishonorable chapters in American legislative history. [Part of the bill] is aimed primarily at getting rid of the crooks and racketeers who have preyed on some labor unions. Let me emphasize as strongly as I can that the AFL-CIO is 100 percent in favor of these provisions. In fact, we believe the bill should go further and crack down on the crooked employers who bribe and corrupt union officials.
>
> But the second half of this bill contains the jokers. Into this section, the big business lobby succeeded in incorporating all the punitive measures against decent unions that they failed to squeeze into the Taft-Hartley Act.

Meany attributed blame for the defeat to a Democrat, the Speaker of the House. In a speech at a labor convention later that year, Meany alleged that the AFL-CIO had discovered that some of its friends were convinced at the outset that the public demanded a tough bill. He said they evidently had been convinced by Speaker Sam Rayburn, who had decided he would not go for a bill that did not contain further restrictions on picketing and boycotts. Fewer than 150 hard-core labor supporters were counted by the union lobbyists as the fight began, he said.

Meany credited the conference committee changes with saving the measure "from being totally oppressive," although he said it still severely restricted organizational picketing and deprived unions of traditional boycott and picketing methods to seek public support in disputes with employers. These and other anti-labor sections, he observed, had nothing to do with eliminating labor crooks—the ostensible purpose of the legislation—but were aimed at preventing clean unions from operating effectively. He called a measure "a fraud upon the American people."

The new law ended the AFL-CIO's own cleanup effort, as Meany recalled for this book:

> Landrum-Griffin practically put our Ethical Practices Committee out of business, although it's still part of our constitution. If we would proceed against a union officer we would be almost making ourselves part of the government setup because anything we'd do, any records we'd make, would be subpoenaed by the Labor Department. Under that act the Labor Department can go into the affairs of any union and they do act on all sorts of complaints.
>
> We can't very well call in unions and interrogate them on things we think are wrong when the law's there. We're in a position where we would be, in a sense, duplicating what the Landrum-Griffin people do. We're always met with the argument: "We can't jeopardize ourselves by talking to you. We're under investigation by a government agency."
>
> As it is now, if you get a fellow doing what Hoffa was doing back in the fifties, he'll say, "We got a law on that and I'm not going to appear before your committee when the Department of Justice is ready to take me on."
>
> I don't think Landrum-Griffin helped [the AFL-CIO cleanup]. Before the law came we were applying what I would call a trade-union morality to the situation.

Meany summed up in more general terms:

> We will never eliminate all corruption [in unions], any more than
> we will eliminate all crime in the community. We don't have an en-
> forcing agency; we don't have policemen; we don't have a battery of
> lawyers and investigators. All the AFL-CIO can do is to try to watch
> the national unions. In turn, we expect the national unions to watch
> their local unions.
>
> The American trade-union movement is about the same, gen-
> erally, as the American people as a whole: we have crooks, we have
> bad people here and there, we have an awful lot of good people.
> Corruption crops up in all walks of life. A lot of corrupt people over
> on Capitol Hill are putting their hands out, collecting money from
> big corporations and from foreign governments. I don't think the
> American trade-union movement is any better or worse than the
> American people as a whole.
>
> But if we are going to do the thing we are set up in business to
> do—to serve the interests of workers—we can't let unions be run for
> the benefit of some outside interest. We do not allow unions to be
> manipulated by government; we're opposed to that. We don't let the
> employer manipulate them. Why should we let some gangster,
> through a connection with some corrupt union official, run the
> union?
>
> There's always a certain amount of petty grafting around and
> things like that. Some unions are under suspicion of working with
> employers and with a very cozy arrangement. A union like that is a
> very nice union—it doesn't disturb the employer, and the employer
> is very nice to the officers. That happens, and you just have to be on
> guard against it. As far as completely eliminating it, you don't get
> too much cooperation from the law.
>
> Take the testimony of Jimmy Hoffa before the [Senate's] McClel-
> lan Committee, under oath. The union involved was in Wayne
> County, Michigan, and the county had a county attorney and a
> prosecutor. This crooked stuff—really stealing money from the
> union—never moved [them] at all. Hoffa was completely secure as
> far as that end of it was concerned. I don't know how or why, or
> what his power was, but you can get away with these things if there's
> no law enforcement. If you had better law enforcement on these
> things, it would be better for all of us. However, I think the trade
> union movement has an obligation to try to keep things just as clean
> of corruption as it possibly can.
>
> Back in 1953, right after I became president, we asserted the right

to look into the affairs of national unions—whether that was possible [under the old AFL constitution] or not, I don't know—but we did assert that right and we did go after that.

Then when we merged with the CIO we made it a constitutional matter; we put it right into the AFL-CIO constitution. So I have a perfect right to call in any union and say, "There are certain things you've got to explain." This was the basis on which we kicked out the Teamsters. We called the Teamsters in and said, "You've got to appear before our Ethical Practices Committee," and they replied. "We will not discuss our business with the Ethical Practices Committee, no matter what the constitution says."

Our argument was that the Teamsters had been part and parcel of the adoption of that constitution and it said they had to come in to be investigated if the [AFL-CIO] president recommended and the Council approved. We didn't convict them of corruption, although everybody felt they were corrupt. We just kicked them out because they refused to abide by the constitution of the AFL-CIO.

I felt we couldn't afford to keep them in because, in the public view, if we kept them in we would be condoning what they had done and what everybody felt they had done. I thought it would be detrimental to the labor movement. It would be a bad situation inside the movement and in the view of public opinion generally. If that happened, I felt we would get really stringent legislation.

I was never sorry that we kicked them out and I am not sorry today they are out, because they've become a big financial institution. I am quite sure that the underworld element is still there in certain phases of handling their pension money. As far as I am concerned, we can get along without them very well.

12

J.F.K.

Kennedy would have been a real great President, but he just didn't live long enough. He was doing quite well and building all the time. He had tremendous personal magnetism; people went overboard for him. He handled the press beautifully.

He got a great deal of credit out of a bad situation in that Cuban Bay of Pigs thing by saying right out, "This is my fault." He didn't attempt to put it over on anyone else, and I think that was a great big plus for him.

But he just didn't live long enough. A lot of the things he was planning Johnson picked up.

That was how Meany summed up the less than three years of the John F. Kennedy Administration. The AFL-CIO leader was closer to Kennedy personally than to any of the other Presidents he dealt with. One Meany associate called it a "favorite-nephew, favorite-uncle" relationship.

Many union leaders had become friendly with Kennedy during his fourteen years in Congress, Meany recalled.

He had been in the House and when he was there he was sort of a playboy; I don't think he worked too hard there. Then he went over to the Senate in 1952 and immediately got national prominence. He was very young. Then he got working on various Senate committees and that's when I met him, back in fifty-six or fifty-seven I guess. He started to pick up quite a few friends in the labor movement during those days.

When Kennedy became President we got along quite well. He knew the labor leaders perhaps better than any other President did; he knew them on a more or less personal basis. But he dealt with me as president of the AFL-CIO; there was no way anyone [in the AFL-CIO] could go around me. This is the way Kennedy worked.

As an example, in August 1962 [Secretary Arthur J.] Goldberg left the Labor Department to go to the Supreme Court and [W. Willard] Wirtz moved up, leaving the Under Secretary post open. Reuther made a play for Jack Conway [a close Reuther aide] without talking to me. We had a list of three or four names which were the official recommendations of the AFL-CIO, and Jack Conway could have been on our list. But Reuther didn't want his name on our list; he wanted Conway as a Walter Reuther appointee, not as an AFL-CIO appointee. This was something that was down deep; this wasn't just a casual thing. Kennedy was very friendly with Conway.

Kennedy called me over and asked, "What about Jack Conway?"

"I know Jack Conway very well," I said, "and he is very capable, but he's not on our list of recommendations because nobody has asked me to put him on."

Kennedy got the point right away.*

The AFL-CIO had supported Kennedy energetically in the election but had taken a neutral stand at the Democratic Convention.

From the opening day of the convention, however, Mrs. Meany had been seen wearing a straw hat with a large "Kennedy" on it. As Meany recalled,

> You see, I wasn't supporting anybody; I wasn't a delegate. There were a lot of AFL-CIO delegates there for Johnson and Hubert [Humphrey] and God knows who else. I took no part in it all, although deep down inside I was very much for Kennedy.
>
> Someone gave her one of those hats and I said, "You know, we are neutral." She said, "You're neutral, I'm not neutral," and she wore the hat through the whole convention.

Meany "was not too happy" about Kennedy's choice of Lyndon Johnson as his Vice Presidential running mate.

* The appointment went to one on the AFL-CIO's list: John F. Henning, then director of the California Department of Industrial Relations. Meany approved the promotion of Wirtz and successfully protested against Kennedy's plan to put Franklin Delano Roosevelt, Jr., into the Under Secretary position. In fact, Meany said, Kennedy made a practice of clearing labor appointments with him, starting with the selection of Goldberg as Labor Secretary.

I had a lot of suspicions. I knew Johnson, but he was a tough politician. I had worked with him to a certain extent, but I didn't trust
him; I just didn't trust Johnson.

At the 1960 convention, Johnson put up a bitter fight to get the
Presidential nomination. He and speaker Sam Rayburn had an idea
that they could stop Kennedy and they tried very hard to get me
away from a neutral position. They wanted me to come out for
Johnson. They wanted me to call a meeting of all the labor delegates
in Los Angeles and tell them they had to go for Johnson on the basis
of his record as Senate leader. Of course, I wouldn't, and we had a
rather disagreeable half-hour.

Kennedy did not give Meany any advance word on the Vice Presidential selection. Asked about a published statement by Jack Conway
that Reuther, Meany and the AFL-CIO Council had argued over the
Johnson nomination in Los Angeles, Meany said:

There was no Executive Council meeting there at any time. The
Council wasn't there. Reuther was operating as a political power; he
had two hundred and fifty to two seventy-five delegates and alternates in the convention. I was there to present our platform requests;
outside of that I was just a tourist. The story that I discussed Johnson with Reuther is absolute nonsense. Reuther was over at some
other hotel; I think I saw him at the convention hall, but he didn't
want any part of me. While I was president of the AFL-CIO, I had
no troops. He kept advertising that he had a couple of hundred delegates and alternates.

Kennedy's nomination was affirmed on a Wednesday night about
eleven-thirty and I was at the convention hall. I was invited to go
meet Kennedy, but I didn't go. He was with his family. I went to
bed. I was back at the Ambassador, and it was the next morning—
maybe around eleven o'clock—that I heard the Johnson story, and I
was disappointed. What did I do? Nothing, absolutely nothing. . . .

The story I got was that Kennedy told Bobby Kennedy to go and
talk to Johnson, and Bobby blew his top; Bobby didn't want any
part of Johnson. Johnson told the story when we were flying out to
Kansas to see Harry Truman in 1965. Johnson signed the Medicare
Bill at the Truman Library in Independence because Medicare had
been proposed first [in 1945] during Truman's Administration. As a
gesture, he took *Air Force One* out there with a lot of people and I was
invited along with some members of Congress.

On the way out, Johnson told us what happened when Kennedy
won on the first ballot late on a Wednesday night. Of course, John-

son was very disappointed and so was Rayburn. They went back to
the hotel, where Rayburn said, "Now if that so-and-so offers you the
Vice Presidency, you tell him to go to hell; don't you have any part
of that. If they come near you, tell them to go to hell." Rayburn was
still boiling over; this was about three A.M.

Somewhere about nine A.M., according to the story, Jack Kennedy
sent Bobby to see Johnson and tell Johnson he wanted to talk to
him, that he was interested in Johnson for Vice President. Johnson
didn't say yes right away; he said to let him think it over. Then he
got a call from Rayburn about eleven o'clock that Thursday morning, and Rayburn said, "I understand he wants you on the ticket
and I think you should go on."

Johnson said, "What the hell! Sam, what were you telling me at
three o'clock this morning? Now you're telling me something different." And Rayburn replied, "Lyndon, I am a much wiser man at
eleven o'clock than I am at three o'clock in the morning." Rayburn,
after a few hours' sleep, got thinking of the practical side of it.

That morning I was at the Ambassador Hotel swimming pool,
having heard the news that Kennedy had picked Johnson. Averell
Harriman came along in a bathing suit an hour later and I was a
little peeved about the Johnson end of it, while I was quite pleased
about Kennedy. Harriman asked, "What do you think of our
ticket?" I remember saying, "Well, it's your ticket, not mine."

But Dave Dubinsky called from New York and took an entirely
different viewpoint than I did. He said, "It's a political master
stroke. This is going to mean that he can win." He was looking at
those [twenty-four electoral] votes from Texas. The final count was
so close that Kennedy couldn't have won without Texas.

As an officer of the Federation, Meany felt he could not take a stand
until the organization officially acted on an endorsement. The Republican Convention nominated Richard Nixon, after the General Board
of AFL-CIO voted to back Kennedy, and Meany threw himself wholeheartedly into the campaign. He organized and directed a special registration drive to sign up new voters and made speeches for the Ken-
nedy-Johnson slate. The registration drive, begun on a crash basis in
August, was widely credited with securing Kennedy's victory. The Executive Council stated that "there is general agreement that President
Kennedy could not have won in the important industrial states, which
provided the bulk of his electoral vote, without the tremendous out-
pouring of new voters resulting from the AFL-CIO registration program."

Meany recalled labor's unprecedented enthusiasm in a recorded conversation with Goldberg for the Kennedy Library in 1965:

> It was rather odd that without anyone passing a resolution, without anyone outwardly promoting his candidacy, [trade union leaders] just seemed to have arrived at a point in 1960 when everybody was more or less for him. . . . He had real tremendous support in the labor movement. It was more than just the routine support that would be given for a candidate whom we endorse. . . . In a great many cases in the past, these endorsements would be sort of perfunctory endorsements. . . . They wouldn't do too much about it and not get enthusiastic about it. But with Senator Kennedy, when he was running, not only did we endorse, but our people were enthusiastically supporting him. . . .
>
> I attribute this to the unique personality of this man. I mean, this man had a way about him. It was simple, direct. He was very easy to talk to; he had an almost non-political approach. He just didn't agree with you because he wanted to be agreeable. He could disagree with much dignity and charm and grace and he could agree with you in the same manner. . . .
>
> I attribute it also to the fact that he was a great man for doing little things that were important. In other words, if you went to see Senator Kennedy about a problem in the midst of a very busy day and he said, "Well, I'll check with you Friday morning," he would check with you Friday morning. If there was a memorandum that was coming, you'd get that memorandum.
>
> He was a great one for keeping in touch with details and he also had a great facility [for] what I would say in political language would be touching base, as they say . . . keeping in touch with people even though he didn't have any particular business at the moment . . . letting them know that he was interested in what was going on. I think this is the reason that so many of our people became, really, emotionally on his side. . . . Even after he became President there was still this same quality about him of taking care of the personal relationships himself.

Meany summed it up in an interview:

> He really was a very attractive human being; he was smart and had a nice way about him. He wasn't in any way abrasive and I was really very, very fond of him.

The affinities of the Kennedy Administration and labor for each other produced a promising experiment, which depended on that unique chemistry. Shortly, after his inauguration, Kennedy appointed the President's Advisory Committee on Labor-Management Policy, composed of seven representatives of the public and seven each of labor and industry. In opening the first session, the President said in part:

"The purpose of this Committee is to give direction to the general movement of wages and prices so that the general welfare of this country can be served. We are breaking new ground. Other Presidents have, of course, attempted at different stages to intervene in the wage-price matter with general exhortations from the White House. These exhortations have not had a very great effect but with your help I intend to get a look at this situation before there is a crisis."

As Meany recalled, the idea of such a committee originated with Arthur Goldberg, the Labor Secretary, although Meany himself had suggested something of the kind to Eisenhower. During the prolonged steel strike in late 1959, Meany had proposed that a national conference of union and industrial leaders be called to "consider and develop guidelines for just and harmonious labor-management relations." Advance conditions laid down by the National Association of Manufacturers, however, had blocked White House efforts to set up the meeting.

Monthly meetings of the Kennedy committee were chaired, in alternate years, by the Secretaries of Labor and Commerce. Top officials of companies such as Ford Motor, Inland Steel, United States Lines, Burlington Industries, Reynolds Metal, International Business Machines, and McGraw-Hill Publishing also served. Labor was represented by Meany, Walter Reuther, David Dubinsky, George Harrison, Joseph Keenan and David McDonald from the AFL-CIO along with the United Mine Workers' Thomas Kennedy.

The group's first report to the White House contained eleven recommendations for a program to cushion unemployment caused by automation. Recommendations included the need for a faster rate of economic growth, improved educational and retraining programs, and adequate unemployment compensation under federal minimum standards. A consensus had been reached on all eleven points, although labor members issued a supplemental report declaring that the proposals should have stressed as well the urgency of shortening the work week if other measures failed.

Another report, on "Free and Responsible Collective Bargaining and Industrial Peace," declared unanimous agreement that "free collective bargaining should constitute the primary procedure by which the essential terms and conditions of employment shall be determined." The group opposed "any governmental imposition in peacetime of substantive terms and conditions on the parties," rejecting any law requiring that disputes be resolved through compulsory arbitration. Voluntary agreement to submit issues to binding arbitration, however, was accepted.*

These and other reports indicated that committeemen had lively debates, which Meany thoroughly enjoyed. For him, they were a continuation of the exchange of ideas among top leaders of labor, industry and the public that he had participated in at the War Labor Board during world War II. But promising though the committee's work was in seeking consensus rather than confrontation, one basic problem remained. As Meany explained:

> The labor-mangement advisory committees have served some purpose any time the President was willing to let them serve some purpose. But it's the old story: You've got an advisory committee to the President of the United States—does he really want advice or does he want you to advise him only at the time he wants advice and does he want you to give him the advice that he wants at the time he wants advice? This is always a big problem.
>
> We had no problems with Kennedy; we had some problems with Johnson. He really hurt the committee; after he became President he just changed management people he felt were Republican, I guess, and he appointed new people. It hurt the committee badly and it really didn't amount to anything after that. But before that I thought it was a very good committee.

The trust that was briefly established, however, did not altogether eliminate conflict between organized labor and the Kennedy Administration. Early in 1962 the Administration presented a couple of ideas of its own—wage "guidelines" and an expressed intention to "define the national interest" in contract talks between major industries and unions. The fuss started when the President's Council of Economic Advisers issued a general guide suggesting that union wage settlements not exceed the average rise in productivity nationwide. This created a

---

* A contention by some members that collective bargaining is impaired at times by "a concentration of power in certain unions" was not incorporated. The AFL-CIO members declared the argument "an example of attributing to others characteristics which are in fact one's own . . . mere name-calling unbuttressed by facts or even any specifications of the nature of the supposed evil."

guideline of around 2.5 to 3 percent a year, although it was conceded there would be variations among industries.

Labor Secretary Goldberg added to labor's alarm the next month by declaring to business executives, "I think government has the obligation to define the national interest and assert [a national policy when that interest] reaches important proportions in any area of our economy." He added that "this is what your government is going to do."

The AFL-CIO president struck back at a press conference:

> If I understand what the Secretary was saying, then I disagree with him. The role of the government is to offer its mediation and conciliation, to do what it can to help the parties reach an agreement, but "to assert a national policy" within which negotiations must proceed is to interfere with free collective bargaining.
>
> Such a course would represent an infringement on free collective bargaining in a free society. This would be a step in the direction of saying that the federal government should tell either or both sides what to do and I don't agree with that.

Meany spelled out his reasoning on the public-interest issue in a later speech:

> Where in the law is the Executive branch of government charged with asserting the public interest in a private dispute between labor and management? And if the government is to assert the public interest, is it the Executive branch or is it the Legislative branch?
>
> It is inevitable that if the government goes in that far to set wages and prices in negotiations between labor and management they have got to go a little further. They have got to decide . . . what is the wage of management? What does the investor get, the person who puts the risk capital in, and what does it all add up to? Well, it adds up to government control, and organized labor in this country is not prepared to go down that road, even a little step.

In response, Secretary Goldberg explained that the government would not "dictate the terms" of agreements and that he opposed wage-price controls and compulsory arbitration. The argument subsided quickly, but Goldberg intervened personally in various labor disputes as mediator—not dictating the terms.

The role of government-as-mediator was put to a test in April 1962 when steel companies raised their prices a few days after signing a new wage contract with the Steelworkers Union, one that Goldberg had declared noninflationary. An angry President called the six-dollar-a-ton price boost "a wholly unjustifiable and irresponsible defiance of the public interest" and moved to investigate to see if laws had been violated. As Meany recalled the dispute:

> The Kennedy Administration was deep into the steel negotiations, which meant Goldberg was in there, and they put pressure on both sides. It got the union to reduce its demands considerably, on the basis of inflation: "We just can't go too high [on wages] because [then] we would get a price rise in steel. . . ." When they finally settled, it was on a wage-increase figure somewhat less than the Steelworkers thought they were going to get.
>
> I am completely convinced that Kennedy, Goldberg and others had been led to believe in some manner by Roger [M.] Blough [the U.S. Steel board chairman] and his gang that there would be no price increase.
>
> Within a very short time after they had concluded negotiations and signed the contract, U.S. Steel announced a rise in the price of steel, and Kennedy blew his top. Goldberg wanted to resign; he felt that he had been put in a very embarrassing position. I am convinced that Kennedy and Goldberg felt they had a commitment, and [Steelworkers President] McDonald felt he had a commitment.
>
> Goldberg was very upset because he had given Kennedy the impression that the steel companies had committed themselves at the bargaining table that there would be no price rise, and I'm quite sure Goldberg believed that. The steel companies said, no, we didn't say anything definite about that. I think that, in order to get a settlement, to get the union to tone down its demands, they gave the impression that there was not going to be any price increase. When they did increase prices, Kennedy yelled blue murder and so did Goldberg and everyone else.
>
> The finance committee of the [U.S. Steel] board of directors, meeting up in New York, made the decision, and sent Roger Blough down here to the White House to explain to Kennedy. They say the meeting with Blough, Kennedy and Goldberg was really something.
>
> Kennedy called me on the telephone and the language he used in describing the steel company was unprintable. He said, "What do you think of these dirty so-and-so's? My father told me these bastards were no good." He was really something. He was just letting off steam; calling me to tell me what he thought.

I talked to both Kennedy and Goldberg at the time and I know they were very, very upset and they were convinced they had been double-crossed. They had argued the public interest on both the union and company.

In fact, I think Blough and the high executives of U.S. Steel even misled their own negotiator, R. Conrad Cooper, the vice president in charge of labor relations. The decision was made on the opening day of the baseball season and Dave McDonald . . . and Cooper were at the opening game in Pittsburgh. They weren't together. When Cooper got the word from New York, he made his way to McDonald's box and said, "Dave, don't blame this on me; I knew nothing about it." In other words, he indicated he had been double-crossed.

U.S. Steel rescinded its increase about seventy-two hours after it was announced, as did other steel companies.

Meanwhile, the Federation and Administration had arrived, on the overall domestic agenda, at a clearer understanding of the national interest. The primary target was racial discrimination of all kinds.

Increased action against discrimination in unions had been adopted by the 1961 AFL-CIO convention after a lengthy debate over whether the resolution's language was tough enough. In opening the convention, Meany had made his own position clear:

> While we may not always agree as to the method . . . let me say quite frankly on the subject [of discrimination] that, as believers in democracy, we of the trade union movement welcome and understand the determination of those in our country who seek to give real meaning to the rights guaranteed by the Fourteenth Amendment. And perhaps we can even understand their impatience.
>
> The goal of the really free American is the goal of the trade union movement. And to put it quite simply as to our obligation, let me say that any union, local, international, or any other union that discriminates in any way on the grounds of race, color, creed or national origin, is flouting the basic principles of the AFL-CIO and doing harm to the trade union movement.

The committee resolution pledged that the AFL-CIO would assure all workers "the full benefits of union organization, without discrimination, segregation, separation or exclusion of any kind." It continued: "As trade unionists, we insist on fair practices in unions, in employment, in housing, in public accommodations, in schools, in citizenship and in every field of life. The AFL-CIO is in the forefront of the civil rights revolution in our land. It is a foremost force in the drive to eliminate and prevent every form of race discrimination and race injustice in the American community. A real democracy has no room for second-class citizenship."

Reporting that "solid progress has been achieved by the AFL-CIO in the past two years, under the leadership of President George Meany, in furthering its civil rights policy in the ranks of labor, in employment, in apprenticeship and training and in the community at large," the committee added:

"But serious shortcomings and deficiencies still persist in all of these areas. The still unfinished task of winning full and general acceptance of nondiscrimination is a challenge to every trade unionist and to every union in our ranks."

The convention called on every affiliate that had not created its own civil rights machinery to do so immediately. Expanded enforcement efforts at the Federation level also were ordered. Noncompliance with the resolution by a national union was to be reported to the Executive Council for appropriate action. AFL-CIO support for a fair-employment law and for federal civil rights legislation was reaffirmed.

The Federation was still pressing the Administration's parallel agenda when Kennedy was murdered.

The extraordinary identity of views that drew Meany and Kennedy together also embraced foreign policy, and especially the tests of the Cold War. In April 1960, Meany and the AFL-CIO Council had gone on record condemning the Fidel Castro regime for moving toward a totalitarian state, taking over the free labor movement of Cuba and abolishing collective bargaining. Meany recalled:

> Castro came in power the first of January 1959. He was supposed to be the great democrat and he ousted [Fulgencio] Batista, who was a dictator, but Batista was an amateur compared to Castro.
>
> Castro invited me to come down there right away. They were going to send a plane up to Miami to bring me over there. I wanted to wait and see what would happen. It was quite obvious from the very first day he got in there that he came in to dictate. He threw the labor leaders in jail and shot some of them; he set up his own labor leaders. God, he really dictated quite effectively. So, of course, I never went down there.

The Bay of Pigs invasion of April 1961 caught Meany by surprise. It was a fiasco, he recalled, but he never attempted to make a judgment as to Kennedy's responsibility.

> I read about it. I think this thing was really in the works before Kennedy was elected; they were training these people down in Guatemala and all that. But Kennedy took the rap for it.

The bond held. Opening the third convention of the AFL-CIO on December 7, 1961—the twentieth anniversary of Pearl Harbor—Meany spoke of dictatorships around the world, including Castro's: "a Communist base ninety miles from the southeast corner of our own country." There was no reference to the spring fiasco.

President Kennedy, appearing on the first day of the convention, referred to himself as "one whose work and continuity of employment is dependent in part upon the union movement." He frankly sought its help:

"Now we are face to face in the most critical time with challenges all around the world; and you in the labor movement bear a heavy responsibility. I occasionally read articles by those who say that the labor movement has fallen into dark days. I do not believe that. And I would be very distressed if it were true. One of the great qualities about the United States, which I do not think the people who are not in the labor movement realize, is what a great asset for freedom the American labor movement represents, not only here but all around the world. . . .

"I want to thank the labor movement for what it is doing abroad in strengthening free labor movements, and I urge you to redouble your efforts. The hope of freedom in these countries rests to a great extent with the labor movement."

Kennedy also thanked the Federation for its support on legislative measures and appealed to it to be ready for future efforts. After a standing ovation by delegates and loud applause indicated he would get continued support, Meany thanked him for coming:

> Mr. President, it is quite obvious from your remarks here this morning, on a wide range of subjects, that you have a tremendous understanding of the problems which deeply trouble and concern the American trade union movement. . . . I am just going to say that we are delighted that we have a Chief Executive in the White House who understands the ideals and the aspirations of our people, where the real welfare of our people is concerned, and merely say to you, "Don't worry about us. We will cooperate 1000 percent."

Meany's continued support of a steadfast Cold War foreign policy was clearly explained in a speech to the Bakers Union in September 1962.

> When you hear someone say, "Something's got to be done about this; we have to find some basis of accommodation to meet these people; we have to find a way out," that someone is preaching a doctrine that could bring suicide to America. There is no way out except to continue this Cold War, to continue to build up America's strength—economically, militarily, and every other way—until the Russians some day see the light and someday realize that they have a contribution to make. They can't make it by dominating and kicking around the rest of the world. . . .
>
> I say to these academic nitwits who think there is something to gain by cultural exchanges, that there are no opposite numbers under the Russian system. Here it is possible for doctors to gather together in an organization, for lawyers, for businessmen and for workers; there are no counterparts in the Soviet Union. When you deal with a committee from the Soviet Union . . . they are agents of a powerful state, under instructions to carry out the number one objective of that all-powerful state. . . . No method is wrong as far as they are concerned: deceit, cheating, lying. There is no moral ethical code there.

Those remarks were made two months and a day before Kennedy announced to a shocked world that the Soviet Union was secretly preparing missile bases in Cuba. U.S. high-flying U-2 spy planes had taken photographs showing the bases with waiting nuclear missiles. After the President showed the photos and announced a naval blockade of the island, to block a further buildup of missiles, a tense period followed, with nuclear war always a possibility. Meany was briefed by the President.

> He called me on the telephone, and that was within about twenty-four hours of the actual confrontation. He filled me in on the whole thing, just told me what was going to happen: if they moved, we were going to stop them. Then, of course, [Nikita] Khrushchev backed down.
>
> It was a gamble that Kennedy felt he had to take; he just couldn't allow them—they were lying to him all the time. It was only two weeks before that [Andrei] Gromyko said, "Oh, absolutely no," as he sat in the White House. At the time Gromyko was telling Kennedy

they had no missile sites, Kennedy had the photographs of the sites. It was one of those things: I am sure it was a tough decision for him to make.

Hell, they had to back down or we had to back down. And if we had backed down, Cuba today would be a fortress pointed right at us. What the hell, the distance from Cuba to our mainland in terms of rockets—for God's sake, they would have had rockets that could just shoot off and key in on every city of the Eastern Seaboard. Of course, they have atomic rockets and all that, but they don't have them there like a land-based carrier.

I felt that he was doing the right thing because the alternative was to capitulate, that's all.

Meany issued a statement supporting Kennedy at the time, in the crucial interlude before the Russians backed down: "In this hour of peril, the President has charted the only possible course for free men. Whatever it costs, the Soviet Union must be stopped and stopped now in its attempt to take over the Western Hemisphere. The President deserves, and he has, the complete, unstinting support of America's organized workers. The President means business and so do we."

Although vociferous and always unflinching, Meany's anti-communism was neither cruel nor vindictive, as he proved before the end of that year. The Soviet Union was in desperate need of American grain to make up for a bad wheat yield and was seeking to negotiate a purchase of some $250 million worth of wheat and wheat flour. Kennedy asked Meany for his opinion, and Meany said yes.

Kennedy asked me what I thought about selling wheat to Russia. This was late in 1962. I told him, "There are two angles to it. One the humanitarian angle—wheat is food, they needed food—and, second, there is a propaganda angle that would please me very much: the great communistic regime has to buy wheat from the United States." It was only three years earlier that Khrushchev was "burying" us and saying, "We'll out-produce you in guns and butter," and all that. That was the only conversation I had with Kennedy on it.

The Russians got their wheat but not Meany's friendship.

I saw Kennedy at the White House some time in late March 1963, I guess, and there had been an announcement in the paper that he was going to go to Europe and would be in Berlin on the twenty-sixth of June. I told him, "I will be in Berlin on the same day. I'm

going to speak to a building-trades convention." He asked, "Why
don't you fly over with me?" I explained, "No, I can't fly over with
you because I will be at the ILO for about two and a half weeks before that, in Geneva." But he told me, "I'll arrange so that you can
fly up to Berlin with me," and I said, "Fine. How about coming to
that convention with me? These are building-trades workers headed
by a good friend of mine, George Leber [later to become Defense
Minister of Germany]."

"Fine, I'll fit it in, I'll jump in there for fifteen minutes," Kennedy
said. So I wired Leber saying to send Kennedy an invitation, he's
going to be at your convention. Well, after about a week I got a
cable that Leber had been turned down, that he got a message that
the President could not fit it into his schedule. Of course, the President never saw his invitation. I went over to the White House and
said to Kennedy, "You told me you would go to that building-trades
convention and you say you won't go." He demanded, "Who the
hell said I won't go?" When I told him, he laughed, "I'll be there."
And he was.

Meany recalled the Berlin interlude with particular pleasure:

> That was perhaps the most eventful day in my whole life—June
> twenty-sixth. I met Kennedy the night before in Wiesbaden and
> flew up in *Air Force One* with him to Berlin. I was standing right in
> back of him when he made that speech to the crowd in what they
> call the Rathaus Square, which is the city hall square, in which he
> said, *"Ich bin ein Berliner!"* Then we had luncheon with all the Ger-
> man officials in the city hall and went out to American University,
> where he made another speech. We left there and reviewed our
> troops, got on the plane and flew over to Ireland.

Meany provided details of the Berlin visit for the Kennedy Library
oral-history collection in 1965. He said that he had delivered his own
speech to an audience of union delegates when Kennedy arrived at the
meeting hall briefly to address the gathering. The hall had been financed by the Benjamin Franklin Society of the United States, as a gift
to the people of West Berlin. In the front of the building was a quotation from Franklin:

> The gist of it was that Franklin said he hoped that he could see a
> world where a philosopher could go any place in the world and find
> freedom and therefore could say, "This is my home, this is where I
> belong, where freedom is." Before the President got there I had

taken a little slip of paper and had copied this quotation from the
wall and gave it to the President. . . . He took that little piece of
paper and he stuck it in his pocket. I don't think he looked at it
again. But when he opened his address he quoted from it. He had
some notes that he didn't use . . . he never even looked at them. He
made about a twelve-minute talk and it was the most effective talk I
think I ever heard on the question of freedom.

And he related it to workers—to workers' unions—the fact that
where workers could get together and form unions and use the
unions, of course, to improve their conditions, that this was one of
the very essentials of freedom. He paraphrased the Benjamin Franklin thing and did it very beautifully.

Speaking at the AFL-CIO convention in November of that year,
Kennedy reiterated his praise for the labor movement and again
stressed its importance to maintaining freedom:

"I am glad to come to this convention, and I think that the AFL-
CIO at this convention, looking back . . . over this century, can take
pride in the actions it has taken, pride in the stand it has made, pride
in the things it has done not only for the American labor movement,
but for the United States as a whole. . . .

"Abraham Lincoln said 100 years ago, 'All that serves labor serves
the nation,' and I want to express my appreciation for the actions
which this organization has taken under the leadership of Mr. Meany,
both at home and abroad, to strengthen the United States, to support
assistance to those who are trying to be free, to make it possible in this
hemisphere for labor organizations to be organized so that wealth can
be more fairly distributed."

That was the last time Meany saw Kennedy. En route from New
York to Washington following the convention, Meany heard of the
fatal shooting in Dallas.

"I don't know about the rest of you fellows," he said when he
reached the office, "but as far as I'm concerned, Washington will never
be the same."

13

LABOR AND CIVIL RIGHTS

We in the labor movement know that you don't have to be a union member to support the doctrine of human rights, but we also know that without human rights there can be no free labor movement.

The record after sixty-four proves that Johnson came through on practically everything [promised in the campaign]. Certainly what he did in the civil rights field was outstanding. He knew Congress; he knew the workings, how everything went. He knew who was on every subcommittee and every committee—the chairman and so forth. He was an expert on legislation; he knew more about the workings of Congress than any [other] President I have ever known. . . . When Johnson was President we enacted a great deal of legislation that was damn important to the American people.

As Johnson took the oath of office, Meany was one of those waiting to see how well the new President would support labor's legislative goals. In 1960, Johnson had annoyed Meany and others in the labor movement by applying heavy pressure in a vain attempt to win their support for his Presidential bid. There also were some bad marks on his congressional voting record dating from a time when he was worrying more about his Texas image than his national one.

Much of the hostility had been eliminated, however, by Johnson's work as chairman of Kennedy's Presidential committee to ensure equal job opportunities for blacks on government-financed projects. Meany had discovered through his own participation in the committee's work that Johnson was a true believer in civil rights in spite of his southern background and some of his earlier votes. But labor as a whole needed reassurance.

Johnson quickly dispelled lingering suspicions. As Meany recalled:

> Kennedy was killed on a Friday. Johnson called me at home on Saturday morning and said he wanted to get together with me as soon as possible. Then the day after he addressed the joint session of Congress he called me at home [six days after the assassination]. I met him at his home out in Spring Valley. He had that place that was formerly owned by Perle Mesta. I rode to the White House with him, talked to him on the way down. It was quite early in the morning. He talked about labor, the Labor Department and different things. He indicated that he was very anxious to go along with a list of things that we were for: federal aid to education, certainly the civil rights business.

At the White House, Johnson took Meany in to speak to the congressional leadership about labor's legislative goals. Then, a few days later, Johnson and his cabinet met at the White House with the entire AFL-CIO Council for a more detailed discussion of labor's objectives and the Administration's. The President's most important objective, it became clear, was passage of the omnibus civil rights bill that Kennedy had sponsored and that was still tied up in the House Rules Committee and was facing a filibuster threat in the Senate. The AFL-CIO leaders said later that they perceived a "sense of urgency" on Johnson's part on that issue. They were also impressed by his position on other issues.

The AFL-CIO's role in the historic fight to enact the Civil Rights Act of 1964 was spelled out by Meany in a 1969 speech:

> In 1963, when President Kennedy called leaders from all walks of life to the White House to solicit support for his comprehensive civil rights act, I was out of the country. But I sent him a telegram from the ILO meeting in Geneva, endorsing the outlines of his program, pledging him labor's support, but also asking that he add a fair employment practices act even though there was some question at that time whether such an act could pass the Congress.
>
> In fact, some of our greatest liberals were very fearful that by pushing for a fair employment practices act as part of the civil rights act we might jeopardize the rest of the bill.
>
> Well, this did not stop the AFL-CIO. We took a very strong posi-

tion, and we are the only major [non-church] institution in America that supported fair employment practices legislation in Washington. . . . The National Association of Manufacturers, the Chambers of Commerce, the Bankers Association—no national employer organization, to my knowledge, supported fair employment practices legislation.

The churches, of course, supported the entire Civil Rights Act of 1964, including the Fair Employment Practices section, but they are exempt, under the legislation, from the application of the section. But we are under the section, and we were the ones, I think, who were responsible for its inclusion in the Civil Rights Act.

President Kennedy was one of the liberals who feared that inclusion of the job-rights provision would doom the legislation in Congress. When he sent his broad civil rights bill to Congress, he attached a letter urging that a separate bill be passed to guarantee fair treatment in jobs for all citizens.

Robert F. Kennedy, the Attorney General, urged Congress not to merge the two measures. Despite all of Meany's arguments at the White House, the Administration sought to keep the employment section out of the main legislation. In Meany's 1963 New Year's statement he insisted that the country favored eradication of discrimination and that his sentiment "must be translated into reality through a federal fair employment practices system."

As sent to Congress by the Kennedy White House, the civil rights legislation prohibited discrimination in public accommodations, education and other areas—but not in employment practices.

The intensity of President Kennedy's feelings—and Meany's—is indicated by the account of lobbyist Andrew Biemiller on a 1963 incident. Biemiller explained that he had prepared a memorandum for Senator Humphrey outlining why the Federation wanted the employment section included in the civil rights measure. He left a copy with a White House aide.

Later that day, Meany—telephoning from Europe—asked Biemiller what kind of a memo he had sent to the White House. Biemiller answered that it said the AFL-CIO "absolutely had to have the FEP [Fair Employment Practices] clause in the Civil Rights Bill," to which Meany commented:

"You sure got Kennedy shook up; he's called me here in Rome and I told him that as far as I know that was exactly what our policy was but I would have you call him."

When Biemiller and Lane Kirkland went to see Kennedy, Biemiller recalled, the President "was like a madman: 'We can't have an FEP in this bill because it will kill the bill! We can't carry that weight on it.' "

As Biemiller insisted that that was not true, Kennedy cited statistics on black employment, but Kirkland and he, Biemiller remembered, both advised the President that the Federation was not changing its position.

The Biemiller memo complained about the failure of the Administration bill to include employment rights, adding: "Probably the one piece of legislation most required in America today is an FEPC [Fair Employment Practices Committee]. The Negro's most urgent need is for job opportunities, and this need is directly related to slums, juvenile delinquency, crime and disease. FEPC will have a tremendous impact on the cultural level of the poor Negro."

Soon after the Administration bill reached Congress in June 1963, Meany told the House Judiciary Committee why the AFL-CIO—and earlier, the two separate organizations—sought creation of an FEPC by law:

> The plain fact is . . . the Negro workers as a whole, north or south, do not enjoy anything approaching equal employment opportunity. . . . we need the statutory support of the federal government to carry out the unanimously-adopted principles of the AFL-CIO. . . .
>
> Why is this so? Primarily because the labor movement is not what its enemies say it is—a monolithic, dictatorial, centralized body that imposes its will on the helpless dues payers. We operate in a democratic way, and we cannot dictate even in a good cause. So, in effect, we need a federal law to help us do what we want to do: mop up those areas of discrimination which still persist in our own ranks.
>
> Second, we want federal legislation because we are tired of being the whipping boy in this area. We have never at any time tried to gloss over the shortcomings of unions on the subject of equal opportunity. Yes, some of our members take a wrongheaded view. . . . But we in the labor movement publicly deplore these few holdouts against justice. We do our utmost to bring them around to the right side. And at the same time, the employers—who actually do the hiring—escape in many instances with no criticism whatever. . . .
>
> When it comes to legislation, it has been the labor movement that has asked for equal employment opportunity laws, applicable to unions as well as to management; while it has been the employers and their associations which, at every level—local, state and federal—have been in bitter opposition. . . .

We support enforceable equal opportunity in employment because it is morally right. Surely, every American is entitled to be judged on his own, on the basis of his ability. He ought to have the same rights on the assembly line, in apprenticeship training or anywhere else that he now enjoys on the ball field. We lost the best of Satchel Paige to ghetto baseball; we need every Willie Mays we can find.

While waiting for Congress to act, Meany stepped up the AFL-CIO's efforts to eliminate discrimination through its own agencies. Among other things, he appointed a five-man committee, with himself as chairman, to work with the White House in more than thirty major cities. He said the aim was to "wipe out discrimination wherever it exists—on the job, in the schools, in the voting booth, in the housing developments, stores, theaters or recreation areas." Staff employees of the Federation and its affiliates were recruited to help. Biracial committees were ordered set up in city and state labor organizations. Construction unions adopted a program aimed at ending discrimination in employment in their field.

Pressure for civil rights legislation had been increased by a wave of riots, demonstrations and attacks on southern blacks that hit various parts of the country in 1963 and 1964. Particularly effective in moving public opinion were two marches: one, led by the Reverend Martin Luther King, Jr., in Birmingham, Alabama, in May 1963, in which police used dogs, clubs and firehoses to break up the peaceful demonstration; and the other, led by A. Philip Randolph, in Washington in August, in which 200,000 peaceful demonstrators participated and heard King make his famous "I have a dream . . ." speech.*

Nevertheless, the legislation remained stalled until the shock of Kennedy's death, when a wave of sympathy for the fallen President combined with Johnson's legislative skills to get things moving again.

The depth of Meany's commitment to the final bill's employment section—which was inserted in the broad legislation by the House Judiciary Committee before Kennedy's death—surprised House Republican Leader Charles A. Halleck. Meany and Biemiller had been sent by Johnson to try to enlist Halleck's support in releasing the bill from the Rules Committee.

* When a reporter asked Meany if he thought King had "moved too quickly" in the situation, Meany replied: "I would be the last one to take the position that the Negroes are shooting from the hip and moving too fast. I think they have been patient for a long, long time. . . . I would not criticize Reverend King for fighting for what I think is right."

When Halleck remarked that "of course" the Federation was not serious about the job section, Meany "let loose a tirade on Halleck the
like of which I had never heard him do before," recalled Biemiller.
Meany demanded to know if Halleck was saying that his Republicans
might vote against that section, adding: "I want that! That's my section; we're the guys who put it in there. You start monkeying with that
title [*i.e.*, section], you're going to be in trouble."

The legislation passed the House with the section in it and on July 2,
1964, was adopted by the Senate; it was signed that very day by Johnson, with the fair-employment provisions intact.

Black leaders, elated by the new law, by far the most far-reaching
civil rights bill ever enacted, were especially exultant over the fair-employment section, although many had been reluctant to make the fight
for it.* As one of them, Bayard Rustin, recalled: "We felt that we had
pushed so much that we couldn't push any more." Soon after the bill's
enactment the AFL-CIO held a civil rights conference to explain the
law's provisions to three hundred union leaders. Meany told them:

> This conference was called because we feel that something must
> be done, that we must have peaceful, voluntary compliance at the
> local level, that the people of the country must get the message that
> is contained in the law: the message that in the final analysis . . . this
> country was founded on the basis of an ideal that all men are equal.
> In seeking this voluntary compliance, we in the AFL-CIO feel that
> we have a part to play and we intend to play that part.

Meany went on to list various examples of what national unions and
central bodies were being requested to do. National unions were urged,
among other things, to assign personnel to take part in area committees
that would assist city central bodies and state federations to develop
their own programs. Each union was told to assign a national officer to
draw up a union-wide civil rights program and develop a community
program in the union's headquarters city. Central bodies were directed
to set up local committees on human rights.

Finally, delegates were asked to draw up an action program to
"eliminate discrimination within our own ranks." Meany said the
AFL-CIO would not wait until the fair-employment section of the law
took effect the next year but would fight for equality of opportunity in

---

* The fair-employment provisions definitely aided the labor movement in its efforts to
eliminate discrimination in the unions, according to Walter G. Davis, who at that time was
assistant director of the AFL-CIO's civil rights department.

hiring, training and promotion from that day. He warned, "We can't let hate groups stand in our way."

As part of labor's assistance in enforcing the Act's employment section, Meany asked Walter Davis to take temporary leave from his Federation post to become deputy executive director of the new Equal Employment Opportunity Commission (EEOC). Davis was there for thirteen months, until Meany telephoned to ask, "When are you coming home?" Thereafter he became AFL-CIO's education director, the first black to head a Federation department.

The Civil Rights Act of 1964 was a landmark for the nation, but although its provisions assured blacks equal access to schools, jobs and public accommodations, the measure nevertheless was only the first on Meany's agenda for domestic reform. The list included Medicare; higher pensions for widows, dependents and the disabled; federal aid to public elementary and secondary education; scholarships and low-interest loans for college students; an expanded anti-poverty program; an improved manpower development and training program; more generous public housing grants; and creation of a Department of Housing and Urban Development.*

In the meantime, however, with continuing violence in the South and an anticipated white backlash there in the election campaign, the Federation and the Administration had to devote their first efforts to securing victory at the polls in November 1964.

Meany told a union meeting early in the campaign:

> There was a time when the problems of the labor movement were fairly simple. You only had one problem. You fought the boss, and he was the root of all evil, and the problem was very simple, a trade union problem of getting a better share of what you were able to produce collectively with the boss, and to get decent working conditions. Now, of course, this is still the major objective of the trade movement, but in attaining this objective . . . you get into all sorts of activities.

The trade-union movement had a lot of problems, Meany continued, listing civil rights problems, community problems, international affairs, jobs, automation and politics among them. "All of these things mean political action," he urged. "We have got to have people in the legislatures, in the national Congress, who understand our problems,

* These were among the bills enacted into law in 1964 and 1965 with labor's help.

who are sympathetic with the things we are trying to do for our people and the country."

Recalling the passage of the Taft-Hartley Act, he said: "We had a fair count. The enemies of labor had the votes. . . . We can't be cryba-bies and say we got cheated. We didn't get cheated. We didn't have the friends in Congress, and that is our fault."

Meany also argued that 1964 "is our greatest year of opportu-nity"—referring to the possibility that the Republicans would select Senator Barry Goldwater to run against Johnson. "Sometimes," he added, "I don't think we could be that lucky, but it is beginning to look as if we might be." He said Goldwater's nomination would make it possible to gain more friends in Congress to add to the "little less than 200 rock-ribbed solid votes that we can count on."

Later, presenting the AFL-CIO's proposals for platform planks to both parties' national committee hearings, Meany reiterated the broader goals of the modern movement:

> The modern labor movement long ago outgrew the role of "spe-cial interest group" in the narrow sense. The AFL-CIO is made up of 13.5 million men and women who live in every state of the Union, who are engaged in virtually every occupation except business pro-prietorship, and whose interests, not only as union members but as citizens, embrace every facet of American life.
>
> This infinite variety is reflected in the ever-widening scope of the AFL-CIO's legislative program, for we try to represent the needs and aspirations of all workers, in all phases of their lives. Thus we are for more clear trout streams, for a humane immigration policy as well as a shorter work week.*

In the meantime the Federation mounted an unprecedented effort to get out the vote, and following Goldwater's nomination at the Repub-lican Convention, which Meany described as reminiscent of Hitler's *putsch,* the full resources of AFL-CIO's Committee on Political Educa-tion (COPE) were thrown behind Johnson and his congressional allies. In fact, at no time, Meany said later, had there been such an identity of interests between organized labor and a government in Washington.

COPE's registration efforts and Meany's campaign speeches derid-ing Goldwater's "extremism" helped Johnson win a sweeping victory,

---

* Regarding the last, and least likely of enactment, Meany once declared, "We are uncon-vinced by the President's observation that a 35-hour week would 'merely share' unemploy-ment. We shall continue to fight for a shorter work week. The only thing that will stop our fight is achievement of full employment."

taking all but Goldwater's Arizona and five southern states. (Goldwater credited his defeat to COPE.) COPE also added, by its own estimate, two new labor friends in the Senate and fifty-one in the House. Of congressional candidates endorsed by COPE, 68 percent were victorious, compared to 60 percent in 1962. The political machine that was the old AFL's answer to the Taft-Hartley Act had come a long, long way in seventeen years.

With the victory won by a massive margin, the coalition of organized labor, the Administration and the Eighty-ninth Congress addressed itself to the remaining proposals on Kennedy's list, a number of which had been bottled up in committees for years.

As Meany declared to his own members after the election:

> To a greater degree than ever before in the history of this country, the stated goals of the Administration and of Congress, on one hand, and of the labor movement, on the other, are identical. I do not suggest that this is "our" Administration or "our" Congress. That would not only be arrogant, it would be absurd. This Administration and this Congress were elected by all the people, of all social, economic and racial groups, in all parts of the country. But because this vast majority endorsed, through their votes, a program we have advocated for so long, we have a special responsibility to make sure that the decision is carried out.

But if the victory had demonstrated the power of a coalition for a the common good, it also had demonstrated the continuing force of political repression in the South, where countless blacks had been prevented from registering to vote.

After the election, Dr. King and other black leaders pressed for strong federal guarantees of the right to vote in order to eliminate southern discrimination against blacks at the ballot box. Meany and the AFL-CIO strongly endorsed the effort, placing voting-rights legislation high on their list. When Dr. King staged a fifty-mile protest march from Selma to Montgomery, Alabama, the following March, seventeen unions and the AFL-CIO headquarters sent delegations to take part. Donald Slaiman, then the AFL-CIO civil rights director, read Meany's message of support at the concluding mass meeting.

Collaboration between civil rights organizations and the AFL-CIO was increased during this period. An informal alliance, begun with the old AFL about 1950, was formalized by lobbyists Biemiller of the Federation and Clarence M. Mitchell, Jr., of the National Association for the Advancement of Colored People. Some eighty other organizations, including church and civil rights groups, joined the campaign to enact the full complement of Kennedy's and Johnson's civil rights bills. The alliance, known as the Leadership Conference on Civil Rights, continued to lobby for human rights over the years—with Meany's strong support.

Following Selma, President Johnson went before Congress in an impassioned plea for voting-rights legislation, to be added to the carefully prepared agenda presented in January. Congress responded with the Voting Rights Act of 1965, enacted on August 6, which authorized federal examiners to register southern blacks—under the protection, if necessary, of federal troops.

Moreover, before the close of that session most of the Federation's broader policy goals had been attained, in a spate of legislative activity unapproached since Roosevelt's New Deal. As Meany said when it was over, it was "undoubtedly the most productive congressional session ever held."

Meany, attributing the success in large measure to increased liberal strength in Congress owing to COPE's efforts and to Johnson's legislative prowess, gave as an example a tactical gambit on passage of the bill to assist higher educational institutions.

> An education bill had passed the House and went to the Senate. Later there were rumblings in the House, and Edith Green of Oregon, who was a very powerful member at the time, announced that when the bill came back to the House she was going to kill it.
>
> This confronted Johnson with a real problem. He set out to pass the House bill in the Senate without changing a single word. That would mean that it wouldn't have to go to conference; it would go through once the Senate passed it. The fellow who handled it in the Senate was Wayne Morse, chairman of a subcommittee.
>
> I recall Johnson calling me at home one morning about half-past seven and telling me there was a meeting of this five-man subcommittee at ten-thirty that morning. He gave me three names, saying, "I want you to get me two votes out of those three; if I get the two, then I'm all right."

Meany decided to try for Senators Jennings Randolph, of West Virginia, and Ralph W. Yarborough, of Texas:

> Johnson wasn't even on speaking terms with Yarborough at the time, and he said Yarborough was trying to get an amendment into the bill to get a couple million dollars for Texas, or something.

"You tell him," Johnson said, "to let the bill go and then come back next year; I'll help him get his two million," or whatever. I called Yarborough and, after a considerable discussion with him, I got his vote.

I called Randolph and had no problem there at all; I got his vote. So we passed the bill out of the subcommittee without changing a single word; it passed the Senate in that form.

Labor's narrower goals, as opposed to its broadly social ones, however, ended up a mixed bag.

Labor felt that Johnson's plan for an expansion of minimum wage coverage to additional groups of workers, but with no increase in the rate of $1.25 an hour, was insufficient. Angry words flew from both sides on this issue at the 1966 winter session of the Executive Council in Florida. Labor demanded an immediate increase in the minimum rate to at least $1.40, with further increases to $1.60 in 1967 and $1.75 in 1968. The President's Council of Economic Advisers, headed by Gardner Ackley, had recommended delaying the $1.60 rate until 1968 or 1970, to curb inflation, and Secretary of Labor Willard Wirtz, speaking to the AFL-CIO leaders, stuck to that position.

Meany threatened political reprisals: "We can make our own way without the Democratic or Republican party. I don't buy the idea that we have to toady along behind any particular party. I don't buy the idea that we have no place to go." (When asked if he would battle with Secretary Wirtz on the issue, Meany cracked, "I hope I get better competition than that.")

Reporters were also informed that, on his return to Washington, Meany would lead a group of Council members to take their case to Johnson. Wirtz countered that "nobody lobbies the President of the United States." Union officials declared the day had long passed when the labor movement went on hands and knees to the President.

"Johnson shut up Wirtz by a telephone call to Florida," publicist Albert Zack recollected. "Johnson announced he would see George when he got back to Washington."

Johnson sent a car to Meany's house the day he returned, to take him to the White House for an evening conference. The conference brought about a new proposal that called for an almost immediate rise in the minimum rate to $1.40 and a year later to $1.60. When Meany telephoned Andrew Biemiller from the White House, he confirmed that the figures were satisfactory to the union leaders most concerned

about the minimum wage. Biemiller told Johnson that he hoped Ackley would not denounce the new bill as being inflationary. Johnson
said Ackley would send word to the Hill that the raises were not inflationary. And Ackley did. Johnson phoned his economic adviser while
Meany was still in the White House family living room.

"Johnson went out of his way," Biemiller said years later, "to bring
George down immediately to act on this thing. There wasn't any question that our relations with Lyndon were so good as to be almost incredible."*

The increases negotiated that night were contained in legislation
signed into law by Johnson on September 23, 1966. The law also
brought some eight million new workers under its net, nearly doubling
the number originally proposed by the Administration.

But even Johnson's repeated exhortation, "Let us reason together,"
could not achieve perhaps organized labor's most burning desire: repeal of Taft-Hartley's section 14(b). The issue came up, together with
everything else, in the opening session of the Eighty-ninth Congress.

Secretary Wirtz strongly supported the AFL-CIO's battle to eliminate the so-called "right-to-work" laws then on the books in nineteen
states, and in the bitter campaign, labor got indications that a secret
deal could be struck to halt a Republican-led filibuster preventing the
Senate from voting on the legislation. Labor was extremely anxious to
repeal section 14(b), which permits states to bar union-shop contracts,
which otherwise are permitted by federal law. (Under the union shop,
the employer agrees to a provision requiring his workers to join the
union and pay union dues.)

By coincidence, Everett M. Dirksen, the Republican leader of the
Senate, was seeking Senate approval of a Constitutional Amendment
that would set aside a Supreme Court decision prohibiting unequal
representation of voters in state legislatures, the so-called one-man,
one-vote ruling.

Meany recalled talking earlier about 14(b) repeal with Johnson, who
was sick in bed with a cold at the time.

> It was about the time Congress was reconvening in 1965, two
> months after his sixty-four election. Andy Biemiller and I saw him in
> his bedroom. He questioned our count on 14(b) repeal [in the

* As for President Johnson's feelings about the Federation, he summed them up in 1965
with these words: "The AFL-CIO has done more good for more people than any group in
America in its legislative efforts. It doesn't just try to do something about wages and hours
for its own people. No group in the country works harder in the interests of everyone."

House] and went over it with Biemiller. Johnson said that it squared pretty well with his information. We said we had about 225 votes and Johnson started to name names: What about so-and-so? That was about the vote we got when we passed the repeal bill in the House.

[Johnson] helped us in the House; he got us half a dozen votes or maybe as high as eight in the House that we wouldn't have gotten—mostly from the South.

Immediately after Meany witnessed the vote in the House, President Johnson called Meany on the Speaker's phone. Andrew Biemiller recalled that the President congratulated them both on their accurate count of the votes and asked them to go immediately to talk to Russell Long, the Assistant Majority Leader of the Senate, to make sure he would support repeal.

Biemiller recounted that Long said "that old guy [A. Willis] Robertson from Virginia" was threatening a filibuster but that Long would "teach him a thing or two." Two days later, Long summoned Biemiller to his office to say, "We're in trouble." Dirksen had agreed to lead the filibuster.

Never before had there been a filibuster to prevent a bill from getting to the Senate floor and never before had the leader of either party led a filibuster. Meany continued the story:

> We passed the 14(b) repeal in the House and it went to the Senate, coinciding with Dirksen's effort to get his Constitutional Amendment. This was a smart move on his part. The Supreme Court had come out with one-man, one vote, which meant that the legislatures of the various states had to reflect the population. For instance, we had legislatures where one member of the state assembly from a rural area would represent 20,000 people while one from an urban area would represent 250,000 people. In was unequal representation. When the Court decision came down, Dirksen came up with his amendment.
>
> This would allow a state with a bicameral legislature—assembly and senate—to have either house elected by some other method than the one-man, one-vote method. That was a pretty cute approach from the point of view of those who controlled state legislatures as in New York, where the state Manufacturers Association and farmer organizations had absolute control of the State Assembly. The Assembly was weighted very much in favor of the rural districts. If they had control of one house, that was all they

needed—if they could maintain this unequal system of representation in one house.

We saw that right away, immediately: it was just as bad as if you
maintain the old system for both houses. So we started a campaign,
and we blocked that amendment—the labor movement was responsible, and Dirksen knew it.

When Andy Biemiller and I went to see Dirksen on 14(b) repeal,
he told us right straight out: "You're in a fight; you're fighting me
and I'm fighting you. When I fight I use everything." He blocked
repeal of 14(b). I don't think he had a damn bit of interest in repeal,
but he knew we wanted it and this was going to show that we
blocked his amendment on one-man, one-vote, and he could block
us on 14(b).

There was some talk, but I never had any direct message from
Dirksen that he would swap. There was the intimation that if we
withdrew our opposition to his amendment he would go along with
14(b) repeal. He killed us with his filibuster. There may have been
an offer; I think they let Andy know. But I never gave it a second
thought. We weren't going to make that kind of a deal with Dirksen
or anyone else. I'm sure that if we had gone to Dirksen and said, "All
right, we'll drop it," we would have been home free on 14(b). He was
very much in favor of this amendment and he was much aware he
would have put it over except for us.

To Meany, the danger to the country threatened by the Dirksen
amendment was far more important than winning a victory on a
strictly labor issue. For the sake of the country as a whole, labor could
take a loss on 14(b)—which it did.*

AFL-CIO lobbyist Biemiller described what happened when he and
Meany met with Dirksen: "Dirksen was pontificating all over the place
about a man's principles. Finally he made it clear to us that if we
would call off the dogs—we had him absolutely cold; he couldn't do
anything on one-man, one-vote—then he would call off his dogs on the
14(b) fight. George said, 'Now, wait a minute! 14(b) is very important
to us, but one-man, one-vote is even more important.' "

An elaboration of Meany's reasoning appears in this speech to the
1965 AFL-CIO convention:

The major political, economic and social problems of the United
State are, to an ever-increasing degree, urban problems—the prob-

---

* Meany earlier had claimed that some congressmen made a deal to get southern votes for
the anti-labor Landrum-Griffin Act in exchange for votes to block civil rights legislation.

lems of people living, working, trying to raise their families in crowded cities and teeming slums. The need for housing, schools, mass transit, clean air and water, recreation and other facilities and services will demand progressive legislation and far heavier public expenditures for those facilities and services than has ever been provided in the past.

Those programs are traditionally regarded by the Old Guard bosses of rural-dominated state legislatures as examples of wasteful extravagance. Those, like ourselves, on the other hand, who are champions of the many rather than the few, must insist that they are a vital, necessary public investment in the future of America and its people.

That, in the final analysis, is what the [Dirksen] filibuster in the United States Senate is really all about. The Senate Minority Leader is conducting a bitter rear-guard action against the relentless advance of the Twentieth Century, to preserve intact the strongholds of political and economic reaction in America, and to prevent or delay the kind of progress that is necessary to meet the new problems and challenges of our modern society.

The trade union movement strongly supports the one-man, one-vote principle and is the most constant and effective advocate of the measures required to provide for the general welfare of the people in this day and age. Therefore, the Senate Minority Leader must assail the trade union movement and place his forces in our path.

The issue of 14(b) repeal and the issue of reapportionment [of legislatures] in particular and progress in general are solidly and inescapably intertwined. There is no illusion about that either in our minds or the mind of the Senate Minority Leader. The filibuster is a punitive and coercive tactic. It is a cynical invitation to a "deal." It is the crafty politician's way of saying: "Come around to the back door. Give up your opposition to the reapportionment amendment and you can have 14(b) repeal."

Well, as badly as I want 14(b) repealed, I do not want it that badly. And the Senate Minority Leader and all his anti-labor stooges can filibuster until hell freezes over before I will agree to sell the people short for that kind of a deal.

Labor lost by seventeen votes in the first attempt to end the filibuster. When Dirksen resumed the blocking tactic the following year, labor lost by fifteen votes and, in the third and final test, by sixteen—killing the repeal measure for that session. Section 14(b) remained on the books thereafter. But Dirksen lost on his Constitutional amendment.

The period of Great Society enactments by then was almost over, replaced by the increasingly divisive issue of United States involvement in the war in Vietnam. Only one other piece of landmark social legislation remained to be enacted and it grew out of a combination of domestic and foreign policy conflicts.

The anti-war movement in the United States had begun in earnest in the fall of 1965 and escalated steadily, as the war did, throughout the rest of Johnson's term. Simultaneously civil disorders in the inner cities increased, fueled both by continuing minority grievances and the general unrest. The grievances crystallized on a demand for legislated fair housing—better housing and open housing. Meany again was in the vanguard, castigating the powerful Washington *Post* for hypocrisy in a letter to its editors in 1967.

An editorial had appeared in the newspaper praising the adoption of a fair-housing law in suburban Montgomery County, Maryland, in which Meany lived. The editorial prompted Albert Zack to report to his chief that classified housing ads with phrases signaling discrimination were appearing in the *Post* despite the editorial.

As an interested resident of the county, Meany sent a letter to the *Post* pointing out that the newspaper could aid the cause of fair housing better by "simply instructing its advertising department to abide by the principles that its editors espouse." He suggested that the paper announce it would accept ads only from those who guaranteed the housing was available without regard to race, creed, color or national origin. The letter did not appear in the paper and no answer was received.

Later, however, Zack mentioned the incident to a *Post* reporter, who apparently complained and prompted a letter to Meany from the paper's general manager, who said it had a policy of banning discriminatory advertising. But, he went on, the *Post* could not require an affidavit of guarantee because this would amount to a form of prior restraint on advertisers. That the paper would regard that "as an abuse of both the authority and responsibility that a free press possesses in the fields of news and advertising."

As it happened, Meany was about to testify before a Senate subcommittee considering a fair-housing bill, one which included provisions barring discriminatory advertising and the one that later became law. Meany read the exchange of letters at the hearing, provoking laughter from the audience, especially with the *Post* press-freedom claim.

The account of the incident may have tipped the scale for enactment, an AFL-CIO lobbyist thought. At any rate, Meany's testimony did appear in the *Post,* together with the *Post*'s earlier "explanation."

That summer of 1967 saw the outbreak of racial riots in Detroit, Newark and elsewhere—riots prompted partly by the housing conditions of blacks, as Meany noted in a radio network speech:

> It has been a summer in which rioting flared in the ghettos and slums which mar our great cities—a summer in which Americans killed each other and our law enforcement agencies had to be supplemented by the bayonets of the United States Army.
>
> No one can condone the riots. . . . Nor can anyone condone the conditions in the slums and the ghettos. . . . Nor should the fact of the riots be used as an excuse for not moving to correct these wrongs. . . .
>
> The tragedy is that only now we are talking about crash programs, and the Congress has yet to adopt the established, recognized, well-researched measures that have been pending before it since last January. Most of these measures, I must add, have been suggested, urged, demanded by the AFL-CIO not for months but for years.

In testimony before the National Advisory Commission on Civil Disorders, the so-called Kerner Commission, Meany said the group ought to study the underlying causes of the riots, and remedies to eliminate them. To ensure the domestic tranquility sought by the Constitution's authors, he said, the nation must create one million new jobs for the unemployed or seriously underemployed on useful governmental or nonprofit projects. He also cited "a broad, multiple need for action on housing." He called for open housing: "The right of any American to buy or rent any available home he wants and can afford, on any block in any community, is essential to the genuine achievement of equal rights and equal opportunity in this nation. . . . The federal government must be the employer of last resort and the landlord of last resort."

On March 2, 1968, the Kerner Commission made its report, agreeing in its conclusions with much of what Meany had said in his testimony and calling specifically for a sweeping program of housing. A month later Martin Luther King, Jr., was ambushed and slain in Memphis, and riots broke out in more than forty cities across the nation. A week later, President Johnson signed the Fair Housing Act, outlawing discrimination in the sale and rental of housing.

In the meantime, the President had again acknowledged his debt to the Federation, in a speech to the biennial convention in December 1967.

"I don't know where a lot of people will be standing in the battle for freedom and progress that lies ahead in the years of the future, but I do know where American labor has stood in the past. I do know where American labor stands tonight. It stands right in the front rank, unflinching and unafraid.

"I believe that you still will be there when the summer soldiers have fled the field of challenge."

Johnson spoke of the past, when labor "fought on a very narrow front" as a matter of "sheer survival—keeping the trade union movement going in the face of bitter opposition." Later, he continued, labor broadened its field: "You took up the fight for the kind of programs that would make this country better for your children than it had been for you. . . . And your President knows what your fight has meant for America in my time."

But the hour was late even then. The anti-war forces had already launched one challenge to the President's renomination and would soon launch another. The political collaboration of Johnson and the Federation on both domestic and foreign fronts would continue a year longer, but the Democratic coalition responsible for the Great Society legislation was no more.

Meany was so sure Johnson would run for re-election that an AFL-CIO movie was made at the White House for showing at union meetings during the campaign. Entitled "Conversation at the White House," it showed Johnson and Meany discussing important issues of the time. It was a lively conversation, with Meany occasionally interrupting the President to get across a point—no rehearsal, no script, no editing afterward.

But owing to Johnson's subsequent withdrawal, the 500 prints were never mailed to affiliates.

WALTER REUTHER

The only anti-Reuther thing I did in my lifetime was preserve my health.

In 1966, Meany, who had suffered increasing physical pain for nearly ten years and had lately been obliged to walk with two canes, underwent major surgery for the reconstruction of a hip socket. He was confined to the hospital for a month and underwent arduous rehabilitation exercises for six months. He was seventy-one years old at the time.

Meany's recovery seemed to some almost miraculous, and the day he put aside the last of his canes—signaling a new lease on life—may have opened the final phase of the internecine conflict long simmering between him and the man who yearned to succeed him, Walter Reuther.

As Meany put it, Reuther never seemed happy being second man in the merged organization. That was evident also to those outsiders who watched the ambition festering. Apparently doubtful about merger from the start, Reuther never could be a team player.

The result was an ongoing war in which Reuther's allegations against Meany, and the AFL-CIO policies, received most of the attention of the press. Meany's public defense was muted because he and other officials believed that, for the good of the labor movement, such disputes should be settled within the family. He agreed to tell his version of the story only a decade after the events:

After we merged, Reuther would go through periods when he was very cooperative, and he was cooperative in a lot of things. But then he would hit periods when you would hear a lot of criticism; he was grumbling.

It was not personal in the sense that he and I had some kind of a feud going. He made a real contribution to the work of the AFL-CIO. We had two or three arguments over a period of eleven or twelve years. He didn't win any of them, so maybe that bothered him; I don't know. I don't know. He evidently couldn't play on a team unless he was the quarterback.

I got along with him quite well. Every once in a while he would come to a meeting and be just growling and very disagreeable, but that would only last a short time.

In 1966, I had been in the hospital in New York for several weeks, and he and his wife came to visit me late in April. They sat in my room an hour and a half on a Sunday afternoon, and my relations with him were just as good as they could possibly be. I got out of the hospital, I think, the first Monday in May. We had a Council meeting that Friday and he was here for it, and I never had better relations with him. It was only a few weeks later when he blew up on the ILO thing [a temporary walkout of AFL-CIO delegates].

Reuther began his union-leadership career as a fighting factionalist in a union noted for its democratic procedures—and its internal battles. He fought for more than a decade to rise to the top of the United Auto Workers. He fought Allan Haywood to capture the CIO presidency, in the only contest for the office in CIO's two decades.

He did not have a chance to keep the AFL-CIO's presidency from Meany at the merger convention, and many—including this reporter—never could see where in subsequent years he could find the votes to win it. Reuther's factional approach to issues lost him the support of most of the former CIO leaders. Being consistently outvoted in the Council did not stop him from harassing Meany with new arguments—not the smartest way to deal with a fighting Irishman who not only became angry at the harassment but was clever at devising strong counterattacks. And had the votes.

Reuther may have thought that Meany's risky hip operation would change the odds. If the surgery failed, Meany could be in a wheelchair for the rest of his life; the Federation might turn to Reuther. But Meany sweated through the painful exercises necessary to recover full health. The vision of the waiting Reuther may have helped inspire him, although he was certain that the UAW president lacked the votes. Meany's real inspiration simply was the desire to return to the active life he loved.

As Meany recovered his normal vigor, Reuther appeared to become more discouraged. He publicly blamed his discontent on the AFL-CIO's policies and on "aging" leadership. (After Reuther complained that Meany was "a complacent custodian of the status quo," Meany told reporters, "I'm now signing my letters, 'sincerely and complacently yours.' ")

Reuther kept saying that he was not seeking Meany's job, but there were frequent indications to the contrary, including planted reports from UAW staffers and friends that Reuther was gaining support for the race. At one period he even courted the suspicious leaders of the building trades, formerly a favorite target.

Some Reuther boosters conceded that he would not be likely to surrender his Auto Union presidency in order to assume the AFL-CIO top post—as required by the Federation's constitution. But when asked privately how he could hold both jobs, one fan said, "We would just change the constitution." To do that, however, requires a two-thirds majority, whereas Reuther was struggling vainly for only half. The old CIO officers served part-time for CIO but drew their pay from their union. The president and secretary-treasurer of the AFL-CIO devoted full time to the Federation post, as in the old AFL.

Rumors of Reuther's intention to run against Meany for the top post never bothered him, Meany said.

It was never serious; it never gave me a second thought for the very simple reason that all they had to do was count. Under no circumstances could he ever get the votes; in fact, he couldn't get all the CIO votes. It was quite obvious I could get all the old AFL votes at any time. Although I didn't have any organized caucus or anything like that, I knew where I was every minute.

Where was Reuther going to get the votes? The ratio was almost two to one, and as the years went on the old AFL unions grew much faster than the CIO, so the voting ratio was always better than two to one, and what AFL union he could ever pick up I don't know. When people talked to me about him, I never gave it a second thought, because, to me, I could count—and that was it.

If he had any idea of getting this job, he didn't plan to give up the auto job; he wanted both of them.

Reuther was not qualified to be the president of the Federation, in Meany's opinion, according to Thomas Harris, former associate general counsel for the AFL-CIO:

"I remember one time George was talking to me about who might succeed him. He asked me who I thought would succeed him if he were to drop dead or retire—disappear from the scene. I said that Walter would make a run for it. He said, 'Yes, Walter would make a run for it but he wouldn't get it, and if he did get it he couldn't handle it.'

"I said that [Council member] Joe Keenan could be elected. He said, yes, Joe could be elected. I said that George Harrison [another member] would be an obvious possibility, although he was getting a bit old. Meany said, 'Harrison could handle it with one hand.'

"Harrison was just about the only labor leader I ever heard Meany express that kind of admiration for. He really thought that Harrison was—and Harrison *was*—a man of real ability."

That was the only conversation the two men had on the subject. "I think the older he got," Harris said, "the less disposed he was to consider the problem."

From his experience advising Reuther at the CIO and Meany after merger, Harris was able to point out crucial differences:

"I think Meany was a lot smarter than Walter was; this is contrary to a very general impression. I think a lot of people have not appreciated how very sharp Meany is. He speaks with a Bronx accent that probably throws people off. He never went to the trouble to get some academic training, as Walter did, but Meany is much quicker than Walter ever was, a much faster mind.

"Walter invariably was outmaneuvered by Meany. Walter certainly had the hope and, I think, he had the expectation, too, when the merger came, that the merged Federation was going to be run by a small executive committee—which was provided for in the constitution.

"It was about six or seven people, and Walter thought that this group was going to run the operation as an oligarchy. Meany perceived right away—I guess he was never in doubt—that the Executive Council, a much larger body, would be a group that he would be able to

dominate much more easily than he would this small executive committee with Walter and Jim Carey in opposition. So he never referred
any important business to the executive committee and it gradually
fell into desuetude.

"Walter was very indignant about that, but that was not an argument that Walter could possibly win in the Executive Council. The
proposition that this small group should be running the operation, and
not the Executive Council, did not commend itself to the Council. So
he had a loser there. Meany finally amended the constitution to abol-
ish the executive committee.

"Meany always liked a good fight. . . . That can be an advantage to
a person in that position. Walter always tended to back away from a
fight or a face-to-face confrontation. Meany's willingness to take one
on, and Walter's reluctance, was one way that Meany maintained
dominance of the situation."

J. Albert Woll, general counsel of the AFL-CIO, thought Meany
had another advantage:

"I think the people looked upon George as being a very stable influence. He didn't vacillate one way or the other. He was like a rock and
they knew where they stood with him. They knew what he would do
and felt safe with him, whereas they didn't feel safe with Reuther.
They didn't know where he would lead them."

Had Reuther won the AFL-CIO presidency, many union leaders
would have found it difficult to work with him—or, more realistically,
under him. He was proud of his liberal reputation; to some non-Communist liberals, he was "the" labor leader of the United States. Meany,
with his background in "business unionism" of the building trades,
was tagged as a conservative by many liberals outside the labor movement. Inside the movement, his liberal credentials were recognized.
But Meany didn't wave the "reform" flag; his influential support for
progressive measures was given quietly. While Reuther announced
high-sounding programs for betterment of the people, Meany was
doing the hard, practical work of promoting social legislation.

In his youth, Reuther was a Socialist, later quitting the party although retaining ties with important Socialists around the world. He
could deliver dramatic, if lengthy, speeches. He could rally the troops
for battle. But he tended to leave the follow-up administrative work to
subordinates.

All of this was so different from George Meany's personality and

operating technique that it was no wonder the two men didn't understand each other. Donald Slaiman, who worked closely with both men
when he was AFL-CIO director of civil rights, thought that Reuther
wanted to be known as a leader of the liberal community and was so
recognized by many. On the other hand, Meany was a leader of the
labor movement. Where he agreed with the liberals, he was *with* them,
but he was not *part of* the liberal movement. He was the leader of the
labor movement, a broad spectrum from far-left liberals to far-right
conservatives. Meany did not do things to win accolades for being a
liberal leader. This meant that, actually, when he was involved in a
civil rights issue, for example, he brought more to it than Reuther did;
Meany brought along conservative labor leaders who trusted him as an
all-around labor leader, not as a leader of the liberal movement. Thus,
AFL-CIO's contribution to civil rights, Slaiman felt, was greater than
that of Reuther's Auto Workers.

The unfair tendency, in part of the media, to label Reuther as a liberal and Meany as less liberal or even middle-of-the-road was a sore
spot in the two men's relationship. On basic trade-union issues they
were in agreement, even on most foreign-affairs issues. Their dedication to fundamental liberal causes such as civil rights was equally
strong; Reuther simply made more of a fetish of his position before TV
cameras.

Former CIO staffer Leo Perlis, who admired Reuther's leadership of
the auto union, was director of the AFL-CIO Community Services Department until retirement in 1980 and thus was familiar with the positions of both Meany and Reuther. He gave this appraisal:

"I don't think basically there was much difference [between them] in
policy or philosophy on the American democratic society, the American economy, the role of the trade union movement—even in international affairs. They were both anti-Communist. I'm talking about fundamental and basic trade union and democratic policies."

Reuther was "a poor federation president and a good international
union president," Perlis said. "In an international union, Walter
Reuther could really run the show and he didn't consider the executive
board or his business agents and district directors as his peers. They
were the subordinates—even the executive board members."

When Reuther complained that the AFL-CIO was not paying
enough attention to organizing the unorganized, Meany outflanked
him by appointing him chairman of the Council's committee on or-

ganizing.* Thereafter, Reuther's leadership of the committee generated a wealth of publicity about his plans for massive special organizing drives but little in the way of results.

The quarrels between the two strong leaders erupted with such fury at the mid-winter Council meeting at San Juan, Puerto Rico, in February 1959 that some of those present thought the AFL-CIO might be breaking apart. Meany conceded when he finally agreed to discuss the subject that there were a lot of arguments there. At one point in the session, he advised James Carey, the former CIO secretary, that henceforth he would deal with him only in writing. That followed a quarrel in which Meany accused Carey of misquoting a Meany telephone conversation concerning one of the disputes:

> Carey was very nasty at that meeting. Reuther and he were trying to upset things. I got there a day late. I had been laid up in bed with a bad cold, and the doctor told me to take another day in bed. I was really not too well when I got there, but they [had] held a meeting the previous day, in which Reuther and Carey tried to take over. So I straightened them out—the way I usually straightened them out—by talking sense to them. Perhaps they knew how many votes they had and how many they didn't have.

He denied reports that Reuther at that time had threatened to quit the Council: "At no time did he threaten to quit." Reminded that Reuther complained publicly about holding the meeting at such a plush resort, Meany said:

> This was a line he had for years. He kept going to Miami Beach, but every once in a while he would make a speech that we shouldn't be meeting there. We met wherever the Council decided to meet; no reason why we shouldn't meet where we liked it. We had an argument one time about Miami Beach and Reuther said he didn't want to mix business with pleasure.
>
> Dave Dubinsky got up and was walking around the table pointing his finger, "business and pleasure? I like to mix business and pleasure." He went after Reuther, who was trying to preserve some kind

---

* Meany's own theory was that organizing was the job of the individual unions, not the Federation's task. From his experience, he said, he knew that it was difficult to get competing unions in the same industry to agree which one would get new members recruited by a Federation organizing drive. A national unit that was involved could—and often did—block an AFL-CIO effort to organize in its field.

of an image that was a little bit ridiculous. He lived the good life. When he traveled he stayed in the best hotels; he had a very active expense account; he liked good meals. But he would always make those speeches that it was wrong for labor leaders to be enjoying life. They claimed in Florida he bought oranges and squeezed his own orange juice for breakfast. I don't believe it.

It was the old hair-shirt argument; you had to preserve the image. But Walter liked to dress nicely and he liked to travel in first-class style, and did.

One of the disputes between Meany and Reuther at the Council session in Puerto Rico was over a Reuther proposal for a "march on Washington" by unemployed workers. Believing that protest parades were ineffective in influencing members of Congress, Meany objected to the idea, but after a long debate a compromise was reached. The AFL-CIO would call a "jobs rally" of union representatives in Washington. It was held April 8 with Meany as keynote speaker.

Another sign of the growing tension appeared at the AFL-CIO's 1961 convention, where Meany felt that Reuther was trying to develop sentiment for a new split in the labor movement. Holding daily caucuses of former CIO delegates, Reuther used as an issue a subcommittee's report on machinery to solve jurisdictional disputes between affiliates. The auto chief was on a Council subcommittee that presented its proposal to the Council after two years' deliberations. The subcommittee majority—Reuther, A. J. Hayes and Joseph Beirne—favored binding arbitration of the disputes, with an umpire empowered to expel a union from the Federation if it failed to accept his ruling.

Meany and other Council members objected to giving an outsider that expulsion authority, normally held only by the AFL-CIO convention. But Reuther refused to compromise on any provision of the plan, and Meany got a motion to discharge the committee. When it was approved, Meany recalled, Reuther pushed back his chair, saying, "Come on" to Hayes and Beirne, but neither moved and Beirne said, "Listen, I'm not going anyplace. The report has been received; we haven't solved the problem; let's go to work." In a few hours a compromise was found: a union that rejected an umpire ruling no longer could use the dispute machinery to protect itself against raids by another affiliate. The convention approved the plan; the Federation was still intact.

Strangely, it was an event in distant Switzerland, rather than the Council quarrels, that Reuther used to intensify his anti-Meany propaganda. On June 1, 1966, the U.S. workers' delegation walked out of the International Labor Organization's conference in Geneva in a protest over election of Leon Chajn, the Polish government delegate, to preside over that year's sessions.

The Communist-bloc nations, Franco's Spain and developing African countries combined to put Chajn in this key position. It was the first time a Communist had been so honored and, furthermore, Poland at the time was under "sanctions" voted by the ILO because of its denial of workers' rights. (Poland told the ILO it should adapt itself to the Communist system.)

The American walkout was temporary—for the June 1966 session only—and did not mean that the AFL-CIO was leaving the ILO. Reuther, however, took very public umbrage, as Meany recalled:

> When this Communist was elected chairman of the conference, his country was under sanctions by the ILO. We wouldn't attend the session; we sort of boycotted it. Reuther made a big thing of that right away. He wrote a letter highly critical of [the walkout] and me, and sent it to the Washington *Post* and some other newspapers. They had it before I got it. Reuther said that this was very undemocratic and all this sort of thing; as long as we lost in the election we should accept the result. We lost due to the fact that our government didn't stand up.
>
> I first heard about the letter when I got a telephone call about seven o'clock in the evening asking me if I had any comment on Mr. Reuther's letter. I said to the fellow, "Mr. Reuther's letter to whom?" He replied, "The letter to you." I asked, "What's it about?"
>
> I wasn't in Geneva in sixty-six when this [walkout] happened, but I was there before that [in 1963] when we all walked out together when a South African came to speak at the ILO plenary session. That was a boycott and the CIO people who were there walked out just the same as the AFL people. (They were all AFL-CIO.) That was evidently all right, but when we walked out on the Polish Communist, that was evidently "wrong."
>
> Reuther's letter came out of the blue; he hadn't said anything to me. I had spent all day [June 3] with him at a meeting, sat right alongside him. We had lunch at the Labor-Management Committee meeting in the Department of Commerce, and he never mentioned the ILO thing to me.

I called a meeting of the Executive Council and brought Rudy [Rudolph J.] Faupl [U.S. worker delegate, from AFL-CIO] back from Geneva for the meeting [on June 16]. Reuther issued a statement to the press telling what he said to us before he said it. There was no way [to avoid a split] after that. The Council heard Faupl and, by an overwhelming vote [18 to 6], approved what he had done.

Reuther tried to justify his opposition and, actually, that was really the start of the break with Reuther. Before that, everything was sweetness and light with Reuther. I was getting along with him great just two days before that.

Reuther's release to the press stated that the issue before the AFL-CIO Council was "not a matter of personalities" but "a matter of policy and democratic procedure." The UAW's leadership, it went on, was "deeply disturbed about the growing negative character of AFL-CIO policy in the field of international affairs."

Delegate Faupl reported that American officials in the ILO were unanimously opposed to electing a Communist ILO president, fearing that the post would be used to increase Communist strength in the governing body of ILO. But, in the showdown, the government representatives decided to "play it in low key."

After Chajn won, Faupl explained, he telephoned Meany from Geneva to say that he could not, "in good conscience, sit in the conference presided over by a representative of a Communist country" and that he was withdrawing the U.S. worker delegation.

Faupl reported that Meany had told him he would do the same thing if he were in Faupl's position but that he should not commit the AFL-CIO to withdrawing from the ILO. Only the Council could make that decision, he warned.

After the AFL-CIO Council meeting, Meany told the press that when Reuther complained that the walkout was contrary to President Johnson's "bridge-building" with the Russians, a Council member reminded Reuther that the AFL-CIO had a policy on it "and we don't believe you can build bridges by recognizing the people who control workers, who oppress workers."

Meany added that he, himself, had to be guided by AFL-CIO policy, regardless of whether or not it conformed to Johnson's policy:

This isn't the only area where we have differences; this is still a free country. We differ with the Administration and have differed for twenty years on their policy of relations with Spain. We don't like the relationship our country has had with Spain . . . we don't like other things on the domestic side, but this doesn't mean that we are opposed to the President and what he is trying to do. It just means that in certain areas we can't agree with him.

As for a Reuther charge that the ILO walkout was planned a week in advance at AFL-CIO's headquarters, Meany called it a "damnable lie." Reuther thought Council members could have been consulted in advance. Meany also told reporters that in the confrontation Reuther "said it is well known that he doesn't like publicity, and he said it without a smile."

When a reporter wondered if the bitter disagreement might hurt Reuther's chances for "higher office," Meany said, "I have no great interest in that. If that happens, I won't be around here."

Reuther's attacks continued at the regular August session of the Council, Meany recalled:

> In that meeting he was making statements about our foreign policy. He had been on the Council for eleven years at that time. Everything we ever did on foreign policy was done with his agreement. Even on the Vietnam situation: at our convention in San Francisco [in 1965] he backed up our report and disagreed with [UAW's Emil] Mazey; they took the floor on opposite sides. So in 1966 he demanded that we review our foreign policy.
>
> We set up a meeting [on November 14] and we gathered all the statements we had made since the merger and we were going to have a great debate. A couple of days before that he said he couldn't come. He didn't show up. He was "too busy." After August of sixty-six I don't think he came to another meeting.

That special November meeting had been postponed once at the UAW president's request. His failure to appear angered Meany and other Council members. One called Reuther "chicken." Meany told reporters that the members present voted unanimously to reaffirm the major policy decisions of recent years.

One of the disappointed members was Paul Hall, president of the Seafarers. He explained: "I thought, well, this Reuther is a little screwed up on some things that I, as one of the few, few internationalists, can take him on. Sailors are really the only internationalists in the whole labor movement, and I'm their representative. I don't know if anybody else in the whole movement was, but I was really looking forward to that opportunity to debate Walter. He didn't show, and to this day I've felt frustrated."

Jay Lovestone, then the AFL-CIO's foreign expert, thought the Reuther criticism of foreign-policy statements was "the biggest fraud" and "disgusting." He added: "Reuther never voted against a single resolution on foreign affairs—but never! Once or twice he even sharpened it, as when Johnson landed troops in the Dominican Republic. We never had any differences, even on Vietnam." Lovestone said drafts of proposed policy resolutions always were given to Reuther several days in advance of meetings to allow him every opportunity to study them and offer revisions.

The Christmas season of brotherly love was barely over when, in early 1967, Reuther began a new series of shock treatments: he resigned from the AFL-CIO's Executive Council, saying his move was unanimously ordered by his executive board. However, Reuther did not quit his post as head of the Industrial Union Department, an important sounding board for him in the Federation. (Later it developed that, during his last months there, the department had drastically drained its treasury by spending more than a million dollars on various programs.)

An attempt to head off the resignation was made by Council member Dubinsky, with Meany's approval. The Garment Workers' president had heard a rumor that the action was about to be taken, and he checked with Meany before telephoning Reuther in Detroit, offering to come out that evening and discuss the problem. Reuther said he was too busy. A few hours later the resignation was announced.

Slightly veiled threats to pull the UAW out of the AFL-CIO followed, in the form of an "administrative letter" addressed to the UAW's local union leaders. This presumably was "keeping it in the family," except that the text was immediately issued in a press release that explained further that the letter outlined "a far-reaching program designed to get the American labor movement off dead center," among other things.

Loss of the UAW, largest of the affiliates, with some 1.3 million members, would be a serious blow to the finances and prestige of the Federation, as Meany well knew. But he never had bowed to such threats in the past. The Executive Council's answer, which came quickly, stressed the point that labor's quarrels should be discussed and settled in a democratic vote inside the AFL-CIO, and not in the public press. The resolution stated in part:

"There is only one limitation upon the extent to which any individual or any organization within the trade union movement can influence the direction of its leadership. As in any democratic order, they must be able to persuade the majority that their complaints are valid, that their proposals are sound and that their alternatives are preferable. Neither size, financial resources, nor extravagance of language can overcome or substitute for that simple basic requirement."

The Council members said they were ready to consider and act upon any complaints or programs proposed, whether "novel or ancient," advanced by any affiliate if offered through "appropriate channels of the AFL-CIO constitution." They added: "We are not, however, prepared to act upon the basis of a kaleidoscope of ever-changing allegations and demands, expressed through press releases, public speeches or circular letters."

Meany read to the Council the resignation telegram he received from Reuther—who gave no reasons for the move except the "order" of his board. Meany explained that no other official communication from Reuther had come to him, although two UAW press releases had arrived.

In a press conference afterward, Meany expressed hope that Reuther would come back to the Council and that the union would remain in the AFL-CIO. He explained that this desire for Reuther's return was his reaction as president of the Federation and not necessarily his personal opinion. When someone asked about the procedure for return, Meany told him to ask Reuther "how he plans to get back," adding, "He is very resourceful." Reporters also were told the Council meeting had been very productive, which he said might have "a possible relationship to the absence of Reuther" as "sometimes some of our members don't talk when Walter is here."

As Reuther's propaganda continued, week after week, it was aimed at Meany personally rather than at the Council's decisions, which were approved by its members. Inside the meetings, Reuther's oratory had been unable to "sell" his ideas even to his old CIO associates.

By February 1967, Meany was described by associates, privately, as certain Reuther had gone so far with his charges that he could not back off from seceding from the Federation. For six months, one aide said, Meany had been attempting to talk things over with Reuther, but the Auto Workers' president refused to accept his telephone calls and remained away from the AFL-CIO headquarters. Associates reported then that Meany did not expect other unions to pull out, because he felt Reuther had no real issue that would convince them to leave.

The door was open, however, if Reuther cared to bring in his complaints, Meany advised the National Press Club. Like the club, he said, the AFL-CIO had procedures for such cases: "We're old-fashioned enough to believe that when any member . . . has a complaint against the people in charge of things, the place to go is to the machinery that is provided under the constitution. . . . If, as and when Walter wants to come and use that machinery, I'll be there waiting to welcome him."

Had Reuther been serious about a democratic showdown over his issues, the December 1967 convention of the AFL-CIO would seem to have been the logical place to get it. Instead, the compliant UAW board decided not to send any delegates to this highest governing body of the Federation. (The union could have sent a delegate or two to present the new "program" for the AFL-CIO, which had been approved by a special UAW convention in April.) The board letter to Meany said officers would be too busy with contract negotiations in the auto industry. It requested that the UAW's program resolution be withdrawn from convention consideration. This prevented a floor discussion and delegates' vote, which, judging by Reuther's track record, was expected to be a strong vote of confidence in Meany.

The AFL-CIO president's reaction to the Reuther complaints and the resulting newspaper "death notices" for the labor movement was revealed in an address Meany delivered to the AFL-CIO convention December 7, 1967:

> The trade union movement is a more vital, a more vigorous and a more effective force for progress today than ever before in its history. I realize that in some quarters it is considered highly unfashionable to express such a view. There are those who write us off as either obsolete or—in the terms of the current cliche—a part of the "establishment," and therefore unworthy of confidence as a progressive element in our society.
>
> There is a common tendency to draw comparisons between the modern labor movement and that of some mythical past period of crusading fervor and dynamic forward motion. Much depends, of course, on how you view the picture. If you are looking for flaws and blemishes, there are always plenty to be found. Take any segment of

labor at any given point in time and something can be found to criticize or vilify—if that is the purpose. But suppose we were to apply the same dim view consistently—disregarding the favorable aspects—to any past period of labor history.

For example, take the Federation of the 1880s and 1890s. It represented a microscopic proportion of the labor force. In addition to the Carpenters, the Cigarmakers and a small handful of other unions that still exist, its roster of affiliates consisted for the most part of such thriving organizations—vibrant with dynamic forward thrust—as the Organ Makers Union, the Umbrella and Walking Stick Workers, the Hair Spinners Union, the Box Sawyers and Nailers, the Architectural Cornice Makers, the Lantern Workers and the Horse Collar Makers National Union.

The Federation's total income in a typical month was about $300 or $400 and its expenses a few dollars less. It had no paid organizers in the field, and its "headquarters staff" consisted of one office boy. It had no friends in the liberal intellectual community. It was, in fact, quite obvious to any well-informed journalist, economist or student that no organization so constituted and so narrowly based and guided could possibly survive the rapid social and technological changes of the time.

Meany then recounted many other periods of peril for the labor movement over the years, and continued:

Now we are approaching the end of the 1960s and things are getting still worse. The new technology is going to wipe us out again—our members are too fat to care about anything but the next television program, and we are too obsessed with the freedom of our brothers overseas to understand the overriding importance of peace in our time. So much for history, as viewed by our detractors. Now let us look at the whole truth. . . .

The essential truth is that—year in and year out—the trade unions of this country, as represented in this Federation of ours, have constituted and will continue to constitute the vital main force of the progressive movement in Ameria. At no time, within my memory, has labor been better equipped and prepared to deal with its problems and responsibilities in society than is the case today.

Never has there been more real unity of spirit and purpose, in substance as well as form—within the labor movement as a whole. Never have we been as active, through so many channels, in the pursuit of human progress as we are today. The evidence is there—

in abundance—for those who care to look without the blinders on. It
points, not to any decline of force and vigor—but to the beginning of
a new and challenging period of growth, change, and response to the
needs and opportunities of our times. . . .

The performance of free collective bargaining as an instrument of
social and economic progress continues to confound the critics and
the soothsayers. While they have been writing its obituary notices,
the working people of America have continued to demonstrate their
faith in that instrument and new groups in our economy are learning to use it to their advantage. . . .

As we know from bitter experience, even Senators go on strike—
our experience with filibusters proves that.

The results of collective bargaining, Meany added, "have brought—
over time—the most profound and revolutionary changes and improvements in the pattern of our national and family life." He listed
numerous legislative goals of the Federation ranging from labor issues
to consumer protection, pollution cleanup and civil rights measures.

On the Vietnam War, one of the issues being raised by Reuther,
Meany explained:

> As far as Vietnam is concerned, we in the AFL-CIO are neither
> "hawk" nor "dove" nor "chicken." We do not pretend to be military
> experts of any kind—armchair or otherwise. Nor are we in a position
> to judge the strategic importance of bombing or other military
> weapons and tactics.
>
> We are trade unionists—and, as trade unionists, we believe in
> human freedom and in democracy—not just for ourselves but for ev-
> eryone who prefers to live under such a system—and I think that in-
> cludes everyone who is in his right mind. We believe that those
> values are worth defending and that they will not survive in the
> modern world unless the richest and most powerful nation on earth
> is willing to help defend them—with its material resources, if possi-
> ble, but with the lives of its fine young men—tragic as that is—if
> necessary.
>
> There is one overriding fact about the Vietnam issue that is and
> must be the primary concern of the AFL-CIO—the existence, in
> South Vietnam, of a genuine free trade union movement. . . .I am
> sure that I do not have to explain to you what would happen to
> these trade unionists and their leaders after a Communist take-
> over. . . .
>
> I am perhaps too young to understand the complex motives of any

American trade unionist who can bring himself to advocate a course
of action that would abandon brother trade unionists of South Vietnam to certain destruction. And, perhaps, I am too simple to com-
prehend how one who takes that position can be called a "liberal."

The standing ovation given those remarks and others indicated how
much support Walter Reuther would have received had he sought to
stir up a "revolt" against the leadership in that hall.

In 1968, Reuther delayed his "divorce" from AFL-CIO but moved
out of the house, as a Federation staff member described it. The UAW
leader withdrew from AFL-CIO affairs and halted payment of per-capita dues to the Federation. But the broadsides from Detroit continued—at least, he was keeping in touch.

An ultimatum was issued by the UAW board on March 2. It demanded that the AFL-CIO hold a special convention in the first or second week of December—even stipulating the timing—for a complete
discussion of the UAW's "program" for the labor movement. The message to Meany ended with the threat of an auto union departure from
the Federation if the convention was not held.

Talking about that period for this book, Meany said:

> Strangely enough, all reports at the time were that Emil Mazey
> did not want Reuther to do what he did. But Reuther insisted and
> Mazey went along with him. In the letter he sent, the ultimatum was
> contained in the last paragraph, and the story I got was that when
> the letter was ready to go out, Mazey said, "Walter, you should take
> that last paragraph out because the AFL-CIO can't take that. You
> can't put a gun up to their heads and give them an ultimatum."
> Reuther said no.

Meany countered the ultimatum by holding a special meeting of his
Council, which unanimously refused the ultimatum but offered the
UAW this:

"You can have a special convention on your charges and proposals—as soon as it is humanly possible to hold one under these two conditions:

"1. That you commit your organization without question to attend
such a convention, if and when called.

"2. That you further commit your organization to accept the demo-
cratically arrived at decisions of such a convention."

The auto board rejected the second condition and announced it would proceed to obtain the convention by the petition route also offered in the AFL-CIO constitution. This would require that unions representing a majority of the Federation's fourteen million members support the UAW demand. Reuther conceded later that they had failed there, too.

UAW's next move was to have its own convention vote to place UAW's per-capita payments for the Federation into an escrow account until December to see if the AFL-CIO held the special convention. Terming that "an act tantamount to withdrawal," the Federation's Council unanimously declared the auto union suspended May 15 and thus barred from all AFL-CIO activities, including the Industrial Union Department.

The UAW had failed to pay its dues since February 15 and the constitution requires suspension if a union is three months in arrears. Departure of the UAW meant a loss of about $1 million a year in percapita dues, Meany said.

He reported that everyone at the Council meeting thought the escrow idea was Reuther's way of withdrawing from the Federation. No one spoke up for Reuther, he added, but said he "regretted this thing very much" although he knew of nothing the AFL-CIO had done to bring it on. The situation on suspension was unique, he said, because "we have never had anyone tell us they were going to stay in without paying," as the auto union proposed to do.

On July 1, Reuther wrote Meany announcing UAW's "formal" disaffiliation and adding new complaints about the conditions imposed by the Council on calling a special convention. Meany's reply included these key points:

> In view of the UAW's record of denouncing the AFL-CIO and advertising its so-called "proposals for reform and revitalization" in the public press for the past two years—while at the same time evading, on various pretexts, every one of the many opportunities presented to it to bring its complaints and proposals to the proper forums of the AFL-CIO, it was only reasonable and prudent to ask the UAW to commit itself to attend and be represented at such a convention, and to give assurances that it would not, at the last minute, decide to perform another disappearing act.
>
> And, since the UAW was demanding a special convention under threat of withdrawal, it was the unanimous opinion of the Executive Council that—in fairness to the other 128 affiliates of the AFL-CIO, all equally worthy of consideration—those affiliates should not be

burdened with the considerable expense and inconvenience of bringing a delegation to such a convention unless there was at least some prospect that the decisions they would make at such a convention would be respected by the organization responsible for putting them to that trouble and expense. Each of those affiliates, after all, would be expected to honor and accept the same decisions, whether they liked them or not.

All that was being asked of the UAW, Meany summed up, was "an agreement on your part to abide by the principle of majority rule in the supreme governing body of the Federation." He then quoted a similar appeal to "carry out the will of the majority" that had been made to a UAW local union in the 1953 UAW convention. Reuther had made that appeal, he pointed out. Moreover, the UAW officers' complaints and demands made to the AFL-CIO, Meany said, "represented a transparent attempt to set up the grounds and excuses to justify to your members your predetermined objective of withdrawal from this trade union movement." He added that the Federation "has no remedy" for Reuther's "apparent unwillingness to live in constructive harmony within an organization in which the rights, the interests and the views of other unions and other personalities are given equal consideration with those of the UAW and its president."

Reflecting on these events a decade later, Meany said:

> Walter wanted to go. We did nothing to compel him to go. He built up this whole situation, starting with the ILO thing. We didn't want him to go out; I certainly didn't want that. He always felt that he had a special position [on the Executive Council], but I can't deny that he did make a contribution. I think he did. But when he got the bit in his teeth in June of 1966—from that day on, he made up his mind that he wasn't going to stay.
>
> A number of the old CIO people went to him and tried to calm him down, but, oh, he wouldn't be calmed down. He ran the Auto Workers and ran it well, as far as I'm concerned, but he ran it. He made all the decisions and he saw that they were approved.
>
> Maybe he was uncomfortable in the AFL-CIO because he was only one member of an Executive Council, which was running the thing. I don't know. People say he wanted to run the show; I don't know.
>
> All I can say is that we issued a "white paper" after he left, and that is absolutely factual. There is nothing in there but facts; it's all spelled out. There was no real reason for the Auto Workers to leave

except that he wanted to leave. He couldn't answer the white paper; he never answered it.

The day they were automatically out because they had run out on their dues—this was all planned ahead of time by Reuther—he, Mazey and [UAW vice president Leonard] Woodcock went over and talked to [Teamster president Frank] Fitzsimmons and formed the "American Labor Alliance" with the Teamsters. Reuther set it up and he got one AFL-CIO union, the Chemical Workers. They donated fifty thousand dollars to the Chemical Workers for organizing purposes, and the Chemical Workers, who were very short of money, were delighted. They took the fifty thousand and joined the Alliance. They didn't stay very long; the Alliance just evaporated.

I never had any doubts that it would go down, because there certainly was no community of interest between the Auto Workers and Teamsters. [Combining] what the Auto Workers stood for and what the Teamsters stood for was like trying to mix oil and water. Because, despite any differences that I had with Reuther—and the differences I had with Reuther were certainly exaggerated—I always recognized the Auto Workers as a damn good trade union, doing a good job, and I looked at the Teamsters as something different. The idea that these two unions would get together was just ridiculous.

On the eve of departure from the AFL-CIO, Reuther sought to get former CIO unions to join his march but received no support from them. (The Chemical Union was from the old AFL.) One of the former CIO leaders who tried to dissuade Reuther was I. W. Abel, then head of the Steelworkers.

Reuther and several associates went to Pittsburgh to discuss disaffiliation with the steel officers, Abel recounted. He and an associate "spent the greater part of a night trying to talk them out of that foolish step, but Walter was pretty much determined.

"Walter at that stage was pretty much taking the position that those of us who had CIO backgrounds were almost morally obligated to go along with him," Abel said. "But we made it plain that we had no intention of doing it. Our real motive was to try to dissuade Walter from taking the step."

Reuther's problem, Abel felt, "was ninety-nine percent personal," although "there might have been, here and there, a difference of philosophy—but there wasn't that much difference. There were very few things with any substance to them; that's why none of the old CIO people followed him out.

"George never made any move to hinder or throw roadblocks at Walter's feet. I think we had a situation where Walter felt that he was the so-called minority spokesman, and so when George made a speech [in the Council], Walter made a speech. When George took a position on something, Walter had to take a little different position to keep reminding everybody that there was the AFL and there was the CIO, that George spoke for one and he spoke for the other.

"But George displayed a tremendous amount of diplomacy. Once in a while he'd get a little gruff, and there was a certain amount of irritant in this thing all the time. Most of the time he would just accept it as a matter of fact that Walter would have to have his say; he let him have his say, and that was it. Jim Carey was more of an irritant than Walter was. Jim just played the devil's advocate; he deliberately tried to aggravate George, and he did a pretty good job of it. But, in spite of that, I don't think Meany let any deep animosity develop; he just accepted Jim Carey pretty much as a little terrier snapping at his heels. He wouldn't hit too hard and couldn't get near him."

Abel recalled Reuther's attempts to hold caucuses of CIO members of the Council to enable him to be "the CIO spokesman." As for Abel's own relations with Meany, he said there had been "no reason for any difference; I have always found him very amenable."

Jacob Potofsky, of the CIO Amalgamated Clothing Workers, recalled a meeting in New York convened by Reuther just before the UAW left the Federation. Officers of various national unions heard Reuther explain his reasons for quitting and his plea that they disaffiliate also. Potofsky told Reuther: "Walter, I advise you against it. If you walk, you're going to walk alone. We are not going to follow you."

"That was the sentiment of all of the CIO unions," Potofsky recalled. He felt that the reason no CIO union went with Reuther was that Meany had "handled the situation in such a way that the merger was real and people adjusted themselves." He said that Max Greenberg, of the Retail, Wholesale and Department Store Union, was another leader at the meeting who urged Reuther not to walk.

The perceptive Paul Hall offered this explanation of the difference between Reuther and Meany:

"The Number One basic difference, in my view, would be in the training, trade-union-wise. Not only did Reuther come to be the president of a tremendous union, but, in the process, he had to go through a lot of infighting—brutal infighting for union leadership. I don't think Walter was ever able to kick that. George Meany could look at that

Council and see a group of equals, Indian chiefs—I'm not downing the Council members, but it is a descriptive word—and see a bunch of people who had to be reconciled on a given issue. I think that when Walter would look over that group he would see them as so many people who would fall one way and some, another. He would try to think how to con them into doing what he wanted.

"I was an admirer of Reuther; I didn't agree with all the things he did. He was a brilliant tactician, but he couldn't ever rise above ground level and take an overview. George can take an overview. It's great to have a person around who isn't a partisan, because a partisan can only see a worm's eye view of any beef, no matter how worthy it may be.

"Reuther, with all of his tremendous oratorical ability and his brilliance—and he had them—could never rise above a situation and say, well, now wait a minute, here are a lot of guys who have honest differences and it's my job not to club anybody or to maneuver them into a situation to get a unanimous vote or a majority. George always knew that the ideal situation was to get agreement and accord. Reuther was the great tactician and Meany was the great strategist. Meany went after the big things. Walter talked a great game on the great big things—and I'm sure had every hope and desire to accomplish them—but the task of coordinating all these Indian chiefs was such that, rather than putting them together into one good team, he had that quality of breaking them apart."

Meany never called his followers into a pre-meeting caucus to map strategy or seek their votes, even when Reuther used that system in early AFL-CIO days, Hall said. Immediately after merger, he noticed a definite swing of former CIO members of the Council from Reuther to Meany:

"George never said to a Council member, 'Why don't you go along with me on an issue rather than with Reuther?' or courted a fellow, or caucused the guys to gang up on somebody. Nevertheless, in a period of time you could watch the shift. . . . It was quite clear in a pretty short period of time that the guy to whom they were looking for the real hard-nosed facts and the real setting-out of positions, was no longer Walter; it was George. George never lifted a finger to do that . . . he never changed a bit. This was a difference in the quality of leadership.

"The kind of leadership that Walter had was a great leadership . . . but he hadn't finished his education. He had just gotten partway through school, but unfortunately he thought he had graduated summa cum laude. . . . The difference was that old George had not only gotten through high school and college, he got his doctorate in human relations."

As for why he thought Reuther left the AFL-CIO, Hall put it this way:

"I just don't think Walter, who obviously couldn't sell certain points of view—none of which were terribly important—could accept the fact that either he didn't have a good case or he had not made a good case. Walter always enchanted and convinced Walter. It wasn't really George—but George was a personification of his frustration. Reuther could not conceive that George Meany could legitimately and properly prevail on the issues that Reuther thought should have been decided otherwise. Walter couldn't accept the fact that maybe George had the better idea or was the better man or was a combination of both."

Reuther's frustration over Meany's improved health was the real reason for the UAW's departure, in the opinion of Iron Workers President John H. Lyons:

"George Meany kept getting healthier. George for a time was looking very bad and acting very aged, with that hip and so forth. Then he had the operation and about a year later he looked fifteen years younger, and acted younger and just as sharp. I think Reuther's withdrawal related more to pique than to anything else. When we really got down and analyzed all of the issues, and put the 'white paper' out, there were no real fundamental issues there . . . no real meat to any of those issues.

"I really don't think, though, that if anything would have happened to Meany in those years that Reuther would ever have been elected. It wasn't just a former-AFL-versus-CIO issue; it was just that too many people in the labor movement couldn't buy Walter Reuther and where they felt that Walter Reuther would take the labor movement."

One of Reuther's problems was his failure to meet socially with other members of the Council, something he apparently thought was a waste of time. Joseph Keenan worked with Reuther for years but felt he didn't really know him because, "he never played golf, he never played cards and you never got to be with him." Keenan thought Reuther had no chance of succeeding Meany even had Meany stepped down, that Reuther couldn't even get the support of other former CIO leaders.

In Council meetings, Saul Miller, AFL-CIO information director, recalled, "Reuther lectured at them and hectored at them a little bit, but he didn't understand that these were fellow union presidents, regardless of whether the union was big or tiny. Meany understands all of this and takes it into context; everybody's opinion is worth something, everybody gets a chance to sound off."

A comparison of Reuther's break and that of John L. Lewis in 1935 emerged at a press conference in August 1969. The AFL-CIO Chemical Workers had just joined the UAW–Teamsters Alliance, the only convert. A reporter asked Meany if the Alliance would result in a major split such as the Lewis move in creating the CIO.

> That's the purpose of it; whether it succeeds or not, I don't know. I don't see any signs of any great success. . . . You take the program of this ALA—if there is any validity to this argument of the AFL-CIO failing in those areas, why wasn't that argument presented to the AFL-CIO? None of the things that he listed as a list of grievances was presented. He never used his position as head of our Economic Policy Committee, as head of our Organizing Committee, as head of the Industrial Union Department (he had carte blanche, nobody interfered with him there); he didn't use his membership on the Council to try to promote these programs. Now he has had the ALA for a year or so—where are the programs? I don't know. . . .
>
> I think that he is interested only in being head of an organization. He would like to be the whole thing. I think so.

When a reporter commented that Reuther already was head of the industrial department, Meany replied, "That wasn't the organization that he wanted to be head of." Why couldn't Reuther win the support of other Council members from the CIO?

> Well, you see, he issued all these administrative letters criticizing. He gave the impression that he was fighting for these things inside the movement. There were twenty-nine men sitting there who knew this wasn't true; every single one of them knew it. . . . That includes everybody from the old CIO. . . . He just became impatient.

The Alliance struggled along almost unnoticed. From the start, Frank Fitzsimmons of the Teamsters kept a close watch on Reuther's programs—and was armed with veto power over the other major partner. The two founders had equal membership on the board, equal voting power, in this strange alliance of such different philosophies.

Reuther was killed in a small-plane crash May 9, 1970. On learning of the tragedy, Meany issued a statement saying: "This is tragic news.

Walter Reuther has made a unique and lasting contribution to the Auto Workers, the American labor movement and the nation. We had disagreements but we worked together as well, and this morning it is the latter that stands out in my memory. All of the labor movement will join in mourning his death and that of Mrs. Reuther."

By early 1972 the Alliance had folded. Afterward, the leadership of the Auto Workers collaborated with the AFL-CIO on legislative efforts and otherwise but had not reaffiliated by the time of Meany's death. Meany made it clear that he felt the Teamsters under Fitzsimmons remained unacceptable. The Chemical Workers reaffiliated with the Federation in 1971.

NIXON AND LABOR

*Nixon was smart and sharp in a lot of ways, but he didn't have balance.
There was something lacking there—look at the way he handled himself
when they discovered those tapes. He went around making speeches denying
this, and then had to admit it; it looked real stupid at the time. I never had
any faith in him, never trusted him, never had any confidence in him as an
individual. You got to know Nixon and he was shifty, he was real tricky.*

After Johnson's speech on March 30, 1968, announcing his intention
not to seek re-election, Meany surprised everyone with his own sudden
move:

Johnson pulled out at the end of March sixty-eight. I saw him at
the White House a couple of days before that; he was at a building-
trades conference the week before and up until that announcement
on Sunday I had no reason to believe he was going to pull out.

When he said he was not going to run, that left things in a mess.
Gene [Senator Eugene J.] McCarthy was campaigning; Bobby Kennedy had jumped in and announced his candidacy. Lane [Kirkland]
and I went over to see Hubert Humphrey and got him to agree he
would run.

In order to bring some order out of the chaos, I announced on behalf of myself and Lane that we [as individuals] were going to support Humphrey. Johnson had left things pretty much in a state of
confusion and we didn't have a chance to call a meeting or anything.
My announcement gave a lot of our people a chance to say to Bobby

Kennedy, "We can't go with you, we have to wait now." Bobby Kennedy was really twisting arms, putting the pressure on individuals, presidents of unions and so forth. McCarthy was putting on pressure, too.

Finally, the AFL-CIO [officially] did support Humphrey and he came very near being elected. He would have been elected that year except he was torpedoed by McCarthy.*

Actually, Humphrey did not have the solid support of the Democratic party. A lot of them were sort of sitting it out. He had solid labor support, but he did not have the solid support of the party, and we always felt that if he had had it he would have been elected.

The Democratic Convention was really a disorderly affair. I was in Chicago. The left-wingers set out to make a shambles of it. They sure did—with what they did \at the hotel and marching up and down Michigan Boulevard and fighting with police. They were really goading the police, spitting at them, determined to create incidents, and the television cameras were there to record those incidents.

When the demonstrations continued around the country during the 1968 campaign, Meany declared: "Humphrey's campaign has been hampered by a concerted, well-planned and well-financed attempt to drown out his voice and his reasoned discussion. In state after state, the same groups of loud-mouthed disrupters—calling themselves liberals—have attempted to keep their fellow citizens from even hearing Humphrey's words."

Another factor that cut into Humphrey's labor vote was the third-party candidacy of Alabama Governor George C. Wallace, who captured some union members' backing, as Meany conceded on "Meet the Press" that September:

The candidates' speeches in the campaign often conceal and camouflage a good deal more about the candidates than they reveal. [George Wallace] makes the same speech every evening, I think, and maybe two or three times during the day—his speech is directed toward all the gripes and all of the grievances that the people of America have. . . .

We do have some evidence that our [union] people are being deceived by Wallace. Wallace pretends to be one thing, but we know Wallace's record. We know the standard of life in Birmingham, Ala-

---

* Robert Kennedy had been assassinated in June.

bama. We know how the Negro and minority groups live in Alabama. We identify Wallace for what he is. And he is a racist, there is
no question about that. He has proved this over the years. Still we
will concede that, along with other Americans, a lot of our members
perhaps are going to be deceived by Mr. Wallace.

In that interview, Meany was asked if he thought Humphrey should
declare his independence from the Johnson Administration:

> I don't think that is necessary at all, and I don't see politically how
> it is possible. After all, there is such a thing as the Johnson-
> Humphrey Administration. If you think a man can run for Presi-
> dent of the United States by repudiating his own Administration, I
> don't buy that at all.

A Gallup Poll showing Wallace with 15 percent of worker-family
support two months before the election occasioned a special AFL-CIO
effort to inform its member of the Governor's record on low wages and
other issues. The same poll gave Humphrey 42 percent labor backing,
with Richard Nixon at 35 percent nationally.

AFL-CIO leaflets widely distributed among workers were aimed at
the Wallace candidacy. Meany praised Humphrey in many speeches
to labor gatherings and over the networks. Talking to one union convention, he outlined his essential position:

> In the last eight years this nation of ours has taken a new di-
> rection, a new forward step, new forward progress, based on human
> values. The question we face as trade unionists in this coming elec-
> tion is, do we want to continue this forward march or do we want to
> accept a fellow like Richard Nixon to lead us? . . .
> His record is there for us to see. We know this man. Nixon helped
> to write the Taft-Hartley Act, and he bragged about it in 1947,
> when he was a freshman in Congress. . . . We keep a score sheet. His
> record shows 59 unfavorable votes and 10 favorable votes. . . . On
> that record, in the years that Hubert Humphrey served in the
> United States Senate, we kept track of 199 votes over a period of 13
> or 14 years. On those 199 votes Hubert Humphrey voted favorably
> to labor 199 times. That is the record. . . .
> Then there is another fellow, who is waging a campaign of hate
> and fear, who promises the American people a police state. . . . To
> me this man represents the very first threat that I have seen . . . of
> fascism in America. We can't afford to have that kind of man. We

are not going to have him, but we can't afford to have Nixon, either.
I tell you that a vote for Wallace is a vote for Nixon. . . .

The get-out-the-vote campaign waged by the AFL-CIO for the 1968 election was termed "unprecedented in American history" by Theodore H. White, the student of Presidential campaigns. White reported that some 4.6 million people were registered to vote through COPE's campaign, 115 million leaflets were printed, more than 24,000 union members manned 638 telephone banks to urge voters to the polls, more than 72,000 volunteers made door-to-door canvasses, and nearly 95,-000 served as drivers, baby-sitters, leaflet distributors and poll watchers on election day.

But the surge for Humphrey fell a fraction of a percent short of success. (Another week, Meany opined, would have put Humphrey over the top.) In any event, Nixon and Spiro T. Agnew were elected, both to leave office in disgrace. But the Democrats retained control of both houses of Congress.

Soon after the election, Meany was invited to meet with the President-elect in his hotel suite in New York:

> I went in there and saw stone-faced [John N.] Mitchell. That's the first time I met him. He was sitting there like a lump of granite, no smile on his face. Nixon was sort of exuberant, sort of bounding around. He talked about a number of things without much meaning, and then he talked about our situs picketing [legislation].* He called in Bryce Harlow and said, "Don't you think we had better get that situs picketing bill [enacted]? I think the building trades certainly helped." He talked about how he hoped to get along with labor, and all that, and he talked specifically about the situs picketing bill.
>
> Then he introduced me to Rose Mary Woods [his secretary] and that was that. It [the meeting] was nothing.

In the introduction, Nixon had remarked, "She's a Catholic, too, George." Recalling that incident, Meany snorted, "What the hell was that? As if that was important to me! What did I care what she was?"

Possible candidates to head the Labor Department were not dis-

---

* The situs picketing legislation was aimed at reversing a U.S. Supreme Court decision barring picketing of a subcontractor at more than one gate on a construction site. Presidents Eisenhower, Kennedy and Johnson had promised to sign the bill if Congress passed it, and Nixon gave the same assurance. (The Taft-Hartley section on which the decision was based still is in the law.)

cussed at the meeting. "We never mentioned Secretary of Labor at all. This was shortly after the election and I hadn't the slightest idea who was going to be Secretary. Three weeks later, I guess, he announced George P. Shultz as Secretary of Labor." Meany continued:

> I had never met him that I know of. I might have been at a meeting when he was present. I had heard of him; he was fairly well-known as an economist at the University of Chicago at that time. He had been an arbitrator and mediator in labor disputes. He made a good Labor Secretary.

Despite disagreements on policies, especially on the legal minimum wage, which Shultz opposed, Meany and Shultz became good friends. In their frequent golf games, economic issues were never discussed, Meany said. The President used Shultz as his ambassador to the labor movement because he, himself, had no rapport with most union leaders, Meany thought.

The fears and misgivings labor had about Nixon stemmed from his background in politics:

> I never trusted Nixon. He was very clever, and just an opportunist. I don't think he was ever sincerely anti or pro anything. When he ran for public office the first time, in California [in 1946], he ran against a liberal [congressman]; the Cold War was just starting after World War II. That was a conservative district and he raised the specter of Communist control; he called [his opponent] Jerry Voorhis a Communist.
>
> He got in and became active in the [House] Un-American [Activities] Committee, and when he ran for the Senate [in 1950] he said that Helen Gahagan Douglas [his opponent] was a Communist too. It was the time, it was the way to get votes. So he got votes and [was] elected to the Senate. He got in with Eisenhower as Vice President—and gradually got away from this anti-Communist stuff.
>
> Finally, after he became President, he wanted to project his image as the great man of peace, so, then his answer to communism was detente—live and let live. He came full circle.

As a peace gesture on a grand scale, Nixon sent a squad of senior officals of the Labor Department, led by Secretary Shultz, to Florida to talk to the AFL-CIO Council at its winter meeting a month after the inauguration. The question of wage controls was at issue—the centerpiece of Nixon's anti-inflation campaign—and the press was eager to know what position Meany would take.

Meany's reply included a reference to earlier Council statements on the subject: "We are not suggesting this; we are saying that if the President of the United States decides that the international situation warrants it," labor would go along. Any controls, he added, should cover "all forms of income and all forms of selling prices on all articles— wholesale and retail."

Nixon's apparent policy on unemployment, which—like controls— later developed into a heated controversy with labor, also came up at the February press conference. Meany was asked about a statement by Paul W. McCracken, chairman of the President's Council of Economic Advisers, suggesting that a slight rise in unemployment might be needed to get economic stability. Meany included Treasury Secretary David M. Kennedy in his reply:

> I don't buy the idea that we have to make that sort of sacrifice in order to achieve a stable economy. I don't buy that idea at all and I don't care whether it is McCracken's idea or David Kennedy's. I don't accept the idea that we have got to conquer inflation by putting more people out of work. I think there is something wrong with a society that seriously contemplates something like that.

Asked for his own inflation-fighting suggestion, Meany said, "I recommend full employment. . . . We have had a Full Employment Act since 1946; let them implement it. I don't think they'd have these problems."

At the same Council meeting, Shultz presented Meany with a letter from the President which appeared to contradict McCracken's comments on employment. The key paragraph, to be quoted frequently by Meany, was:

"We must find a way to curb inflation, which robs working men and women and their families of hard-earned gains. And we must do this without asking the wage earners to pay for the cost of stability with their jobs."

Meany told reporters he thought the Nixon assurance was directed at statements by Secretary Kennedy to the effect that he hoped to curb inflation with a minimal increase in joblessness. The letter, Meany said, "pretty well states our position that we should not ask the wage earners to pay for the cost of economic stability and the halting of the inflation spiral by losing their jobs."

In another friendship bid, top Administration officials attended a three-day conference of the AFL-CIO in White Sulphur Springs, West Virginia, in April. The objective was to exchange views, but neither side was persuaded by the other's arguments. The unprecedented meeting was never repeated, in any administration.

Still another briefing—this time including a talk by Nixon—followed the next month when Meany and twenty-two other Council members spent ninety minutes at the White House discussing a variety of issues with high officials. Meany told reporters that Nixon had "said nice things" about organized labor and had seemed concerned about American workers losing their jobs when U.S. companies moved their factories to Mexico.

But all the attention from the White House did not stop the AFL-CIO Council from complaining publicly only a week after that briefing that Nixon's tax reform proposals would not do enough to relieve the tax burden on middle-income Americans. Meany commented that Nixon was proceeding cautiously, "maybe too cautiously" on some problems.

Administration policies still were confusing in the fall of 1969, Meany explained when asked in a news conference to "size up" the Nixon record:

> Well, I have been trying and trying—and waiting and waiting—
> and up to the present time I just can't size it up. He seems to come
> out with statements, he has a little bit for everybody, even if you are
> on opposite sides. . . .

Reiterating his support of the Administration on Vietnam, Meany scoffed at a suggestion by Labor Secretary Shultz that labor leaders should modify their wage demands because inflation would not continue forever and high-cost contracts would price employers and union members out of the market. Saying he did not "buy that," Meany admitted there might be some logic in the suggestion but said that if Shultz were the head of a big union and made such observations to his members, he would not be head of the union next year. It is a practical situation, he added, and members insist on getting more money to meet inflationary prices.

Meany's riposte was an AFL-CIO campaign for still another new idea: national health insurance, as he mentioned in a 1969 speech:

> Now, we have no objection to people making a decent income—doctors, or anyone else. How could we object? It is the very purpose of the labor movement to try to obtain decent incomes for as many people as possible. So we think that doctors deserve to get an adequate income commensurate with their talents and their services.
>
> But we think there is something indecent about a small group of people making a lot of money out of the misery of other people. And I am afraid that is what is happening in America today. This indefensible escalation of medical costs is depriving millions of Americans of the health care they need.
>
> This profiteering by the providers of medical care has had its worst effects in Medicare and Medicaid. Labor fought hard for the establishment of these two programs. Although they are somewhat different, they both have a single goal—to provide medical care to people who cannot afford to pay for it themselves. . . .
>
> But what has been happening? Some doctors and other health practitioners have pounced on these programs as if they had been legislated as get-rich schemes for the medical profession. And, instead of controls being placed on fees and charges paid under these programs, the burden has fallen on the disadvantaged people the programs were supposed to help. . . .
>
> There is an answer. It is one the labor movement has advanced for many years, but we are more determined to achieve it today than ever before. That answer is national health insurance, a program that would provide comprehensive health care for every American.

The first showdown between the Federation and the Nixon White House came in August 1969—over Nixon's nomination of Judge Clement F. Haynsworth, Jr., to the Supreme Court. The historic clash demonstrated the AFL-CIO president's willingness to take on a fight against extremely heavy odds, for not since 1930 had organized labor sought to interfere with a High Court appointment. Labor at that time, with the National Association for the Advancement of Colored People, blocked Herbert Hoover's elevation of Judge John J. Parker to the Court.

The Haynsworth showdown evolved in this way, Meany recalled:

> Nixon nominated Haynsworth for the Supreme Court, and we took that on. That, to us, was sort of a declaration of war. We looked

up Haynsworth's record. He was very closely connected with the southern industrial complex, which is headed up pretty much by the J. P. Stevens Corporation. His record as a judge didn't show him to be what we thought was the type of man who should sit on the Supreme Court—the racist overtones and the whole background.

We just went out and worked about as hard as we could. We assigned [Thomas E.] Harris, our house legal counsel, to look up this thing, and he fed material to senators. I testified before the Judiciary Committee over in the Senate. All the rest of 1969, we were campaigning and getting votes against Haynsworth. We went all out and we came up with the votes.

Hell, by the time our convention was held in September of sixty-nine, in Atlantic City, we had forty votes pledged and twenty-five still in the doubtful stage. During that convention, I can remember going to the telephone to call senators during the morning, afternoon and evening.

The night before the vote was taken we had an absolutely accurate count; we knew where every vote was going except four.

Before that battle began, rumors had alerted the AFL-CIO to the impending appointment. Judge Haynsworth's federal court record was familiar to the labor movement because of his rulings against the Textile Workers Union and in favor of textile corporations.

Meany sent a letter to Nixon explaining the evidence that the AFL-CIO had gathered against the nominee. Later, when the appointment was announced officially, more protests immediately went to the White House from labor, civil rights organizations and others. Leaders of black organizations such as the NAACP privately expressed doubts that the appointment could be blocked in the Senate, but Meany insisted on making the effort. The Leadership Conference on Civil Rights, in which the AFL-CIO was a key member, spoke out against the nomination on behalf of its black, labor, religious and civic organizations.

At the start of the planning, publicist Albert Zack recalled, Meany asked his chief lobbyist, Andrew Biemiller, "Andy, how many votes would we get automatically?" Biemiller replied, "About eight." When Meany asked, "If we worked hard could we get sixteen?" Biemiller agreed. "So, if we worked very hard could we get twenty-four?" Again, agreement. "Let's work even harder than that," Meany concluded.

Meany's own judgment on the relative importance of the evidence against Haynsworth proved to be correct, according to Thomas Harris. One line of attack was to point up evidence of a conflict of interest, while the other was to stress the judge's decisions on labor and civil rights cases. Meany thought the conflict of interest angle would carry more weight with the senators, as it did. Labor, however, presented both lines of evidence in its testimony.*

Meany's subsequent sparring match with Chairman Sam J. Ervin, Jr., before the Senate Judiciary Committee was the first serious blow to Haynsworth's nomination. Ervin, a lawyer, had once represented the Darlington Mills textile firm in a case before the U.S. Supreme Court and was expected to be sympathetic to the nomination.

Under questioning by Ervin, Meany admitted not knowing that the Darlington firm began operations in 1886, prompting the Senator to tell him, "Well, that is a fact." Meany's retort was, "I don't remember it."

"Well, don't you know it failed in 1937?"

"No, I did not; I am sorry to hear that."

Ervin wondered if Meany knew that the firm "had a very rocky road, economically."

"I don't know. I know the people that worked for the mill had a very rocky road."

The Senator launched into a long explanation, filling a printed page, and then asked a question, bringing Meany's reply: "I don't know. You lost me about 20 minutes ago. You read a 30-minute speech and then you want me to express an opinion about it."

When Ervin demanded to know whether Meany contended there was any bias in Judge Haynsworth's opinion in a 1961 Darlington Mills case, he was told:

"You argued the case before the Supreme Court and now you are still speaking for your client. The lawyer for the other side is here and if you want to retry the case, try it with him."

The Senator replied that he was "not speaking for my client" but as a Senator. He said he had had no connection with the Darlington case since 1964.

---

* In preparing the case, Harris remembered that the Textile Workers Union, in an earlier case that Haynsworth had decided for the company, had received an anonymous tip that the judge had a conflict of interest. According to the report, not verified at the time, Haynsworth owned a financial interest in a firm that was profiting from its vending machines placed in the textile mills of the chain having controlling interest in the Darlington, S.C., mill involved in the court case. This objection developed into a major factor in Haynsworth's rejection by the Senate.

As to why the AFL-CIO opposed Haynsworth, Meany testified in part:

> In the final analysis, we believe the crucial test is whether the nominee is fit to sit on the nation's highest court. By that yardstick, we say Judge Haynsworth should not be confirmed. . . . His decisions prove him to be anti-labor. He has demonstrated indifference to the legitimate aspirations of Negroes. He has demonstrated a lack of ethical standards, while on the bench, that [disqualifies] him from consideration for promotion. . . .
>
> We submit that Judge Haynsworth lacks the ethical sensitivity a Supreme Court Justice should have. He sat on a case involving an old client. He had a large interest in a concern that was doing business with that client, and was soliciting more business. He did not tell the union of these interests and he did not disqualify himself.

Meany told the 1969 AFL-CIO convention that the nomination was part of the Nixon "Southern strategy" aimed at re-election in 1972:

> Nowhere is this new Southern strategy . . . more apparent than in the nomination of a mediocre jurist from South Carolina to the United States Supreme Court. . . .
>
> During his twelve years on the federal bench, Judge Haynsworth sat on seven cases involving labor-management relations which have been reviewed by the United States Supreme Court. In all of these seven cases Judge Haynsworth took the anti-labor position. In all seven cases Judge Haynsworth's position was repudiated by the United States Supreme Court. In six of the seven cases the reversal was unanimous. In the seventh case one lone Supreme Court justice supported the position of Judge Haynsworth.
>
> This means that Judge Haynsworth's philosophy on labor-management problems is out of tune with that of all segments of the Supreme Court, liberal and moderate as well as conservative.
>
> But the most important of our charges is that Judge Haynsworth has displayed a disregard for those ethical standards we believe essential for a justice of the highest court of the land. Judge Haynsworth had a major conflict of interest in a labor-management case, the Darlington case, involving an affiliate of the AFL-CIO. He did not disclose his financial interest to the union litigant or apparently to his colleagues on the court. He cast a deciding vote on behalf of the employer and against the union. . . .
>
> [Despite various disclosures] the Justice Department . . . continues

its refusal to see anything improper in his actions. The Attorney General [Mitchell] tried to minimize the seriousness of the opposition by saying that any nomination would have been attacked even if one of the twelve apostles had been nominated.

Speaking for the AFL-CIO, I might point out to the Attorney General that we did not in any way oppose the nomination of Chief Justice [Warren E.] Burger, quite well-known as an eminent jurist, albeit somewhat of a conservative.... This statement about the twelve apostles is rather an unfortunate analogy. It might be said that if the twelve apostles were all brilliant lawyers, had been editors of the Harvard Law Review and clerks to the Supreme Court justices, and were recommended by the Bar Association, Mr. Mitchell still would not have regarded any of them as eligible for the post.

In the first place, they were all poor. Furthermore, they preached the philosophy that a rich man could no more enter the Kingdom of Heaven than the camel could pass through the eye of a needle. They were the followers of a humble carpenter, and they were dedicated to the cause of the meek, the lowly and the underprivileged. They were quite obviously unsuitable for the post, any post, under this Administration.

And with their ethnic background they would even have had a hard time getting by [South Carolina Senator] Strom Thurmond.

Blocking Haynsworth seemed almost impossible, but Meany was determined, as a matter of principle, to press the fight. He got deeply into the action himself, with telephone calls to senators and trips to the Hill to talk to them individually. Any senator appearing at the AFL-CIO convention, an aide recalled, was taken into a side room by Meany and asked where he stood on Haynsworth. Senator Fred Harris was one who got a long Meany lecture why "that is one that can't be ducked." Harris voted Meany's way.

In the end, Haynsworth was rejected by a 55 to 45 vote on November 21, 1969.

Nixon's next choice was another southern federal judge, G. Harrold Carswell, of the Fifth Circuit Court of Appeals. When it was announced in January 1960, nearly everyone expected the appointment to go through; many senators would not want to cast a second vote against a court nominee. But Meany said, "His record as a racist was worse than that of Haynsworth."

AFL-CIO staff members were unable to find enough labor-management cases handled by Carswell to show his position in that field, but they knew his record on civil rights cases. The NAACP had gathered the evidence in protesting Carswell's elevation to the federal appeals bench.

That record and other material gathered by the staff was shown to Meany by Zack, who explained that some of the Federation staff thought labor should sit out this fight after winning the only two challenges in this century. The AFL-CIO, staffers felt, should not jeopardize its record by trying another challenge.

"Oh, hell, two out of three isn't a bad record!" Meany exclaimed. "We've got to fight this guy."

Zack said, "It was really Meany who started that fight when all the others didn't have any stomach for it at all."

A draft of a statement criticizing Carswell, but not mentioning what the AFL-CIO would do about it, was shown to Meany, who added a tough conclusion. It accused the President of "still using Supreme Court nominations for partisan political advantage, instead of seeking a justice worthy to wear the mantle of Holmes, Brandeis or Warren." He added: "On the basis of what we know of Judge Carswell's background and philosophy, we believe he does not meet the high standards for Supreme Court membership. We are opposed to his confirmation. We hope he is rejected by the Senate."

One reason for Meany's decision to make the fight was revealed later when a reporter asked him if he had any evidence that Carswell was anti-labor. The reply: "No, except my long experience indicating that a judge who is anti-Negro is also anti-labor."

Biemiller remembered that when Meany asked him how many votes there were against Carswell, he replied, "I don't know. Having just licked Haynsworth, it will be a letdown and there may be trouble." Meany said, "I don't care if you only have five or six votes, I want that fight made. He's no good."

In a statement to the Senate Judiciary Committee, Meany called the appointment "a slap in the face of the nation's Negro citizens," adding: "It can only be considered to be the result of a studied attempt to find a federal judge whose civil rights record is recognized by the Negro community to be even worse than Haynsworth's was shown to be."

An added push for the labor campaign came from more than 400 prominent attorneys—including deans of twenty-three university law schools—who issued a statement holding that Carswell "does not have the legal or mental qualifications essential for service on the Supreme Court." The entire law faculty of some schools joined in the declaration; in all, there were 334 law professors from forty-five universities.

Finally, on the eve of the Senate vote, Meany wrote each Senator: "It is now entirely clear that Judge Carswell is anti-Negro and is utterly without distinction as a judge and a lawyer. His 1948 white-supremacy diatribe has repeatedly been affirmed, not repudiated, by his actions." Meany was referring to remarks attributed to Carswell favoring racial segregation.

Senators voted 51 to 45 to reject the nomination. Nixon soon appointed Judge Harry A. Blackmun, of Minnesota, who was confirmed 94 to 0. Meany filed no complaint on that appointment.

Ironically, while Meany was fighting to keep so-called racists off the Supreme Court, the Administration was accusing the AFL-CIO building trades of racist tendencies in hiring for construction projects. On June 27, 1969, the Labor Department unveiled its Philadelphia Plan, supposed to become a model for other cities.

Under its provisions, a contractor bidding on a project financed by federal funds had to promise to make a good-faith attempt to meet a "goal" of black employment based on the ratio of white-black population of the city. Meany described to reporters why the AFL-CIO Council opposed the plan:

> The general view of the Council members is that the plan won't work. It's directed toward seven trades in the construction industry—seven highly-skilled trades. . . . The reason we feel it won't work is that, very frankly, there are not enough [black] members—even though these unions do have apprenticeship programs and are training numbers of non-whites.'. . .
>
> There is another question: the question of whether or not this order does not violate the provisions of the Civil Rights Act of 1964, which takes a firm stand against using a quota system. . . . We believe it is a quota system, although they try to conceal it. . . .
>
> But, the practical problem is how do you get [specified] percentages of non-whites in these skilled trades? No matter what the attitude of the union, no matter how friendly the union may be to the idea, how do you get them on the job when [non-whites] just don't exist in the area . . . who have gone through the apprenticeship program and who have attained these particular skills. . . .
>
> Do you say to the contractor, put on people who are not skilled? Well, of course, this is completely impossible because the contractor couldn't possibly do his job that way. He has to bid for his work and if he doesn't have skilled people to do the work he certainly would not be able to meet his cost estimates, as far as labor costs are concerned.

Meany attacked Labor Department figures on the number of blacks already in these construction unions in a speech:

> I believe it is necessary that we set the record straight if we are going to end discrimination and go beyond it and expand real opportunities for minority citizens and youth. . . . I don't know where these [government] figures are pulled from, but in practically every case we investigate we find that they are not accurate. . . .
>
> Then here is another misconception that you hear about the construction industry: that it has very few minority members and those that they do admit are put in only what they call the poorly-paid and dirty jobs. Well, I don't know what they mean by poorly-paid jobs. The lowest pay that I can find in the Philadelphia area . . . is $4.25 an hour, and that is the lowest paid laborer—not all laborers, but the lowest paid laborer. And as far as their being put on the dirty jobs, well, I don't know of any clean jobs in the construction industry, and I have been around quite a while—they are all dirty jobs.
>
> When the Equal Employment Opportunity Commission began to study white-collar jobs in major industries, they found out (and I want to stress this) in every city that they looked at, that minority group participation was lower in white-collar industries than it was among the blue-collar skilled groups. . . .
>
> But still we find the building trades singled out as being "lily white," as they say, and some fellow the other day said it was "the last bastion of discrimination." Now this is an amazing statement, when you figure how small the participation of Negroes and other minorities is in, for instance, the banks of this country, in the press, on the payroll of the newspapers and the communications media, and I think there is one Negro in the United States Senate. . . .
>
> I resent the action of government officials—no matter what department they come from—who are trying to make a whipping boy out of the building trades.

One day Meany asked Donald Slaiman, then the director of the Federation's civil rights department, to give him all of the material he had on the Philadelphia Plan. When Slaiman produced it—"thousands of pages of material"—and explained, "I know you can't read all of this, but I'll tell you what's in there," Meany replied, "No, give it to me. I'm going to make a speech at the National Press Club on this."

For three days Meany studied the documents and transcripts of congressional hearings, Slaiman recalled. Then Meany had Slaiman listen to the speech he had prepared—with his notes on small cards. Slaiman asked a few questions and Meany asked for more information. From those cards, Meany delivered his message to the Press Club, including these excerpts:

> I have seen more misinformation and confusion about the Philadelphia Plan from columnists, editorial writers and from public officials than anything I have seen or heard in a long time. . . .
>
> The Philadelphia Plan is a concoction and contrivance of a bureaucrat's imagination. It makes tremendous publicity. It attracted a lot of attention and when it gets right down to operating, there is no substance to it whatsoever. . . .
>
> In 1963, the Kennedy Administration gave up—and I say this advisedly—gave up on the question of including a fair-employment practice clause in the Civil Rights bill. The AFL-CIO did not give up. We went ahead on our own, with the cooperation of Clarence Mitchell of the NAACP, and we were able to have this clause included in the bill, despite the fact, as I say, that the Kennedy Administration despaired of getting that clause in. They felt they might jeopardize the bill if they insisted upon it.

The AFL-CIO had decided five or six years before the Philadelphia Plan was born, he explained, that the only way to get blacks properly into these skilled jobs was through the apprentice system.

> We found out . . . that, contrary to the opinion of a good many people, we did not have a situation where large numbers of minority groups were knocking at the door. This was just not so. . . . That is why we set up this so-called apprentice Outreach program. . . .
>
> Perhaps the biggest drawback of the [Philadelphia] Plan is that it diverts attention from the real, solid task of training and qualifying minority workers for a permanent place in the ranks of skilled workers who are available and qualified for employment on all the construction work in an area, not just the federally-financed work.
>
> So I can say to you we don't like this Plan. We feel it is political in nature. We feel that it was put forth on the basis of very poor information. . . . We won't get in its way. We know it will fall of its own dead weight. . . .
>
> We make no apology for our attitude and our work in this field. We make no attempt to deny that there was discrimination in unions, lots of unions in this country; that the trade union movement in this country really is a picture of the whole country. We

have Southern members. We have members with all sorts of prejudices, not just prejudices against the color of a person's skin.

I am convinced that [the Philadelphia Plan] was an attempt to
offset the Administration's very, very poor record on civil rights—a
very bad record over the last year—by taking a crack at the building
trades.

The Philadelphia Plan along with a rising unemployment rate nationally and other problems prompted Meany to grant a press request
for his analysis of the President's first year: "Well, I would say his first
year, from the labor standpoint, is sort of a great big 'goose egg,' as we
say in baseball." Asked then if he thought the increase in unemployment was alarming, he responded:

Yes, it is alarming because, while President Nixon said that he
was going to stop inflation without punishing the workers, without
any increase in unemployment, most of the leading economists expect an increase in unemployment as a result of the anti-inflationary
actions of the Administration. I would say that most of the members
of the Administration, including some Cabinet members, subscribe
to the idea that you cannot curb inflation without causing unem-
ploymnent. . . .
The layoffs that have been made and the announcement of future
layoffs by some of the big corporations indicate that there could be a
very sharp rise in unemployment in the next few months. . . . If it
jumped to 6 percent, that would be quite a rise, I think. The way it is
going now . . . I think that is a distinct possibility.*

The U.S. invasion of Cambodia in April of that year created an out-
burst in the country, but Meany reiterated his support of the Administration's policy of gradual withdrawal. However, his agreement with
the stated aims of Nixon and Secretary of State Henry Kissinger's policy did not deter him from pressing in on the economic front.

While Nixon was briefing the AFL-CIO Council on Cambodia,
Meany took advantage of the opportunity to give him a copy of a
Council statement, just adopted, dealing with the White House's eco-
nomic policies. As Meany told the press,

I described it briefly and gave the President a copy, and asked him
if he wouldn't read it and he said he would. I told the President that

* From 4.2 percent in February, when Meany was talking, the unemployment rate reached
5.9 percent in November of that year and 6.2 percent the following month.

it was a pretty comprehensive statement. It went into various phases of the economy—inflation, unemployment, high interest rates and so on and so forth. Also, we made some suggestions as to how we might work our way out of this situation.... He promised that he would look at it very carefully.

Did Meany, he was asked, think the statement would change the minds of Administration economists?

Well, I think eventually facts may change their mind. I am familiar with it. I have known Arthur Burns for years and the course they are following—the so-called monetary-fiscal policy, tight money, and so on and so forth—has been Arthur Burns' idea for many years as to how you should curb inflation: you curb it by preventing your economy from being over-heated or, if it is over-heated, you cool it down a little.

Now, this is his theory and this is subscribed to, I am sure, by McCracken, by Dave Kennedy and others. We point out that this theory—and it is the theory that President Nixon adopted when he went into office a year and four months ago—is not working on two counts. And on the third count it is causing great hardship.

It is not working on the question of inflation. We still have inflation. It is not working on the question of unemployment; we have rising unemployment and we were told that this would not be a condition which would prevail to the accompaniment of these monetary and fiscal policies. Insofar as the interest rate is concerned, it has practically stopped the housing industry in its tracks. We think this is bad. We think it has affected everyone in America who would like to own his own home.

In an August news conference, Meany didn't see any improvement in the economic field but found a few pluses in other Nixon actions:

I think our relations with the Nixon Administration are just about as good as we could have expected. I wouldn't say we have any romance or love-feast going on, but I think he has been responsive in some areas. Of course, he is still, I would say, much more on the conservative side of things than his predecessors Johnson and Kennedy. I would say that the relationship has been fairly good.

We, of course, agree with him to a great degree on his efforts to end the war in Southeast Asia through the building up and developing the ability of the South Vietnamese to take care of themselves. We are in agreement with that because, frankly, we don't think there is any disagreement about getting out—getting our people out of Southeast Asia. . . . But we think he has a practical plan to get them out. The plan makes sense. Whether it works or not is another thing, but, up until now, it appears to be working. . . .

We find that in the field of government employees [Nixon] has certainly been more liberal than any man in the White House before him because he has come out for collective bargaining for government employees at every level. He has come out for extending to government employees practically all of the rights that workers have and unions have in the private sector. So we think this represents progress.

On several other issues, however, Meany was critical of the President. Nixon, he said, "is obsessed with the idea of balancing the budget" by trying to cut back on educational programs enacted before he entered office. The AFL-CIO, he said, does not think "he should be balancing the budget at the expense of America's young people who need education."

Nixon also got bad marks on his civil rights policy "because he is obviously attempting to carry water on both shoulders." Meany accused him of trying to do, on the record, what civil rights groups expect, and, at the same time wanting to "keep Strom Thurmond happy" but "he just can't do both."

The political allegiance of workers is shifting to some extent, Meany told the reporters, but "not so much that people are looking to the Republicans." He thought they were "looking less to the Democrats because, actually, the Democratic Party has disintegrated." It has almost "become the party of the extremists" to the extent that the New Left group has taken over the Democratic party:

> As they take it over and as they move more and more to the left— and I mean away over to the left—I think, more and more, the Democrats are going to lose the support of our members.
>
> Our members are basically Americans. They basically believe in the American system, and maybe they have a greater stake in the system now than they had fifteen or twenty years ago, because under the system and under our trade union policy, they have become "middle-class." They have a greater stake.
>
> You can be quite radical if you are involved in a labor dispute where people are getting 30 cents an hour, because [if you pull a strike] all you lose is 30 cents an hour. But [when] you have people

who are making $8000 or $9000 a year—paying off mortgages, with kids going to college . . . you have an entirely different situation. . . . They have obligations that are quite costly—insurance payments and all that sort of thing. So this makes the strike much less desirable as a weapon.

Naturally, we wouldn't want to give it up as a weapon but I can say to you quite frankly that more and more people in the trade union movement—I mean at the highest levels—are thinking of other ways to advance without the use of the strike method.

What did he have in mind as an alternative?

Well, voluntary arbitration, for instance. . . . We don't make policy for our unions; our unions make their own policy and we try to coordinate it—but what would be wrong with a union signing an agreement for, let's say, two years and then saying that at the end of two years all the basic conditions of this agreement will prevail except wages, and that wages shall be the subject of collective bargaining? And, if, after a certain length of time there is no agreement between the parties, the American Arbitration Association will make a final and binding decision. I am not saying that this is what should be done. . . . I say this is one possible way. . . .

You are hearing a lot more people talking about [voluntary arbitration] than ever before. You see this is not compulsory arbitration because, if the two parties come to the table and agree in advance that they are going to do something, that is not compulsory. Now, of course, for many years a great many of our unions have [had] agreements with employers which refer to arbitration all items on which there is disagreement as to what the contract [means].

We have agreed to set up a small committee to meet with the representatives of the American Arbitration Association to explore this whole idea. Actually, what it adds up to is that while strikes have their part and all that—and we certainly have advocated for years that you have got to have the right to strike—we find, more and more, that strikes really don't settle a thing. . . . Where you have a well-established industry and a well-established union, you are getting . . . to the point where a strike doesn't make sense. . . .

When you have an area where an employer doesn't want to have anything to do with a union, or listen, then, of course, you have to strike. But those areas are certainly not as numerous as they were some years ago.

Another subject at the news conference was the relation between the Administration's first "inflation alert" and the National Commission on Productivity, created by Nixon that July. Meany, one of the panel's twenty-three members, revealed the dispute that arose when the Commission was asked to make public somebody else's "alert":

> There is no relation, really, between the Productivity Commission and the so-called "inflation alert," despite the way the President connected them. . . . I can say to you that there is unanimous feeling on the Productivity Commission—and it is the one thing that they have agreed to so far in the one-day meeting—that they should not be the medium to release the inflation alerts that are prepared by McCracken and the Council of Economic Advisers. . . .
>
> The Commission still has the function of exploring the whole question of productivity to see, (1) what can be done to spur industries where they are not really working at this question of trying to increase productivity, and (2) to explore what ways and means there might be for government to help in this area of increasing productivity. We have no quarrel, as far as labor is concerned, with this approach. If productivity can be increased, fine. . . . The Commission is made up of people from the trade union movement, people from business, people from government and people from the general public.

Did the government members go along with the decision?

> Yes, without question. This thing is open and shut. We sit down and we are told by the President that we are to release this inflation alert. We have never seen it. We have never seen a draft of it. We are at our first meeting and in comes McCracken and opens the thing up and, in effect, delivers it to us. But we haven't had a chance to read it or anything, and then he goes through a ten-minute or fifteen-minute resume of what is in this document, which measures 188 pages. Now, the response of the Commission was: Do what you want with it but don't saddle us with it because we had nothing to do with it.
>
> Now, on the other hand, if they wanted us to take this thing and study it for a month and then do our own research to try and justify it, that would be different. But the way the thing was worded—and this came out of the President's statement when he announced he was going to set up the Commission—we would release the inflation alert.

What was Meany's personal opinion of the alert document?

I did not get a chance to read it. I thumbed through it very quickly and I found what I was looking for and what I was suspicious of—that this was a device of McCracken and others to put pressure on certain areas of the economy—either on the workers' side or on the employers' side. I . . . saw what I expected would be in there, and that was a paragraph about construction workers. It was a very, very short paragraph that consisted of two or three sentences and it said the price of structures [has] gone up considerably in the last few years because (1) wages have gone up tremendously and (2) the construction industry doesn't seem to have any real plan for increasing production. And that was it.

Meany added that if McCracken sought to explain the increased cost of construction, he would need to look beyond wages and productivity to check the cost of land, financing, mortgage money. McCracken, he said, only mentioned the two things.

In a TV interview the following month, Meany was asked if labor's evident dissatisfaction with the Democratic party meant that the "great coalition" was being destroyed:

> There never was any great coalition; we just happened to see eye to eye with the Democrats on a great many issues, and the party really has fallen apart mostly at the local level. . . . I think you find more and more the so-called left-wing Democrats are asserting their influence within the party.
>
> As far as labor is concerned, we've been pretty consistent in the things that we advocate. We've had a liberal program of social security, civil rights, and all of these things, and we're still working down that street, we're still in the same line we've been in for many years. . . .
>
> Actually, at the top level [of the party] you've got your Democratic National Committee, and you've got your ADA [Americans for Democratic Action] group which—some of them are really saying, in effect, they'd like to see the Democratic Party go down to a real defeat so it could be rebuilt. And you've got your Congressional forces in there—and there's no real cohesion, at the present time anyway.

When asked to identify the left-wing groups, Meany said he didn't mean people in Congress but he did mean "a good many" in the ADA, including Professor John Kenneth Galbraith, the economist.

Where was organized labor going to go, politically?

Organized labor is going down the same street, supporting the same type of candidates it has always supported. The difference is that in most cases in the past, where we supported a Democrat, he had a good, live, Democratic machine in his locality, which made our job that much better. And when I say that the Democratic Party has disintegrated, I mean in a number of . . . Congressional districts where the candidate is obviously entitled to our support. We're going to give him that support, but that is the only support he's going to get, because there is no machine. . . .

Meany was also asked about criticism of the labor movement by young people.

What has the young generation got to demonstrate to any other generation—not just my generation but the people in the 40–45 year, 50 year—what have they got to demonstrate that they know the answers? I listen to what a lot of these young people are saying—they are not all speaking with one voice—they have complaints—but I have yet to find out that they have the answers.

I don't know, and surely the behavior of some of these young people—destroying American institutions. Take an old American institution like Columbia University in New York, they made a shambles out of that . . . seized the administration building, a lot of destruction and rioting. Now, this doesn't demonstrate to me that they have the capacity to lead the nation, to tell the older generation what to do. It just doesn't make sense.

In September the embattled Meany and the embattled Nixon got together to celebrate Labor Day at the White House, with several thousand others. Union presidents and their wives had been invited to join the President and Administration officials and their wives for dinner. An additional four thousand lesser union chiefs and staff members, with their wives, attended an after-dinner celebration in the garden.

Realizing the political reason for the dinner, Meany felt he had been trapped by Nixon's invitation, delivered by Labor Secretary James D. Hodgson, who had replaced Shultz when the latter became head of the Office of Management and Budget. As Meany recalled:

Jim Hodgson came to me and said the President wants to do something big for Labor Day. He wanted to give real recognition to labor; it was something that was never done before. I certainly was not in a position to say to him, no, please tell him not to do this. At the time Hodgson spoke to me I knew we were not on very good terms with Nixon. This was after the Carswell-Haynsworth thing.

This was all Nixon's idea. He made a speech at the dinner and I made a speech, and, of course, it was a speech in a very light vein. I didn't speak about anything serious; I kidded him a little, but it was not unfriendly because it was that sort of an occasion.

The Labor Department made that into a pamphlet and the Republican National Committee [later] sent it out, including my speech, as a sort of campaign document. The big thing was that labor was at the White House. There was a political angle in his mind right from the very start. Now, who would think of having a dinner, taking a verbatim record of the dinner, and sending it out as a booklet? Nixon would think of it.

We thought he was trying to make it appear as if he wanted us over there because he liked us, and he really wanted us over there to use us.*

That dinner, needless to say, did not stop Meany from blasting away at his host's policies in a news conference as the 1970 congressional campaign warmed up:

Well, this has become quite a campaign. What we're getting now from the highest level of the Administration is a lot of what I would call calculated deception, Madison Avenue double-talk. It seems every action, every statement . . . the last few days is directed at the election. And they are talking particularly about the economy. I think at least they should tell it like it is. . . .

We in the trade union movement, who have always been very practical, go by the record as it is. And in the twenty months of the Nixon Administration, from the official figures, January 1969 to September 1970, we find this is the record:

Consumer prices are up 10 percent.

Unemployment has risen from 2,675,000 in January of 1969 to 4,607,000 in September of 1970 . . . a 72 percent increase. . . .

The buying power of the factory worker's weekly pay is down 2 percent. . . .

---

* Probably one reason the Republicans publicized the Meany speech was that he had included a comment that Franklin Roosevelt "was just as tricky a politician as anyone who bore the name of 'Tricky Dick' could be." It came in some rambling, ad lib, remarks about various Chief Executives, including the fact that he had had differences with "any President who ever sat in the White House since I came down here."

The AFL-CIO's efforts to stress the economic issue met with general success during the elections in November 1970, although labor lost two good friends in the Senate races plus another in the primaries. Nineteen of the 31 candidates endorsed by COPE for the Senate were winners, as were 203 endorsed in the House contests and 19 in gubernatorial races.

Meany tagged the results, by and large, a plus for labor, with Nixon failing to "control the elections pretty badly in Florida, California, Illinois, New Jersey and in other places." He concluded, too, that the electorate had rejected Nixon's economic policies, adding: "I would think the President would want to change his game plan."

The "game plan" was revised early in 1971 as Meany had predicted, but the AFL-CIO Council declared the new one "presented no basic change in policy—merely a change in rhetoric." Meany was caustic at a union dinner:

> All in all ... the Nixon-Burns "game plan" for the country's economy—after two years—was a miserable and complete failure. So now we have a "new game plan." We are going to psych the economy toward prosperity by the middle of 1972. Well, 1972 is important. That is when we elect a new President. And we are presented now with what can be called mini-expansion measures, pie-in-the-sky revenue-sharing, plus a barrage of optimistic rhetoric.
>
> And what about the architect of this prolonged recession with its increasing unemployment, combined with the steady rise in living costs? What does Dr. Burns have to say now from his ivory tower as the chairman of the Federal Reserve Board? ... He has new ideas for the future. He knows how he can solve our problems and he has found a very convenient whipping boy in the process. And who would the whipping boy be? Surely you can guess. Organized labor, the favorite whipping boy for eggheads of big business from time to time over the years.

Meany went on to mention suggestions made by Burns in a January speech in California, including repeal of the 1913 Davis-Bacon Act—which sets wage rates on federally financed construction—and compulsory arbitration of labor disputes in key industries.

Burns, he said, also proposed revising the minimum wage law to permit employers to hire teenage labor at a lower wage than the regular minimum. Meany thought it would provide jobs for youths by taking the work from their fathers. Another proposal called for faster tax depreciation allowances for business on the cost of new equipment.

Then, Meany recounted, Burns later suggested that "the time had come for Congress to take away some of organized labor's powers and stop 'subsidizing strikes.' " Meany continued:

> So the good doctor . . . wants to take us back into the last Century when industry's answer to the aspirations of workers for a decent wage and a decent standard was the starvation method—starve them out. And he stated to the [Senate] committee that labor had become so powerful that members of the unions suffer from the union policies. . . .
>
> This gentleman, who never met a payroll in his life and who never worked with his hands for wages in his life, is telling Congress that unions are too powerful.

Meany praised America's high-wage economy in another speech replying to Burns:

> What has sustained this great dynamic economy that we like to boast about? We talk about the American standard of life. We talk about the good things that our people can buy. . . . They come from a high-wage economy and they come from no other kind of economy.
>
> And if we want to turn this thing around, as Dr. Burns and some of his friends want to do, to a low-wage economy, then you will have a low-wage country and America will not be the first world power that she has been in the past. . . . Those people who advocate low wages do not understand that 95 percent of the things we manufacture we sell here. If you destroy the wage structure, who is going to buy them? There are not enough people getting $10,000 or $20,000 a year to buy all the things we can make.
>
> You've got to look to the little guy, and here is where the unions come in. Here is where the union has played its part in raising the wages, raising the mass purchasing power of this country that made this country a great nation, and we are going to try to keep on doing just that in the future.

When Nixon subsequently suspended the venerable Davis-Bacon Act fixing pay scales on federal construction, one of those most shocked by the action was his Labor Secretary, as Meany recalled years later:

> Hodgson was down in Florida trying to work out this agreement [on wage restraint] with the building trades. He was making considerable progress when out of a clear sky Nixon threw a monkey wrench in the whole thing by suspending the Davis-Bacon Act. It threw the whole industry into chaos.

That only lasted about thirty days; he had to retract on that one, but he left Hodgson high and dry. I talked to Hodgson that night and he was practically crying. He said, "I don't know what—nobody told me this." This was another one of those shocking surprises that Nixon liked.

Meany explained the theory behind the Davis-Bacon Law in a speech soon after it was suspended. He said the principle had been established in the laws of many of the states long before Congress enacted the federal statute:

> That theory is still sound: that public money should be used to keep up wages and to keep up conditions ... the suspension of Davis-Bacon in late February was a punitive action. ... It was designed to punish the construction workers because some people in the White House felt that the wages were too high.
>
> The action was taken against workers in one industry. It made no contribution at all to meeting the major problem of inflation. It was in no way directed to the major causes of construction costs—to the financing and interest charges, the cost of materials, contractors' profits, and the cost of the land.

On the day Nixon reinstated the Davis-Bacon Act, he set up the Construction Industry Stabilization Committee, consisting of representatives of the unions, contractors and the public. It was assigned the task of preventing excessive wage increases in that industry.

Then a Nixon surprise for the whole world was made public on July 15, 1971: he would visit Communist China—the People's Republic of China—at the invitation of Premier Chou En-lai. Arrangements had been made by Kissinger in a secret flight into China via Pakistan. As Meany recalled,

> Nixon announced it late Sunday afternoon or evening. About ten o'clock that night the reporters who had been trying to get to him found where he was: in Perini's restaurant on Wilshire Boulevard [in Los Angeles].
>
> This thing had just hit the press. It was a big sensation, and Nixon actually danced on the sidewalk when he came out of the restaurant—danced a little jig—he was so happy with his great success. His great success was that he was going to China. This was when he started a campaign to project the image of Nixon as the great fighter for peace.

As far as Meany was concerned then, Nixon's trip was the opening shot of the 1972 campaign. The second shot, he stated in the summer, he suspected was that "controls are indicated as the President's way out." Meany concurred in that wisdom with reservations, saying that increases in prices had prompted union members to seek higher wages to make up for what they had lost in inflation since the last contract.

> I don't see any other way to bring this [cycle] under control now—and these controls would not have to be permanent. What you have here in this country is a high-price psychology. There are any number of cases where prices are just raised because it is the thing to do; everybody is doing it.

Would the Federation accept wage and price controls without profit controls?

> No. . . . We want it across the board. If we make the sacrifice, we want the others to sacrifice, too: profits, dividends, everything in the form of income. You know, when the Steelworkers get an increase of 30 percent over three years that is called terrible, that is inflationary. When three, four or five million stockholders of a corporation get a 50 percent increase in their dividends nobody pays any attention. And if the Steelworkers' increase is inflationary, what about the others?

Meany elsewhere declared: "I can truthfully say to you that we have in Washington today the worst economic mess since the Hoover Depression of 1930."

That mess was to grow steadily worse and result in one of the toughest battles of Meany's life.

16

MEANY AND
WATERGATE

Out of a clear sky, Nixon put on this wage freeze, tried to nullify our contracts with employers by executive order, and all of that. So we had a real knock-down, drag-out fight with him.

Nixon's re-election in 1972 was foreshadowed in various ways, all of them more or less repugnant to Meany. The first was Nixon's wage freeze, a right-about-face decreed on August 15, 1971. Another was Nixon's state visit to China. A third was serious Democratic disarray and a final omen was a hint that labor's hard-won Occupational Safety and Health Act (OSHA), enacted in December 1970, was to be selectively enforced by the Administration in order to extract campaign contributions from industry.

Nixon's announcement speech on the initial ninety-day freeze, to be followed by a long-range program, reminded the Federation chief of the Russian habit of replacing one "Five Year Plan" with another, he told the 1971 AFL-CIO convention:

> [On August 15] came the big flip-flop. From "positively no controls" to a wage-price freeze. Again, no apology from the President, no explanation, no *mea culpa*, nothing like that. It just didn't happen. It reminds me of the years in the Soviet Union, the '20s and '30s, when they had the Five Year Plan to bring more consumer goods to their people, to make life a little better. Of course, you know they re-

write history, those people; they even rewrite the arithmetic tables. They had five Five Year Plans in ten years.

So now we have a new plan to curb inflation after two and a half years of failure. . . . On August 15 the President put on one of his usual, scintillating performances, a very, very beautiful act. The market went up. He inaugurated Nixon's new prosperity. He didn't explain what the hell was wrong with the old prosperity, because when he came in we only had 3 percent unemployment. We now have 6, and 2.2 million more people are unemployed.

Yes, the market went up and then it went down. It reminds me of the story of the farmer who went into town to hear a new minister preach and came back and told the neighbors. He said, "Oh, what a beautiful sermon! This man is terrific! He is wonderful." The neigh-- bors said, "What did he talk about?" The farmer hesitated and said, "You know, he didn't say."

That is what happens to the market. It goes up, you know, when his performance is terrific . . . and they say, "What did he say?" And then it goes down.

Well, the President talked that night about equity. We had told the President time and time again that we would cooperate in any program to meet these economic problems that was equitable. . . .

So, on the fifteenth of August, the President proposed a program. We got to looking at the program and, very frankly, we were looking for equity. What we found was rank discrimination against those in lower economic circumstances in favor of big business. It was just as simple as that.

The proposed [90-day] wage freeze was very simple to enforce. Every employer was an enforcer and happy to be an enforcer. The price freeze—no plans for that except the Internal Revenue Service, and they enforced it over the telephone. . . .

But when we looked at this program, we saw a $3 billion investment tax credit for business. This was on top of $4 billion he gave them in May of 1971. . . .

Whatever philosophy [Nixon] has is based on the idea that, if you make the fat cats a little fatter, somewhere along the line the poor simpletons are going to profit by it. His slogan is "Profits, profits, profits."

The day after the Nixon television "performance," Meany announced that he was calling the AFL-CIO Council into special session three days later to consider the new program.

We will ask Administration spokesmen to outline in detail all aspects of the President's decisions and to answer the many and perplexing questions he left unanswered in his speech last night. . . .

Only seven weeks ago, the President's newly-appointed chief economic spokesman, [Treasury] Secretary [John B.] Connally, had solemnly assured America that none of these actions were contemplated. And less than two weeks ago, in a press conference, the President himself had cast cold water on similar proposals.

The AFL-CIO has, since February 1966, said that if the situation warrants extraordinary overall stabilization measures, the AFL-CIO would cooperate so long as such restraints are equitably placed on all costs and incomes—including all prices, profits, dividends, rents and executive compensation, as well as employees' wages and salaries. . . .

The President's program simply does not meet that test.

We have said that we are prepared to sacrifice as much as anyone else, as long as anyone else, so long as there is equality of sacrifice. That pledge still stands. But this program, as it relates to the domestic economy, is certainly not equality. While the President studiously avoided any mention of profits and interest rates—the two most inflationary factors in the economy—his chief spokesman has made it quite clear that these will not be controlled.

After a Shultz-Hodgson meeting with the AFL-CIO leaders, Meany said, "Mr. Shultz tried to explain the various phases of the President's program. He tried to indicate that it was forward-looking." But Meany doubted that he convinced anyone.

When you embark on this road you don't turn back so easily. . . . To me, it smacks of a program that means an eventual attempt to impose government controls on industry and labor, because in the final analysis, they can't control labor alone. They will have to control the whole works, if that is the road they are going to take.

Looking back at that period for this book, Meany summed up why he thought the freeze was unfair:

Number one, the freeze would have prevented us from negotiating any wage increases, and number two, what is more drastic was the fact that it nullified wage increases that were already agreed to—a good many of them in contracts that had been negotiated with government participation in some way. These wage increases were declared null and void from the White House. We felt that that was not only unfair, it was illegal. In fact, in December of that year, Congress passed a bill, and Nixon signed it, validating all those contracts that he had nullified.

At a news conference, Meany informally suggested creation of a tripartite board like the War Labor Board of World War II. He indicated he favored such a board to rule on wage-contract disputes after the freeze ended. He stressed that the board should have authority to write its own rules and said that union leaders would not serve if they were there only to provide window dressing:

> The one plan I don't think will work: if they are going to bring management and labor in for some sort of window dressing and leave the power in the Department of Justice or leave it in the hands of Connally or Arnie Weber or somebody like that—that we won't buy, because we are not going to go into that sort of a swindle.
>
> If there is going to be government control, it is going to be direct. It is not going to be camouflaged by saying we have a labor-management setup here.

(As events unrolled, Meany was drawn into "buying" exactly that kind of board, and Arnold R. Weber's hat switch from director of the Cost of Living Council to neutral "public" board member could be called part of a swindle.)

In the news session, Meany predicted that unions would fight to collect the deferred wage boosts that would be left in employers' hands by a ruling of the Cost of Living Council:

> The Council says that there can be no bargaining after the freeze for what you lost during the freeze. Well, this is absolute nonsense. How the hell can they tell anyone, if the freeze is off? You go in and you bargain, and you bargain for any damn thing you think you can get. . . .
>
> If I was the head of a union and had one of those contracts, the very day the freeze was over I would say, "Mr. Employer, come on—give it to me." No negotiation. Go on strike that very minute for violation of contract. Now, that would be my approach.

If the regulations after the freeze prohibit unions from doing that, he added: "Then, of course, we've taken a long, long step towards fascism. If they bar negotiations, hell, that really gets right down to government control."

There was a lot more in the Nixon "package" revealed August 15 than the wage-price freeze, Meany pointed out to reporters:

> The overall picture is of a President doing everything he can to encourage business, bribing them, in effect, with tax gimmicks, but taking the cost of it out of the federal government employees, the cities and their needs, and out of the poor and the whole country.
>
> This is the basis of our position, right from the start, that this action on the part of the President was discriminatory. . . . We have been saying that we felt the only way we could stop this inflationary splurge was by putting on restraints of some kind. We didn't change our mind when the President made this announcement. We still feel this is the way to go, but we felt that, looking at the whole package, he was putting the load on the poor people, the load on workers.
>
> Actually, in a sense, it was Robin Hood in reverse—he was robbing the poor to help the rich. We just couldn't buy that, and as far as cooperation is concerned, we are not cooperating.

A TV questioner later suggested that perhaps labor leaders were "out of step" with their members because a poll of union members reported that some 65 percent favored the Nixon program, and Meany shot back:

> Just a minute! Sixty-five percent of our members answered a question: "Do you favor President Nixon's program to create more jobs and bring down prices?"
>
> Well, who wouldn't vote for that? But if you said to them: "Do you favor President Nixon's program to provide employment and bring down prices and that penalizes a million government employees and that cancels out contracts and that takes money from the welfare program and from the cities" and so forth—that is a different thing.
>
> You see, the news media have never touched on these things the President did that night. They have never referred to the other things. All they refer to is that he freezes wages and prices. He has done more than freeze wages. If he had just frozen wages and prices I would have been the first one to say amen, because for several years I have been saying this is the thing that he should do.

Early in the freeze period Meany and other union and employer members of the President's Productivity Council were invited to the

White House to confer with Nixon—and with advisers Connally, Shultz, McCracken, Burns, [Herbert] Stein, Hodgson, "and all of these other fellows who make a career of managing other people's lives," as Meany put it in his speech to the AFL-CIO's convention later that year:

> In response to the President's desire for what he called some kind of fair mechanism to curb inflation without rigid government controls, we told them that we would suggest the establishment of an independent voluntary agency free from government control, of a tripartite nature, similar to the War Labor Board of World War II.
>
> We told him very simply that we would not accept government control under the camouflage of an agency that pretended to be voluntary and independent, and we urged him to study the history of the War Labor Board—the tripartite setup—and also a similar setup that was in existence for a short time during the Korean conflict.
>
> In the meantime, he created what was known as the Cost of Living Council under the chairmanship of "Big John," the big oil man from Texas [former Texas Governor Connally]. And they continued to hand down decisions restricting every type of activity of workers and their unions while prices were being controlled by the IRS over the telephone. We were getting new rulings every day from the Cost of Living Council, and the hatchet man there was a fellow by the name of Weber, John Connally's asssistant. He made all sorts of rulings. Oh, some of them were contradictory, but there were none of them friendly. I'll tell you that. . . .
>
> He made seven or eight rulings on [pay raises for teachers] and we kept a little box score on him. It was no, no, maybe, yes, no, yes, no. And I don't think he knows yet what those rulings were.
>
> So then came the birth of Phase Two. Obstetricians, I think, would refer to it as a breech presentation.
>
> And surely it was a case of confusion compounded. October 5th, came a bearer of good news, Brother Hodgson. The President had agreed to our plan for an independent voluntary agency. They wanted five, five, and five: Five industry, five labor, and five public. They specified that . . . of the five labor one would be Teamster, one would be Auto.
>
> I said, "Fine, that's okay with me." I said "Jim, will you put this in the form of a memo? Because I would like to get these fellows together and let them see what this is. I think it is all right." So he said, yes, he would do that.

Meany telephoned the news to the presidents of the two independent unions, Leonard Woodcock of the Auto Workers and Frank Fitzsimmons of the Teamsters, and to AFL-CIO union heads I. W. Abel of the Steelworkers and Floyd E. Smith of the Machinists. They and Meany would be the labor members of the Pay Board. Meany arranged for them to attend a breakfast meeting with Hodgson on October 7, as he told that year's fall convention delegates:

> That is the day the President made the announcement over the television. That was quite a day. On the morning of October 7, we met and Jim Hodgson brought over his memo and distributed it. This was a setup and we read it very carefully. There were a few words there that bothered us. So we said, "Jim, does this mean that the Pay Board has got to be—?"
> "No, no, no."
> "Well, how about that word 'review'?"
> "No, that doesn't mean anything."
> "Well, can they veto the standards?"
> "Oh, no." He was very convincing. . . . Well, that was very good; so we were convinced.
> Then we were invited over to the White House to the meeting of the Productivity Council and we listened to Mr. Shultz and he gave us no cause for believing that Mr. Hodgson was wrong. The five of us came back to the AFL-CIO office and we drew up a short statement in which we said that, under these conditions, we would cooperate and try to make the President's plan work. Then the radio and the TV and the newspapers started to come out and they all contained the same language: Cost of Living Council veto power over the so-called Pay Board. This caused us some difficulty.

The labor leaders, therefore, waited to hear the President's own speech, hoping to get some clarification of the Board's real power. When Nixon was halfway through his address, Meany telephoned AFL-CIO's Albert Zack saying, "Don't put that statement out, Al. We got a fast deal out of this one. So we are not going to say anything tonight." Zack was at the office, prepared to telephone the statement of acceptance to reporters. Meany and the other leaders talked to Shultz the following day:

> [We] tried desperately to get him to say [whether] they do or do not have a veto power and, of course, we thought we were talking to the head man, but we found we weren't. He had evidently been de-

moted, and he advised us to listen to Secretary Connally's TV show.... We were assured that Connally would clear it all up.

But Connally did not clarify the possible veto power; he ducked the issue three times in the press conference. The confusion prompted Meany to call the AFL-CIO Council into special session on October 12 and he invited Woodcock and Fitzsimmons to attend. Just before the meeting, Shultz and Hodgson came to Meany's office bearing a new Nixon memo, this one signed, "RN." (Taking no chances that Nixon would later deny the memo, Meany had photocopies of the memo with the "RN" approval distributed to the press.)

Meany told the convention that one section said the Cost of Living Council "will not approve, disapprove, or serve as an appeal level for case decisions made by the Pay Board and Price Commission and it will not approve, revise, veto or revoke specific standards or criteria developed by the Pay Board and Price Commission." Meany also said:

> Well, this was quite definite and it had the initials on it, and I guess they knew damn well I wouldn't take anything [less definite] from them after what I had been through, so they brought this in. So we made a simple decision: We will try to help make the President's mechanism to control the cost-of-living work; we will serve on the Pay Board; we will establish our own watch dog units to monitor prices; we will continue to oppose the President's tax measures in the Congress; we will continue to fight for full employment. [Woodcock and Fitzsimmons agreed with the AFL-CIO position.]
>
> Well, I received a phone call of appreciation from the President that afternoon. Boy, I should have known better; that should have really made me suspicious.
>
> Then, on Saturday night, I received a phone call from Jim Hodgson. Now they are getting ready to set up the Pay Board. I was out having dinner [at a restaurant] when I received the call.... It came from the White House—you know, very impressive. This business of the Cabinet people using the White House—somebody comes up and says, "Mr. Meany, the White House is calling." You think you are going to get the President, and you wind up with Hodgson.

Hodgson asked if Meany knew a judge named Boldt in the state of Washington. When Meany said he did not, Hodgson suggested that he check on him because he was being considered for the chairman's post at the Pay Board. In recounting it, Meany said that if he had known then what he discovered later, "I would have sent a glowing letter recommending that fellow in the highest terms, and then he would have surely been turned down."

Less than three days later, he went on, Hodgson called to advise him to forget Boldt, as "he is totally and completely unfit for this job. He has absolutely no experience in this field and he just couldn't handle it at all."

Meany recalled thinking that "that is the end of Boldt," but two days later Hodgson informed him that Boldt was going to be chairman: "I said, 'What the hell are you talking about? He is going to be chairman after your description?' He said, 'Well, there are some people around there that don't agree with my estimate of his abilities—and, besides, we couldn't get anybody else.'"

The judge turned out to be Federal Judge George H. Boldt, and other public members of the new Board were Arnold R. Weber, the former director of the Cost of Living Council; Neil H. Jacoby, economics and business professor at the University of California at Los Angeles; William G. Caples, Kenyon College president; and Kermit Gordon, president of the Brookings Institution.

Meany's colorful and biting descriptions of the so-called "public" members of the Pay Board—contained in interviews for this book, and in the convention speech—went this way:

> Nixon set up the Pay Board deliberately; as Arnie Weber said, it was set up to "zap" labor. You look at the composition of the board. . . . The five labor members were labor leaders and the industry people were industry people, but the public members were not public.
>
> Nixon took a federal judge, gave him a leave of absence and appointed him chairman. Well, the judge is on the federal payroll and he certainly is neutral in the sense that he doesn't know a damn thing about labor and management. But he has someone right at his elbow who takes care of him and answers all the questions. . . . Every time we asked him a question, in comes Mr. Weber.
>
> Nixon took the fellow who had been trying to horsewhip us before that, Arnie Weber, and made him a public member. Arnie Weber is in the government one day running the Cost of Living Council and the next morning he was a public member.
>
> Then we move to a gentleman, quite a nice man, by the name of Caples. His whole life has been spent in industry—executive vice president of Inland Steel Company, his entire career spent on man-

agement's side of labor-management relations, a former vice president of the National Association of Manufacturers. The last two years, however, he is the president of Kenyon College; he has retired from his business life.

This would be like taking one of our old-timers who spent his whole life on the labor side and give him a title of emeritus and say now he is neutral, he can be a public member now.

Then we have Dr. Neil Jacoby, a conservative economist from the Council of Economic Advisers under Arthur Burns in the Eisenhower Administration, and he helped to fashion those two recessions that we had in those days; for the past twelve years and up to the present moment a director of the Occidental Petroleum Company. How is that for a neutral? He was supposed to be an economist and he had written a lot of anti-labor stuff. God, he was anti-labor! So he was in there as a public member.

The only public member who really could qualify as a public member, as a neutral public member, was a fellow from Brookings, Kermit Gordon, and he was just as conservative as the industry men. . . . He could be properly classified as a public member who was very, very much on the conservative side.

In other words, this was a Nixon setup, it was a board that he was going to control. It really was a frame-up. . . . It adds up to a stacked deck. It adds up to playing with loaded dice—just as simple as that. There is no hope, or very little hope, for equity.

I knew that from the very start. I didn't want to go along, but they appointed "Red" Smith, Abel, Woodcock, myself and Fitzsimmons. Of course, Fitzsimmons was outside of the AFL-CIO and so was Woodcock, so I called Abel and Red Smith and said we're being framed up; this is a setup, the public members are anti-labor, and I don't think we should sit on it.

They disagreed with me. They said, "We've got to answer to our membership and we just can't walk out on this without giving it a trial, even though we know it's a setup." I had no membership to answer to, in the sense that I had to answer to individual members. That made my mind up: as long as they were willing to go on, I went along. Woodcock was willing to go along. But nobody had any illusions about it. We did the best we could, but we knew we were framed and set up right from the start.

Prior to the Pay Board appointments, Meany had been saying he was willing to serve on a board similar to the War Labor Board, on which he was the leading labor member. The Nixon so-called "public

members," however, were different from those on the World War II
board, he said, and were so lacking in neutrality as to discredit the new
board.*

Meany felt that Secretary Connally had been given the job of holding down the wage decisions of the Pay Board through his Cost of Living Council. Connally also seemed to be the architect of the latest
game plan, Phase Two, Meany recalled, adding, "It was quite obvious
that Connally was a strong man and that Nixon was attracted to people like Connally. In fact, at that time, I think Connally thought Nixon
was going to make him the next President. I wonder if he's disillusioned on that today?"

In spite of the labor members' doubts, they undertook to keep their
promise to try to make the Pay Board work. Meany described the first
formal meeting to the convention delegates:

> I discovered within two minutes that Hodgson was right [about
> Chairman Boldt]. We discussed organizational matters and we ad-
> journed in about an hour. Then we met the next morning and again
> discussed organizational matters and then we adjourned for four or
> five days to November second, in order that the government statisti-
> cians could come up with some economic facts that we might need.
> They came up with some facts. . . . Then there came four days of
> complete frustration. I want to tell you, I've been around a long
> time—I don't have to tell you that; you read that in the paper. . . . In
> all my experience never have I gone through a more frustrating, de-
> basing experience, I would say. I have been insulted by experts in
> my time.
> The employer section was run by Mr. Roger Blough. He wasn't
> the spokesman, but he was running the show. I have a suspicion he
> was running the public group, too. This is the fellow who was chair-
> man of the board and president of the United States Steel Corpora-
> tion, who in 1962 was accused of double-crossing the Steelworkers
> Union, and of double-crossing the steel industry officials who nego-
> tiated with the Steelworkers Union. [Their agreement] was sold to
> the union on the basis of being a non-inflationary contract. As soon
> as the union ratified it, Mr. Blough went off to his so-called price
> committee of U.S. Steel and he raised the prices. So this was the fel-

* The original public members of the War Labor Board were William H. Davis, a New
York lawyer and labor mediator; George W. Taylor, an economics professor at the University of Pennsylvania; Frank P. Graham, president of the University of North Carolina, and
Wayne Morse, dean of the University of Oregon Law School. Those public members "were
really public members," Meany recalled. "There was no White House influence there at
all."

low, who is now retired. . . . He runs an organization that is dedicated to bringing wages down.

The five employer members of the Board caucused openly with the
public members, Meany said. "They just left us off to one side and they
made the decisions, and we just had to take it. It was a real frame-up."

When the first major policy decision was being discussed, stalling
was the order of the day, with caucuses and conferences, Meany said:

> We kept asking for a vote, and the judge said, "No, I have got to
> study these things. I don't agree with the labor proposal and I don't
> agree with the industry proposal." He was asked if he would please
> tell us what he didn't agree with in our proposal or even in the in-
> dustry proposal. He said, no, under no circumstances would he di-
> vulge his disagreement.

A crucial session, scheduled for eleven o'clock one morning, did not
convene until four that afternoon. The delay was deliberate, Meany
felt, with the public and industry members—who left labor sitting in
the office while they went out together for lunch—"trying to goad us
into walking out." When the meeting opened, labor's demand that a
vote be taken was rejected.

All the members knew that Meany had reservations to go to Florida
to speak at a convention of the building trades. However, he delayed
his departure and advised the other members he was ready for further
meetings. At that point, he thought, "they understood they weren't
going to force us to walk out" and the stalling ended.

At last, on November 8, the public and industry members were prepared to vote on proposals from each of the three sides. The employer
proposal, Meany said, "was really unnecessary because it was practically identical with the so-called public proposal." Labor wanted existing union-management contracts to be honored in all their terms,
while the public members proposed to allow payment of deferred raises
only in a few cases. The exceptions would be made for some members
of some big unions. Labor held that all unions, big and small, should
get the increases in their pre-freeze contracts.

Labor was outvoted 10 to 5, by the public and employer members.
The Board also adopted a new general rule allowing pay raises in new
contracts to go to 5.5 percent. The denial of the retroactive raises,
Meany complained, "took money that was legally and rightfully due
workers and put it in the hands of employers."

In his report to delegates at the Florida convention, Meany said the other members "didn't even give us credit for getting a licking." The minutes recorded only the successful motions by public members and failed to list the defeated labor motions.

At the ensuing convention, Richard Nixon's speech launched a White House propaganda stunt seeking to discredit Meany. But, as the meeting opened, the big question facing the delegates was whether they should instruct their three members on the Pay Board to stay on, or walk off. Meany, in his opening address, set the stage for that decision.

The AFL-CIO president also accused public members of the Board of attempting to split the labor side by privately telling each member that he would be "taken care of" in later rulings. Also, heads of unions were told that their own unions' wage increases would be allowed to exceed the formula. Meany said his vote was solicited by a public member's offer to assure him, off the record, that "they would not challenge any contract that was not over 8 percent." It was "a little under-the-table deal," Meany said.

The "deal" was rejected as the labor members kept a solid front.

The public side of the panel, Meany recalled in an interview later, promised that approval would be given for settlements above the 5.5 percent level in the longshore, coal, railroad and aerospace industries negotiating late in 1971.

Labor's chief complaint, according to Meany, was the Board's refusal to validate the existing wage contracts and their pay raises. Labor members were quoted as telling the other Board members that, if contracts were validated and retroactive pay raises allowed, the 5.5 percent standard would be accepted.

At the AFL-CIO convention, Meany warned delegates that the nullification of existing contracts "threatens the future of our whole economic system." If such bargaining contracts can be set aside by "a presidential edict," he said, no other legal contract "is sacred."

Pay Board Chairman Boldt, he continued, "is for the sanctity of contract, but he says there is a vital principle involved here. And I said, 'What the hell is the vital principle?' He says, 'We've got to go along with the President.'"

The convention delegates voted to keep their men on the Pay Board at least temporarily, while continuing efforts to get legislation reinstating the contracts providing for deferred raises.

The strategy behind Nixon's visit to the convention was transparent, Meany recalled.

> Nixon came to our seventy-one convention and claimed he was insulted. It was all Chuck [Charles W.] Colson's little idea. I invited Nixon to speak as a routine matter in September and got no word at all—no answer one way or the other until eight-thirty on the evening before we opened. That Wednesday evening I had a call from George Shultz, who said, "The President would like to address your convention at noon tomorrow." I just said, "The President can't address the convention at noon tomorrow," because we were wrestling with what we were going to do on the wage freeze. We were really blasting him on that.
>
> We had a breakfast meeting scheduled for the morning the convention opened and we had an Executive Council meeting set for twelve o'clock. The breakfast meeting was a committee meeting to come up with a statement on wage policy. The noon meeting of the Council was to take that statement and make it a recommendation to the convention. [Administration officials] knew our whole schedule and they knew that we had the breakfast meeting and the convention opening at ten o'clock with the governor of Florida, local dignitaries and all that sort of thing. They knew we had a Council meeting at noon.
>
> When I told Shultz the President couldn't speak at noon, he said, "Well, how soon could he?" I said he could address our convention at three o'clock. We'd be ready for him at three o'clock. He said he would call back. He finally called and said Nixon decided to come on Friday. When he came I left the platform, went to the [back stage] office, met him and, with an escort committee, brought him up to the stage, sat the escort committee behind him. When he was introduced he got a nice hand; people stood up and gave him polite applause. They were not enthusiastic.
>
> He told the audience that food prices were going down, adding: "If you don't believe it, ask your wife," and three thousand people laughed in his face. That unnerved him; he started perspiring. He got himself all up emotionally. He was perspiring and he was really almost incoherent at times.
>
> His escort committee and I were supposed to go out with him when he got through. When he got through, I took the mike to thank him, I turned around and, boy, he was running off the stage. His escort committee was sitting there; they hadn't moved. He didn't sit down.

The Secret Service lowered the ropes and he went into the crowd. [White House] TV men were photographing him. He pushed into the crowd, and the crowd started to mill around. People in the back started to come all the way over, everybody started to crush into him. That's when I asked them to take their seats.

From the platform I could see that he plunged into the crowd and then I could see that everybody in the back and to the left were all coming over to the front right—all pushing over. It looked like the whole crowd of three thousand people was going to be compressed into that corner. I got a little worried.*

Afterwards, he went back to [his home in] Key Biscayne and announced he was going back to Washington. Everybody that had come down with him had plans to stay until Monday. So, Friday afternoon, they were all trying to get reservations on planes to come back to Washington. He turned his plane around, came back to Washington.

Within an hour Chuck Colson was on the telephone talking to the wire services, newspapers and networks telling them, "Don't you know that Nixon was insulted by the AFL-CIO?" and all this. They spread the impression that he was insulted, and, of course, he wasn't. Secretary Connally made a radio statement criticizing me.

A *New York Times* article reported that within an hour after the President spoke at the convention Devan I. Shumway and Alvin Snyder, White House "communications" aides, had been briefed on the "discourtesies" and had quickly contacted the news bureaus to "make sure their correspondents in Florida had not missed these aspects of Mr. Nixon's appearance."

At the next session of the convention, the following Monday, Meany again addressed the delegates:

I have the impression the President did not come here to make a speech. He came here to contrive a situation under which he could claim that he had been unfairly treated. . . . I am proud of the conduct of the AFL-CIO. We respect the office, we respect the man that holds the office, and we are going to continue to do that. However, that doesn't mean that we have got to be subservient to the man who holds the office. This does not mean that our respect for the President and his office calls for us to submit to something that we

---

* Meany asked the delegates to return to their seats, and Nixon rushed out of the hall with his White House TV crew, which had entered just before he did and had taken pictures only of him shaking hands with delegates. After the President departed, Meany cracked, "We will now proceed with Act Two," to heavy applause.

consider unjust. Otherwise, our pride in America and its institutions would be meaningless.

This is still a democracy . . . not a monarchy. And the respect for the President and the respect for our rights as Americans is part and parcel of the entire American way of life to which we are committed without reservation.

A copy of a mysterious memo describing the White House plot was left at Meany's office soon after the convention. At the end of December, the text appeared in a newspaper column by John P. Roche, who stated it had been written by George T. Bell, a special assistant to the President and aide of Colson. Dated November 19, 1971 (the day Nixon spoke), it summarized a telephone call Bell had received from White House aide Pasquale Jiuliano and read as follows:

"Mr. Jiuliano called at 9:30. He is at the AFL-CIO convention. Pres. Nixon is going to speak at 10:30 A.M. They will chastise him, and that will be the best thing that could happen. Geo. Meany will be trying to make himself look like a big deal; but the Am. people will see the spectacle; and decide for themselves on the merit of what Mr. Nixon is trying to do. Mr. Jiuliano will use the same experience he did when he invited Gov. [George] Romney to an AFL-CIO meeting to speak B-4 [before] he was elected Gov. of Michigan. It was televised and the labor group gave Romney a rough time of it. But in the end he won.

"Mr. Jiuliano will give Mr. Bell a full report on his return from the meeting. He thinks it will make President Nixon look greater in the eyes of the Am. electorate. Mr. Bell wants Mr. Jiuliano to call him after Nixon speaks and let him know how things went. Discreetly and indirectly to get the reaction of others."

Four of the five labor members of the Board finally resigned in March 1972, after the Board ruled against dock workers on the West Coast. But much more than one dock decision prompted the departure, Meany recalled:

> We got very shabby treatment from this combination of five employers with five who were supposed to be neutral, and were not neutral. They were making decisions and shoving them down our throats. We finally walked off when they refused to give the West Coast longshoremen credit for productivity gains, which were enormous since their last agreement.
>
> Fitzsimmons didn't have to give me a reason [for not going]. I think he had made a political deal with Nixon and I think the politi-

cal association with Nixon lasted right up until Nixon resigned. I think it went back to when Nixon, in a conference with him, agreed to commute Hoffa's sentence. But I never talked to Fitz about any of that stuff.

Nixon's answer to the labor walk-off was a revamped Pay Board. He announced the next day that he was reconstituting the Board as an all-public panel, with the five original public members plus holdover members Fitzsimmons and Rocco Siciliano remaining to "advise" the public members on the viewpoints of labor and industry, respectively.

Meany meanwhile had other things on his mind in late 1971 and one was Nixon's plan to visit the Red Chinese early the next year. Before the event, Meany had these pungent comments to make at a Washington labor dinner:

> When you look back . . . at the President of the United States, this was the No. 1 anti-Communist that this country had. I know because I was No. 2. I didn't like being No. 2 but I concede he was No. 1. Do you remember his early campaigns? Oh, he was the most ferocious anti-Communist this country ever saw. And his technique in running for election was to charge the other person with being soft on Communism. He believed in freedom. He believed in a free society. He was against tyranny. . . . Well, now he is a realist—someone who accepts things as they are. Back in the '30s we were told you have to accept Hitler; you have to be a realist. . . .
>
> So now we have 1971 realism. We don't see much wrong with Mao Tse-tung. We don't see much wrong with Russian Communism. You have to be realistic. It's all right. We have our friend [Vice President Spiro] Agnew. He doesn't see anything wrong with . . . a military dictatorship in Greece. . . .
>
> We [in AFL-CIO] don't buy the idea that you can compromise with a military dictatorship in Greece just because Spiro happens to be a Greek. We don't think you can compromise with human freedom in dealing with the Soviet Union or with the Chinese Communists, and we don't see any future in playing around with Fidel Castro. Perhaps the President seems to feel that this is a new America where good faith doesn't mean anything; where truth is no longer meaningful.
>
> Well, I am old fashioned . . . I believe in decency. I believe in fair play. I believe in truth. I don't believe there is any future in a policy of deceit. And, as far as the American trade union movement is concerned, we are not prepared to compromise our principles on the

ground of expedience or on the ground of realism. . . . I think the labor movement is going to go on after the Connallys and a few more like that have gone down the road to oblivion.

A few days after the China trip in February 1972, the President and Kissinger briefed Meany at an eighty-minute breakfast meeting in the White House family quarters. Kissinger revealed that he had gone to Peking through Pakistan, secretly, to arrange beforehand for the Presidential visit.

When Nixon later asked Meany if he had any questions, Meany said: "So that's why we helped out the stinking Pakistanis—to get you into China!"*

Meany's deep-seated feelings about Communism, and especially U.S. involvement in the Vietnam War, emerged during a magazine interview in early 1972 when he was asked if he wanted to see Nixon defeated in November.

> It all depends on who the Democratic candidate is. I don't want to see him defeated by somebody who is advocating surrender. I don't believe in surrender in Vietnam. There's one point, one deep end I will not go beyond. I will not go with a guy who advocates surrender, and this has nothing to do with the labor movement; it has nothing to do with Nixon. This is me. I will not go with a fellow running for President of the United States who advocates surrender in Southeast Asia.

Asked about his opposition to New York's Mayor John Lindsay as a Presidential candidate, Meany replied: "What a mess he has made of my city," and charged that he had "advised kids to resist the draft." He added, "I can't buy that kind of a guy . . . I'm that old-fashioned."

Asked in another interview which Democratic candidate was advocating surrender, Meany replied: "I'm not saying anyone is advocating surrender. . . . But the way these guys are going, by the first of September, who knows, they may be advocating not only surrender but give Hanoi Texas as a gift." When a reporter amended that to include: "providing they would take Connally with them," Meany said, "I'd throw him in."

The real problem for Meany, however, was George McGovern,

* The India-Pakistan war of the previous year had occasioned sharp comment from Meany in a news session: "No one has explained to me yet why this Administration has to support Pakistan—a military dictatorship that was guilty of the worst kind of oppression and cruelty—and why we supported them against the people of Bangladesh and against India."

whose mostly young supporters had turned an anti-war protest into a
raid on the Democratic party. In spite of Nixon's grandstanding in
Moscow in May 1972, which was still reverberating when five men
were arrested on June 17 after a break-in at offices of the Democratic
National Committee in the Watergate apartment complex in Washington, Meany chose to withhold support from the Democrat. He explained in a speech after the Democratic Convention:

> This convention will go down in history as the convention that
> nominated the candidate who chaired the commission that made up
> the rules that governed the selection of delegates who selected the
> candidate. The so-called McGovern commission was supposed to
> produce the most democratic convention in the history of the par-
> ties. . . .
>
> Let's take a look at this "grassroots" convention. [From] Califor-
> nia, the McGovern delegation was made up as follows: 53 college
> students, 18 white-collar miscellaneous, 45 managerial representa-
> tives, plus professors from colleges, plus an additional group of 37
> teachers, 35 people from the poverty program staff, 20 political of-
> fice holders, 24 owners of small businesses, 19 retired people and 9
> trade union officials. Nine—3.2 percent of that delegation was made
> up of trade union officials, and this is the convention of the party
> which, history shows, from the Roosevelt days up to now, had its
> bone and sinew furnished by the American trade union movement.
>
> In July, *Life* magazine came out with a breakdown of the Oregon
> delegation . . . the delegation to the convention that was nearly per-
> fect, according to the so-called McGovern reformation. It had . . . 6
> students, 5 teachers, 4 businessmen, 4 lawyers, 3 writers, 2 bureau-
> crats, 2 editors, 2 officeholders, 2 homemakers, 1 social worker, 1
> newspaper indexer, 1 retired Army officer and 1 secretary.
>
> No bricklayers. No steelworkers, and, worst of all, no plumb-
> ers. . . .
>
> Thirty-nine percent of the delegates at the convention held post-
> graduate college degrees. . . . Thirty-one percent had family incomes
> of over $25,000 per year, according to the *Washington Post.* So this
> was a real classy convention. It was a convention of the elite.
>
> Oh, 300 labor delegates managed to get there, but only one,
> [Steelworkers'] President I. W. Abel, was allowed to address the dele-
> gates.
>
> We listened for three days to the speakers who were approved to
> speak by the powers-that-be at that convention. We listened to the
> gay lib people—you know, the people who want to legalize mar-
> riages between boys and boys and legalize marriages between girls

and girls. . . . We heard from the abortionists, and we heard from the people who look like Jacks, acted like Jills, and had the odors of johns about them.

Finally, after considerable pressure, President Abel was allowed to make a seconding speech for [Senator Henry M.] "Scoop" Jackson.

Senator McGovern, chosen by the convention to head the Democratic ticket November 7, got the support of part of the AFL-CIO union leadership, but Meany steered the Federation itself to a neutral position in the Presidential race. Abel was one of the union presidents who agreed with him; as Abel explained in 1976:

"After the nomination [Meany] and I sat down and talked about it. We decided that the best bet would be to concentrate on Congress and forget about the Presidential election, and that is what we did. If we hadn't, I am afraid we would still have Dick Nixon in the White House.

"Even a lot of the fellows who went all-out for McGovern now appreciate our position and the futility of theirs. But it is one of those things: they felt so strongly about Nixon that they were ready to support the Devil, just as an opposition. George and I looked at it more from the standpoint of constructive effort. We felt very strongly that in no way could you defeat Nixon with McGovern. We would have had a hard time in seventy-two defeating Nixon with either Hubert [Humphrey] or Scoop Jackson. With McGovern and the kind of supporters he had, we recognized it as a hopeless situation; we did feel that we could save the Congress and maybe stop some things that way."

The showdown on an endorsement came July 19, when the Executive Council voted 27 to 3 in favor of a neutrality policy on the Presidential contest, with each union permitted to decide for itself on an endorsement or neutrality. The Federation would concentrate its COPE efforts on electing friendly members to Congress.*

At a press conference after the meeting, Meany declared, "I will not endorse, I will not support, and I will not vote for Richard Nixon. I will not endorse, I will not support, and I will not vote for George McGovern. If Norman Thomas [frequent Socialist candidate] was only alive—"

Meany said he would like "to defeat both of them, if that were possible." Asked why he dropped his early plan to give Nixon's defeat top

* The strategy of concentrating on Congress proved to be correct. While McGovern carried Massachusetts and the District of Columbia, 217 of the 362 House candidates endorsed by COPE were elected and 16 of 29 endorsed for the Senate won.

priority, he replied, "Because a man named George McGovern got the Democratic nomination." At the time, insiders reported that Meany and others on the Council felt that the Democratic party had been taken over by the "New Politics" faction and that labor had been ousted from the party it had aided so long.

McGovern's labor supporters pointed to a COPE voting score of sixty-three "right" votes and only nine "wrong" in his House and Senate careers.

Meany's own reasons for opposing a McGovern endorsement by the AFL-CIO, itself, included attacks made by the Senator on labor's embargo of grain shipments to Russia during the Johnson Administration. Meany recalled,

> He was denouncing us in the Senate of the United States, telling us we should mind our own business, denouncing me personally and denouncing the AFL-CIO. He said it was none of our business where the wheat went, and so on. We had direct evidence of his tie-in with the big grain millers—and I mean direct evidence, documented evidence.
>
> Under those circumstances, as far as I'm concerned, as long as McGovern lives he could never get my support. Of course, he can go back to South Dakota and get the support of labor there, as he did in the last election [1976]. That's up to them; when he's running for the Senate, the decision as to support comes from his own home state. We don't make that decision. But when he's running for either President or Vice President of the United States, then the AFL-CIO itself makes the decision.
>
> In addition, I don't think that McGovern was ever fit to be President, any way that you look at it.*

Meany returned to the subject of McGovern on the CBS "Face the Nation" show in September:

> He's attacked labor publicly on the floor of the United States Senate. He's attacked me . . . called us labor brokers. After he had the nomination, he announced in Rapid City . . . that his campaign was going to be based on a determination to cut the power of big labor and big business. Now, if labor has power and big business has

---

* Long afterward, when a reporter asked which Presidential nominee got his vote in that election, Meany said, "Nobody. And he was a pretty good candidate; he really was the best candidate."

power, I don't think it's any compliment to labor to be compared with big business. Whatever power we've had, and we've used it over the years, is to build up the standard of life . . . not only of people who belong to our unions but people in all walks of life.

Was Meany, by indicating he was more angry at McGovern than at Nixon, being "more neutral" toward Nixon than toward McGovern?

For a long time before [McGovern's nomination] I spent more time perhaps than any man in America criticizing President Nixon. . . . The assumption is because I criticized President Nixon that I would accept anybody who'd run against him, and that was a wrong assumption. . . . Now the reason that I stress our position on McGovern [is that] there is where the attacks are coming— [his saying] that we should be supporting the Democratic candidate—and I don't buy that.

Meany's opposition to McGovern never flagged, but Nixon's victory didn't make Meany happy, either; the bright side for him was COPE's success in preventing the Nixon tide from also sweeping over Congress. The Republican campaign, Meany thought, reeked of money and corruption and he was angered by the attempt to promise slack enforcement of the Occupational Safety and Health Act for employers who contributed to the GOP campaign. Recalling Nixon's involvement with the OSHA regulations, Meany said for this book:

I think he tried to use it politically. When Nixon was starting to get ready for his campaign [in 1972] and raise funds, he actually sent word out that he wanted a message to go out to employers that it would be a good thing if they made a contribution to his campaign. They might not have as many OSHA inspectors around. I think it was when Shultz was in Treasury. [Lawrence H.] Larry Silberman, Under Secretary of Labor, was involved and he and Shultz wouldn't have anything to do with it—but it actually came from the White House: the suggestion that this would be a good way to raise funds for Nixon; everybody had to get in the campaign; and that one thing that would be looked on with a great deal of favor [was] if the employer could be told that there wouldn't be such strict enforcement.

A Meany aide said that the idea of using OSHA came from Charles Colson at the White House and was put into a confidential memo by Assistant Labor Secretary George C. Guenther. A former Labor De-

partment official recalls that Senate investigators later uncovered the
memo sent by Guenther to Silberman.

As a deluge of revelations about deceit and corruption in the Nixon
White House poured from the press and from Senate investigations in
1973, George Meany began the most important crusade of his career.

The AFL-CIO was the first national organization to demand Richard Nixon's ouster for the far-reaching crimes lumped under the name
"Watergate," beginning with a bungled third-rate burglary and extending to corruption of the Presidency itself.

Following the first disclosures by former Nixon aide John W. Dean
III of Nixon's personal involvement in the attempted cover-up, and the
President's public denial, the AFL-CIO Council took its stand on Watergate, on May 8, 1973, noting that "the American people have been
profoundly shaken by the Watergate revelations and the related scandals that reach into the upper echelons of the White House. . . .

"It is indeed a subversion of political democracy when one party,
because of its access to vast and excessive sums of money, can exercise
the advantages of wealth and power to pervert the Justice Department
and the White House itself to undermine its opposition and cement its
grip on the reins of government. . . ."

In a personal comment over TV later, Meany said:

> In all the excitement, I think we must not forget the American
> system of justice. We must see to it that the rights of individuals are
> protected. And we must remember that everybody concerned is in-
> nocent until convicted by due process of law.
>
> However, it is obvious that the revelations thus far have shaken
> public confidence in the integrity of their government. There is
> ample evidence that there was illegal use of huge sums of money to
> cover up crimes that were designed to maintain the political power
> of the Administration.
>
> The sordid picture of high Administration officials, operating
> from the White House, passing out hundreds of thousands of dollars
> in cash—this cash from campaign contributions—for illegal politi-
> cal espionage is indeed shocking. Confidence in government can
> only be restored by letting the American people know the whole
> truth. Then Congress can take the necessary action to preserve our
> free democratic political system. That system can survive if we know
> the true picture—no matter how bad it is. . . . Any additional at-

tempts to cover up will only further diminish public confidence in
government.

At a press conference following disclosure in the Senate hearings of
secret taping of the Oval Office, Meany again condemned the President and his staff:

> I feel very keenly about the whole question of privacy. . . . There is
> no right in the office of the President or any other office in govern-
> ment . . . to say that they can tape a conversation and keep a record
> of it . . . without [a person's] knowledge. Because this means, in ef-
> fect, that the government in power is saying, "We, because we are in
> power, in order to maintain our incumbency" —as somebody put it
> quite delicately—"we can break the law."
> Let me tell you, if the government can break the law, that is the
> end of democracy in this country. If they can break it and burglarize
> your home, then they can commit any crime. I don't buy that. . . .

At another press conference, Meany likened the Nixon way of soliciting campaign contributions from big business firms to gangster
strong-arming:

> What was going on in Watergate was not campaign collection;
> what these people were doing was extortion. They were going to big
> corporations and saying, "Get it up, get it up. You want to do busi-
> ness with the Government, you have got to get so much up."
> They were putting a tax on the corporations. Hell, it was just like
> the old gangster regime where they came around down the street to
> tell the storekeeper, "You are going to stay in business? Fifty dollars
> a month." The next one, $100 a month. As far as I'm concerned, the
> morals of this committee to re-elect Nixon were not any better than
> the morals of the gangsters.

Nixon's refusal that fall to turn over key Watergate tapes to the special prosecutor, Archibald Cox, raised other questions:

> I think the President is wrong in trying to assert that he had some
> special privilege . . . he talks about the right of privacy that gives
> him the right to surreptitiously tape conversations in the Oval Office

or on the telephone, and then gives him the right to do with those tapes as he sees fit. . . .

If the Supreme Court finally tells him that he has got to either give up the tapes or allow them to be listened to by the judge [and] if he still refuses, as he indicates, I think the Congress will have to impeach him. . . . I think they will start impeachment proceedings. . . .

The long-range importance of Watergate, Meany told a labor convention that fall, was more than a clumsy break-in:

Watergate is not just a question of somebody breaking into the office of the opposite political party in a very clumsy way and getting caught. It is not a question of the cover-up. Of course, there was a cover-up, and how far up the ladder that went we may never know. . . .

The long-range importance is the effort, the deliberate effort, being made to corrupt the American political system, to make it impossible for anyone to assume high office in this country unless they were bought and paid for by the great corporations of America. That is the sad picture we face. . . .

Think of what Maury [Maurice H.] Stans was trying to do—the treasurer of the Committee to Re-elect the President—taxing people having government contracts, taxing people on the percentage of their net worth. It was no longer a question of a contribution; you were really bribing your way into influence when you sent your money in. And collection became a matter of extortion, just plain and simple. So I think this is the lesson that we have to learn, and I think we have to change the American political system so that people are more important than money. . . . The first thing . . . is to provide for public financing of federal elections and to bar private contributions.

The AFL-CIO president itemized the score in the Watergate scandals in opening the October 1973 convention of the Federation:

The Vice-President of the United States [Spiro Agnew] has resigned. The wordy strongman of law-and-order—the nemesis of permissiveness—stands before the nation as a convicted felon, a tax-dodger.

Two members of the President's Cabinet are under indictment for conspiracy, perjury and the obstruction of justice. These are criminal charges—and they have been brought against the former Attorney General of the United States, John Mitchell, the man who was supposed to be the chief law enforcement officer of this country, and they were brought against the former Secretary of Commerce, Maurice Stans.

Four members of the White House staff have also been indicted, among them the President's chief domestic affairs adviser. A dozen more officials of the Administration have either resigned or been fired in connection with the White House scandal.

The President of the United States has, himself, been accused of tax avoidance, shady real estate deals and illegal—even criminal—abuse of presidential power....

Guilt is for the courts to decide. But responsibility is for the people to decide and, I think, the people have reached a verdict. The verdict is that this Administration has cast a dark shadow of shame over the spirit of America. After five years of Richard Nixon, this great and once-proud nation stands before the world with its head bowed—disgraced—not only by its enemies abroad, but by its leaders at home.... This torn and tattered Administration has lost the moral authority to lead, either at home or abroad....

In the final analysis, let us keep in mind that the Watergate and the cover-up itself was paid for by the great corporations of America....

The turning point occurred during the weekend recess of the Federation's convention: the so-called Saturday Night Massacre. In order to stop special Watergate prosecutor Archibald Cox from going into court to force the release of the White House tapes, Nixon ordered Attorney General Elliot L. Richardson to fire Cox. Richardson refused to do so and resigned. Deputy Attorney General William D. Ruckelshaus also refused and was fired. Solicitor General Robert H. Bork, as Acting Attorney General, dismissed Cox.

One of the most frightening Nixon actions also took place that night: he sent FBI agents to padlock the special prosecutor's office and take possession of the Watergate evidence there. It reminded many of Hitler's storm troop activities.

As soon as Meany heard of these events he called a special session of the Executive Council for early Monday morning. At the convention that day—while most of the nation remained in shock—delegates adopted the Council's statement, read by Meany, calling for the President's resignation or impeachment. In part, it stated:

We believe that the American people have had enough. We therefore call upon Richard Nixon, President of the United States, to resign.

We ask him to resign in the interest of preserving our democratic
system of government, which requires a relationship of trust and
candor between the people and their political leaders.

We ask him to resign in the interest of restoring a fully functioning
government, which his Administration is too deeply in disarray to
provide.

We ask him to resign in the interest of national security.

If Mr. Nixon does not resign, we call upon the House of Representatives forthwith to initiate impeachment proceedings against him.

The statement also asked Congress to hold up consideration of
Nixon's designated Vice President, Gerald Ford, pending disposal of
accusations against the President, "who has placed himself on the
brink of impeachment."

With that "indictment" the AFL-CIO launched the campaign to remove Nixon, but the Federation did more than pass a resolution.
Meany and his top staff people soon began drawing up their own "articles of impeachment" when Nixon made it clear he had no intention
of resigning, as Meany recounted:

One of the most important things we ever did in the labor movement was when we drew up our articles of impeachment and published them all over the country, week by week for the next three
and a half or four months—published them, documented them.

We had nineteen charges under which we claimed he should be
impeached. When the [House Judiciary] committee finally came up
with the articles of impeachment they had eighteen of our nineteen
charges on their list. We put on a campaign to get him the hell out of
there, and we finally did get him out. We were way ahead. We had
our articles of impeachment out and published them all over the
country before the Judiciary Committee of the House ever had a
meeting on the thing—before they were even organized.

Meanwhile, referring to the President's "dangerous emotional insta-
bility," Meany had called upon Congress "immediately to establish by
law an independent office of special prosecutor, completely removed
from the President's authority."

Following Leon Jaworski's appointment as independent prosecutor,
but with Nixon claiming the President could not be indicted, and refusing to answer a subpoena, the only recourse, Meany said, was impeachment. But there, Meany shortly explained on television, as far as
the Federation was concerned, the matter had to lie.

We are not lobbying on Capitol Hill for impeachment because we feel that impeachment is a very serious thing and we feel that each member of the House should make up his own mind on the basis of the information they'll have before [them]. So, we're not lobbying in the sense that we normally lobby for a piece of legislation. . . . We don't conduct any polls. But my general feeling is . . . that the votes are there for impeachment. . . . I would be very much surprised if [Nixon] finished the term.

Things were bad all over, Meany indicated, as he touched on foreign affairs at a labor dinner:

I see our friend Henry is on the road again. He doesn't like to spend too much time in the White House and who the hell can blame him? Anyway, he's in Moscow now. When he arrived at the airport he made a very optimistic statement. He said that he expected to see concrete progress on a number of outstanding issues. Then the Russian ambassador, Mr. Dobrynin, also told the newsmen that he was optimistic. Then [Leonid] Brezhnev said, the day before Henry got there, that he was optimistic.

Frankly, when this gang gets optimistic, I get pessimistic.

Then Henry really went overboard; he got aesthetic. He proposed sainthood for Brezhnev. Of course, he included the fellow down in Washington, too. He said that Brezhnev would go down in history with President Nixon, the co-architects of detente. They are going to give them a joint award—the Joseph Stalin Peace Award.

I am not sure whether that is good or bad. But I can agree, at least in part, with his statement; Mr. Brezhnev and Mr. Nixon will go down in history.

The 1973 Arab oil embargo and its effects had by then been all but submerged by the Watergate hearings.

In April 1974, under pressure from the House Judiciary subcommittee considering impeachment, Nixon voluntarily released several censored tapes to the public, prompting this response from Meany:

A week ago Monday, the President came out and said, "I want to take my case to the American people. And I'm giving the American people these transcripts." Now these were transcripts of tapes that the House Judiciary committee had subpoenaed. He was refusing to give them the tapes. And he was, in a sense, attempting to bypass the House Judiciary Committee by going to the public. . . . So, we have the transcripts, and we feel that we are part of the American people.

I personally feel, and I am quite sure that this reflects most of the people on our Executive Council, that the transcripts hold back a great deal of information that the President evidently doesn't want to give the American people and which he ought to give to the House Judiciary Committee. The transcripts really strengthen the case for impeachment. . . .

I personally would prefer his resignation. I want to get Watergate behind us. Not in the same sense as he does, but I want to [get] this man behind us . . . out of the White House. . . .

I got sick to my stomach at one point reading the transcripts, but I went back at them. Here we are presented with something that reminds you of the high executive committee of "Untouchables, Incorporated," deciding what to do. To protect the American people? To bring justice to this situation? No, no, to protect themselves. Actually talking about "hush money." Actually discussing [it] with the President of the United States . . . to see these four men from the seat of power, from the Oval office, talking about perjury, talking about how you can withhold the truth without committing perjury. And then hear the President say to John Dean: "We have got to get after these people. We have to get after our enemies."

Well . . . the potential enemies were everybody who was not in that room . . . including public officials. And saying, "We are going to go after them. We are going to use the power that we have. We are going to use the IRS. We are going to use the government agencies to get after these people . . . just as soon as this election is over." And then John Dean saying, "This is an exciting prospect."

Is there any need to elaborate? I think the transcripts speak for themselves and I think they say without question that this man is no longer fit to be President [and] the best thing he could do for his country, for the office, is to resign.

By August, the House Judiciary Committee had voted three articles of impeachment and, as the mid-summer meeting of the AFL-CIO Council began on August 5, reporters were questioning Meany about what kind of a President he thought Gerald Ford would make.

I wouldn't make any prediction on what Mr. Ford's policies might be. . . . I think Ford would be an improvement because there would be a certain confidence in his integrity that we have evidently lost with the present occupant of the White House. . . .

I have confidence in [Ford's] integrity. And I think most of the American people would be willing to chip in and try to help us over this problem which would surely ensue if the President is convicted [by the Senate]. I think there would be a certain amount of national unity displayed, and I think that Vice President Ford, if he becomes President, would have that kind of support.

And I am sure that at least he would have the support of the trade union movement insofar as we could consistently support him in view of our problems and our policies. Vice President Ford is a conservative . . . but we have lived in this country with conservatives before, and the conservative with integrity is far better than what we have now in the White House.

I don't know whether President Nixon is conservative or radical or what he is, and I'm sure that he himself doesn't know.

I don't agree with those who say that there is something undemocratic about resigning or that resigning is a terrible thing. Resigning resolved the Spiro [Agnew] problem and nobody seemed to get excited. I have not heard anyone say that the country is in very, very bad shape because Spiro resigned, and, if the President resigned, I don't think it would be as shocking to the country.

Would Meany favor granting the President immunity for any Watergate crimes he might have committed? Meany replied, "I would have no interest in seeing the President have any further troubles. All I want of the President is [for him] to just go away."

New disclosures on additional tapes released by Nixon on August 5 prompted more of his congressional supporters to turn against him. Nixon admitted that he had originated plans to get the FBI to stop its investigation of the Watergate break-in for political reasons. Meany told reporters the news reinforced his opinion that Nixon should resign.

Meany's voice by then, of course, was far from the only one urging resignation, and Nixon resigned on August 9—three days after Meany spoke out. Ford was immediately sworn in as President. Looking back at the Nixon Presidency years later, Meany ridiculed the foreign journeys in particular.

There is always a political connotation to them: the fellow in the White House feels that by making a trip abroad he is the man who is pushing for peace and this is good for his political image here at home. Some of the trips abroad were really just set up for that purpose.

The Nixon trip to China and the following one to Moscow shortly

afterwards, I think, had a certain angle for domestic consumption—
to prove to the American people that Nixon was the great advocate
of peace. When Nixon got in trouble on Watergate and was proved
to be a crook and completely dishonest in regard to his obligations as
President, many people said, "Look at his accomplishments in foreign affairs."

What were those accomplishments? When you make a trip, is that
an accomplishment? When you sign an agreement, is that an accomplishment if the other side doesn't keep it? So the whole thing, as
far as I am concerned, is a fraud. . . .

The very fact that you make the trip is a concession and a propaganda victory for the Soviets, who live on propaganda. If you make
an agreement in which you make concessions and they make concessions, and you keep your agreement and they don't—that's a loss.

Or, as Meany said in a speech in 1974:

We are going to judge the Nixon Administration on its deeds. . . .
Deeds like two-digit inflation that eats away at your members' paychecks like a flash fire. This administration has set a whole host of
economic records—the kind of firsts America can do without:

The highest prime interest rate in history.

Not one, but two recessions with soaring inflation and high unemployment.

The biggest decline in the buying power of the workers' paychecks
on record.

More discarded "game plans," Freezes and Phases than in all previous administrations combined.

The biggest housing crunch in years.

New inflation records practically every month.

The worst energy crisis in history. . . .

The Nixon-Kissinger foreign policy is one of "buying" treaties,
agreements and what-have-you. The price of the Vietnam cease-fire
and withdrawal of American troops was an offer of massive financial
aid to North Vietnam. The price of detente was to sell wheat to
Russia at a loss so that Russia could sell it to other countries at a
profit. And we are supposed to be the capitalists!

The American people are still paying for detente. Go to the su-
permarket and look at the price tags on bread, pasta and cereal
products and you'll see the price of detente. Or, in the famous words
of President Nixon to our 1971 convention: "Ask your wives."

17

MEANY AND FORD

Ford was a pleasant fellow and we had good contacts with him, but he would very pleasantly say no to anything that represented a liberal point of view. His Administration was a failure. What he did was to follow the real right-wing, conservative line—which is the big-business line—and he stuck to that pretty religiously.

He is a very nice man, but he is completely out of touch. . . . Just the same as Arthur Burns. Unemployment is a statistic to Arthur Burns, he doesn't know anything about it. He has no poor friends.

As far as George Meany was concerned, the Administration of Gerald Ford got off to a fatal beginning. The issue that killed it at the outset was whether Nixon, having resigned, should face prosecution for Watergate. The issue was raging throughout the country when reporters asked about it in late summer:

> I don't think anybody wants to see Nixon go to jail. But I feel that there is no escape from prosecution. . . . The law is there and I don't think there is any legal way out. . . . People have been indicted. People have had to plead guilty. People are in jail and people are facing trial.
> And how can they proceed with the trial of [John D.] Ehrlichman, [H. R.] Haldeman and Mitchell for obstruction of justice when we have a President of the United States who has practically admitted

335

obstruction of justice under the very same circumstances? What I am saying is, while I don't want to see Nixon in jail, I don't know how under our system of law it is possible to say he will not be given his day in court.

I don't think anyone would argue against a pardon by Ford . . . as long as the thing is cleared up legally.

Seven days after that last comment, the President issued an unconditional pardon to the man who had appointed him Vice President. Meany promptly told a union convention why he thought Ford had acted too soon:

President Ford's unconditional pardon of former President Nixon, for any and all offenses that he may or may not have committed while occupying the highest office in the land, raises serious questions about the integrity of our judicial system based on equal justice under law. . . . I had assumed that the normal legal processes in the Watergate case would proceed, with those charged or under suspicion of breaking the law receiving the due process guaranteed under the Constitution.

I had the feeling that President Ford might exercise his right to pardon our former President, if he were to plead guilty or to be convicted of a crime. And I'm sure that if that happened many Americans would have approved the action. But now we have a situation where one citizen, who has not been indicted or legally charged with any crime, is given an unconditional pardon against any and all possible offenses.

[This] could have the effect of completely halting [the Watergate] investigation, and the final effect would be that the American people would never get the truth about the involvement or non-involvement of the Chief Executive. This also can lead to a widespread consensus that we have a dual standard of justice in this country— one for those in high public office and one for those who do the bidding of those in high public office.

I'm afraid the Watergate nightmare is still going to be with us for some time as the result of President Ford's action.

President Ford ran into another Meany verbal buzz-saw in less than a month after the Nixon pardon. Someone had convinced the new Chief Executive that, as his second "accomplishment," he ought to launch a national drive against inflation.

Ford began his ineffective "Whip Inflation Now," or "WIN" campaign with a "summit" conference to receive ideas from all segments of the country. At the September 1974 conference, Meany broadened the agenda in his customary frank manner:

> We in labor don't intend to limit our advice and counsel to the problems of inflation alone. Because, as bad as inflation is, it is only a portion of America's economic problem. . . . Workers are equally scarred by recession. Recession and rising unemployment spell certain disaster for working people. . . .
>
> We will cooperate with an equitable program to bring the economy into balance. We will join with every other segment of the American economy in taking the necessary steps to fight inflation— if the policies are based on equity and fairness and evenly applied to all segments of the economy. . . .
>
> We are in a recession now. And yet, Mr. President, your advisers seemingly want to use the same policies which, for five and a half years, have been taking America downhill.

The AFL-CIO's program for reversing the trend, as outlined by Meany, included lower interest rates, loosening of the money supply, more public service jobs, and a halt to budget-balancing that cuts out vital services for the poor, the aged, the handicapped and minorities.

Meany's impression of the summit, as he gave it in a speech soon afterward, was:

> Job creation and tax reform were two of the most widely-supported proposals that came out of the summit hearing. From labor, from business, from financiers, from economists, there was general agreement that the government must move against unemployment, starting with the creation of at least a half-million public service jobs. . . . One area on which the delegates to the summit were practically unanimous was that the Nixon tight-money policies have to be abandoned.

In November, jubilant over their increased majorities won in both Houses of Congress, Democrats were talking about their new "mandate," but Meany told reporters that he had drawn a different conclusion:

> I don't know what the mandate was. I have an idea that the election was a national reaction to the failure, to the immorality of the American political leadership. The most significant thing about the vote the day before yesterday was the fact that it was down

to the very, very lowest level in many, many years. And I don't think it was a vote of approval for any political party. . . . It was a natural reaction on the part of the American people to vote against the party that happened to be represented by the people in the White House for the past five years. . . .

I think it was a vote against Richard Nixon . . . against Arthur Burns . . . against everything they represented . . . against inflation. I don't think it was a vote for the Democratic party at all. And I don't think the Democratic party has any mandate. Because, you know, when people get an idea that they've got a mandate, somehow or other, they don't think straight anymore. . . .

Oh, I don't believe in this mandate stuff. . . . A guy runs for office and he wins and he suddenly has a mandate. You know, if he had a few less votes he'd have had nothing. So I don't buy that at all.

One of the main reasons for the Republicans' losses was further deterioration of the economy, and in January the President got some advice from an emergency meeting of the AFL-CIO General Board. Opening the session, Meany declared that the nation's economy "is in the worst shape it has been in since the Great Depression." Attacking Ford's State of the Union message, he termed its economic program the "weirdest" one he had ever seen:

To fight inflation, he proposed to increase the cost of living.

To fight recession and stimulate the economy, he resurrected the old, discredited "trickle-down" theory of economists that Arthur Burns first learned before the 1930 Depression.

For those who are suffering the most—the unemployed, the aged, the sick and the poor—he proposed even more suffering.

The President's proposals were very disappointing. They were based on statistics, computer profiles and economic models, but not on human needs. Unless an adminstration looks at people as flesh and blood, and not as simple statistics, its proposals will not be good enough for the American people.

The AFL-CIO's "Action Program to Put America Back to Work" adopted by the union leaders at the January session included proposals for "an immediate tax cut of at least $20 billion, primarily for low- and middle-income taxpayers, to stimulate the economy through added purchasing power." Congress was urged to consider the unanimous recommendations the previous fall of the President's Labor-Management Advisory Committee, which Ford had ignored in his own suggested program.

Without yielding, but to try to appease Meany, Ford brought Harvard's John T. Dunlop back into the government as Secretary of Labor, replacing Peter J. Brennan. Dunlop, who had excellent relations with Meany and the labor movement, had performed fact-finding and other chores for various administrations back to World War II.

Meany indicated at a news conference the extent of his break with Brennan. He said he had not been inside the Labor Department building since Brennan became Secretary but had had good relations with Under Secretary Richard F. Schubert, "who ran the Department, actually."*

At that conference and others during 1975, Meany praised Dunlop frequently, with glancing blows at other economists—except those on the AFL-CIO staff:

> I know John Dunlop very well. I've known him for a quarter of a century and I've never had any trouble getting along with him, and I assume I'll get along with him as Secretary of Labor.

> John Dunlop is a hard worker. He is knowledgeable, he has had a lot of experience, he's an economist, he puts both feet on the ground, he's a very practical man . . . he is very easy to talk to; I don't see any problem with him. . . . I'm sure he would want to get his own thoughts over to the Administration and I'm sure some of his own thoughts would coincide with our thoughts.

> He is certainly compassionate. He understands the problem. And despite the fact that he is an economist, basically, I have great confidence in him.

> John Dunlop is not only a good, hard-working Secretary of Labor, in his own right he's a damn fine economist. I think he's a better economist than some of those other guys they have over there [in the Administration]. And this is not just an opinion; this is something I think can be established over the years: that John Dunlop is a competent, first-class economist.

* Nixon appointed Brennan Labor Secretary in 1973, but Brennan, who had been head of the New York Building Trades Council, soon won Meany's enmity by testifying in Congress in support of Nixon's minimum wage proposals that were opposed by the AFL-CIO. During Shultz's time in the Nixon Administration, Shultz was Meany's contact with Nixon, and Meany said that, when Brennan became Secretary, Meany was told that practice would continue "and not to pay any attention to Brennan."

But as for the President: His priorities "all point to big business," Meany told reporters.

> He's a nice guy. He's a likeable guy, a very, very straight, truthful guy. There's nothing tricky about him. On a personal basis, it's pretty hard to come to dislike him. . . .
>
> He's had 25 years as a conservative Congressman from a conservative district. I don't think he paid too much attention to what was happening to the country during those years. . . . He came to the Presidency without the proper experience. I don't think his legislative experience meant a great deal over those years. . . . His priorities all point to big business. They all point to helping business. . . .
>
> My main quarrel with the President is this fetish that he has on the budget: that the budget deficit can't go up, and it can't go beyond a certain level. Now, this isn't the way the American economy works. This is not the way a family lives. If a family lived this way, you wouldn't send your kid to college until he got to be 30 because it would take until he was 30 years old to save the money. . . . You wouldn't buy any new furniture until you had the money in the bank. There would be no expansion of business until the money—the profits—had piled up, and you would never be borrowing. There'd be no interest rates. Arthur Burns would be out of business. . . .
>
> The big corporations in this country go out and borrow billions of dollars to expand, to move along. This country is a great big corporation. Why shouldn't we borrow money to expand at times when we need to borrow money? Why should we put a line and say: That's it, we're not going above that?
>
> I would say if we had $100 billion deficit this year and that enabled us to bring down the unemployment rate from 9 percent to 5 percent, this would wipe out $64 billion of that $100 billion deficit right away, because that would be what you'd get back from people going to work. . . .

Meany told the reporters that Ford was out of touch with the people and with reality:

> I think President Ford is about as decent a man as I ever met. I don't think he thinks of the American workingman as an enemy but [because of Ford's] background and his experience over the years as a conservative following the conservative line . . . he's become completely insensitive to the real problems that the American worker faces.

If he felt some compassion for this problem . . . he would not try to solve it by saying to the American worker, "It's too bad, sonny boy, you've got to stay out of work for another three or four years and then everything is going to be just all right."

His economic philosophy, if he has an economic philosophy, is of the last century. At least, he doesn't conceal it.

I'd give him one plus: you can talk to him. He doesn't tape you when you talk to him. He's frank and open. But his domestic policies are going down, downhill all the time. On the international scene, he goes visiting, and I don't know whether these visits are doing any good or not. They tell us that we are just as strong as ever overseas. I just don't believe that. I don't think anyone overseas believes it. But it sounds nice when he says it. All in all, I don't think he's made any great record of progress at all. . . .

As Ford was completing his first year in the White House, Meany responded to a question about Ford's accomplishments:

I think that he's served the interest of the big banking institutions . . . of the big corporations. I think he has served the interest of those at the top of the economic ladder. He has completely failed to meet the problems of the American worker . . . he's doing nothing to really bring an end—a real end—to the recession, and I define a real end of the recession as getting people back to work. He's telling us, in effect, that in order to fight inflation we've got to accept unemployment—widespread unemployment—for the next four or five years.

But despite Meany's opposition to Ford's domestic policies, he continued his support of the Nixon-Ford Administration's phased withdrawal from Vietnam.* His appraisal of U.S. Vietnam policy over the years, however, had changed.

It was in late 1974 that Meany's change of heart on Vietnam surfaced, during an appearance on the "Dick Cavett Show." Cavett asked if Meany believed he had been right in backing Johnson and Nixon on that war; the reply was a curt "No." After Meany conceded that he had been wrong at the time, the surprised host asked, "Is it hard for you to admit that?"

"No," said Meany. "If you're wrong, you're wrong and I've lived a

---

* The withdrawal was completed in April 1975.

long time and I've made a lot of mistakes . . . I've been wrong plenty before."

In a later press conference a reporter asked Meany what he would have done differently had he known during the war what came out later. "I'd have publicly criticized the people who were deceiving me . . . Richard Nixon, Henry Kissinger—just to name a couple." Did Johnson deceive him? "Possibly."*

He said he was deceived about the chances of peace and added: "I didn't know they were going to bomb the civilian population. If I had known that, I wouldn't buy that. I didn't know about the secret bombing of Cambodia, and many other things."

When a reporter suggested that there were Americans who opposed the war at the time on the very same grounds, Meany exclaimed:

> No, they didn't oppose it on those very grounds because they, too, were deceived. They didn't know the inside information that we know now—that has come out in Congressional hearings and through other sources since then. They couldn't have known. There were a great many people who were opposed to our policy on the ground that they wanted to see Hanoi predominate, and, of course, that was never my position. It's not my position today.
>
> I wanted the South Vietnamese people to have the right to determine what kind of a government they wanted without the use of violence and force. And, you know, one of the things that we were told by Henry Kissinger and Richard Nixon was that detente had settled that problem: "This is one of the first fruits of detente." Well, that was January 1973; this is February 1975 and you can see how well that agreement worked.†

---

* Later, in 1976 Meany said, "I think Johnson felt the same way we did: that we could win the war. This was the idea that the military people evidently were promoting. I don't think Johnson deceived us. I think Nixon did."

† In 1976, Meany went further, predicting that, in the future, labor leaders would no longer automatically endorse Presidential military actions abroad:

"Under our system, the President is Commander in Chief and, when he makes military decisions that affect United States interests all over the world, the inclination—as far as I'm concerned—is to support the President. If he decides that we need to keep American troops in a certain part of the world—that this is in the American interest—he's the one who has the information; he has all the expert knowledge. He has the Joint Chiefs and everything else.

"So we start off, basically, very much on the side of the President and, unless something happens that indicates the President is not doing his job, we support him. This has been true for years; we supported World War II, we supported our government in Korea, we supported our government in Vietnam. It is pretty hard, under our system, not to support the President, because he has the responsibility under the Constitution. He represents civil-

Meany was also unhappy about the domestic scene in 1975.

At the Federation's biennial convention in San Francisco in October, Meany's printed report to delegates on domestic issues was described by him as "the gloomiest ever presented to an AFL-CIO convention in this organization's twenty-year history." On the AFL-CIO's own future, he was optimistic. But he termed Ford's Administration "a government of negativism" through "nihilistic use of veto power." In his opening address, he elaborated:

> Given our present circumstances, it is not enough to have a new President—we need a new philosophy. We need new policies, we need new directions for America. It is not enough to have a nice guy in the White House. It is not enough to have a new leading man—if the play is no good. You have got to write a new script, and you have got to get a whole new set of characters.
>
> The sad fact is that, when it comes to economic and foreign policies, President Ford is still playing by the old Nixon script. And, by and large, he has retained the same cast of characters who first set American policies on the wrong track—domestically and internationally—six and a half years ago.

Relations deteriorated further in January 1976 after Congress had passed legislation to kill the so-called situs picketing ruling of the Supreme Court, which unions in construction work had been trying to eliminate since 1951. In a deal engineered by President Ford through Labor Secretary Dunlop, these unions had agreed to accept new restrictions on collective bargaining in return for ending the decision's severe limitations on picketing.

But Ford reversed Ford and vetoed the legislation on January 2, 1976. Meany explained the background of the problem for this book:

---

ian control of the military, which is a basic American principle.

"But I don't think that's going to be the situation in the future, because of what happened during Nixon's period, where we were backing up Nixon on this. Now we realize that in a good many places he wasn't telling us or the country the truth.

"When you figure that the President of the United States would deceive his own people on these vital matters—for instance, on the bombing of North Vietnam. In December of seventy-two, when he started to bomb Hanoi and Haiphong harbor, we were led to believe that they were bombing only military installations. They were not; they were doing what was done in World War II: you would bomb cities indiscriminately.

"So I would say that if this happened again, labor's support of the President on military actions would certainly not be automatic. In the past, with the vast majority of the people and with labor leaders, it was automatic: you supported the President. Of course, the assumption was that he was reporting to the people and telling us the truth. Looking back on those Nixon days, I don't know how often we got the truth."

You have a general contractor. He subs out different things to subcontractors, but he has control all the time. He is the single employer. What the court's decision said was that the building trades on strike against a subcontractor can only picket the entrance he designates, or the contractor designates, as the entrance for these employees and subcontractors. The union can't picket any other entrance.

This doesn't apply to any industrial union and the court said, in effect, "Congress may not have intended the law to operate this way, but it is the way the law is written. On the language of the law we've got to decide that you can't picket more than one entrance, and if any changes are to be made they should be made by Congress."

Every President from Eisenhower on—Eisenhower, Kennedy, Johnson, Nixon and Ford—said that this [court decision] was wrong and should be changed. Ford said it should be changed, but he tied a condition to it. He said, "I will sign the situs picketing bill if you give me another bill that lays down certain conditions for collective bargaining, to bring some sort of order into collective bargaining in the construction industry."

Those conditions were met. He did agree to do away with the situs picketing rule and sign the bill. Of course, when the time came he changed his mind because of the political situation.

I don't think [the picketing section] is life-or-death to the building trades. I don't think it's perhaps as important as the other section of the bill vetoed by Ford, which had to do with collective bargaining. But it is an emotional thing. The building trades are saying, in effect, "Why should we be barred from doing the very thing that the industrial unions are permitted to do under the law?"

Meany recalled how Ford and Secretary Dunlop had worked on the draft legislation, and what followed.

Dunlop and Ford were in complete agreement on situs picketing; Dunlop testified on the bill, and the bill that passed was practically written in the White House by Dunlop. He actually wrote it with Ford looking over his shoulder and approving every word of it.

Before testifying on the legislation on the Hill, Dunlop insisted that Ford sit down there in the White House and listen to his testimony. He told me that he read his testimony—every word of it—to Ford before he went to the Hill. So there was no real difference between Ford and Dunlop on the merits of the legislation.

I still think the bill Dunlop drew up [that] was passed and then vetoed was a very, very good bill. While it addressed itself to the situs picketing thing, it also addressed itself to the whole business of collective bargaining in the construction trades. It would have represented something really progressive there, but Ford vetoed it because of the very, very strong opposition of the right wing, the Birchites, [Ronald] Reagan, and because he felt that, if he signed it, it might cost him the nomination [in 1976]. He turned around and vetoed it. And it cost him the election.

John Dunlop didn't promote the idea of the situs picketing bill; it was promoted by Ford, and Ford laid down some pretty stringent conditions accompanying the adjustment of the picketing situation.

Dunlop negotiated with the building trades, with the contractors' association, with the members of Congress. He finally came up with a bill that was approved by the workers and approved by the contractors and he got it through Congress. It was Gerald Ford's bill. Then Ford had a change of heart.

Ford called Dunlop in and said, "I don't know what this is going to do to me politically." I understand that Dunlop said, "What's politics got to do with this?"

Ford said, "It might cost me some primary states because of the opposition of Reagan and the Right-to-Work Committee." Actually, there was evidence that [opponents of the measure] had raised considerable [campaign] money for Ford but held it back, saying, "You veto the bill and you'll get the money, and if you don't, well, you don't get it." They didn't put it in writing, but everybody felt that this was the situation.

In the building-trades situation, Ford promised the unions, gave his word to Bob Georgine [head of the Building Trades Department of AFL-CIO] and then failed to keep his word. Ford repudiated Ford.

This was very hurtful for Ford because the building trades worked very hard for Carter [in the 1976 election]. Had Ford signed the bill, a lot of those unions would have felt obligated to work for Ford. I don't think there is any question he would have had the support of, if not all the building trades, certainly a large portion of it.

Meany said at the time, "We in the labor movement believe that a man's word is his bond. Now the President has shown what his word is worth" and "proved himself too weak to stand up to right-wing political pressure."

Secretary Dunlop resigned after making what he called "a professional judgment" that he no longer could be effective in the atmosphere created by the veto, and Meany boycotted the White House until a final visit at the end of Ford's term.

By January the 1976 Presidential election campaign had begun, with Ford challenged within his own party by Ronald Reagan and, in the other party, by a number of mostly congressional Democrats.

Late the previous year, Meany had allowed a reporter to lure him into guessing who, in each party, had the best chance to win. Regarding Ford, the likely Republican candidate, Meany said:

> Supposing Reagan knocks him off in three or four primaries— how can he run? And . . . I don't think Ford is going anywhere. I think the more he appears on the radio or the more he appears in his press conferences the worse he gets. . . . He just doesn't have it. I mean he doesn't have the attraction. . . . He's mentally lazy. I think he lets other people do his thinking for him. . . .
>
> I know Reagan. I've known him for years. I knew Reagan when he was way over . . . when he was a fellow traveler . . . and then he moved a little [to the right] and he got active in trade union affairs and he became president of the SAG [Screen Actors' Guild]. And then General Electric picked him up and put him on the payroll [as TV commentator] and he went way over . . . the whole spectrum. No, I've got no respect for anyone like that.
>
> But I'm a very practical person. As a candidate, he is very, very effective . . . and I think when he goes head-to-head with Ford, he'll murder Ford.

But whatever the Republicans did, Meany felt the Democrats had a good chance to recapture the White House because more voters considered themselves to be Democrats.

> If the Democratic party comes up with a candidate who can receive the united support of the Democratic party [its] chance of winning the election in November 1976 is quite good. . . . If they come up with another George McGovern, forget it. We'd have another repetition of 1972. If they come up with a live, attractive Democratic candidate, I think they've got a good chance.

When asked to name a good candidate for the Democrats, the AFL-CIO president said he could not recall all the announced candidates but suggested, "Start with Jimmy Carter and Fred Harris"—not a bad prediction still ten months in advance of the convention! Carter, who had been campaigning energetically for many months, was not Meany's personal choice at the time, but Meany had been keeping a close watch on him.

After Carter captured the nomination at the Democratic convention, Meany led the AFL-CIO Council in a quick endorsement of the Carter-[Senator Walter F.] Mondale slate. He did not wait for the larger AFL-CIO General Board to act on it, as was the custom.

Meany explained to reporters:

> The die is pretty much cast. There is no longer any doubt who the Democratic nominees are. . . . And as far as [the later Republican convention] is concerned, it's Tweedle-Dee Ford and Tweedle-Dum Reagan, or the other way: Tweedle-Dee Reagan and Tweedle-Dum Ford.
>
> No, we know who the candidates are and I'm sure everybody in the country knows who they are. I think it's going to be Ford against Carter.
>
> I've talked to [Carter] and I think he is a very warm human being. I think that he is not satisfied with things as they are. I think he wants to change things . . . the whole economic picture. And that's what we want to do.
>
> Now, of course, when you get down to details, I'm quite sure that there will be points of disagreement if he's elected President. But his overall purpose is our purpose—to put America back to work. . . . We will give him all-out support of the AFL-CIO. We'll give him all the support that we can legitimately and legally give him through our COPE organization, through our state federations, through our national unions, through our COPE area committees—the entire bit. And the reason I say it will be all-out support is the fact that I cannot find anyone, at any level, in the official family of the American labor movement who is going to be for Gerald Ford.   .   .   .
>
> I think it's a well-balanced ticket. Mondale is an out-and-out liberal. And while Carter certainly hasn't got any record here in Washington, he has a record as Governor of Georgia. I think, if I were to classify the two men, I would say that Mondale is not as conservative as Carter. I think it should make a very good team. . . .
>
> I think it is going to be a much tougher race than the polls show it to be at the present time. I think running in primaries [is different] than appealing to people in a general election. . . . I don't buy the idea that there is going to be a landslide for Carter. If I were to bet today, I would bet, yes, he would win.

Would Meany personally have preferred another candidate getting the nomination?

> Oh, I had half a dozen preferences, as it were, but very early in the primary campaign it developed that those half a dozen weren't

going to make it. And, as far as I am concerned, I'm very happy with Carter. I think he's going to make a very, very intelligent candidate . . . a wide-awake candidate . . . the type of candidate that will attract the American people. I think his approach is going to be new. . . .

Answering a question about possible cooperation between COPE and the Democratic National Committee on a campaign to get more people registered to vote, Meany said:

When I talked to Mr. Carter on the thirtieth of June, I gave him a memorandum on this whole subject of registration, and pointed out to him that COPE has been very, very active in this field with Frontlash [a youth group], the A. Philip Randolph Institute, and the [National Association of] Senior Citizens. I also pointed out to him that the last election in which the Democratic National Committee took a direct interest in a registration and get-out-the-vote campaign was in 1960 with the election of John Kennedy.

Now, he took this memorandum and said he was going to look it over. I'm quite sure that he is going to take a far greater interest in registration than some of the previous candidates.

The new nominee did take that memo to heart and had the Democratic Committee set up a special registration unit, while COPE's campaign was much more extensive than earlier drives.

Practical political know-how—and "troops"—also were supplied to Carter by the AFL-CIO. Enthusiasm was sky high at a meeting of its General Board, consisting of the heads of more than one hundred affiliated unions, on August 31. In opening it, Meany urged maximum support for Carter, summing up the situation this way:

We are here today because we have had enough.

We've had enough of government policies that increase unemployment, feed inflation, cause recessions and create misery and hardship.

We've had enough of government by veto, by stalemate, by inaction, by deceit and by pardon—a government that just drifts along, with no leadership, no firm policy, foreign or domestic.

America deserves better. And we are here to do our level best to see that America gets better.

Candidate Carter, in his speech to the General Board that day, promised, among other things, to "put our people back to work"—

which, he said, was "the most important thing of all." He had kind words about Meany:

"I also want to say here today that President Meany and all of you in the labor movement, historically, for many decades in this country, have been in the forefront of the crucial issues that have affected the individual human beings that comprise America. In the area of civil rights, in the area of adequate wages for those who in the past have been deprived. . . . Your great president and you have always insisted upon a strong national defense; on jobs for our people; and, perhaps most important of all, the quiet dignity of human beings."

Following the Republican Convention, Meany became an "issue" in the minds of some second-string speakers on the Ford team, especially his running mate, Senator Robert J. Dole of Kansas, and Agriculture Secretary Earl Butz. The Secretary told the Republican platform committee, for example, "If Jimmy Carter is elected President of the United States, George Meany would have a key to the front door and the back door of the White House." One of Dole's contributions to this level of oratory was a "warning" that Meany would be running the country if Carter won. Recalling the Republican oratory in that campaign and later, Meany saw a double standard:

> This talk of labor's power—to begin with, if labor has this great power, what is it used for? It's not used to make me rich, it's not used to make profits for somebody. It's used to help the little people of America.
>
> We're active as a lobbying agency over on Capitol Hill and, in our setup in this country, in order to protect yourself you've got to have a lobbying group. We lobby openly. The big corporations lobby under the table. They don't appear, they just throw their money around. I'm sure they have been breaking the law, but there's nothing much that can be done about it, because there are too many people over on Capitol Hill involved. Take all the corporations that broke the law on political contributions to Nixon.
>
> We observe the law; we're very much aware that we'd be very vulnerable if we didn't observe the law. We lobby for anything and everything that affects the ordinary citizen. Very little of our time is spent lobbying for things that affect the labor movement exclusively. The great bulk of our activity is in consumer legislation—legislation that will protect the ordinary citizen. We've got fourteen million members and that means we've got fourteen million consumers.

Our lobbying activity is fairly effective and, if that's an example of labor's power, it's all right with me. The idea that I can tell the President of the United States what to do is complete nonsense. This business of campaigning is rather odd: "If Carter's elected, George Meany is going to be looking over his shoulder," or "George Meany is going to be running the White House," and so on.

Down through the years with all of these Presidents, I have never had any trouble getting an appointment to talk to the President. The basis for that, I think, is that we are the largest organization of private citizens in the country, with fourteen million individual members. I feel that if we have problems and they are serious enough to be brought to the attention of the President, he should consider the problems and make a decision. The President can do as he likes; there is no compulsion. I don't know of any big business organization that doesn't have access to the President, and big corporations seem to have no trouble talking to him.

Ford doesn't hesitate to use whatever influence we have if it happens to suit him. In December of 1974, when the question of arms aid to Turkey was up in the House, it was being blocked by Ray Madden, the chairman of the Rules Committee. He wouldn't listen to the President of the United States. He wasn't the least bit impressed by Kissinger's argument of the importance of this arms sale. He wouldn't listen to [House Speaker] Carl Albert; he wouldn't listen to [Thomas P.] Tip O'Neill [House Majority Leader].

Madden was blocking the legislation by the very simple expedient of not calling a meeting of the Rules Committee. He knew if he called a meeting the votes were there to report out this legislation.

President Ford called me on the telephone and asked if I would call Ray Madden and ask him to do one thing: not to favor the bill—it was quite obvious he was opposed to it—but to ask him to call a meeting to find out if they wanted to report the bill out.

I called Madden and he was, oh, very grumpy about it. He didn't appreciate my call, but I said, "Ray, I think you owe it to your committee to call a meeting and find out where they stand." He agreed. He wouldn't do it for the President, for Kissinger, for Carl Albert, or for Tip O'Neill, but he called a meeting at my request.

The votes were there to report the bill out, of course. Ford called me up to express his great appreciation.

Dole raised the specter of labor's power again in his national television debate with Mondale, but his performance was so caustic and partisan that, by general agreement, he lost the debate. Meany thought that Carter won in the aggregate the three Presidential debates:

Looking back at the campaign, I think Carter got the best of the debates. I don't think the first debate really was any great victory insofar as the substance of the debate was concerned. Nor do I think that the third debate was; in it they were both very, very cautious.

In the second debate, however, I think Carter made quite a bit of progress, and Ford was talking loud, but he was definitely on the defensive as to his policies. But the important thing about the debates from Carter's point of view was that he was practically unknown nationally. The primary campaign brought him to some public attention, but, compared to Ford, he didn't have the national exposure. He was at a disadvantage even when the primaries were over.... The ninety-minute debates put Carter into the homes of millions of Americans, who had a chance to look at him, to listen to him. He came through as a highly intelligent, sincere individual. That was a big plus for Carter.

Although Carter's stand on some of the issues was not clear, Ford's stand on the issues was contradictory at times.

On the eve of the election Meany confided privately:

I listened to Ford last night in his press conference. He first stated that on this Arab [oil] boycott he was the first President that ever did anything—the first one. Then, five minutes later, in the same conference, he's defending Kennedy, Johnson, Nixon—saying they tried to do something about it—and attacking Carter because, he said, Carter was downgrading Kennedy, Johnson and Nixon on this question.

I don't know why Ford called that press conference. He calls a press conference and puts himself on the defensive right away—on the defensive on this [oil boycott] and on the defensive in apologizing on what he said was really a routine action in blocking the Patman resolution to investigate the [Watergate] break-in. That was long before Watergate became a scandal. It was when Watergate was just a break-in, a stupid kind of thing, and the general public didn't know what was back of it.

[John] Dean and those fellows knew what was back of it. Dean is absolutely right that Nixon sent word over to Ford [then House Minority Leader]. Ford claims that he met with these members of the House Committee on Banking and Currency at their request. Now, that's a lot of baloney. Anytime he would meet with the sixteen Republican members of the committee would be at his request, not theirs. He said they called on him for advice and, routinely, he said that he didn't think they should go for the resolution calling for an investigation.

On Nixon's orders, he lined up the sixteen Republicans and six Dixiecrats to throw out the resolution. But, at that time—it was September 1972—Watergate was not a scandal. [Now] Ford calls a press conference and puts himself on the defensive.

Carter's biggest asset is that the vast majority of the American people have no respect for Ford. He has no class; he's a fumbler. He comes through as a symbol of mediocrity. On the other hand, Carter is a mysterious figure in lots of ways. I think the election is going to be close.

There's no change in the Ford philosophy at all; none at all. If he gets elected we're going to have four more years of the same, and, frankly, I think that the economy is going to go downhill. It is in a shaky position right now; it could go bad again.

Somebody explained the Wall Street situation—with the market dropping off tremendous amounts in the last few weeks. Somebody explained that what's bothering Wall Street is they figure *either* Ford or Carter is going to be elected.

The November 2 election gave Carter the closest electoral-vote in sixty years—297 to 241—and only 51 percent of the popular vote. Meany again confided his view of what produced the victory:

In elections as close as this there are any number of things that now are viewed as crucial. The black vote was crucial, if Carter didn't get the black vote it's quite obvious he couldn't have made it. The labor vote, I think, was important.

Designation of Dole as Vice President hurt Ford. Dole didn't come through well, and in the debate with Mondale, in which he was exposed on national TV, Dole came through very badly. This opinion seemed to be shared by a lot of people. After that debate I ran into a number of people who said, "My God! Think of that man being a heartbeat away! Can you imagine him as President?"

That was another negative for Ford and a plus for Carter. The American people, more than ever [no longer look] at the Vice President as some kind of useless appendage to the Presidency—someone who doesn't mean anything. Look at the number of Presidents who have been Vice Presidents: Nixon, Johnson, Ford. So I think in the designation of the Vice President, it is not so much what duties he gets. When people are voting for a Vice President they are thinking: Is this man qualified to be President?

On that score, Dole just did not meet the test. Mondale came through as a calm, straightforward individual who was discussing the issues and putting forth his very definite point of view.

The one thing, however, that hurt Ford more than anything else was something that happened two years earlier and that was the pardon of Nixon. Here's a man who, as President, violated his oath of office and I'm quite sure violated the law in many cases, tried to cover up, and lied to the American people time and time again. He was forced to resign, but all of a sudden he's absolved from all possible questions. The people wanted to know the full truth, but when he was pardoned by Ford this shut the thing off; he was home free. I think there were hundreds of thousands of Americans who still felt at the election that this was wrong. Ford lost enough on that one act to lose the election.

Ford was a politician, and in my book he was a low-grade, mediocre politician. He represented his district for a quarter of a century; he was Minority Leader [of the House] for a good period of time. He never made a serious contribution to the work of Congress. He was just a political hack; he did the things he was supposed to do as a Republican politician.

I can't forget his spirited defense of Nixon when Ford was Vice President. He was telling people that he knew Nixon was innocent, that he had information, the evidence that proved beyond a question, as far as he was concerned, that Nixon was innocent. I question that. I assume he was really following his old political philosophy; he was a Republican Leader and became a Republican Vice President. He was trying to protect in every way he could a Republican President who had quite obviously violated the law.

I don't think that is honest. On the other hand, to say that Ford is basically dishonest would be wrong. I don't think there is any evidence that he did some of the things that Nixon did, but I question whether his actions—when he must have known how deeply Nixon was involved—were completely honest.

Ford put on what I would call a pretty good campaign. American campaigns basically, over the years, consist of trying to fool the electorate. I think Ford played that part of it; he put on a vigorous campaign. Some of his propaganda turned around and hurt him. TV spots which they showed over and over again in the last ten days of the campaign had him sitting there with a little group around him and he was saying, "Isn't it wonderful that we've turned this country around? Everybody is feeling good about everybody else. The economy is on the upswing and things are going great."

It wasn't true. The American electorate is highly intelligent, very selective in their voting. The idea of pounding into them the propaganda that everything was all right—people knew the economy was not on the upswing.

Ford during his two years in office pretty much ignored the problem of the unemployed. He kept pointing to the fact that we have seven and a half million people unemployed but look at all the people we have employed. That is rather a stupid argument, because that's not much comfort to the fellow out of work. The fact that during his two years he pretty much ignored the blacks and their problems hurt him tremendously.

Labor's situation in this election really was unique; just nobody in the labor movement was for Ford—no national officer, no local officer. I don't know of a single officer in the thousands of local unions throughout the country who was for Gerald Ford.

The reasons why, Meany thought, were obvious.

His Administration was a failure. Despite all the propaganda, we have more people unemployed. [As for] all this business about the economy turning up—every indication right now is that Carter is going to inherit an economy that's really very bad. Inflation is not being licked; the unemployment situation is not being taken care of. Our inner cities are bad; more and more people are living below the poverty line. All of this has happened not only during the Nixon Administration but, surely, during the Ford Administration.

People need homes and can't buy them. Our great American cities are deteriorating rapidly. The federal government certainly has a stake in the preservation of our great cities.

Ford did nothing about those problems; he ignored them. His ideas were the same as McKinley's: Keep big business happy, keep big business healthy and wealthy and profitable and everything is going to be all right. But business is profitable, big business is doing quite well, according to all the records—and still we've got these millions of people unemployed. We still have this disastrous inflation.

Among the Ford mistakes, in labor's view, were his failure to act on the serious unemployment problem and his excessive use of the veto power. The record of his first two years in office made him a "do-nothing President," AFL-CIO lobbyist Biemiller wrote in late 1976.

Fifty-three vetoes in those two years set a new record in the history of the Presidency; Ford's yearly average exceeded that of any previous Chief Executive. Only ten of those vetoes were overriden by Congress. Four vetoes involved important job programs that would have provided more than two million additional jobs. One of these programs was resurrected in a scaled-down form by the legislators, who this time passed it over a veto.

This unprecedented abuse of the veto authority amounted to a Presidential effort to impose minority rule on government, Biemiller thought. All Ford needed was the support of one-third plus one of the members of either the Senate or House to override the wishes of the congressional majority.

For the year 1975 the average unemployment was 8.5 percent of the labor force—the highest since the start of World War II—with 7.9 million workers idle by government count. The AFL-CIO estimated the true figures at 11.6 percent unemployment and 10.85 million idle workers; the Federation included those too discouraged even to seek work and those forced to work part-time. But, by either count, Ford was ignoring a major disaster.

AFL-CIO's COPE had broken all records of its own in its effort to elect Carter, Meany said:

> We got out more literature, registered more voters, got more voters to the polls. We had a larger telephone bank by far than ever before to get out the vote.
>
> The building trades made an effort in every single building-trades council in this country. They registered people—they sent them literature, got them out to vote. This is unique for the building trades. They don't as a general rule engage in this sort of work—registering and getting out the vote. This year they did, to a tremendous degree.

Of the 28 senatorial candidates endorsed by COPE, 19 won election. In House races, of 365 candidates supported by COPE, 262 won. Nine of the 14 nominees endorsed for state governorships also won, giving the AFL-CIO a 70 percent success score.

Early in the morning after the election, while returns were not complete, Carter telephoned Meany and then called three days later to express appreciation for AFL-CIO's support. Meany said it was "a very short, pleasant conversation," with no discussion of labor's problems or proposals.

At a press conference a few days later, Meany was asked what role he expected to play in the Carter Administration. "Elder statesman," he replied with a broad grin. But, as things turned out, even that role was denied him.

THE CARTER YEARS

We in the labor movement worked hard for the election of Jimmy Carter and Walter Mondale because we believed America needed a change in the philosophy of government. . . . The nation needed and wanted a government of compassion, whose primary concern would be the welfare of the American people.

If you remember last year's campaign, the number one issue was jobs. . . . I don't remember that he [Carter] made a great issue of balancing the budget last year, and now this seems to be the big thing. . . . The thing we ought to do is try to get the American people back to work.

When Jimmy Carter moved into the White House on January 20, 1977, the occasion ought to have been one of the happiest of George Meany's four decades in Washington, the beginning of a climactic chapter to his career. Candidate Carter's speeches had appeared to promise the liberal approach labor had been waiting for throughout eight years of Nixon-Ford conservatism. A revival of AFL-CIO's power in Congress and the Administration was expected both by union leaders and by their political opponents.

But for Meany the euphoria was already gone. He had assumed that, with a Democrat elected to the White House, labor now had an opportunity to obtain progressive legislation that was killed by Ford vetoes. But that was not so.

At a November press conference, Meany had been asked what

he thought the first order of business for the new Administration should be:

> The first order of business for this country is to do something about the economy, and . . . the number one priority for everybody is jobs for American workers. . . . Unemployment has gone up again. Inflationary pressures are still pushing upwards. . . .
>
> Something must be done to stimulate the economy, to reverse a good many of the bills that [Ford] vetoed, which we felt would have been helpful. I'm sure some of those bills will be repassed by the Congress, and I hope that the Chief Executive will act favorably upon them. . . . Outside of jobs, we have no priorities. We have a real program of legislation . . . that affects our people not just as workers but as consumers and citizens. . . .

As a stimulus to the economy, Meany said he would prefer a tax cut for low- and middle-income families rather than the Ford policy of "trying to stimulate the profits of the large corporations, [which] doesn't work." (He did not know then that the new President's tax-cut plan would be closer to the Ford model than to Meany's.)

When the issue of wage and price guidelines was raised by a reporter, Meany said, "I'm quite sure when the time comes we'll be ready to talk to him (Carter) about it." He reiterated the Federation's opposition to wage-price controls and said, "The record will show that the demands of the unions, especially in this period of high inflation, have been quite moderate."

Did Carter owe a debt to the AFL-CIO for its help in winning the election?

> In a close election such as we've just come through, you can point to any number of factors. You certainly can point to the labor vote, which turned out in great numbers. I think President Carter was elected by a broad cross-section of the American people. . . . The blacks made a tremendous contribution. There's an indication that all of the so-called minority groups made a contribution, [including] the ethnic groups throughout the country.

When Meany then was asked about his choice for Labor Secretary, he said he expected discussions with the incoming Administration on that and hoped "that we will be able to have some bearing on the selection." Asked about John Dunlop, he thought Dunlop, among others, would be acceptable, that Dunlop had "made a real contribution over there" as Ford's Labor Secretary and "is outstanding."

Meany's strong support of Dunlop was communicated to Carter by Lane Kirkland in December, while Meany was home recuperating from a cataract operation. "We put forward the name of John Dunlop for the Secretary of Labor and we declined to suggest alternatives that we would put in competition with a man we felt was the best available candidate," Kirkland recalled. He added that it was normal procedure for the Federation not to provide a list of alternatives for someone it recommended, "at least until we were clearly notified that our candidate was not acceptable."

But Dunlop's prospective appointment was opposed by some black leaders and women activists, and Carter suddenly solved the impasse by nominating a forty-eight-year-old University of Texas economics professor and manpower expert, F. Ray Marshall, to head the Labor Department. Meany was dumbfounded, but his public reaction was mild.

> Ray Marshall has had a long and distinguished career in the academic world as a labor economist whose views are liberal, informed and sensible. We have worked closely with him in the past in programs to enhance the employment opportunities of the underprivileged. He will have our full cooperation in the effort to achieve full employment, full production and a balanced economy.

A major difference in goals between Carter and the AFL-CIO became public even before the Georgian was inaugurated. Carter announced a plan to stimulate the economy with a package costing thirty billion dollars over two years and featuring tax cuts and rebates. Three days later, the Federation unveiled its own proposal for expenditure of thirty billion in one year and stressing direct job-creating programs.

Carter's program, the AFL-CIO said, was "too small, takes too long and is too ill-advised" to provide the required boost to the national economy.

At his confirmation hearing as Labor Secretary, Marshall told senators that he too thought Carter's program was too small and should provide additional money for jobs. He and Meany had already conferred several times since the announcement of Carter's choice, and agreed in general. Meany said privately at the time:

> I think he is a very solid fellow, good, and his philosophy toward his job is very good. He has wide experience except in one field: in the field of collective bargaining. I don't think that that's too impor-

tant if he has a good man in the Federal Mediation and Conciliation Service who does that job. For instance, if he had a fellow like [W. J.] Usery—who did that job well [for Nixon and Ford]—it doesn't call, really, for anything to be done by the Secretary of Labor. Marshall has very good experience in manpower, apprenticeship training, urban affairs and things like that, and we look for him to do a good job.

Meany also looked to the Congress for support but already, in January, saw a potential for conflict.

> Congress, during the Nixon years, really got pushed around. But I think this is a different situation; you have different leadership in Congress to begin with. You've got a strong man in the Senate and in the House. When you look back at [Carl] Albert and [Mike] Mansfield, neither one of them was strong.
>
> So there may be some problems between Carter and the House, but I've got the feeling that he will adjust to them quite quickly. He isn't going to let himself get into the position where a feud develops between Congress and the White House.

By February, Secretary Marshall was ready to concede there were differences between the AFL-CIO and the Carter Administration. Meany agreed, but again in a conciliatory way:

> That's a fair estimate of the situation. After all, you don't get complete agreement on everything. For instance, the disagreement we have on the stimulus package is reasonable. I feel the Carter Administration has come down too heavily on the use of tax cuts in order to stimulate employment.
>
> Our emphasis, of course, is the other way: the emphasis should be on public service jobs, housing, youth programs and things of that type, which we feel will provide jobs much quicker than any tax incentive.
>
> Then ... there are certain parts of the tax package that to me don't make sense at all. I don't know why big business should get a windfall that they don't need. ... I don't see why people in the upper bracket should get $50 [a proposed rebate] that they can flip at the first head waiter they see. ... We take a position that any tax rebate or relief should go farther down the economic ladder than that. But I don't think there are major differences.

There were, however. The specter of wage controls had appeared early in the Carter Administration when a reporter said the President was proposing that unions and employers give prior notification of wage demands and company offers. The issue, destined to become one of the most heated points of argument between the White House and the AFL-CIO, prompted Meany to make this response about voluntary "prenotification":

> We are absolutely opposed to it, absolutely, completely opposed to it, even if Billy Carter wants it. We will oppose it. We will not cooperate.... It would destroy collective bargaining. If unions are compelled to notify the federal governmenrt two or three months in advance, what happens if you make a settlement at midnight the day the contract expires?
>
> No, this would destroy our flexibility at the bargaining table, and we are completely and absolutely opposed to it. And, actually, it's just a foot in the door. Notification—then the next thing is voluntary guidelines. From voluntary guidelines to government-imposed guidelines and, the first thing you know, wage-and-price controls. And, to us, that's a disaster ... on the basis of our experience....
>
> There are some people in the Carter Administration, I think, that would like to go this route. A fellow by the name of Alan Greenspan [a former Ford aide] is still over there, but he's changed his name to Charlie Schultze. He'd like to go this route and he's very timidly approaching it. But we're wise to him.
>
> [Administration officials] haven't taken any firm position. These are little trial balloons they are throwing up.   .   .. I can tell you Ray Marshall doesn't go for it.... He feels the same way we do about it. Whether the President has expressed himself on this or not, I don't know....

When informed of another press account that Carter reportedly disagreed with the reasons for Meany's refusal to cooperate on prenotification, Meany said:

> That's what makes horse races.... I'd be glad to talk to him at any time. This prenotification doesn't seem to make any sense. What, just what can they accomplish? Let's say one of the negotiating committees of one of our large unions has a meeting prior to negotiations, what can they gain by having to expose all of their wage demands in public before they get to the bargaining table? ...
>
> I don't know how they are going to carry [prenotification] out on either side. I find no sentiment among our people to cooperate at all.

As for Meany's own idea of how to deal with inflation:

> Put the people back to work. One of the greatest contributions to inflation is the expenditure of money that is not accompanied by production of some kind. Production, wages, paying taxes—that's the answer to inflation. And the most inflationary thing now is unemployment. . . .
>
> Interest rates are an inflationary item. . . . Where is the increase in productivity of a bank that is charging 5¾ percent, 6 or 6¼ percent to their prime borrowers and then, overnight, they have a meeting and say, "Well, we are going to raise it half a point." Had the productivity of the bank increased to take care of that half a point? No. It's completely arbitrary. So I think another area where we can help inflation is to bring down interest rates.

To get action on inflation, Meany said, "requires leadership from the White House. I think the White House can do something about interest rates . . . about home mortgages. . . . I had a mortgage a few years ago of 4½ percent; I have one now of 6 percent. Why should somebody else have to pay 10 percent just because Arthur Burns appeared on the scene?"

Inflation and unemployment were not the only problems for the Federation; it had a list of legislation for Congress, including amendments to the basic law governing labor-management relations. This law, the Wagner Act, over the years has been revised—mainly in favor of management—by the Taft-Hartley Act and the Landrum-Griffin Act, and now the AFL-CIO hoped to remedy some provisions it considered to be grossly unfair to labor. The labor-law-reform drive turned into a gigantic battle between employers and organized labor.

Meany was asked by a reporter how difficult it would be to get their list of laws enacted:

> The history of remedial legislation—improvement of the condition of the ordinary people in this country through legislation—is that you keep working at it. . . . You keep plugging away. You lose. You come back again the following year. Sooner or later, the logic of what you are trying to do gets through, and you accomplish something.
>
> Now, we have a program. We are going to try to get Congress to enact our program. They may enact some of it, but they may not enact a whole lot of it. But [as for] that portion that they do not

enact, [we] will be back at the next Congress and the next Congress until we make these improvements. . . . I'm never discouraged, because in this area we have no timetable. . . .

The fact that we are going into this broad effort to reform the labor law indicates that we have a chance in the Congress and in the White House. We are not going to live in the fear that we had of the constant vetoes in the past few years. It indicates that we feel the time is good.

To what extent did Meany think Carter's attitude toward the legislative program of the Federation "should be influenced by a sense of debt to organized labor?"

"I don't think it should be influenced at all by a sense of debt to organized labor," Meany said. "I think it should be influenced by a sense of justice to organized labor and to the American worker."

Another questioner asked if the AFL-CIO expected Carter to "get out in front" in the drive to get the labor law reforms, and Meany replied:

We haven't asked him to get out in front of it. We expect him to look at it fairly. We feel that when we make these changes there is no reason to believe that he would be unhappy about these changes. I don't look for vetoes.

All I ask of him is a fair appraisal of our problems and an opportunity to present those problems. I don't ask for any commitments on these things. I didn't ask him for anything when he was running for office, and I'm not asking him now. If these bills come up, I certainly will present him with documentary evidence indicating why he should sign these bills. But I'm not looking for any advance commitment.

Doubts about the Administration's goals, or the lack of them, were not allayed by a meeting in March between the President and Meany. The latter called it "just social," with no substantive matters discussed. For about an hour, he said, the President "was just sitting there smiling, being very social and very happy with himself." After Carter left, Mondale and other aides listened to the AFL-CIO's arguments. (Kirkland, who attended several of the private White House conferences, said they tended to be "rather formal, a little stiff," compared with sessions with Johnson and Ford.)

In fact, labor had several disappointments in store, and the first oc-

curred shortly thereafter. A mistake in strategy and a violent anti-
union campaign heavily financed by business produced a surprise defeat in March when the House of Representatives voted down the situs
picketing bill that Congress had approved fifteen months earlier and
Ford had vetoed.

Union strategists had assumed that the measure would win quick
approval and were concentrating on preparing for an expected filibuster in the Senate. But a coalition of Republicans and conservative
Democrats was galvanized by the massive pressure campaign; the construction trades again lost their attempt to wipe out the Supreme
Court ruling limiting their right to picket construction sites. As in earlier legislation, the measure also would have established machinery to
promote stability in collective bargaining in the industry.

In another disappointment for organized labor—and the working
poor—the Administration proposed to boost the $2.30-an-hour mini-
mum wage only to $2.50. Meany immediately protested that the plan
was "shameful" because $2.50 was 38 cents an hour below the pov-
erty-level figure set by the government itself. "This is a bitter disappointment to everyone who looked to this Administration for economic
justice for the poor," Meany stated.

The AFL-CIO had been urging Congress to boost the minimum rate
to at least $3 an hour, with automatic increases yearly to keep the rate
at 60 percent of the average factory worker's wage; and, at a subsequent White House luncheon, Meany and other AFL-CIO officers
urged the President to reconsider labor's proposal on the minimum
wage.*

To offset the growing pressure of the business lobby and reinforce
the White House and Congress, the AFL-CIO joined with groups of
blacks, women and church leaders in a broad coalition supporting a
progressive minimum-wage law. They founded the Coalition for a Fair
Minimum Wage, and Meany addressed it as follows:

> Administration spokesmen say the minimum wage can't go higher
> because that would damage "business confidence." Frankly, we are
> more concerned with the confidence, the health and the well-being
> of low-wage workers who must spend every dime they make on food,

---

* Carter had requested the meeting to discuss changes in the labor-relations law, but the
AFL-CIO Council members took the opportunity to air other grievances about Carter programs. Among other things, they accused the President of not living up to his campaign
promises, and, at a separate White House gathering the same day, complained about
Carter's foreign-trade policies.

clothing and shelter for their families. As a matter of fact, I can't think of a better boost to the confidence of intelligent businessmen than 10 million American workers with more money to spend in the marketplace.

Until now, what the President has been saying to these workers is, "Business will feel better if you are poverty-stricken." We think that is indecent. We can't believe that a President concerned with human rights will not reconsider and view this issue with compassion and concern.

But if he doesn't reconsider, then the Congress must do better.

By April, when asked to characterize his relationship with the Carter Administration, Meany gave a one-word answer: "Correct." The reporter pointed out that labor did not like Carter's original minimum-wage proposal, his refusal to put a quota on imports of inexpensive shoes, and his economic stimulus package. Meany agreed and added: "So we're hoping to get around to some things that we will like. We're in there trying—that's all I can tell you. And any time we feel that we're not satisfied, we're going to speak up."

The reporter then asked whether Meany had anticipated that kind of relationship.

I listened very attentively to Governor Carter when he was running for office and I noted one thing: In his campaign he spoke quite well about his overall objectives, but I noticed that he was not specific, and I certainly am not surprised that he is not specific now in making promises. But he has the power to act on these things and we're going to use all the persuasiveness that we have to try to get him to act favorably.

But, as far as breaking any promises, he hasn't broken any specific promises because, frankly, if you go over his campaign, he never made any specific promises to anyone.

As part of the lobbying effort, Meany appealed to the AFL-CIO's affiliates to help convince Carter and the Congress that more progressive laws were needed:

We are not going to be stopped. The fight is going to be even tougher than we thought. But fight we will, until our goals are won. . . .

Arrayed against us are the traditional, well-financed foes of progressive legislation and workers' rights. They have already shown their tactics will be hate, fear, and emotionalism—ignoring at every turn the facts and the compelling case that can and will be made for reforms.

The need for a counterattack was perceived to be so urgent that the AFL-CIO Council authorized an assessment of one cent per member each month for six months to help finance it. This special tax on affiliated unions was unusual, emphasizing the leadership's grave concern about the resurgence of reactionary forces.

Carter then turned to the unofficial Labor-Management Group, which had evolved from a Presidential advisory panel during the Ford Administration. Carter asked the Group, headed by John Dunlop, to work with government officials in holding down inflationary pressures. Meany announced acceptance of the consultation plan, saying the Labor-Management Group "would be willing to discuss with the President's advisers in a voluntary, non-official manner the major economic problems facing the nation." But he added, "The labor movement believes one of the major problems is mass unemployment and we will address ourselves to this problem as well as inflation and all other economic issues on a regular and continuing basis."

After a consultation session with Treasury Secretary W. Michael Blumenthal, economic spokesman for the President, and Marshall, the group of eight labor and eight industry officials declared:

"The Group commends the President for the main themes of his statement on inflation: There are indeed 'no magic solutions in the battle against inflation,' and 'making progress in dealing with this problem has to be a long-term task.' The President has well avoided the course of controls and guideposts which had proved counter-productive."

Thus, the industry officials as well as labor leaders went on record in opposition to guideposts and controls—months before the AFL-CIO quarreled with the White House over the putting into effect of guidelines under another name.

Before that crisis developed, however, additional shocks hit Meany and other labor leaders as the President's policies were revealed—and sometimes soon revised—in early 1977. By the time AFL-CIO Council members gathered for their May meeting, Meany had sharp words for the Carter record in a news conference:

> He has been working on his image, and I think he has been doing quite well on that score. And, according to Pat [Patrick H.] Caddell [Carter pollster], that's supposed to be the big idea. . . .

He is going to reform welfare, which he promised in his campaign—and that's all the substance to that. Now, of course, he
promised in his campaign he was going to do it immediately and
now he says it can't really be done for several years. . . .

Frankly, I think it is a little too early to judge, for, after all, it's
only three months—the so-called honeymoon period. I think he has
done a lot of talking about a number of things, but so far very little
action.

Was Meany "a little disillusioned" with the President? he was asked.
He said it was "a little too early to make that judgment." Another
questioner wanted to know if labor had "anything to be happy about"
with the new Administration so far. The answer: "No." Was he hap-
pier with Carter than he would have been with Ford?

"I don't know. When I look at this Administration, there are some
disappointments. On the other hand, we still have a great big plus—
and that great big plus is that we got rid of Ford."

Carter, personally, "is a great guy," he went on. "But that doesn't
mean that I agree with the things that he is doing."

> I'm very, very unhappy . . . and very disappointed on his position
> on minimum wage, because all during the campaign he indicated
> that his first priority . . . was the people, especially the little people of
> America. And this to me is all wrapped up in this one question of
> minimum wage. If he has no compassion for these millions of people
> who work below the poverty level, then I have reason for my disap-
> pointment.

The fate of the Federation's labor law reform proposal at that time
was uncertain, Meany indicated. He was reminded that in February he
had called the congressional climate good for some of labor's legislation and was asked what had changed. "What's changed is we got a
good licking on situs picketing; that's one thing that has changed."

There followed a period of give-and-take. In July, Carter made a
move that some businessmen did not like: He bowed to arguments of
the Coalition for a Fair Minimum Wage and called upon Congress for
a new first-step minumum rate of $2.65 an hour—15 cents higher than
his first proposal. The Coalition agreed to this compromise, coming
down from its $3 rate proposal.

On another front, the Administration seemed to have abandoned
the idea of seeking early-warning notices on wage demands but was

hinting about another gimmick. Meany privately elaborated on labor's position:

> You certainly couldn't have collective bargaining, as we know it, if the government were to inject itself into the process, even in a small way, three months or so or even a month before the final decision.
>
> From the practical point of view, the way the big unions and big corporations bargain collectively, there is just no way you can have prior government consultation on the wage demands—you don't know what the wage demands are! When you go to the bargaining table it's not just the wages [that are involved], it's the fringes, it's all sorts of things that enter into collective bargaining.
>
> There's no way you could get a union, three months before they go to the bargaining table, to give a figure. In fact, you couldn't get the employer to say what he'll offer. The union says we want this, and the employer says no. When it's half past eleven on the last night, with a half hour to go—that's when they finally lay the real stuff on the table.
>
> I'm quite sure Charlie Schultze's idea of controlling inflation is to control wages. He tries to hide it but everything he does and everything he says indicates that. He talked about prior notification—holding up wage increases for a certain amount of time so that the government could do some jawboning, and then he went to just notification, itself.
>
> Now he talks about consultation, just consultation. Well, there is nothing to stop him. There doesn't have to be any agreement in advance; there doesn't have to be any set government policy.
>
> They can consult any time they want to consult. For instance, last week he did some consulting with Bethlehem Steel—nothing to stop him. Of course, Bethlehem Steel went right ahead with its price increases and he issued a statement saying that it was too bad, what a horrible thing it was. So what?

During his meetings with reporters after the Executive Council sessions in late August, Meany noted an improvement in Carter's track record but said it was far from a perfect record:

> We have reached an agreement on the minimum wage. The President came up a little on his proposal; we came down on ours. We came down a little more than he came up. . . .
>
> He is backing our labor law reform proposal. . . .

I have to give him some pluses on the energy business. I think he hit that .'. . . it is something that he tried to bring home to the American people: the crisis in energy. I don't think he succeeded, but I don't think that's his fault. At least, he tried to impress upon the American people the need for conserving energy, and, up to now, I don't see where the American people are really captured by the idea of conserving energy. In fact, a good many . . . don't believe that there is an energy shortage, or any possible energy shortage. And I think that is dead wrong. . . . There is a great possibility of an energy shortage. [Carter] is trying—trying a little too hard in some cases. . . .

He has failed to really face up to the real economic problem of this country, which is permanent jobs. On the other hand, I have to give him a plus on trying to do something on temporary jobs . . . the youth employment bill, and, of course, the public works bill, where he finally agreed to $4 billion after he originally proposed $2 billion. These things are all temporary panaceas . . . sort of band-aids put on the problem.

The real problem is jobs—full-time jobs; jobs in private employment; jobs with good wages that would have kept the country going. . . . I don't think that we have made any great progress in the last year in solving the real problem: the twin problems of jobs and unemployment, and inflation.

Black organizations which, like labor, had helped elect Carter, were complaining that the President had not kept his promises to them, a reporter told Meany, getting this response:

If you remember last year's campaign, the number one issue was jobs. Now, my quarrel with the President—and I'm sure this is the quarrel the black organizations and the poor have—is that during the campaign he raised the expectations of these people, and they are disappointed. I'm sure they have reasons to be disappointed.

I don't remember that he made a great issue of balancing the budget last year, and now this seems to be the big thing—"We have to balance the budget by 1981" and if we do, all of our problems will be over. There will be dancing in the streets in the ghettos—and I think Moscow might even put up a white flag of surrender, if we balance the budget. . . .

The thing that we ought to do is try to get the American people back to work. I think the greatest crime being committed today is being committed against the black community, against the black teenagers and against the white teenagers. The number one priority in 1976 was jobs. I'm not saying that the President is unconcerned.

I'm sure that he is concerned, but I think his priorities should be reordered . . . the number one priority again should be jobs. . . . He should look at the real crux of this whole economic situation, which is jobs. We are never going to get out of this rut that we are in unless we get people back to work.

Meany scorned, as politically inspired, optimistic Administration projections showing lower rates of inflation and unemployment. Referring to the previous day's action of the Federal Reserve Board in increasing the rediscount rate, he said, "This is our old friend Arthur Burns." Burns's action, he said, meant a tightening of the money supply and higher interest rates for new housing and projects for business and governments—adding to the unemployment problem. "I'm wondering," he went on, "when somebody in this government is going to take a look at this man and retire him, and see if we can't get our economy moving again. I think he is a disaster."

Meany said he would like to see someone new making Administration economic policy, someone who would not follow the old philosophy "If you keep the big corporations wealthy, everything is going to be all right."

Meany also criticized Congress:

> Quite a few of the new House members are not paying attention to their own leaders. . . . We just keep plugging away at what we think is good legislation, and we do have the cooperation of the leadership.
>
> But that doesn't mean that the leadership can automatically turn over to us the membership of either the House or the Senate. I think that Tip O'Neill and Bob Byrd [Senate Majority Leader Robert C. Byrd] are well-seasoned, good legislators. They know the Hill—and they are leading—but there is no guarantee that they can get the members of their own party to go along with them on everything that they advocate.

In a TV interview on Labor Day, 1977, Meany appraised Carter in a new light:

> I think the President is a conservative. I don't think he's quite as conservative as Ronald Reagan or quite as conservative as Gerald Ford or Nixon—people like that. . . . He wants to push the economy forward. My complaint is that he's not giving the attention to the real problem, the job problem [that] we expected he would. He

seems to have some idea that his greatest accomplishment would be balancing the budget by 1981, and I don't know just how much [of] an accomplishment that would be. I'm not opposed to balancing the budget, but what price do we pay . . . in human terms?

I would still think we've got a friend in the White House despite the fact that he's not, perhaps, doing . . . all the things we think he should do.

Inflation cannot be blamed on the labor movement, Meany said in reply to a question.

We are the victims of inflation. I don't think that we can be held responsible for it. People keep trying to tie wages to inflation, and I think the wage increases—certainly those we've had in the last five or six years since inflation became a real problem—are the result of inflation. . . . Every study showed that there has not been what we call the wage-price push, the wages pushing the prices up, although some of the economists around try to pretend that is so.

Meany's "happiness" index regarding his relations with Carter did not rise much between Labor Day and October. In a TV interview that month he thought he saw a change, reported some pluses and "definite minuses." When asked if labor would support Carter if the election were the following month, he replied, "I think so . . . when we consider the alternatives."

The President's stand on human rights, he decided, had been "kind of muted, let's say, for some months now." He confessed to being "a little bit confused by the foreign policy," because he had trouble reconciling Carter's position on human rights with "the obvious overtures that are being made to dictatorial countries to bring about what they call normalization of relations." Also, he deplored the President's planned visits to "countries where there's no such thing as even a vestige of human rights."

In opening the AFL-CIO's biennial election convention in December, Meany again gave Carter more credit than he did Carter's opponents. He praised Carter's human rights policy as "the greatest foreign policy initiative attempted in this half-century" but accused businessmen of objecting to the stress laid on such rights because of their interest in profits to be made in trading with Russia.

On the domestic front, he pointed to the President's endorsement of the full-employment bill but warned that a promise "is not enough";

what was needed were comprehensive, effective programs that would meet the "reachable" goal of a 4 percent unemployment rate.

At the time, the nation's unemployment was 6.9 percent. Meany said that the 1977 budget deficit could have been virtually wiped out if unemployment had been reduced to the proper level. He put the cost of having ten million jobless workers at $61 billion.

Attacking advocates of the supposed need to build up "business confidence" through tax relief for corporations, he said that "the way to restore business confidence throughout America is to set a goal of four million new jobs a year" for the next four years. "With that kind of a commitment, the President would meet both of his major goals: full employment and a balanced budget."

Carter did not make a personal appearance at the convention, although he was invited; he sent a brief message, delivered by Secretary Marshall. In it, he said that the AFL-CIO's endorsement of his candidacy in 1976 had been important in the election "and is important to me today." Conceding that labor's views would not always match his on issues, he said, "but at the end of four years, I am confident that the issues on which we agree will far outweigh our momentary disagreements."

Meany summarized the Federation's case for and against Carter's actions in his report of the two years since the previous convention. Minuses outnumbered the pluses:

> On the economic front, the President proposed a sound measure to deal with youth unemployment, and a stimulus program, which, while less than adequate, was a substantial improvement over the approach of the Nixon-Ford years.
>
> Most of President Carter's programs represented major steps toward the direction of labor's own programs in each area. Even in energy, where we differed on several key points, the President dramatically and correctly stated the depth of the crisis facing the nation and offered a sweeping, detailed program to meet that crisis. . . .
>
> It is still too early, however, to grade the Carter Administration. For, the pluses, and they are many indeed, are clouded by the continued slack in the economy and high rate of unemployment. Realistic action to meet these problems has been stymied by an apparent shift of priorities away from the President's number one campaign issue—jobs—and toward the number one issue of the conservative opposition: "balance the budget."

Turning to the future, Meany warned of the growing threat posed by right-wing lobbyists and their supporters in Congress:

> The past two years have shown increasing evidence that some businessmen, who publicly express support for the principle of collective bargaining, are in fact working covertly to subvert this institution of democracy. Employer challenges to collective bargaining have never been greater since the late 1930s. When these business leaders who proclaim their respects for the rights of their employees to bargain collectively act in concert to defend such immoral law-breakers as J. P. Stevens by seeking to gut labor law reform, we are left no alternative but to question their good word.
>
> When business leaders engage in gutter tactics and mudslinging, promote libelous and maliciously false advertising, and provide financial assistance to the extreme right-wing hate-mongers, then we question their decency. . . .
>
> If major business leaders persist in defaming the labor movement in order to protect those businesses which refuse to obey the law, it will bring into question the value of seeking greater labor-management cooperation. Without mutual trust and respect, there is no basis for cooperation.

In the biennial election of AFL-CIO officers, no one was nominated to run against Meany or Kirkland, and the thirty-three candidates for vice president also were chosen without opposition. Thirteen of the candidates would be serving their first full term, in Meany's continuing campaign to bring younger union presidents to the Council table.*

A few weeks after the convention, Senator Hubert Humphrey died, and the AFL-CIO with the other fifty-nine national organizations in the coalition stepped up their drive to enact the full-employment bill bearing his name. The Humphrey-Hawkins bill, as weakened somewhat to win White House support, established a "national goal" of providing useful employment at fair wages for all persons able and willing to work. Its interim goal called for reduction of the unemployment rate to 4 percent within five years. (Congress later watered it

---

* One of those going on the top body for the first time was William W. Winpisinger, head of the Machinists Union. He had been quoted in news stories suggesting that Meany should retire because of his age. Some of Meany's associates wanted to keep Winpisinger off the nomination list, but Meany insisted that he had a right to go on. Any critic of Meany, of course, could have run against him, but it was obvious that he had the overwhelming support of the delegates. No hint of rebellion reached the floor during the four-day convention.

down further before passing it in the 1978 closing rush; it was reduced to more symbol than substance. But the 4 percent jobless rate was retained as a goal.)

As 1978 began, industry went to war against the labor movement with powerful weapons of computerized mailing lists, unlimited funds and propaganda. The assault far exceeded the business effort that had killed the construction picketing bill of 1977. It was the right wing's biggest assault on labor since big business fought Roosevelt's New Deal.

The principal target was a relatively mild piece of legislation aimed at closing loopholes in the basic labor law governing collective bargaining. (To obtain Carter's support, labor had had to tone down its original proposal, but even so, the attackers exaggerated its effects and its contents.) But before that warfare got underway in earnest, Meany had to deal with a new Administration attempt to deliver its own blow at collective bargaining over wages. The President called on labor and industry to cooperate in a voluntary program to hold pay raises and price increases to less than the average of the previous two years. The new gimmick was called "deceleration." Meany expressed labor's suspicions in a January statement:

> We certainly agree that inflation must be contained and reduced, and we applaud the President's rejection of advice to tamper with collective bargaining through wage-price controls. Guidelines, in any form, are of course a step down the road toward controls.
>
> Negotiated wage increases have barely kept pace with inflation caused by events and actions that had nothing to do with wages—such as huge increases in the price of energy, interest rates, food, housing and the continuing inflationary pressures that result from the economic waste created by unemployed workers and idle productive capacity. . . .
>
> The AFL-CIO and its affiliates have always been willing to meet and confer with Administration officials on all matters of mutual concern, and we shall continue to do so in the future. We cannot and will not, however, support the proposition that government should define the terms and results of collective bargaining through any variation of guidelines, generalized or industry-by-industry. We are concerned that the Administration approach—proposing a two-year average base period for "deceleration"—appears to lead in that direction.

Labor criticism of the Administration escalated at the February meeting of the Executive Council. Meany told reporters why the council objected to the latest wage-restraint idea:

> We have had a year now dealing with Charlie Schultze and Mike Blumenthal. And they first were talking about voluntary guidelines—and didn't get any takers. And then they were talking about consultations . . . before you go into collective bargaining. . . . Now they come up with this idea of deceleration. This is a new word, and the idea is you are supposed to keep price and wage increases below the level of the last two years and try to bring them down.
>
> All of these ideas are a step toward . . . wage and price controls— and we are opposed to controls, period. No matter what form they take. [The President] keeps saying that he is not in favor of controls, and Mike and Charlie keep saying, "Well, we have to do something."

After Carter had completed his first year in the White House, a reporter asked Meany what kind of report card he would give him. Meany said he noticed that a poll of students scored Carter at C-plus. He rated Carter at C-minus. But, he went on:

> I don't want to be overly critical at this stage, and I think that the President is trying pretty hard. . . . He has come up with some progressive ideas [but] he could do more in the job field. . . . We want some direct appropriations for jobs: public works, public service jobs, youth jobs, mass transit, housing and guaranteed loans for cities.
>
> All of these things would produce jobs and none of these are in the President's program at the present time. He's depending on tax incentives to business, and there's no indication that tax incentives to business have created any jobs. We are in complete disagreement with the idea that he can solve the country's problems by giving additional goodies to the business community in the way of tax breaks and tax incentives.

More conflict arose over a three-month-old national coal strike. Meany thought that the President had been right in not intervening in the early stages but felt the time for strong action had passed weeks before the White House did move in to urge a negotiated settlement. When asked what he would do if he were President, Meany responded: "I'd seize the mines and lay down conditions the miners would accept" because "that's the only way you are going to get coal." Asked if he would guarantee the operators a profit, he replied, "No."

When it developed that his advice had not been sought by the Administration in this crisis, a questioner asked if other Presidents had consulted him about similar strike situations. Meany replied: "I don't think Lyndon ever had a national strike of any kind without telephoning me or talking to me about it. . . . There was much more interest in those days in what I thought." Asked why that was so, he said, "I have no idea. I don't spend my time trying to analyze why somebody else does something. If they do it, I just more or less accept it. Now, if you want to find out why they do it, you ask them; don't ask me."

In that exchange, he indicated that Carter was having trouble with labor, black organizations and other groups because he did not seem to realize the importance of consulting with major segments of society through their leaders.

In response to a question about the labor movement's recent switch from a strong "free trade" position to one it called "fair trade," Meany explained:

> We think that the present trade policy of our country is one that is slowly but surely converting America into a service-industry country, and there is a possibility that we will lose our position before long as a major manufacturing nation—not only to foreign competition but to competition from American corporations who produce overseas.
> We think this is a bad thing. We think it has to be turned around: we are losing too many jobs in this area. . . . If all of our manufacturing is going overseas, then we are going to be reduced to shining one another's shoes, that's all.

AFL-CIO strategy on foreign-trade laws had been revised, Meany explained. Instead of seeking in one piece of legislation all its proposed corrections, the Federation would try to get Congress to act on a series of separate measures. Putting it all in one bill, he said, "doesn't seem to be in the cards as far as Congress is concerned." He added:

> People from the academic world [tell us] that we have to have free trade, and, if we don't, that the consumers are going to lose certain benefits. [But] we don't have free trade today. We were free traders. The American labor movement was traditionally oriented to free

trade, starting way back to the time of the Hull reciprocal trade pacts.

Actually, what we have now is that we are trading in a world where practically every country has various devices and various methods of protecting their own people . . . and we are theoretically the only free traders left. We feel that the time has come when we should no longer look at the word "protectionism" as a bad word. We are looking for protection. . . .

We are competing with the Japanese, who have taken our technology, and their trade is government-supported. We are dealing with companies that get subsidies. We are competing with countries that dump. . . . We are sort of standing back, Simon-pure, and saying, "Well, we are for free trade."

Much of Meany's time in 1978 was devoted to the largest legislative effort ever conducted by organized labor and its allies—to counter the unprecedented lobbying drive by business groups, whose computerized mailing lists were soliciting millions of personal contributions and letters to members of Congress. To compete with the greatest volume of "issue" mail Congress had ever seen, the AFL-CIO generated more than two million cards, letters and telegrams to the legislators, plus thousands of personal visits by union members. The increasingly evident imbalance in the basic law was what prompted the labor movement to make its all-out drive. As Meany explained:

Go back to the original history of the National Labor Relations Act, which came into being for two basic reasons. One was the La-Follette Civil Liberties Report in the early thirties, after a couple of years of exhaustive testimony. Volume after volume of testimony painted a very sordid picture of the activities of American employers.

Those were the days when the hiring of strike-breaking agencies was routine. They hired them not just when they had a strike; they hired them as a matter of business policy.

Then the Depression came and got worse and worse; the attitude of people in public office toward workers and those suffering from the Depression took a radical change. Labor was very definitely the underdog. It was as a result of those two factors, at least in my opinion, that they got the Wagner Act.

That Act states very clearly it was set up to correct an imbalance. In the field of collective bargaining, the authors of the Act said in effect, the power is all on the employers' side, and we've got to redress that, we've got to balance that off.

When the Wagner Act went into effect, I think it's reasonable to say that, in the first few years, the balance went the other way. The original members of the Board and the staff people were very pro-labor, and the employers felt they were not getting a fair deal. The pendulum had swung the other way. When the time came, the employers planned to get back, and they got the Taft-Hartley and Landrum-Griffin acts.

We don't have goons or the thugs anymore; we've got lawyers [to contend with]; the imbalance has gone completely the other way. Any employer who is willing to give the time and effort can keep the union from operating effectively in his plant. I don't care how strong the union is. If the employer is determined to stop the union from operating in the plant, he won't bargain, he'll get all sorts of decisions against the union, he'll drag things out on appeals.

The classic case is J. P. Stevens. He has been cited time and again; he's broken the law time and again, and still he has very effectively kept the union out of his textile plants. They say the workers don't vote for a union. Under the circumstances in which elections are conducted and the pressure put on the workers, it's surprising that any worker stands up and votes for the union.

We feel that an imbalance has been created, and we want to get the law back to where it is even-handed on both sides. For instance, take the injunction procedure. The union can be subjected to an immediate injunction by the Board, but the employer can't be. An unfair labor practice by a union—injunction right away. The employer knows that he can be cited and he can go to the trial and drag the thing out for months. We are going to try to change that.

The Administration bill, to change the unfair sections of the law, passed the House by a big margin: 257 to 163. But the real battle was just beginning. Senate conservatives lacked the votes to defeat the Carter measure and therefore began a filibuster to prevent a showdown. Meany tried to argue with reasonable businessmen by publishing an open letter to American business leaders in *The Wall Street Journal*—the first time the AFL-CIO had used the employers' bible for advertising. The letter read in part:

The Business Roundtable, the U.S. Chamber of Commerce, the National Association of Manufacturers, the so-called National Right-to-Work Committee and others, including extreme right-wing organizations, have publicly committed themselves to defeat the labor law reform bill. They seem to feel the only way to achieve this

is to defame the trade union movement, and misrepresent the
bill. . . .

Every business leader knows—or should know—that President
Carter's labor law reform bill will have no effect on those companies
with established labor relations. There will be no changes in relations between unions and management where contracts are in force.
The bill will have no effect even on those companies which oppose
unions but obey the law and act according to the rules.

The bill's clear target is the lawbreakers.

Against the huge sums spent by opponents of reform, the AFL-CIO's
expenditure of $1.4 million was pitiful indeed. Thus efforts of the Sen-
ate leadership and the AFL-CIO failed to break the filibuster and on
June 16 the measure was sent back to committee to die. The supporters
of reform tried in six cloture moves to obtain the needed sixty votes;
they started with only forty-two; their peak was fifty-eight, and another Senator was willing to switch to their side if they could get the
sixtieth vote.

Meany's reaction to the defeat became public at his first press conference at the August Executive Council meeting in Chicago where
members discussed the outcome. In response to a question on what the
Council decided, Meany said: "We decided we lost," and added:

I presume we will have to wait for a new Congress if we are going
to try to pass the labor law reform. . . . Labor law reform as we presented it to the Congress is dead for this session. [Opponents] joined
with the right-wing, anti-labor forces which were opposed to anything for labor, opposed to anything that would help the minorities,
opposed to anything that would make life a little better for the people in the inner cities. And I think it is part of a class warfare. . . .
There seems to be a resurgence of the right-wing feelings throughout
the country, and we have had this before, and I'm sure that we are
going to combat it.

One result of the dispute over changing the labor law was destruction of the Dunlop Labor-Management Group. Late in 1978, Meany
explained why no meetings had been held for some months and none
was in prospect:

The employers on that committee—despite the fact that they privately told us they did not oppose what we wanted to do on labor
law reform—did nothing to support us. We knew that they threw

their money into the Roundtable and the opposition. That's the reason [for not meeting]; it's just as simple as that.

Talking to reporters in August about the failure to break the filibuster on reform, Meany had said the opposition in Congress was too tough, but Carter's lack of experience in dealing with Congress was a factor.

> The situation of the Presidency made some kind of contribution, because, actually, we do not have a strong President in his relations with Congress. And I think that this is due to the inexperience of the people in the White House, beginning with the President himself. I don't think he has been able to deal with the Congress in control of his own party. So, while I certainly don't blame President Carter for the setbacks . . . if he were a stronger President—stronger in relation to Congress—I think he might have been helpful to us.

Efforts to get a new "report card" grade for Carter failed:

> I don't think we should try to rate him on that basis. He didn't like that. And I wouldn't want to hurt his feelings. . . . I would say that the relationship between the AFL-CIO and the White House is better than it was six months ago . . . I'm always ready to work with the President. After all, he is the only President that we have.

At its next meeting, in October, the AFL-CIO Council called for a mandatory program of controls for all phases of the economy. This was labor's surprise reply to the Administration's latest plan to reduce inflation: so-called "voluntary" wage and price standards. Any firm violating the standards could be punished by a denial of federal contracts—a weapon which, if used, could mean losing millions of dollars in sales. Employers were expected to hold wage-fringe increases to 7 percent annually. The price standard was vague, complicated and elastic—and did not cover such inflation-causing costs as food products, medical services, interest rates or energy costs.

Immediate public confusion over the reasons for the AFL-CIO decision was one result, especially since many media accounts failed to disclose details of the Council's statement, which said in part: "The AFL-CIO Executive Council agrees with President Carter's conclusion that inflation is the nation's No. 1 problem, supports his determination that prompt remedial action be taken, and concurs with his contention that austerity must be shared equally by all Americans. . . .

"While the program demonstrates the President's desire to address the problem of inflation, the plan his advisers have devised is unfair and inequitable and the end result of their ill-considered proposals could well be another recession, with mass unemployment, which at least one Administration spokesman is already predicting.... Since the President's economic advisers have so far rebuffed suggestions for changes to make this third anti-inflation program more equitable, we now believe the time has come for mandatory, legislated economic controls."

The Council urged the President "to draft a legislative program of full economic controls covering every source of income—profits, dividends, rents, interest rates, executive compensation, professional fees, as well as wages and prices."

The Council also proposed that Carter call a special session of Congress to enact a detailed program of controls, not a standby authorization for the President to set his own rules. It promised the Federation's support for a fair, legislated program.

The statement was approved unanimously by the Council members after Meany made an impassioned plea for mandatory controls. Several members reported that it was one of the best speeches they had ever heard him deliver, and that he had laid down the facts of the situation without indulging in personalities or attacking Carter.

From the Council table, Meany went to answer reporters' questions, such as whether labor would cooperate with the President on his program:

> We are going to cooperate with the President to try to bring down the inflation rate. We are not going to dictate to our 60,000 collective bargaining groups as to what they will lay on the bargaining table.... I expect them to do what they think is right for their membership.... It could mean that they would adhere to the guidelines. It could mean that because of special circumstances they want to go beyond the guidelines. The figure on the guidelines is not the problem.
>
> The problem here is equity ... fairness. The program of the President's ... attempts to control wages and keep wages down. It controls nothing else—nothing else. That does not attack the problem of inflation....
>
> We want everything that goes into the cost controlled and then, maybe, we will get a handle on this inflation and, when we do, we can remove the controls and get back to normal. But the way we are

going now is this piecemeal approach to control wages and then come up with a formula which nobody contends will be able to control prices. . . .

This is not a wage-price-push inflation. Nobody's made that contention, including Charlie Schultze. Now, if wages are not the cause of inflation, how in God's name are we going to stop inflation by controlling wages?

Meany ridiculed Carter's short-lived suggestion that Congress enact a "real wage insurance program" that would affect workers who accepted the 7 percent ceiling on pay raises but then found inflation had exceeded that figure. They would be reimbursed by the government for the excess rise. A member of Congress had tagged this as the "carrot and stick approach," prompting Meany to say:

Nobody knows how it is going to work. And I'm a little bit skeptical about something that is referred to as the "carrot and stick" approach. . . . Now, the carrot and stick approach is used on a beast of burden, and it works quite well. You know, you get him a carrot and then beat him a little bit with the stick. But I never heard a horse say that he approved of the idea.

Meany explained that he had been meeting with the White House economic advisers on their proposals for curbing inflation:

I've been meeting with these characters for the last two months and I've been looking into their eyes, pleading and crying, "Will this work?" And every time they say, "Oh, no, no! Don't put me on record. I don't know whether it will work or not." Poor old Charlie Schultze. They're for it but they don't know if it will work or not.

I feel that we have to face up to this problem, and the way to control inflation is to control it. Not to throw cream puffs at it but to . . . control every phase of it. Now, if they don't buy that, we will try to see if we can get Congress to buy it.

Elaborating for this book, Meany put it this way:

During World War II, we controlled inflation. We had a large number of people working in Leon Henderson's price agency. They reached down to the retail level, and we had rationing of certain things. But the thing worked fairly well. They say that Henderson had sixty-three thousand people working for him, and, if you do the same thing now, it would possibly take two hundred and fifty thousand people. But when you take the cost of that and you put it against the cost the American people are paying every day, the amount involved is very little. . . . Maybe it costs you five billion dollars a year, but what's five billion?

[Carter spokesman Robert] Strauss keeps talking about austerity. . . . If austerity is to mean anything, the people of the country have to be convinced that everybody is involved. . . . That's the reason that we take the position that the only thing that will work is something across-the-board that involves everybody. . . .

In the big, thick fact sheet [government officials] put out, they make this statement: "While wages are not responsible for the inflation that we have today, moderation of wages is part of the cure." Now, you figure that one out! That's exactly what they say. . . .

Carter's method of conducting what he termed "consultations" with labor and other groups before drafting his anti-inflation plans was vastly different from President Johnson's system, Meany added:

[Carter's staff system] is almost an impossible system. Everything terminates with him. The best example is the way that we tried to work with him on inflation. At no time since he became President has there been any consultation on any issue affecting labor *before* he made a decision. You would always talk to him after he had made a decision.

When he set up his committee on inflation in August, he asked us to set up a committee to work with him. Between the fifteenth of August and the nineteenth of October, I guess we met maybe five or six times. At no time was there a definite discussion, because everything they laid on the table was tentative. You would argue about it and they'd say, "Well, it's not final; the President hasn't passed on it."

During all those meetings, I kept reminding Ray Marshall that I wanted this [labor] committee to talk to the President before he finalized whatever he was going to do. Marshall said, "Yes, I'm sure we can arrange that." This went right on; we would go to these meetings; we would discuss something. We would sort of disagree with them and they'd say, "It's not final; it's all tentative."

In the last couple of meetings, working papers were laid on the table and they were numbered. We were told we had to return them; we couldn't take them with us. When we left about one o'clock on October nineteenth, nothing had been finalized. The President had set the date for his [broadcast] talk for October twenty-fourth. Again

I said to Marshall: "We want to see the President before he makes his final decision." He looked at me queerly, saying, "Oh, you want to see him before he makes his speech?" I said, "Yes. What the hell do you think I've been talking about?" He said, "I didn't understand it that way."

Of course, he was lying; he had gotten the word that the President didn't want to see us. He said he would take it up at the Cabinet meeting. We still had five days to go before the speech, but that was the end of it. An assistant said the President could not fit me into his schedule.

Now, the difference between him and Johnson is: you could go over and see Johnson on any proposal that was coming up and he would give you the line where he wanted to go. He listened to you and in some cases he would make adjustments, concessions. When you left him, you knew what he was going to do.

With this fellow, everything is tentative until he makes the final decision. In this case everything was tentative until a couple of hours before he made his speech. How are you going to deal with people like that?

Meany heaped equal scorn on some White House staff people he had known:

It's the attitude of people like Colson, the attitude of Haldeman and Ehrlichman, and to a lesser degree the other people who go to work for the White House. It's like they are working for an emperor. It's the President against the world, and they look almost with contempt at anybody who doesn't agree with them.

You've got that now; you've got that with this little White House crowd there—the little special-interest group, I guess you could call them. There are no two ways; it's the man's way, and anything that is said has to be complimentary to the man. They would never admit that he ever does anything wrong. It's an ongoing propaganda, day-in, day-out. And they look upon outsiders with contempt.

Disagreements over policy, however, did not prevent the President from sending cordial greetings to Meany's eighty-fourth birthday dinner, held to honor Meany and raise money for one of his pet charities, the "No Greater Love" organization. He was an early supporter of the organization formed by professional athletes to help the thousands of children of Vietnam War servicemen killed or missing in action.

Meany advised the crowd that someone had said people should "grow old gracefully and quietly," and he had "thought a lot about that and bought half of it." He said also, "Being eighty-four is not so difficult. Just hang on, keep going, and you'll get there."

But election day, 1978, was not so pleasant for Meany, as labor suffered a net loss of supporters in both Houses of Congress. Before the results were in, Meany had these thoughts:

> The Watergate effect really has not diminished. There are other things, but I think there is an absolute contempt on the part of the American people [regarding] people in public office. They don't give a damn for senators or congressmen; they've gotten to the point where [they believe] all representatives of the people are crooks. One thing responsible for a great deal of this is Watergate, because every American with any common sense knows that the President of the United States was crooked; he was a lawbreaker. No matter what happened, you can't wipe that away. This runs deep and people say, "My God, our President was a crook and he wasn't punished."

A crucial showdown between Carter and Meany occurred on January 12, 1979, and led directly to an important "first": the so-called national accord promising labor a voice in administration decision-making on national issues. The accord turned out to be Meany's last big achievement, one that would have far-reaching effects on American labor after his death.

The January meeting had been arranged by Labor Secretary Marshall in an effort to improve the soured relations between the Administration and the AFL-CIO. On the way into the White House, Meany and seven AFL-CIO vice presidents found reporters and cameramen waiting in the pouring rain. Meany, acting as a business agent for the press, complained to a Carter aide, who promised to bring them in under cover.

After the meeting, Meany told the media: "I think we cleared the air and we will be able to communicate better." He said that communication rather than specific issues was the purpose of the conference.

Later, others reported that Carter conceded that communications between the Administration and the AFL-CIO were in a mess and that AFL-CIO Council members should feel free to telephone him at any time. This apparent attempt to go around the Federation's president was rejected immediately. Members said that this was not the way to deal with an organization, that Carter should deal with their president and not through the vice presidents. Reportedly, Carter agreed to this, promising to consult with Meany before reaching a decision—not afterward.

Meany suggested that the President delegate to subordinates some of the decision making but got no response.

Lane Kirkland's recollections of that January meeting surfaced at a press conference in October after the signing of the accord. He tied the accord to the the January session, where, he said, labor "expressed some dissatisfaction with the fact that we were frequently getting surprised by positions taken in areas of very direct concern to us, winding up in battles that could have been avoided with proper advance notice and consultation."

Kirkland explained that it had been agreed that periodic meetings of AFL-CIO officials and top Administration officials headed by Mondale would be held and that the President would be available for further consultation if requested. It was during the subsequent meetings, held about once a month, that labor learned that the Administration was considering revised guidelines on wages and prices to go into effect after the end of the first-year program, Kirkland said.

He added that when asked if the AFL-CIO would be willing "to embrace" new rules, labor representatives said they would if "we negotiate them." The Administration was told: "You're talking about something that goes to the heart of the responsibilities of trade unions in representing their members, and you've dealt with that in a unilateral way in the evolution of your guidelines.

"We were granted an audience and our views were disregarded, and you went ahead and did what you pleased, and we don't regard that as an appropriate basis for cooperation. The basis for a cooperative effort must arise out of a negotiated understanding. Negotiations are quite different from being granted an audience, or even being consulted. Negotiations involve the exchange of considerations—relevant considerations. The consideration you seek from us is participation in a program of wage restraints, and we have some considerations, and here's a little list."

During the eight months from Meany's January demand for better contact with the President to the national accord signing, Meany had to contend with the usual media curiosity about the President's "report card." As a reporter at the opening news conference of the February Council meeting began his query, Meany cut him off in mid-sentence, saying he was not going to make that mistake again. Another reporter tried again, asking if Meany thought "Carter's performance" had improved in the past year. Answer: "No." Was there anyone whom Meany would prefer to see on the Democratic ticket in 1980? "Yes, Harry Truman. I wish he was here."

Two members of the AFL-CIO Council had told reporters they thought there should be a "moderation of the criticism of President Carter," a reporter told Meany, adding that it appeared to be a reference to his comments. He was asked if he had heard from the two men, Sol C. Chaikin, president of the Ladies Garment Workers, and Glenn E. Watts, president of the Communications Workers. Meany said that "Glenn did make a statement some time back that he was unhappy with the fact that I criticized President Carter" but that he had not heard from Chaikin.

At times, he continued, there is dissent in the Council when a resolution is proposed, but "when the time comes to approve the resolutions there is no indication that they want to formally go on record in opposition." Sometimes a member wishes to be so recorded and is. Any union, he further explained, is free to take its own position, even if contrary to the AFL-CIO position. Regarding the two members' complaints voiced outside the Council meeting, he said:

> Some of our statements that we adopt here will be critical of President Carter, and I like the way we operate in this country . . . and that's the privilege to criticize anybody in government from the top to the bottom. I'm sure that Chick Chaikin and Glenn Watts would certainly not want to put a muzzle on the Executive Council or on me insofar as our thoughts regarding labor's problems [are concerned].
>
> Certainly I don't think anyone is immune from criticism, including myself. . . . I think [the President] was elected to represent the people; I don't think that he is ordained by the Almighty. I think he is human and he makes mistakes and, frankly, I will continue to comment on those mistakes.
>
> The funny part of it is the President doesn't seem to be upset about it. I talked to him yesterday afternoon and he was quite pleasant about things, and asked me how the meeting was going. I told him it was going quite well. And I'm sure at that time he had gotten some of the reports that came over the radio.

Meany also was asked if the Federation was heading toward a "break with Carter" in view of his critical statements, to which Meany replied:

Mr. Carter is the President of the United States. He's the only President that we have. We worked like hell to get him elected. That doesn't mean that we have to agree with everything that he brings up. And when we don't agree to everything that he brings up, that doesn't mean that we're approaching a break, that we're going to put him on an enemies list or anything like that.

We're dealing with the President; we deal with every President whether he's a Republican or a Democrat . . . and we deal on the basis of the old American tradition that we have a free right to talk; we have the right of freedom of speech; he's got the right to criticize us. And I don't think that that should be interpreted politically under any circumstances.

A suggestion that Meany be chosen AFL-CIO's "chairman of the board" if he retired from the presidency had been made privately by one Council member, according to a reporter, who then asked Meany if he would "accept" the post.

"They have a chairman of the board," Meany replied. "Here he is."

So the game was played out: "Sir, you're now eighty-four years old. Have you given any consideration to retiring at the end of this year?"

Meany said he had been thinking about retirement "for a number of years" and "I'll keep thinking about it for a number of years."

When asked if he would run for re-election at the November 1979 convention, the AFL-CIO chief replied: "I don't know. You give me your telephone number and I'll let you know. Don't call me. I'll call you."

A decision not to reintroduce the labor law reform bill in the new Congress was made by the Council at its February 1979 sessions. Having come out of the 1978 election with five fewer friends in the Senate, Meany conceded that it would be useless to risk another filibuster with the same bill. Instead, attempts would be made to get approval of separate sections of the bill.

The Council also authorized a double-barreled attack on the Administration's wage-price standards—further exacerbating the still chilly relationship with the White House. Attorneys were instructed to file a lawsuit challenging the legality of the penalties that could be imposed against employers who did not confine wage and fringe increases to the 7 percent standard. At the same time, the AFL-CIO moved to set its own monitoring system to report price increases. Meany announced the lawsuit first:

We have decided that we're going to test the government sanctions angle of the anti-inflation program. . . . After the President announced the voluntary program, there were statements made and efforts made to intimidate employers on the wage side of the thing by telling them that—while the program was voluntary—if they did not adhere to the wage guidelines they would be subject to government sanctions; and if they happened to have government contracts the contracts would be canceled.

[The law] that's on the statute books—that was enacted right after the Nixon fiasco on controls and freezes—says that there shall not be any mandatory controls.

Turning to the price phase of the government program at his news conference the following day, Meany described a telephone call he had received February 19 from the President, seeking cooperation in holding down prices:

He called up asking for cooperation on the price side. Which I would say is a recognition on his part that the price side of the anti-inflation program isn't going too well. I told him that we would cooperate, and that I had already written [Presidential inflation adviser Alfred E.] Kahn about ten days ago offering our cooperation. If you recall, Mr. Kahn made a speech [in which] he said he would like to have the cooperation from consumer groups monitoring prices at the retail level.

I wrote Mr. Kahn, and told him that we had the machinery, that we had a number of central bodies throughout the country with thousands of people who would be glad to assist in helping him to monitor retail prices. So, I told the President that and he said that that was good. He also said that Vice President Mondale would be in touch with us to see what can be done to get labor's cooperation on the price side. And I'll tell you we will be quite happy to cooperate.

But, a reporter reminded Meany, Kahn had expressed concern elsewhere about vigilante groups checking prices. Meany replied:

Oh yes, I'm sure there's a little worry there about that, because one thing Mr. Kahn would never do [is] make the business community unhappy. But he did say it—that he wanted help—and we are offering that help. Now, if he feels that that help is going to develop into vigilante groups, then, that's too bad. . . . I don't have the same reservations about offending the business community as Mr. Kahn has. . . .

Immediately after the lawsuit of the AFL-CIO and nine of its affiliates was filed in U.S. district court in Washington on March 13, 1979, Meany reported to a news conference:

> The Administration has said that companies that are violating its so-called "voluntary" wage guidelines will be denied federal contracts. We believe that "penalties" for "violators" clearly make the wage controls mandatory and not voluntary. Since there is no statutory basis for this action, we have asked the court for an injunction prohibiting the use of such tactics. . . .
>
> In our opinion, the President of the United States has every right to ask the American people to "voluntarily" do anything the President believes is right for the country. But, when he asks employers to "voluntarily" hold the wages of their employees to seven percent or less and then backs that up with the denial of contracts if employers don't "voluntarily" go along—then he has instituted a "mandatory" program. It is obvious that the denial of contracts is an enforcement weapon primarily for wage controls, since the price guidelines are, for all practical purposes, non-existent.

The AFL-CIO won the first legal round when the district court ruled that the President had no constitutional right to threaten violators of his guidelines with denial of federal contracts. However, the Administration won in the appeals court, and when the AFL-CIO sought review of that ruling by the Supreme Court, the High court, in its final action of the term, declined to review.

But by then the embattled chieftain was seriously ill. His wife, Eugenie McMahon Meany had died in March, at the age of eighty-two, following a long illness. Her death was a staggering blow. Although in the past, in news conferences and private chats, he had joked about being "bossed" by his wife—something that seemed incredible to those who try to judge character from a TV screen—the jokes covered up a deep, mutual devotion, an Irish togetherness, tenderness, that had sustained this "tough" labor leader for six decades. When half of the partnership died, his whole life was shattered.

Dignitaries attending the funeral mass included Rosalynn Carter, Vice President Mondale, Labor Secretary Marshall, Senators Edward M. Kennedy and Charles M. Mathias, as well as members of the House of Representatives, diplomatic corps and AFL-CIO Council. Each of the Meanys' fourteen grandchildren participated in the service.

Three weeks later, only hours after having been thoroughly chilled at the outdoor signing of the Camp David accords by Israel and Egypt, Meany was rushed to the hospital, suffering from a recurring bronchial ailment he had had since boyhood. He was back at work three days later, but more serious health problems followed. On April 22 he was hospitalized again for treatment of bursitis of the knee.

He had to miss sessions of the Executive Council in May, only his third such absence in his twenty-three years as AFL-CIO president. After a month of hospital care he returned home, but continuing therapy also kept him away from the August 1979 Council meeting.

Meany was able to pay a brief visit to his office on August 15, for the first time in about four months. He used a wheelchair to get from the car to the suite but switched to crutches while visiting with other officials.

He was not well enough, however, to attend a Labor Day picnic that the President held for more than a thousand labor movement guests.

The issue of Meany's health was very much on the minds of the AFL-CIO Council members at their August sessions, where Lane Kirkland presided and held the press conferences. The familiar cigar and bulldog face was replaced by a cigarette in a short holder and by a much fuller head of hair, but positions voiced by the secretary-treasurer—and in the Council resolutions—followed the Meany pattern.

Unable to ask Meany the standard query about his retirement, reporters tossed it at Kirkland: What was Meany's latest thinking about retirement this year?

"George Meany is well on the road to recovery from an ailment that has primarily affected his right leg," Kirkland responded. "He is in the process of exercising to build up the strength in that leg—progressing quite well. . . . What his plans are, he will declare in his own good time."

Pressed as to whether he expected to run for president or secretary-treasurer at the upcoming November convention, Kirkland said he expected Meany would decide whether to seek re-election "on the basis of what he finally ascertains about his physical capacity and what he thinks is good for the American trade union movement, and I would not want to have that decision in any other hands. I think it's in good hands."

If Meany did not seek re-election, would Kirkland seek the post? For the first time he stated flatly that he would seek the presidency if Meany did not: "Well, I believe George Meany is mortal, although that remains to be proven. I have no objective evidence of that. I would hope that his physical condition would permit him to carry on for as long as possible. I regard George Meany as a tremendous resource to the American trade movement, and I think if at some time mortality does overtake him, it will be a great loss.

"His physical capacity—his body and his legs—are not what he leads with. . . . It's his mind—and his mind is as clear, vigorous and forceful as ever, which means that it's superior to most of ours."

Kirkland added that, should a vacancy occur at some future date, "if nominated I will run; if elected, I will serve. I don't know of any first mate who was worth his salt and respects his trade who wouldn't like to be captain, and I'm no different."

The former first mate on American merchant ships, in answer to another question, said it was absolutely not true that the business of the Federation had been neglected while Meany was ill.

Two months later, on the evening of September 27, Meany telephoned the expected word to Kirkland: He would attend the Executive Council meeting the next day and tell the members that he was not going to seek re-election. But he was too ill even to attend the meeting, and Kirkland, in an emotional encounter, had to deliver the message himself.

Just prior to the AFL-CIO's convention, at which Kirkland was elected president, Meany took a sentimental journey to the convention of the Maritime Trades Department in a Washington hotel. Delegates rose, cheered, whistled and applauded—and some tears were seen—as he was pushed to the front of the platform in his wheelchair.

"I am delighted to be here," he began in a strong voice. "I am delighted to do anything these days." Typically, he rejected any idea of "going over past memories, because that doesn't get you anywhere." Instead, he talked about the present: "The Administration is still shying away from the only fair way to control inflation, and that's to control everything." As for the future, he said, "I'm quite sure that the Federation is in good hands. . . . We may have one-track minds, but it's a pretty good track."

As the subsequent AFL-CIO convention convened in November, the President was meeting the crisis over the seizure of the American Embassy in Iran. Early in that takeover, Meany, in one of his last official statements, had strongly backed Carter's handling of the problem—a typical example of Meany's ability to support a U.S. President in a foreign crisis, although differing sharply with him on domestic issues. And in Carter's speech to delegates he lavishly praised Meany's career and then embraced him.

Some 323 trade union leaders from 68 countries joined the 895 delegates from 95 national unions and various other affiliates for the November convention. About 650 media representatives recorded Meany's emotional farewell address. Appropriately, a telegram from Aleksandr Solzhenitsyn, the great author-dissident, was read at the final session:

"Dear George Meany. You can be envied: You have amply fulfilled your life's mission. Keep up your good spirits. I embrace you warmly."

But Meany was not present to hear the telegram read. Immediately after nominating Kirkland and seeing him elected unanimously, Meany tapped the gavel on the mahogany block—one he had used in countless meetings since the Carpenters Union had given it to him fifteen years earlier. The block broke in half. Meany gave a final wave to the delegates and left the platform for good.

19

HUMAN RIGHTS

No society that scorns human rights generally will make an exception on trade union rights. And so, ever since Samuel Gompers, American labor has vigorously urged the promotion of democracy and human rights as the heart of U.S. foreign policy.

Meany led the United States out of the International Labor Organization (ILO) in 1977 because that United Nations agency had been converted into a political sounding-board for Communist-bloc nations. Technically, President Carter took the action, but Meany and the AFL-CIO—backed by the U.S. Chamber of Commerce—pressured the White House into ending four decades of membership in the tripartite body. Had the Administration declined to pull out, the AFL-CIO could have seriously weakened the U.S. delegation by refusing to nominate the American worker delegate. (Under the rules of the ILO, the dominant labor movement in a country selects a worker representative and the leading employer organization chooses a business delegate. A government representative is the third delegate.) The U.S. employers' side probably would have refused too.

The required two years' notice of intent to leave the ILO had been filed by Secretary Kissinger, acting on behalf of President Ford. It listed four complaints against the organization having to do particularly with Soviet-bloc actions. During the waiting period, the United States had made every effort to get the ILO to return to its original

393

purpose: improving the wages and conditions of the working people of the world. But the coalition of Soviet-bloc (and some nonaligned) nations had refused to make sufficient changes in its tactics.

Part of the problem, as Meany pointed out, was that certain participating nations had no free trade unions; Communist and right-wing dictatorships controlled their so-called labor movements. The employer delegations sent to the ILO from these countries usually were government agents, like their worker counterparts.

Meany's strict antitotalitarian views had prompted him earlier to lead the AFL-CIO in withdrawing from the ICFTU (International Confederation of Free Trade Unions), which American labor had helped organize. One problem then—the year was 1969—was the growing flirtation of Western Socialist labor leaders with the "labor movements" of the Soviet bloc—which had been refused membership in the ICFTU from the beginning. AFL-CIO conventions had approved Meany's position against exchanging fraternal visits with the government-run unions of Russia and its allies, and the ICFTU also had adopted that position, but many union officials in Western Europe were increasing their "bridge-building" with the bloc movements. So the American Federation withdrew.*

Thus, when the United States left the ILO, the American labor movement was unrepresented in the two chief world organizations for union cooperation. To fill the vacuum, AFL-CIO unions expanded their activities in the worldwide "secretariats," in which unions in a particular industry cooperated on labor matters affecting their own field of work, and direct AFL-CIO assistance to free labor movements in developing nations, increased after the withdrawal from ICFTU, was further stepped up.

Under Meany's leadership, schools were set up by the AFL-CIO to train union leaders of the developing nations, teaching them the importance of democracy and free labor unions. Also, the U.S. Agency for International Development, or AID, helped finance housing projects and other programs to assist workers and their unions. To Meany,

---

* Meany also had other reasons for advocating the pull-out, including what he called "a bit of financial chicanery" by ICFTU officials. When Meany demanded, and got, a look at the books, he forced the ICFTU to return to the AFL-CIO some $818,000, he recalled—part of the money American labor had contributed to a fund for aiding developing labor movements in Asia, Africa and Latin America. Instead, some of it had not been spent for organizing but had been "hidden" in other funds to be used for pensions for the world organization's employees, Meany contended. He further accused Socialist union leaders of using ICFTU to spread Socialist doctrine to the new unions.

these programs among the new unions were the Federation's most important accomplishment in the foreign field:

> We have helped workers in the newly emerging countries; we have made a great contribution in Latin America, Africa and Asia. It's a slow process. In Africa we devoted a lot of our energy [to] bringing vocational skills to the workers, as well as helping them build unions. Take Latin America: We bring [workers] up here and give them a course in how our movement works and how it fits into the American economy. We stress the idea of union freedom—freedom from government, freedom from employer domination, freedom from any outside domination. We leave it to them to set up their own type of union. More and more, the unions are beginning to look a little bit more like our unions, but we don't impose our type of unionism on them.

The education in democracy and in free trade unionism helped to combat the efforts of Soviet Russia to spread communism in Latin America through its workers. It was part of Meany's opposition to all forms of dictatorship—a position that to some observers seemed extreme. It was, however, entirely consistent and Meany's independent course in international labor had followed years of restraint. Recent developments, moreover, had borne out his long-held view that Soviet-bloc unions were in fact agencies of the state.

From the time the Soviet delegation returned to the ILO in 1954, over Meany's objections, the Soviets had worked diligently to politicize that forum. Despite Meany's criticisms, the Communists and their allies became increasingly powerful, until in 1966 they succeeded in electing the Polish Communist delegate as presiding officer of that year's sessions. Their power kept growing as more third world delegations and others joined with the Soviet bloc. Four years later, the new director-general, Britain's C. Wilfred Jenks, appointed a Russian to the important post of assistant director-general. This was the first time, Meany told reporters, that the Russians had "reached a spot where they could exert a tremendous pressure on the employees of ILO."

When Meany, along with representatives of the State Department and employers, described this development to a subcommittee of the House of Representatives, the AFL-CIO did not ask that the country's dues payments to the ILO be withheld. Meany told the panel, "We have no desire to destroy or withdraw from the ILO, but if it continues in the trends it is going now, we have no further interest in it." Congress temporarily withheld the American payments to ILO. (The U.S. had been paying 25 percent of the annual budget, the largest contribution of any country.)

The AFL-CIO subsequently issued a strong attack on Communist activity in the ILO. Meany said the Council wanted to alert the public to the "gradual transformation of the ILO from an economic and social-welfare organization, dedicated to workers' rights and workers' welfare, into a political instrument."

Thereafter the uneasy alliance continued, until in 1975 a combination of Communist, Arab and third world nations voted at that year's sessions to allow the terrorist Palestine Liberation Organization to be represented by "observers." AFL-CIO protests that the PLO did not represent any country and was dedicated to the destruction of an ILO member, Israel, were ignored. Irving Brown, the U.S. worker delegate, along with Secretary-Treasurer Lane Kirkland and the rest of the U.S. delegation, then walked out in protest and were joined by the American governmental and employer delegates. The U.S. and Israel boycotted the rest of the conference.

A few months later, the United States' formal notice of intent to withdraw from the ILO was filed. The member states and officers of the ILO, Meany cautioned, must decide whether it is to continue "to be smothered in the suffocating spirit of accommodation with totalitarianism of the left and right" or is to resume its proper role.*

A phase of the "accommodation" Meany referred to was the detente agreement signed by Nixon and Brezhnev in 1972, an agreement Meany deplored as one-sided at a luncheon at the National Press Club two years later. Recalling Franklin Roosevelt's agreement with the Russians at Yalta after World War II, he cited a young politician who denounced that settlement as a sell-out to Russia, calling it "treason." Meany added:

> Those words were spoken by Richard Nixon almost twenty years ago. Was he a prophet? Was he twenty years before his time? Or was he then, and is he now, an opportunist without deep beliefs or large

---

* The subsequent U.S. withdrawal—opposed by the State Department but endorsed by Carter on the advice of the Labor Department—soon yielded the desired reforms, and Meany, at his last Executive Council meeting in November 1979, supported the Council's decision to return to the ILO. Later, the formal announcement of reaffiliation was made by the government. Meanwhile, ICFTU had gone into terminal decline. Meany said in 1977 that it "still has a headquarters and I guess they're getting enough money in from dues to pay their salaries and stuff like that. The organization is dead."

ideals, cynically indifferent to the cause of human freedom? And, more frightening still, has he refashioned American foreign policy in his own image?

What alternative short of war did Meany see for detente, he was asked:

> The alternative . . . is what they tried to sell to the American people a couple of years ago: cooperation between the Soviet Union and the United States in pursuit of peace, cutting down on the arms race, using our influence, wherever we have influence, to see to it that these wars don't break out which might cause a global war. . . .
>
> The idea that they [the Soviets] would throw the bomb—I don't buy that at all. I think that they have the same urge for self-preservation that we have. But I think they are great poker players . . . much better poker players than Henry or Dick, and they have been playing their type of poker for a long time.
>
> Now, what we need in the future is an open and above-board relationship with the Soviet Union—give-and-take, some old Yankee horse-trading methods. Some collective bargaining, if you please. But, unilateral concessions—in other words, appeasement—is not the answer. . . .
>
> In dealing with these people: cash on the barrelhead—give-and-take. If we've got technology they need, let's find out what they've got that we need. Maybe in return for our technology . . . and our financing . . . they would help us bring peace to the Middle East. . . . And let them let their people go.

Meany's repeated public condemnation of the Kissinger brand of detente provoked criticism in many quarters, as he acknowledged to the Senate Foreign Relations Committee on October 1, 1974:

> I suspect, Mr. Chairman, that you are not altogether unfamiliar with my views on this subject. They have been reported in the press, sometimes quite colorfully. Let me read to you from an editorial in a little newspaper called the *Torrington, Connecticut, Register,* under date of May 24, 1973—and I quote:
>
> "Once upon a time, labor in this country was in the vanguard of the liberal movement in foreign policy as well as domestic. But not any longer. Today its liberalism stops abruptly at the water's edge. On issues involving normalization of relations with the Communist world, the AFL-CIO as represented by aging George Meany, often makes the U.S. Chamber of Commerce sound like a cabal of wild-eyed Bolsheviks."

Well, aging or no, I have no desire to undertake a defense of the
Chamber of Commerce from the charge of wild-eyed bolshevism. I
might suggest, however, that what you see in their eyes isn't the Red
Flag. It's dollar signs.

But, more to the point, I cannot help but wonder what has become of the word "liberalism." I always thought that liberalism had
to do with the defense of freedom—and that the defense of feedom
did not stop at the water's edge. Now, I don't know how many liberals would accept the clear implication of this editorial that liberalism is to be defined as a softer or friendlier attitude toward totalitarian powers, whereas conservatism means a harder or more hostile
attitude toward totalitarian powers. . . . I don't see any necessary
connection between a liberal commitment to social and economic
justice at home and a policy of appeasement of Communist sup-
pression abroad.

We live in strange times. We live in a time when a man whose
whole political career was built on rabid anti-Communism can become President and overnight be transformed into the chief advocate of unilateral concessions to the Soviet Union.

We live in a time when the president of Pepsi-Cola is transported
into ecstasy by Leonid Brezhnev, about whom he says he was tremendously impressed "by the candor and sincerity of this man and
by his clear commitment to pursue not only peace, but also . . . the
enrichment of life in his country."

This is Don Kendall talking. He's the man whose company fills
the airwaves with jingles about "feeling free."

Reiterating that he was opposed not to genuine detente but only to
this Nixon-Kissinger version, Meany explained his objections to the
Senators:

I discovered something interesting. I discovered that this detente
has suddenly become very ambiguous. Suddenly this great idea—
this "conceptual breakthrough," to use one of Secretary Kissinger's
favorite phrases—is like gossamer. You can't grab hold of it. I wondered how we could have gotten so excited about something that
wasn't much of anything anyway. . . .

What has happened is that, as public disillusionment with detente
mounts, its proponents are retreating into a rhetoric of dampened
expectations, of fuzzy ambiguity. You might call it a revolution of
falling expectations. At least two members of this committee have,
in my judgment, contributed to this process of obfuscation through
excessive refinement.

Meany offered definitions that had been given by Chairman J. William Fulbright and Senator Frank Church, as well as Kissinger himself, and then summed up:

> A common thread runs through all these definitions of detente. They all boil down to the same thing: detente is the avoidance of nuclear war. Detente is the imposition of restraints so that the two superpowers don't blow each other up. If this is the meaning of detente, then I have a question. What is the difference between detente and cold war? Isn't cold war also an avoidance of hot war?
>
> If we have decided that this is all detente means—just that both sides restrain themselves—then what's all the fuss about? Why the vitriolic attacks, by Senator Church among others, on the "old-time cold warriors"? Perhaps we owe the cold warriors an apology. . . .
>
> The American people thought they were buying something more. To them detente meant not just something negative but something positive—not just restraint but cooperation. Cooperation not only to reduce armaments, but to further world peace. To prevent small wars.

Because of detente, "the cause of human rights is in a recession, a worldwide recession," Meany told an audience in 1975:

> I'm not blaming all of the world's troubles on Henry Kissinger, but I'm saying, in the final analysis, the cause of human rights in this world is dependent on the strength, the economic strength, the military strength, the moral strength of the United States of America. If we falter, freedom is shaken everywhere. . . .
>
> I believe, advisedly believe, sincerely believe, that Dr. Kissinger has presided over an era which has seen a decline of American strength—military, economic and moral—of unprecedented proportions. . . . One outstanding example of America's "great influence and standing" in world affairs is the United Nations vote to give recognition to the organized murderers known as the Palestine Liberation Organization. In opposition to this action by the UN, the United States was able to pick up four votes out of a total of 120-odd nations. Four votes; the Dominican Republic, Bolivia, Israel and ourselves.

But the signal defeat of detente, Meany believed, was the Yom Kippur War of 1973. As he recalled for this book:

> If [the Soviets] hadn't violated the detente agreement there would have been no Yom Kippur War, because they could have prevented it. They not only didn't prevent it, they encouraged it. The day after

the Arab sneak attack by Egypt, [Soviet Premier] Brezhnev was on
the air with a message to all the Arab countries: Don't leave the
Egyptians to fight alone, this is your fight, and so on.

   The very minute the attack started, they started to resupply the
Egyptians with massive amounts of military hardware [to replace
what] they lost in the initial hours of the onslaught. Despite that, I
remember one statement Kissinger made right at the height of that
thing—within a few days after we started to resupply the Israelis. He
said that the Soviets acted with great restraint, and that was a damn
lie. They didn't act with any restraint at all.

   But Meany's harshest condemnations of detente related to the chill-
ing effect it had in the West on critics of Soviet policy toward Russian
dissidents. He was particularly outraged by the Ford Administration's
refusal to receive Aleksandr Solzhenitsyn at the White House following
the Nobel laureate's expulsion from the Soviet Union in 1974.

   Soon after Solzhenitsyn reached Switzerland, Meany wrote inviting
him to visit the United States under AFL-CIO sponsorship. Solzhenitsyn was unable to come then but later accepted a renewed invitation.
He knew of Meany's efforts to free Russian dissidents, although he discovered only on the trip that Meany in the 1940s had arranged for
publication by the Federation of a "Gulag" map, identifying the loca-
tion of Russia's infamous prison camps. When the renowned author
arrived in 1975 the AFL-CIO welcomed him with a dinner attended
by 2,500 guests.

   During preparations for the dinner, at which Solzhenitsyn spoke,
Meany and AFL-CIO public-relations director Albert Zack discussed
how to invite the President. Zack suggested that Meany simply pick up
the telephone and give Ford a personal invitation, but Meany's knowledge of politics told him otherwise.

   "No, Al," he said firmly, "I'll write to him, because if I phoned,
Ford would say, 'Don't invite me' to save himself embarrassment.
Then, if the press asks why Ford isn't here, I can't say, 'Well, he said
not to invite him.' So, I'll write him and it's up to the White House to
explain why he turned it down."

   In any event, Ford did not attend, although two of his Cabinet
members did—Secretary of Defense James R. Schlesinger and Labor
Secretary Dunlop. Kissinger subsequently told reporters that the
Nobel Prize winner's views were a threat to world peace and that that
had been the basis of his recommending against a Presidential chat.

The advice had gone to Ford in the form of a memo from Kissinger's executive secretary. In recommending rejection of the AFL-CIO's invitation, the memo stated that it would be "an occasion for outspoken anti-Soviet rhetoric." Meany divulged a portion of the memo at a Senate Foreign Relations Committee hearing, although he didn't explain how he had obtained it: "The Soviets would probably take White House participation in the affair as either a deliberate negative signal or a sign of Administration weakness in the face of domestic anti-Soviet pressures. We recommend that the invitation to the President be declined and that no White House officials participate."

Anticipating the possibility that pressure might be exerted to have Ford receive the Russian author, the memo suggested that if some concession became necessary, Solzhenitsyn could be invited to any large social function at the White House or to an outside affair attended by the President. But no visit to the Oval Office.

Solzhenitsyn's speech excited attention but also generated some criticism from people who misunderstood his position on detente—something that Meany clarified in an interview at the time:

> Detente is a fraud. I would like to see genuine detente. I would like to see a genuine give-and-take with the Soviet Union. I would like to see genuine cooperation. But we don't have anything like that at all. What we have is this phony detente that was supposed to relax tension. We carry out our part and they violate every phase of it, every phase of the agreement, as they have violated every agreement . . . they signed with any other nation in the last 60 years. . . .
>
> I'm for real detente and, of course, if you read what Mr. Solzhenitsyn says, this is his position, too. He is for genuine detente. He said so quite plainly. He's not for a confrontation with the Soviet Union. He's a man of peace; he's not a man of violence. He suffered, he spent eleven years in the Soviet prison camps and he was put in there because, while he was in the Soviet army . . . he wrote a letter to another soldier . . . who had been a school boy chum of his. In that letter he said that he questioned the judgment of Stalin. He was critical of Stalin. That letter was opened. They gave him eight years in jail and then they gave him three more for good measure.

Asked to cite violations of agreements by the Russians, Meany ticked off various treaties of friendship with Soviet neighboring countries which, as he said, were "followed by invasions." Another agreement he listed was the United Nations' Declaration of Human Rights, which "spelled out very, very definitely that any person shall have a right to leave any country, including his own, and go to another country." However, he pointed out, the Soviets "keep tens of thousands of Jews prisoner in the Soviet Union, refusing to let them migrate." He added:

> And in the name of detente we accept all that, their propaganda, their abuse—we're the capitalists, we're the aggressors, we're the oppressors of the world and so on. . . . It's never stopped for one minute and in return we give them American taxpayer money at 6 and 7 percent to help out their economy. . . .

Interestingly—considering his common-sense approach to problems—Meany's concern for human rights in Russia and his opposition to unilateral detente were widely interpreted as aspects of a macho chauvinism. Even President Carter, who had enjoyed Meany's full support in the campaign for greater human rights in the Soviet Union, was surprised to find Meany parting company with the super-patriots in other respects.

In 1977 the AFL-CIO Council voted unanimously to endorse Carter's Panama Canal treaties turning over the Canal and the American Zone to Panama in the year 2000. Meany explained his position at a press conference:

> My general attitude is that there is no particular reason for us holding onto territory 2000 miles away just because we built the Canal on somebody else's land back in 1904. I don't think the history of American involvement in the Canal is anything that Americans can be proud of. I'm talking about the way the Panamanians were treated and the way we actually financed the revolution and sent in American troops when these people pulled away from Colombia. . . . That was in the days of gunboat diplomacy, as they called it.

Carter had telephoned Meany before the Council meeting to seek labor's support for the treaties. Meany had immediately assured him of it.

> He just called up and said he hoped we would support the treaties. I told him that, as far as I personally was concerned, I was in favor of relinquishing our control over the Zone. I said I felt, as a matter of principle—to uphold America's long-standing principle

that we didn't want to own anybody else's territory or control anybody else—that we should go along with the treaty. We've never been a colonial power.

Four months before he died, the AFL-CIO's magazine, *The Federationist,* published an article in which Meany outlined labor's human-rights policy:

> From its founding, the American labor movement has stood for justice, freedom, equality and human dignity—human rights.
>
> To us, human rights are absolute qualities, not relative quantities. They cannot be measured in degrees or percentages. They cannot be quantified in terms of some political victims released—so long as any remain in jail. Human rights cannot be considered a body count of emigrants or as an empty basket in a diplomatic agreement. . . .
>
> The first rights to be taken away by dictatorships of the right and the left are those which are the lifeblood of both free trade unions and democracy: freedom of speech, freedom of association and assembly.*
>
> You cannot have a trade union or a democratic election without those rights. Without a democratic election, whereby the people choose and remove their rulers, there is no method of securing human rights against the state. No democracy without human rights, no human rights without democracy and no trade union rights without either. That is our belief, that is our creed.

That creed helped guide Meany's actions at home as well as abroad, as was testified to by the Reverend Benjamin L. Hooks, director of the NAACP, at the AFL-CIO's 1979 convention:

"George Meany is no ordinary man. He is a determined and vigilant fighter for the working man. He is a careful and deliberate champion of human and social justice. He is a close and dear friend of civil rights and a passionate advocate for the under class. In history of the great men of the American scene who have shaped the world events and the national spirit, George Meany stands tall and prominent. . . . He has been a leading human and civil rights advocate. Every piece of civil rights legislation in this century was enacted with the active support

---

* Meany's record of defending human rights—at home and abroad—went back to 1933 when he attended an AFL rally in New York that launched an anti-Hitler campaign. Over the years since then, the record is consistent: He attacked right-wing as well as Communist dictatorships; he opposed Franco's Spain, Latin American military governments and the racial policies of South Africa.

and leadership of George Meany and organized labor. . . . He has been a strong advocate of women's rights. . . ."

Human and civil rights, protected by a democratic system, were values Meany had cherished throughout his adult life, and when he shortly died, after a debilitating illness, his loyalty to them was attested to by tributes from all over the world, from statesmen, leaders of national and international labor organizations, workers and citizens with no affiliation with a labor union.

Tributes of a more personal kind—prayers, a silent vigil—were paid at the casket by thousands of his friends, fellow union members and officers, those who had worked with him in civil rights campaigns, politicians and strangers who respected what he stood for, although they knew him only on a TV screen. For two days they passed through the mural-lined lobby of the AFL-CIO headquarters, past the honors awarded to Meany by a President, by the governments of Germany and Italy, by universities and countless other institutions.

President Carter headed a long procession of dignitaries attending the funeral mass at Washington's St. Matthew's Cathedral. Vice President Mondale, dozens of members of Congress, foreign ambassadors, labor leaders from other nations, Democratic Presidential candidates Edward M. Kennedy and California Governor Edmund Brown, and Governor Hugh Carey of New York were present. Others included leaders from the business community, notably David Rockefeller, the chairman of Chase Manhattan Bank, Russian dissident Alexander Ginsberg and rank-and-file members from Meany's home plumbers local in the Bronx.

The Meany era had ended, but the basic principles that guided him and the Federation remained. He left behind many monuments, especially the George Meany Center for Labor Studies (the name was chosen by the Council members). The center, situated on a forty-seven-acre campus just outside Washington, had been established by Meany because he foresaw a need for special training for union leaders, who would face new problems in the 1980s.

The labor movement's future also was on his mind as he delivered the last of his annual Labor Day speeches, four months before his death:

> In the eighties, I am confident there will be a strong growth of unionism among groups previously considered not interested in union representation. . . . They will make up their own agenda of

concerns. They will structure their unions and choose their leaders to achieve their goals. And the face of labor may change, just as it has changed with each new period of growth in the labor movement.

But the basic goal will not change. It is—as it has always been, and I am sure always will be—to better the standards of life for all who work for wages and to seek decency and justice and dignity for all Americans.

AUTHOR'S NOTE

Valuable insight into Meany's character and career was provided in taped interviews with family members and close associates (listed with their positions at the time of the interviews):

I. W. Abel, Steelworkers president
Alexander E. Barkan, COPE director
Andrew J. Biemiller, legislative director
Irving Brown, AFL-CIO European representative
Sol C. Chaikin, president, Ladies Garment Workers
Nelson H. Cruikshank, former AFL-CIO Social Security director
Walter G. Davis, education director
William T. Dodd, former Bronx union associate
Murray H. Finley, Clothing Workers president
Robert A. Georgine, Building Trades Department president
Arthur J. Goldberg, former U.S. Supreme Court justice
Matthew Guinan, Transport Workers president
Paul Hall, Seafarers president
Thomas F. Harris, member, Federal Election Commission
Fred K. Hoehler, Jr., director, George Meany Center for Labor Studies
Joseph D. Keenan, former AFL-CIO Council member
Lane Kirkland, AFL-CIO secretary-treasurer
Eileen Lee, Meany daughter
Ernest S. Lee, international affairs director
Jay Lovestone, former international affairs director
Genevieve Lutz, Meany daughter
John H. Lyons, Iron Workers president
Regina Mayer, Meany daughter
William H. McClennan, Fire Fighters president
Saul Miller, publications director
Morris S. Novik, long-time Meany friend
Rudolph Oswald, research director

Leo Perlis, community services director
Jacob S. Potofsky, former Clothing Workers president
A. Philip Randolph, former president Sleeping Car Porters
Bayard Rustin, director, A. Phililp Randolph Institute
Bert Seidman, AFL-CIO Social Security director
Albert Shanker, Teachers Federation president
William Sidell, Carpenters president
Donald Slaiman, civil rights director
Virginina Tehas, Meany's secretary
J. C. Turner, Operating Engineers president
Martin J. Ward, Plumbers president
J. Albert Woll, general counsel
Albert J. Zack, public relations director

Officials and staff members of the Federation generously aided in this project, with special assistance rendered by Thomas R. Donahue, Sandra Gray, Hilda Julbe, Doris Kelenson, Michelle Kikta, Robert C. Mayer, Saul Miller, Mary Petock, William Pollard, Rosemary Ruane, Edwin M. Schmidt, Jean Y. Weber, Steve Yarmola, Kenneth Young, Lee M. White and Allen Y. Zack. Special thanks also go to Frank Alexander, Paul J. Burnsky, Ann Cassin, Joseph G. Clark, Harry Conn, Margaret Ernst, Henry C. Fleisher, Frank Fernbach, Msgr. George G. Higgins, Oscar Jager, Karl A. Limbach, Eli Oliver, and A. H. Raskin.

CHAPTER NOTES

Useful sources included the books of verbatim proceedings of labor conventions, cited in chapter notes as "N.Y. Fed 1935" for New York State Federation; "AFL 1935"; "CIO 1935," etc. Meany's news conference transcripts are listed as "press conf." and his speeches as "sp."

CHAPTER 1

13—Prayer: AFL-CIO 1979, Pt. I, p. 10.
20—Canal Zone: press conf. Aug. 29, 1977.
22—Lobbying: Murray H. Finley;
   Not in awe: "Dick Cavett" show, ABC-TV, Dec. 19, 1974.
23—Where he stands: Andrew J. Biemiller.
25—Progress: sp. May 7, 1952, at City of Hope dinner.
27—Chandeliers: Eileen Lee;
   Never heard: Genevieve Lutz;
   Footnote—gift: Regina Mayer;
   So engrossed; NBC "Today" show Jan. 22, 1974;
   Daughters: Regina Mayer, Eileen Lee, Genevieve Lutz;
   Looked like: Eileen Lee.
28—No popularity contest: Public TV, "The MacNeil-Lehrer Report," Sept. 4, 1978.

CHAPTER 2

31—Grandson: sp. Nov. 20, 1976.
34—Memory: Eileen Lee;
   Math: press conf. May 7, 1975, at Society of American Business Writers;
   Sleep problems: Genevieve Lutz.
35—Only interest: AFL 1953, p. 620.
38—First meeting: sp. Industrial Union Department, June 7, 1957.
40—Dock job: sp. Oct. 29, 1971;
   Everybody saved: Eileen Lee;
   Courtship: *Good Housekeeping* June 26, 1957.
   Dances: Eileen Lee.
46—Attitude: sp. Dec. 3, 1957, at Building Trades convention, p. 183.
47—Member in trouble: press conf. Aug. 28, 1969.
48—Tradition: sp. Pennsylvania State Federation, 1952.
51—First idea: interview, Nov. 6, 1953, *U.S. News & World Report.*
52—Foreign policy: sp. June 4, 1970, Retail, Wholesale and Department Store Union.

CHAPTER 3

56—Election: N.Y. Fed 1934, pp. 39, 55; *N.Y. Times* Aug. 30, 1934;
    At that time: Ingalls; *Herbert H. Lehman,* p. 132.
61—Highlight: press conf. Aug. 28, 1969.
62—Herbert Lehman: Ingalls, *op. cit.,* p. 2.
66—Radio speech: *N.Y. Times* Aug. 10, 1935.

CHAPTER 4

70—Political motives: *U.S. News & World Report* Nov. 6, 1953.
74—Mine union plight: Alinsky's *John L. Lewis,* p. 61.
76—Contention: *ibid.,* p. 68.
77—Directives: AFL 1934, p. 587, 598.
78—Lewis joined: press conf. Aug. 28, 1969.
79—Debate: AFL 1935, pp. 522–538.
80—Footnote: Alinsky, *op. cit.,* p. 78.
81—Relations: press conf. Aug. 28, 1969;
    Charter revocation: AFL 1938, p. 103. Ladies Garment Workers withdrew from CIO
    in 1938, rejoined AFL in 1940.
85—No desire: AFL 1955, p. 3.
86—Membership: AFL 1947, p. 151;
    Negotiations: CIO *News* Dec. 22, 1937; AFL 1952, pp. 521–23;
    After a number: sp. AFL 1952, pp. 521.

CHAPTER 5

90—Campaigning: N.Y. Fed 1936, p. 23.
92—Bills: *ibid.,* 1937, p. 85;
    Minimum wage: *ibid.,* pp. 106, 113.
98—New York Branch: AFL 1938, p. 404.
101—In August: N.Y. Fed 1939, p. 57;
    Third Term: *ibid.,* p. 186.

CHAPTER 6

106—Green: AFL 1939, pp. 554–558;
    Nomination: *ibid.,* pp. 582–585.
109—Four days: sp. AFL-CIO Industrial Union Department convention, 1957;
    Emergency: AFL Council minutes Dec. 1941.
110—Industry-Labor: Thomas Holland, unpublished report on labor-management conferences, p. 38;
    AFL delegates: National War Labor Board Termination Report, 2nd Vol., p. 1038.
113—NWLB: *American Federationist* Apr. 1946;
    Dispute: AFL Council minutes May 1943.
115—Sacrifice: AFL 1944, p. 515.
    Answer: sp. June 8, 1944, to Labor Research personnel.
116—Production: sp. N.Y. Fed 1943.
117—A few days: AFL Council minutes June 17, 1942.
119—Reaffiliate: Alinsky, *op. cit.,* p. 275; AFL Council Report, 1943, p. 19; AFL Council
    minutes Aug. 1943;
    Meany report: *ibid.,* Jan. 1944.
120—Failure: AFL 1944, p. 123;
    Footnote: AFL Council minutes May 1943.

CHAPTER 7

125—Description: sp. Apr. 19, 1960, to AFL-CIO Conference on World Affairs.
126—Policy: sp. to National Press Club, quoted in *AFL News Reporter,* Dec. 19, 1952;
    Propaganda: sp. Aug. 4, 1954, to AFL Labor Institute at Rutgers University.
127—Excesses: sp. Feb. 26, 1955, to Jewish Labor Committee.

129—Praise: Dubinsky-Raskin's *David Dubinsky*, p. 256.
131—Raising Money: AFL 1942, pp. 230–231;
    Were asked: sp. Aug. 4, 1954, to AFL Labor Institute.
132—Delegate: sp. Sept. 12, 1945, to British TUC; *N.Y. Times* Sept, 13, 1945.
135—Result: AFL 1946, p. 70. Footnote: *ibid.*, p. 71;
    Italy and France: sp. Mar. 19, 1964, to Bond Club, New York.
136—European workers: Irving Brown.
137—Stalin: sp. Dec. 5, 1947, over Mutual Broadcasting System;
    AFL course: sp. Mar. 13, 1951, to Catholic Labor Alliance;
    Nearly all: Taft's *Defending Freedom* p. 125.
138—ICFTU: sp. June 26, 1949.
139—ORIT: AFL 1951, p. 71; ICFTU 1951, p. 33.

CHAPTER 8

140—Conference: Thomas Holland report, *op. cit.,* p. 68.
143—Coal strike: Rayback's *A History of American Labor,* p. 393.
147—As Congress: sp. Apr. 16, 1947, National Broadcasting Co.;
    Footnote: Labor Secretary W. Willard Wirtz sp. at AFL-CIO 1965, p. 87.
150—Lewis-Meany debate: AFL 1947, pp. 486–98.
153—Summed: sp. June 2, 1967, to National Press Club.
156—1948 race: AFL Council minutes Aug. 1948.
157—Results: AFL 1948 p. 514;
    No compromise: *ibid.,* p. 532;
    Taft bill: *U.S. News & World Report* Jan. 13, 1950.
158—Labor Committee: AFL 1951, p. 51; *N.Y. Times* Sept. 29, 1951;
    Defense program: sp. N.Y. Fed 1951.
160—Shocking: sp. Sept. 17, 1952, at AFL banquet.
161—American Federation: sp. Nov. 9, 1952 to National Council of Christians and Jews.

CHAPTER 9

162—Accepting: minutes, AFL Council Nov. 25, 1952.
164—Six days: "Reporters' Roundup," Mutual Broadcasting System, Dec. 1, 1952;
    Goal: sp. Dec. 2, 1952, to National Council of Christians and Jews;
    sp. Dec. 19, 1952, to National Press Club.
165—Reuther speech: CIO 1952, p. 486.
166—Survey figures: AFL 1953, p. 85;
    Cost: sp. May 14, 1954, at conference, quoted in *AFL News Reporter* May 21, 1954.
167—Withdrawal: *AFL Federationist* Aug. 1953; *N.Y. Times* Aug, 13, 1953.
168—Interview: *U.S. News & World Report* Nov. 6, 1953;
    Agreement: AFL 1954, p. 56.
171—Short way: Cormier and Eaton, *Reuther,* p. 325;
    Both sides: Goldberg's *AFL-CIO: Labor United,* p. 86;
    Pressure: *U.S. News & World Report* Dec. 3, 1954.
172—McDonald: CIO 1954, pp. 407–409;
    Reuther: *ibid.,* pp. 418–419;
    Telegram: *ibid.,* p. 410.
175—Agreement: Goldberg, *op. cit.,* p. 89.
176—Name: minutes, unity committee meetings May 2 and July 20, 1955;
    Footnote: *AFL News Reporter* July 22, 1955.
178—AFL meeting: AFL 1955, p. 3;
    Reply to Randolph: *ibid.,* p. 361;
    Closing: *ibid.,* p. 450.
179—CIO's final: CIO 1955, pp. 301, 326;
    Speech: AFL-CIO 1955, Pt. I, p. 25.
181—Program: *ibid.,* p. 172.

183—IUD: AFL-CIO Council minutes Dec. 1955 and IUD 1955;
    Membership: *AFL-CIO American Federationist* Mar. 1980.

CHAPTER 10

188—Asked: sp. National Press Club, quoted in *AFL News Reporter* Dec. 29, 1952;
    Told Council: AFL Council minutes Jan. 2, 1953.
191—Hutchinson's *The Imperfect Union,* p. 387;
    Committee: AFL-CIO 1957, Pt. II, p. 45;
    Ike: AFL-CIO minutes June 1956;
    McClellan: sp. IUD conference June 7, 1957.
192—Recalled: sp. Nov. 1, 1957 IUD convention;
    Thought we knew: sp. IUD convention Dec. 1, 1957;
    Pointed out: Jan. 14, 1957, letter to Edward V. Wandersee, University of Pennsylvania faculty;
    Declaration: AFL-CIO Council minutes Jan.–Feb. 1957.
194—Details: *ibid.,* Mar. 29, 1957.
195—Not a case: *ibid.,* May 20, 1957. pp. 470–476.
196—Next: AFL-CIO 1957, Pt. II, pp. 470–476.
197—Soon after: AFL-CIO Council minutes Oct. 1957.
198—Summation: AFL-CIO 1957, Pt. I, p. 94;
    Vote: *ibid.,* p. 105;
    Fear: AFL-CIO 1959, Pt. I, p. 468.
199—Footnote: AFL-CIO 1961, Pt. I, p. 210.
200—Valente: AFL-CIO 1957, Pt. I, p. 485;
    Testimony: hearings of Senate Select Committee on Improper Activities in the Labor and Management Field (McClellan Committee), Pt. 9, pp. 3347–3355.
201—Bakers: AFL-CIO 1957, Pt. II, p. 506;
    Cross: *ibid.,* Pt. I, p. 230.
202—Arguing: *ibid.,* p. 217;
    Meany: *ibid.,* p. 240.

CHAPTER 11

203—Dealing: AFL 1953, p. 115; *AFL News Reporter* Mar. 6, 1953.
204—Chat: AFL Council minutes Nov. 25, 1952.
207—Durkin: AFL 1954, p. 476;
    Following: *ibid.,* p. 480;
    Eisenhower: *ibid.,* p. 513.
    Record: AFL 1954, p. 23.
208—Nevertheless: AFL-CIO Council minutes Aug. 1956.
209—Board: *AFL-CIO News* Sept. 1, 1956;
    Letter: AFL-CIO release Sept. 25, 1957.
210—Relationship: Arthur Goldberg–Meany tape for John F. Kennedy Library.
211—With the onset: AFL-CIO 1959, Pt. II, p. 370;
    Footnote: *ibid.,* p. 371.
212—On the Hill: *ibid.,* p. 371.
213—Aftermath: sp. Sept. 7, 1959, at Salt Lake City rally.
214—Blame: sp. to Metal Trades convention 1959.

CHAPTER 12

217—Closer: Albert J. Zack.
219—Argument: Cormier-Eaton, *op. cit.,* p. 374.
220—Endorsement: AFL-CIO 1961, Pt. II, p. 264.
    Rather odd: Arthur Goldberg–Meany tape for John F. Kennedy Library.
222—Purpose: White House release Mar. 21, 1961;
    Suggestion: letter to Eisenhower Nov. 9, 1959;

Automation: *AFL-CIO News* Jan. 20, 1962;
Bargaining: White House release May 1, 1962.
224—National interest: Goldberg sp. Feb. 23, 1962, to Executives Club, Chicago;
Meany press conf. Feb. 26, 1962, quoted in *U.S. News & World Report* Mar. 12, 1962;
Spelled out: sp. April 16, 1964, to Operating Engineers;
Role: Goldberg in *U.S. News & World Report* Apr. 16, 1962.
226—Discrimination: AFL-CIO 1961, Pt. I, pp. 18–19, 475–476.
227—Revolution: *ibid.,* pp. 475–76;
Condemnation: AFL-CIO Council May 4, 1960.
228—The bond: AFL-CIO 1961, Pt. I, p. 14;
Kennedy: *ibid.,* pp. 49–50, 52;
Meany: *ibid.,* p. 58.
229—When you hear: sp. Aug. 21, 1961, to American Bakery and Confectionary Workers.
230—Statement: AFL-CIO release Oct. 22, 1962.
231—Meany provided: Goldberg-Meany tape for Kennedy Library.
232—Kennedy: AFL-CIO 1963, Pt. I, pp. 129–133;
Shooting: Biemiller.

CHAPTER 13

233—We in labor movement: sp. Apr. 11, 1978, to National Conference of Christians and Jews.
234—In 1963: sp. Sept. 24, 1969, to Building Trades.
235—President Kennedy: Zack and Biemiller;
Biemiller memo: June 10, 1963.
236—Soon after: July 17, 1963, to House Judiciary Committee.
237—While waiting: AFL-CIO 1963, Pt. II, p. 49; *AFL-CIO News* July 27, 1963;
Footnote: *ibid.,* May 18, 1963.
238—This conference: sp. Sept. 2, 1964, at AFL-CIO civil rights conference;
239—There was: sp. May 11, 1964, to Furniture Workers.
240—Footnote: AFL-CIO release Jan. 5, 1964.
241—To greater degree: sp. Jan. 11, 1965, to AFL-CIO legislative conference.
243—Reporters: Zack;
Johnson sent: Biemiller.
244—Footnote: AFL-CIO 1969, Pt. II, p. 487.
246—The major: AFL-CIO 1965, Pt. I, p. 26.
248—An editorial: Zack;
As it happened: Aug. 23, 1967, to Senate Fair Housing subcommittee.
249—The account: Biemiller;
That summer: Sept. 4, 1967, National Broadcasting Co.;
In testimony: Oct. 24, 1967.
250—"I don't know": AFL-CIO 1967, Pt. I, p. 669;
Meany was sure: Zack and Biemiller.

CHAPTER 14

251—Only thing: Zack.
253—Letters: Zack.
259—Strangely: Rudolph J. Faupl report to AFL-CIO Council June 16, 1966.
260—Reuther: UAW release June 16, 1966;
After Council: press conf. excerpts quoted AFL-CIO radio program, June 19, 1966, American Broadcasting Company.
261—Reuther charge: Associated Press June 17, 1966;
November meeting: *U.S. News & World Report* Nov. 28, 1966.
262—Attempt: Dubinsky-Meany tape for Dubinsky autobiography;
Threats: UAW release Feb. 9, 1967.
263—AFL-CIO resolution: Feb. 20, 1967;
Press conf.: United Press International Feb. 24, 1967.
264—Open door: sp. June 27, 1967, to National Press Club;

Reaction: AFL-CIO 1967, Pt. I, p. 7.
266—Vietnam: *ibid.,* p. 16.
267—In 1968: AFL-CIO 1969, Pt. II, pp. 420–422;
    Meany countered: *ibid.,* pp. 424–427.
268—UAW's record: *AFL-CIO News* July 13, 1968.
274—Comparison: press conf. Aug. 28, 1969;
    Statement: AFL-CIO release May 10, 1970.

CHAPTER 15

277—When demonstrations: Meany editorial, *Federationist,* Oct. 1968;
    Candidates' speeches: "Meet the Press," Sept. 22, 1968, National Broadcasting Co.
278—Last eight: sp. Oct. 8, 1968, to Iron Workers.
279—Get-out-the-vote: White's *Making of the President 1968,* p. 365.
281—Meany's reply: press conf. Feb. 17, 1969;
    "I don't buy": *ibid.,* Feb. 18, 1969.
282—All the attention: *AFL-CIO News* Apr. 17, 1969.
282—Administration policies: press conf. Aug. 28, 1969;
    Scoffed: *ibid.*
283—Insurance: sp. Nov. 13, 1969, to IUD conference.
284—Before battle: Zack;
    Protest: *AFL-CIO News* Aug. 23, 1969.
285—Sparring match: Senate Judiciary Committee hearing Sept. 18, 1969.
286—Meany told: AFL-CIO 1969, Pt. I, pp. 13–16.
287—Blocking: Donald Slaiman.
288—A draft: release Jan. 27, 1970;
    One reason: press conf. Feb. 16, 1970, quoted in *AFL-CIO News* Feb. 21, 1970;
    Appointment: statement to Senate Judiciary Committee Feb. 7, 1970.
289—Finally: *AFL-CIO News* Mar. 28, 1970;
    Philadelphia Plan: U.S. Labor Department release June 27, 1969;
    General view: press conf. Aug. 8, 1969.
290—"I believe": sp. Sept. 24, 1969, to Building Trades.
291—More misinformation: sp. Jan. 12, 1970, to National Press Club.
292—The Plan: press conf. Feb. 16, 1970;
    Cambodia: release, May 1, 1970;
    Described it: press conf. May 12, 1970.
293—In August: press conf. Aug. 25, 1970.
294—You can be: *ibid.*
297—TV Interview: "Face the Nation," Sept. 6, 1970, Columbia Broadcasting System.
299—That dinner: press conf. Oct. 20, 1970.
300—AFL-CIO's efforts: COPE memo Dec. 7, 1970; *U.S. News & World Report* Nov. 16,
    1970; press conf. Nov. 9, 1970;
    All in all: sp. Mar. 12, 1971, to Sheet Metal Workers.
301—Praised: sp. July 19, 1971, to Longshoremen's Association.
302—That theory: sp. Apr. 19, 1971, to Building Trades conference.
303—Any other way: press conf. Aug. 9, 1971;
    Meany declared: sp. Aug. 2, 1971, to Plumbers.

CHAPTER 16

304—Flip-flop: AFL-CIO 1971, Pt. I, p. 15.
305—"We will ask": release Aug. 16, 1971.
306—Shultz-Hodgson: press conf. Aug. 19, 1971.
307—News conference: Sept. 2, 1971.
308—Overall picture: *ibid.;*
    "Issues and Answers," Sept. 5, 1971, American Broadcasting Co.
309—In response: AFL-CIO 1971, Pt. I, p. 17.
310—That is the day: *ibid.,* p. 18;
    Labor leaders: Albert Zack;

Desperate: AFL-CIO 1971 Pt. I, p. 19.
311—Quite definite: *ibid.*
312—The judge: *U.S. News & World Report* Nov. 8, 1971;
Meany's colorful: AFL-CIO 1971, Pt. I, p. 21.
314—Footnote: NWLB Report Part Two.
315—"We kept asking": AFL-CIO 1971, Pt. I, p. 23;
Labor was outvoted: *U.S. News & World Report* Nov. 22, 1971.
316—Public side: *ibid.,* Feb. 21, 1972;
At convention: AFL-CIO 1971, Pt. I, p. 26;
Convention delegates: *ibid.,* p. 58.
318—*N.Y. Times* Nov. 25, 1971;
Addressed: AFL-CIO 1971, Pt. I, p. 317.
319—Memo: press conf. Feb. 14 and 17, 1972;
Text: *AFL-CIO News* Jan. 8, 1972.
320—Look back: sp. Oct. 29, 1971, to Carpenters.
321—A few days: AP Mar. 10, 1972;
Deep-seated: *U.S. News & World Report* interview Feb. 21, 1972;
Footnote: press conf. Feb. 15, 1972;
In another interview: press conf. Feb. 14, 1972.
322—Speech: Sept. 18, 1972, to Steelworkers.
323—Not endorse: press conf. July 14, 1972.
324—Sept. 3, 1972, Columbia Broadcasting System;
Footnote: press conf. Feb. 20, 1975.
325—Meany aide: Zack;
Former official: Joseph A. Loftus in *Neiman Reports,* Autumn 1976.
326—Following first disclosures: press conf. May 8, 1973;
Personal comment: May 22, 1973, National Broadcasting Company.
327—Feel keenly: press conf. Aug. 1, 1973.
What was: press conf. Aug. 30, 1973;
Nixon's refusal: *ibid.*
328—Watergate is not: sp. Oct. 11, 1973, to Metal Trades;
The Vice-President: AFL-CIO 1973, Pt. I, pp. 14–16.
329—"We believe": *ibid.,* p. 267.
330—Meanwhile, referring: release Oct. 24, 1973.
331—We are not: "Washington Straight Talk," Apr. 5, 1974, WETA-TV;
I see our friend: sp. Mar. 27, 1974, to Machinists;
A week ago: press conf. May 9, 1974.
332—I wouldn't make: press conf. Aug. 5, 1974.
333—I don't agree: press conf. Aug. 6, 1974.
334—We are going: sp. June 5, 1974, to Retail, Wholesale and Department Store Union.

CHAPTER 17

335—Nice man: press conf. Feb. 17, 1975;
Not want Nixon jailed: press conf. Aug. 29, 1974.
336—No one opposes pardon: "Issues and Answers," Sept. 1, 1974, American Broadcasting Company;
Seven days: sp. Sept. 10, 1974, to Brotherhood of Electrical Workers.
337—We in labor: AFL-CIO transcript Sept. 17, 1974;
Job creation: sp. Oct. 8, 1974, to Clothing Workers;
Mandate: press conf. Nov. 7, 1974.
338—To fight inflation: sp. Jan 23, 1975, to AFL-CIO General Board.
339—Meany indicated: "Face the Nation," Feb. 9, 1975, Columbia Broadcasting System;
I know John: *ibid.;*
Hard worker: press conf. Feb. 17, 1975;
Compassionate: press conf. May 7, 1975;
John Dunlop is: press conf. Aug. 28, 1975.
340—As for the President: *ibid;*

A decent man: press conf. May 7, 1975.
341—One plus: press conf. June 6, 1975;
   Served interest: press conf. July 30, 1975;
   Despite opposition: "Dick Cavett" show, Dec. 17, 1974, American Broadcasting Company.
342—Later press conference: Feb. 21, 1975.
343—Biennial convention: AFL-CIO 1975, Pt. II, pp. 1, 2.
345—In labor movement: *AFL-CIO News* Jan. 3, 1976.
346—Supposing Reagan: National Public Radio 1975;
   If Democratic party: press conf. Aug. 28, 1975;
   Asked to name: *ibid.*
347—Die is cast: press conf. July 19, 1976;
   Half a dozen: *ibid.*
348—Talked to Carter: *ibid.;*
   Here today: sp. Aug. 31, 1976, to AFL-CIO General Board.
354—Among mistakes: *AFL-CIO News* Sept. 4, 1976.
355—For the year: *ibid.,* Jan. 17, 1976;
   Of 28 senatorial: AFL-CIO 1977, Pt. II, p. 302;
   What role: press conf. Nov. 10, 1976.

CHAPTER 18

356—We in the labor movement: statement Nov. 3, 1976;
   If you remember: press conf. Aug. 30, 1977.
357—First order: *ibid.,* Nov. 10, 1976;
   In a close election: *ibid.;*
   When Meany: *ibid.*
358—Ray Marshall: statement Dec. 21, 1976;
   A major difference: *AFL-CIO News* Jan. 15, 1977;
   At his confirmation: Washington *Post* Jan. 14, 1977.
359—Fair estimate: press conf. Feb. 21, 1977;
   There were: *ibid.*
360—That's what: *ibid.,* Feb. 22, 1977.
361—Put the people: *ibid.;*
   To get action: *ibid.,* Feb. 24, 1977;
   The history: *ibid.,* Feb. 22, 1977.
362—We haven't asked: *ibid.;*
   Labor had several: *AFL-CIO News* Mar. 26, 1977.
363—In another disappointment: *ibid.;*
   Administration spokesmen: sp. Apr. 27, 1977, to Coalition for a Fair Minimum Wage.
364—By April: press conf. Apr. 13, 1977;
   We are not going: *AFL-CIO News* Apr. 9, 1977.
365—The need for counter: *ibid.;*
   Carter then: statement Apr. 15, 1977;
   The Group commends: Group statement Apr. 19, 1977;
   He has been working: press conf. May 4, 1977.
367—We have reached: *ibid.,* Aug. 29, 1977.
368—Black organizations: *ibid.,* Aug. 30, 1977.
369—Quite a few: *ibid.;*
   TV interview: "Morning News," Sept. 5, 1977, Columbia Broadcasting System.
370—Meany's "happiness" index: "Face the Nation," Oct. 2, 1977, Columbia Broadcasting System;
   In opening: AFL-CIO 1977, Pt. I, pp. 5–6, 19.
371—Carter did not appear: *ibid.,* p. 70;
   Meany summarized: *ibid.,* Pt. II, p. 2.
372—The past two: *ibid.,* p. 11;
   In the election: *ibid.,* Pt. I, p. 367; *AFL-CIO News* Dec. 17, 1977;

Footnote: AFL-CIO staff members.
373—We certainly agree: statement Jan. 20, 1978.
374—We have had: press conf. Feb. 20, 1978;
    I don't want: *ibid.;*
    More conflict: *ibid.,* Feb. 24, 1978.
375—When it developed: *ibid.,* Feb. 23, 1978;
    We think: *ibid.,* Feb. 21, 1978;
    People: *ibid.*
377—The Business Roundtable: *Wall Street Journal* May 7, 1978.
378—I presume: press conf. Aug. 7, 1978.
379—Talking to reporters: *ibid.,* Aug. 2, 1978;
    Efforts to get: *ibid.,* Aug. 7, 1978;
    At its next meeting: press conf. Oct. 31, 1978.
380—We are going: *ibid.*
381—Nobody knows: *ibid.;*
    Been meeting: *ibid.*
384—January, and reporters in rain: Martin J. Ward.
385—Lane Kirkland's recollections: Kirkland press conf. Oct. 16, 1979;
    During eight months: Meany press conf. Feb. 19, 1979.
386—Two members: *ibid.,* Feb. 20, 1979.
387—Carter is President: *ibid.;*
    When asked: *ibid.,* Feb. 19, 1979;
    A decision: *ibid.,* Feb. 23, 1979.
388—We have decided: *ibid.,* Feb. 22, 1979;
    [The law]: *ibid.,* Feb. 19, 1979;
    He called up: *ibid.,* Feb. 20, 1979.
389—The AFL-CIO won: *AFL-CIO News* June 2, 1979; AFL-CIO 1979, Pt. II, p. 307.
390—George Meany is: Kirkland press conf. Aug. 6, 1979.
391—I am delighted: Maritime Department transcript Nov. 13, 1979.
392—Some 323: *AFL-CIO News* Nov. 24, 1979;
    Solzhenitsyn telegram: AFL-CIO 1979, Pt. I, p. 402.

CHAPTER 19

393—No society: *Federationist* Sept. 1979.
395—From the time: AFL-CIO 1971, Pt. II, p. 123; press conf. Aug. 4, 1970;
    When Meany: AFL-CIO 1971 Pt. II, p. 124.
396—AFL-CIO subsequently: press conf. Aug. 4, 1970; *AFL-CIO News* June 21, 1975;
    A phase of: sp. July 15, 1974, to National Press Club.
397—Meany's repeated: Hearings Oct. 1, 1974.
399—Because of detente: sp. Jan. 15, 1975, to Jewish Labor Committee.
401—Advice had gone: Meany testimony to Senate Foreign Relations Committee, Dec. 8,
    1975;
    Detente is a fraud: "Irving Kupcinet Show," Aug. 14, 1975, Public TV.
402—My general attitude: press conf. Aug. 29, 1977;
    Called up: *ibid.*
403—From its founding: *Federationist,* Sept. 1979;
    That creed: AFL-CIO 1979, p. 198.
404—Meany era: sp. Sept. 3, 1979 over Columbia Broadcasting System.

BIBLIOGRAPHY

Alinsky, Saul. *John L. Lewis, An Unauthorized Biography.* New York: G. P. Putnam's sons, 1949.

Cormier, Frank, & Eaton, William J. *Reuther.* Englewood Cliffs, N.J.: Prentice-Hall, Inc., 1970.

Dubinsky, David, & Raskin, A. H. *David Dubinsky: A Life With Labor.* New York: Simon & Schuster, 1977.

Goldberg, Arthur J. *AFL-CIO: Labor United.* New York: McGraw-Hill Book Co., Inc., 1956.

Hutchinson, John. *The Imperfect Unions: A History of Corruption in American Trade Unions.* New York: E. P. Dutton & Co., 1970.

Ingalls, Robert P. *Herbert H. Lehman and New York's Little New Deal.* New York: New York University Press, 1975.

Rayback, Joseph G. *A History of American Labor.* New York: Macmillan, 1959.

Taft, Philip. *Defending Freedom: American Labor and Foreign Affairs.* Los Angeles: Nash Publishing, 1973.

White, Theodore H. *The Making of the President 1968.* New York: Atheneum, 1969.

INDEX

Abel, I. W., 270–71, 310, 313, 322, 323
Ackley, Gardner, 243, 244
"Action Program to Put America Back to Work," 338–39
Actors Equity, 164
ADA (Americans for Democratic Action), 297
Adams, Sherman, 203
aerospace industry, 316 ,
Afghanistan, Soviet invasion of, 21n
AFL (American Federation of Labor), 41–179
  absence of serious organizing in, 46–47, 71–73, 76, 79, 84
  Amalgamated Clothing Workers admitted to, 75
  anti-Nazi campaign of, 16, 52–53, 127–29, 403n
  autonomy doctrine of, 180, 185, 186, 188–90
  Big Split in, 15, 69–87
  Building Trades Department of, 45, 166, 177
  Central Body of, 50–52, 53, 56, 64–65, 96, 156
  CIO and, see CIO
  Communist infiltration of, 124–25
  constitution of, 82n, 107, 149, 150, 151n, 180, 188, 216
  corruption investigated in, 185–91, 215–16

AFL (cont.)
  doubts about merger in, 176–77, 178
  Executive Council of, 67–68, 69, 70, 75, 76, 77, 78, 79, 82, 102, 108, 109–10, 114, 117, 118, 119–20, 132, 148–49, 150, 151–52, 154, 155–56, 159, 160, 162, 163, 167, 173, 174, 178, 186–89, 227
  federal unions in, 148, 149, 152
  foreign policy views of, 16, 52–53, 124, 126, 127–39, 204
  Gompers' philosophy and, 18, 44, 45n, 88, 90–92, 100
  international relations committee of, 131
  at labor-management conference (1945), 140–41
  legislation advocated by, 20, 48, 60, 61, 62–64, 92, 98
  lines of advancement in, 55, 105, 106, 107
  Meany as president of, 14, 30, 45n, 162–79, 188–91, 204–8, 215–16
  Meany as secretary-treasurer of, 14, 16, 26, 104–22, 131, 140–61, 185–88
  Meany's platform for, 160–61, 163, 164–65
  membership of, 79, 86, 87, 106, 120n, 149, 166, 183
  at Miami meeting (1955), 173–76